AF361451

Protectors or Praetorians?

Protectors or Praetorians?

PROTECTORS OR PRAETORIANS?

*The Last Mamlūk Sultans and Egypt's
Waning as a Great Power*

Carl F. Petry

STATE UNIVERSITY OF NEW YORK PRESS

Published by
State University of New York Press, Albany

Marketing by Bernadette LaManna
Production by Laura Starrett

For information, address State University of New York Press,
State University Plaza, Albany,
New York, 12246

Library of Congress Cataloging-in-Publication Data

Petry, Carl F., 1943–
    Protectors or praetorians? : the last Mamlūk sultans and Egypt's
    waning as a great power / Carl F. Petry.
       p.   cm. — (SUNY series in medieval Middle East history)
    Includes bibliographical references and index.
    ISBN 0-7914-2139-2 : $59.50.—ISBN 0-7914-2140-6 (pbk.) : $19.95
    1. Egypt—History—1250–1517. I. Title. II. Series.
    DT96.7.P47   1994
    962'.02—dc20   94-2925
                                            CIP

10 9 8 7 6 5 4 3 2 1

To the memory of Claude Cahen

CONTENTS

ACKNOWLEDGMENTS

The research supporting this study, and its companion volume—*Twilight of Majesty: The Reigns of the Mamlūk Sultans al-Ashraf Qāytbāy and Qānṣūh al-Ghawrī in Egypt*—was initiated by a grant from the National Endowment for the Humanities in 1981, administered through the American Research Center in Egypt. Over a period of ten months, I began examining several hundred endowment deeds (*awqāf*) drawn up or appropriated by Sultan Qāytbāy, his wife Fāṭima, and Sultan Qānṣūh al-Ghawrī, and now kept in the Egyptian National Archives (*Dār al-Wathā'iq al-Qawmīya*) or the Ministry of Pious Endowments (*Wizārat al-Awqāf*), both in Cairo. I returned to that city in 1985 with the support of the United States Information Agency, possessing a keener sense of what these sources contained and at least an equivalent level of energy, to look at documents I had passed over in 1981. I am very grateful to Madame Sawsan ʿAbd al-Ghānī and Ustādh Ḥusām al-Dīn Kenj ʿUthmān, curators of the respective collections, who extended such a warm welcome and guided me through the idiosyncrasies of cataloging notations. During both stays in Cairo, the ARCE was my academic home, providing much more than logistic services. As for so many others who have conducted their research in Egypt, this institution was indispensable to the successful completion of my own.

In 1988, I received a fellowship from the John Simon Guggenheim Foundation, which allowed me to spend a year reading through the chronicles that yielded the study's narrative data. Two all-too-brief months of that year I spent in Istanbul examining Egyptian manuscripts from the Mamlūk period housed the Sulaymānīya Library. Its staff, and, in particular, the director, Dr. Muammar Ülker, exceeded any assistance I could have hoped for by temporarily transferring texts not readily accessible to foreign scholars from other libraries. The productivity of this most pleasant sojourn I owe to their hospitality.

This analysis of the Mamlūk regime in the decades preceding its conquest by the Ottomans represents the outcome of my current thoughts about its condition at the end of the Middle Ages. While a subject of such complexity is never definitively portrayed, those hypotheses the study offers have benefited from comments and suggestions of colleagues who have followed my project as it developed. In particular, I wish to mention Muḥammad M. Amīn, Jere

Bacharach, Jonathan Berkey, Bruce D. Craig, Jean-Claude Garcin, R. Stephen Humphreys, John O. Hunwick, Donald P. Little, Ivor Wilks, and John E. Woods. Their advice has been more valuable to me than they may realize. While the responsibility for shortcomings in the analysis is mine, its insights reflect their contributions on many occasions.

The staff at SUNY Press, and in particular Christine Worden, acquisitions editor, and Laura Starrett, who supervised production of the book, may take credit for its expeditious processing and attractive design.

The four maps are reproduced from my monograph, *Twilight of Majesty* by permission of the University of Washington Press.

A statement on transliteration. The Library of Congress System has been used for most Arabic terms. Tā' Marbūṭa is rendered "a" rather than "ah"—and "at" in construct. Words common in English usage, such as Mecca, Medina, or Koran, appear in their more conventional forms. The frequent occurrence of Turkish, and to a lesser extent Circassian or Persian, personal and place names raised special problems of transliteration, since these were not written uniformly by Egyptian authors. I have consistently rendered them as they appeared in the Arabic chronicles, rather than attempting to approximate their forms in the original languages. The variant "Qānṣūh" rather than "Qānṣawh" is used throughout. For background on the Mamlūk system of nomenclature, see D. Ayalon, "Names, Titles and 'Nisbas' of the Mamlūks," *Israel Oriental Studies* 5 (1975), 189–232.

ABBREVIATIONS

AI	*Annales Islamologiques* (IFAO, Cairo)
AW	Wizārat al-Awqāf (Ministry of Pious Endowments), Cairo.
BSOAS	*Bulletin of the School of Oriental and African Studies* (London).
DW	Dār al-Wathā'iq al-Qawmīya (National Archives), Cairo.
EI¹, EI²	*Encyclopaedia of Islam,* first and second editions (Leiden: 1913–1938, 1954–).
GAL, Suppl.	*Geschichte der Arabischen Litteratur,* two volumes with three-volume supplement by Carl Brockelmann (Leiden: second edition of original two volumes, 1943–1949; Supplement, 1937–1942).
IC	*Islamic Culture* (Hyderabad).
IFAO	*Institut Français d'Archéologie Orientale du Caire* (Cairo).
IFD	*Institut Français de Damas* (Damascus)
JA	*Journal Asiatique* (Paris).
JAOS	*Journal of the American Oriental Society* (Baltimore)
JARCE	*Journal of the American Research Center in Egypt* (Evanston).
JESHO	*Journal of the Economic and Social History of the Orient* (Leiden).
REI	*Revue des Études islamiques* (Paris).
SI	*Studia Islamica* (Paris).

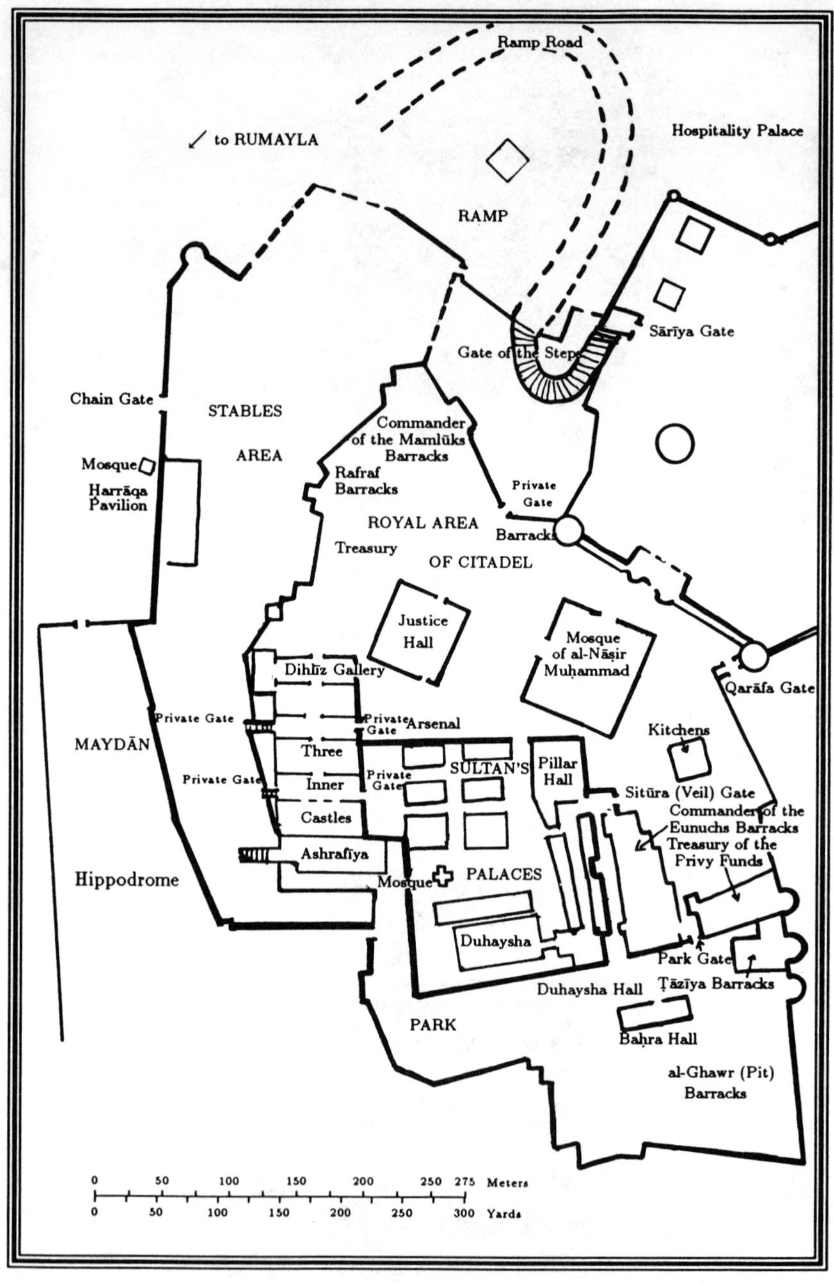

The Citadel of Cairo

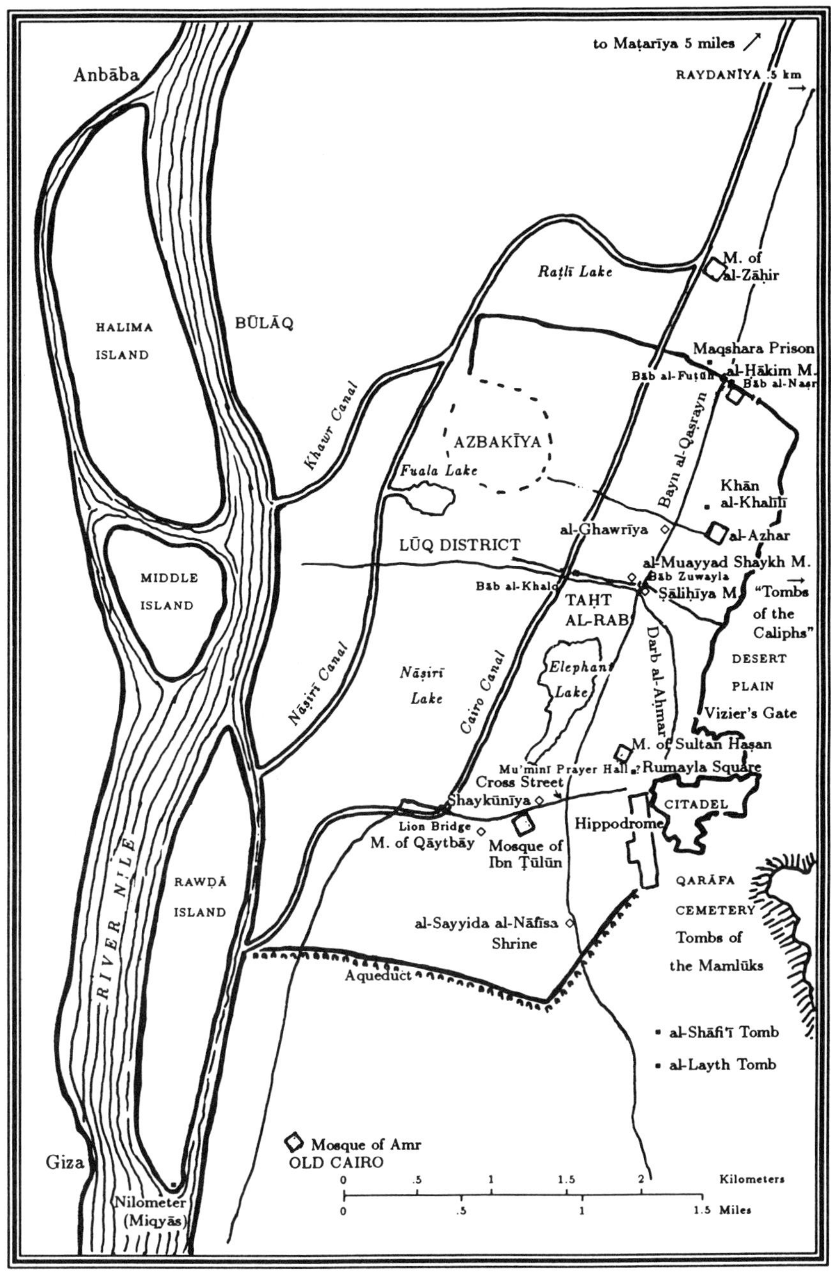

The City of Cairo

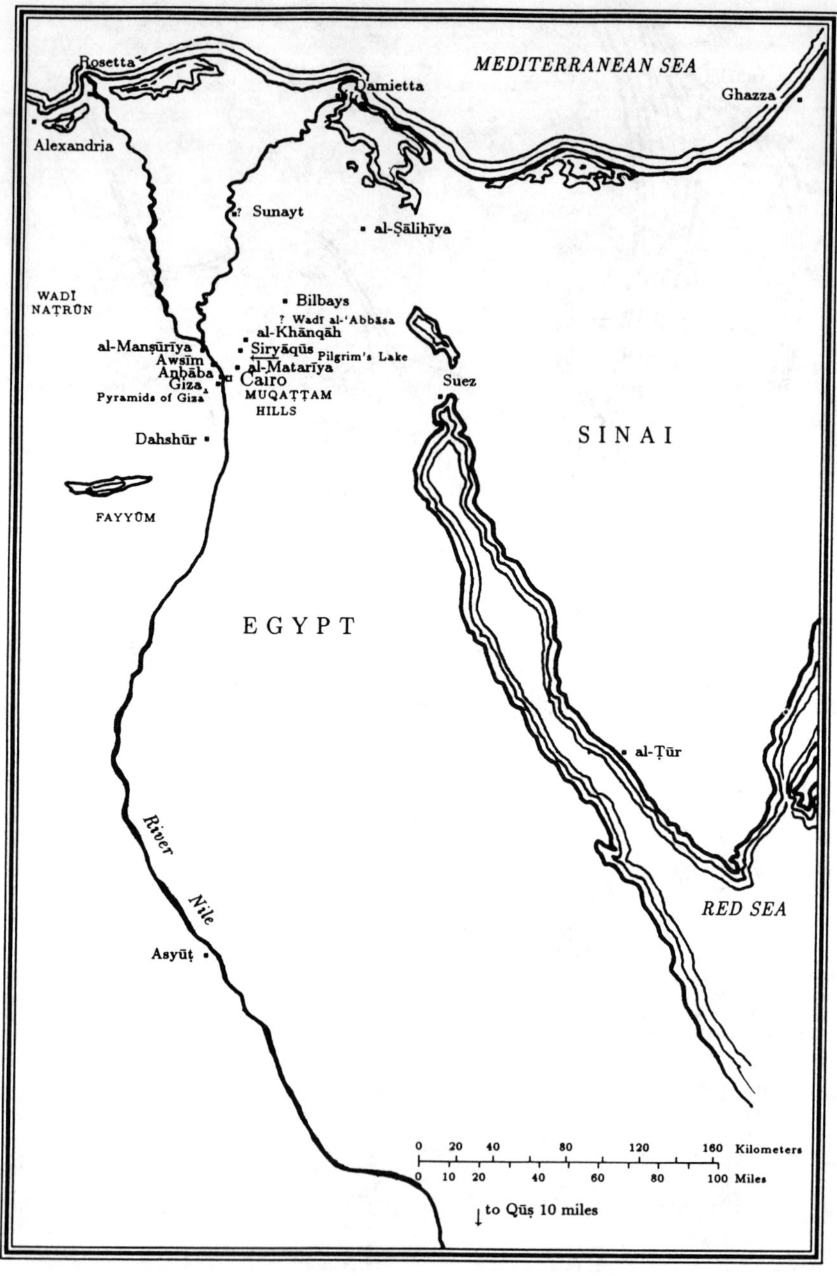

Egypt and Sinai

Southeast Anatolia, Syria, and Palestine

1

INTRODUCTION

In 1937, Philip Hitti typified the opinion of his generation's Arabists about the legacy of Mamlūk authority with the following:

> Mamlūk Egypt began its history under proud and triumphant rulers who had cleared Syria of the last vestiges of Frankish dominion and had successfully stood between the Mongols and world power. By the end of the period, however, with its military oligarchy, factions among the dominant caste, debased coinage, high taxation, insecurity of life and property, occasional plague and famine and frequent revolts, both Egypt and its dependency Syria were all but ruined. Especially in the valley of the Nile persistence of outworn ancient superstition and magic, coupled with the triumph of reactionary orthodoxy, hindered scientific advance. Under these conditions no intellectual activity of high order could be expected. . . . Mental fatigue induced by generations of effort and moral lassitude consequent upon the accumulation of wealth and power were evident everywhere.[1]

While chroniclers who dwelled on the Mamlūk regime's abiding dilemmas gave a scholar of Hitti's stature ample ammunition for such an assessment, their comments reveal a more vibrant milieu than these lines bespeak. Anyone who pores over the historians' myriad depictions of militarist strife, abuse of the commons, and fiscal exploitation cannot but acknowledge the prevalence of "hard times" in the later Mamlūk Empire. Yet these commentators' remarks rarely indicate a lapse in "intellectual activity of high order" or the onset of "mental fatigue." Quite the contrary, the characters who charted the regime's course emerge as pragmatists coping with trying conditions of state service they accepted as normative. Although their solutions to vexing challenges may

have aimed more at short-term expedience than long-range reform, their stratagems tell us much about how ambitious individuals in later medieval Egypt
pursued their fortunes and guarded their realm in the face of adversity. Their
behavior, therefore, merits examination on its own terms as the reasoned response persons immersed in a sophisticated non-Western society devised to
transcend its crises.

This study explores overt policies and covert ploys adopted by Egypt's
military and civilian elites to shore up the Mamlūk Sultanate in its final decades. Its purpose is twofold. First, it unravels the complex events of this era
(A. H. 872–922/C.E. 1468–1517), beset as it was by external threats and
internal dissension, to present a coherent picture of the times. So far, this pivotal episode in Egypt's history, the country's last phase as an independent
power before the modern age, remains untold in a comprehensive way.[2] Second, the analysis deciphers tactics adopted by the sultanate's bureaucracy to
meet its autocrats' demands under straitened circumstances, while simultaneously fattening purses of its more adroit members. The dynamics of patron-
client ties and their hidden rationales lurk behind every aspect of the inquiry.

Superficially, the work tells a tale of two monarchs: al-Ashraf Qāytbāy
(r. 872–901/1468–1496) and Qānṣūh al-Ghawrī (r. 906–922/1501–1516).
The author acknowledges flaws attendant in an analysis focused on autocrats
at the summit of their society, for all their prominence in a lengthy roster of
sovereigns over the millenia. Yet both men attained their offices by merit
rather than inheritance. Each was a seasoned professional soldier who advanced
to the top by a combination of martial talent, political acumen, and inscru-
table fate. While the two contrasted markedly, each was a high achiever in the
military caste he entered as a slave cadet. Their careers thus convey those values their peers regarded as essential for distinction. Both monarchs interacted
closely with a host of associates: Mamlūk comrades, civilian clients and grasp-
ing subordinates who rose from diverse levels of society and virtually all its
categories. The two therefore accumulated intimate knowledge about those
they admitted to their retinues. Although each can justifiably be castigated as
a tyrant, neither was ignorant of burdens their policies imposed on the masses
who footed their bills. Most other personalities who figured in the contemporary sources were discussed in conjunction with their ties to one of these individuals. A study centered on these rulers' careers thus illuminates aspirations
and machinations of all those who consorted with them, high or low.

The study does not claim to reconstruct the political economy of the
Mamlūk State in these turbulent years. Copious as they are, its data can only
hint at broad trends in the economy or the regime's responses to them. The
analysis does probe, in-depth, attitudes, motives, and goals of those who plotted the regime's economic course and set its political tone. Recovery of a mindset is sought here, the disposition of a ruling caste that regarded its realm and

all who inhabited it as an apanage, a personal possession to be tapped at will. Their mentality had a powerful conditioning effect on all social groups that came in contact with them. That arrogance, brutality, and parasitism imbued the Mamlūk's behavior, none acquainted with their legacy can deny.

Yet despite their excesses, the Mamlūks hardly disdained matters of state security, mass prosperity, public welfare, or spiritual piety. On occasion, they showed genuine compassion for suffering endured by even the meanest of their subjects. In the prospect of their own destitution, they sustained a rich program of cultural endowment. Egypt's military caste may warrant condemnation for its legacy, but it cannot be simplistically dismissed as petty. When their facade of arrogance is pierced, these praetorians' behavior reveals a peculiarly vulnerable coterie of officers and troops who, using standards their forebears enjoyed, saw their own integrity and well-being threatened. Moreover, this elite regarded many of the ad hoc bonds linking it with civilian dependents as egregiously compromised by the latter's duplicity. One discerns a corrosive sentiment of mutual betrayal, a lack of trust on both sides infusing acts which, on the surface, seem wantonly cruel or irrational. The behavior of those who loom large in the following chapters suggests a deep-seated conviction that neither side was any longer fulfilling its part of a clandestine bargain. Those in positions of dominance would not curb their demands, while subordinates closeted the lion's share of gleanings they were forced to forfeit to retain their privileges. We thus contemplate a paradox in the conduct of Egypt's elites. An absolutist stance by the sultanate, with undisputed claims on state assets, was qualified by nagging paranoia over the trustworthiness of its own agents of exploitation. This study seeks to explain this paradox and, by so doing, expose the essence of a clandestine partnership under severe strain.

The enterprise is prefaced by brief political summaries of the two autocrats' reigns (chapter 2).[3] These sketches are followed by discourses on the objectives of the sultanate's foreign policy, the performance of its military institution, the productivity of its economy, and the strategies it mounted for its survival.

The essay on foreign policy (chapter 3) addresses the sultanate's defensive posture. Motives are offered for the regime's obsession with maintenance of the international status quo. Aspirations of the sultanate's foreign competitors are compared according to the disparate challenges they posed. The Mamlūk caste (chapter 4) is considered in the context of its renown for combat effectiveness and sordid reputation as a leech on society. The Mamlūks' excesses as a self-centered interest group fully aware of their patron's beholden dilemma are considered in light of their anger over a perceived decline in lifestyle and status. The regime's economic sectors: agriculture, artisanship, and commerce (chapter 5) are examined according to the proclivity of each to concentrate its creative energies on concealment, hoarding, and preservation of existing assets rather than dabbling in more lucrative but higher-risk ventures. The evidence available depicts no precipitous decline in output but instead heightened attempts at extraction. The certainty of confiscation promoted a static attitude toward productivity, a conviction that higher profits merely attracted government harassment. Bedouin predation merits mention as a gauge of the regime's waning control over its hinterlands.

The final sections form a unit on clandestine strategies. Chapter 6 addresses the Sultanate's traditional means of coping with endemic crisis by either its circumvention, or, more likely, its manipulation for gain. It identifies the regime's schemes for coercing service from civil clients and enhancing its revenue from subjects skilled at passive resistance. Mounting frustration on both sides explains the tensions marring ties between master and minion. Chapter 7 speculates on the sultanate's attempts at overcoming crisis through innovation. It discerns tentative steps toward new procedures of recruiting soldiery outside entrenched bastions of Mamlūk power, of exploiting adroit clients, and of garnering hidden funds. Hypotheses are submitted about the sultan's attempts at creating a private fisc by laundering trust (*waqf*) properties. Inchoate as these experiments may have been, those with a vested stake in the established order rejected them vehemently as deviant and dangerous.

Many of the behavioral patterns apparent in bureaucratic or magisterial procedures of this era long outlasted their medieval progenitors. Whatever their implications for Egypt's current problems of development, they evolved indigenously long before Europeans exerted any significant influence. However they are interpreted, these tendencies emerged from myriad references by contemporary observers steeped in traditions of their culture with no sense of inferiority before the values of another. Indeed, comments about malaise occupy much of their chronicles' space, along with descriptions of factional rivalries and foreign affairs. Those who would discount the consequences of such patterns must also discredit the opinions of those who evaluated Egypt's condition in their own time. These candid observers, who did not gloss over unsettling episodes, deserve serious consideration of what they had to say.

But if the following analysis dwells on seemingly short-sighted responses to adversity, it does not ignore creative impulses of actors prominent in their design. Noted historian Eliyahu Ashtor, who contributed so much to our understanding of the economy in Mamlūk Egypt, yet so little to why it faltered, summed up his perceived limits of inquiry: "It would however be unreasonable to claim that this change in industrial structures is a satisfactory explanation of technological decline. Sometimes great innovations are made by individuals without being helped by a powerful organisation. They are indeed historical questions which the historian can raise but not answer."[4] This book aims at answering some of them.

The Sources

The study rests on views of several chroniclers, who left detailed accounts of the regime's activities, and archival documents, which list charitable endowments of Qāytbāy, his spouse Fāṭima, and Qānṣūh al-Ghawrī. Of the contemporary authors, four contributed the majority of the monograph's narrative data: Jamāl al-Dīn Yūsuf ibn Taghrī-Birdī (813–874/1411–1469), Nūr al-Dīn ʿAlī ibn Dāʾūd al-Jawharī al-Ṣayrafī (819–ca. 900/1416–1495), Zayn al-Dīn ʿAbd al-Bāsiṭ ibn Khalīl al-Malaṭī (844–920/1440–1514) and Abūʾl-Barakāt Muḥammad ibn Iyās (852–930/1448–1524).

The first was the son of a Mamlūk amīr who died in the author's infancy.[5] Raised in the households of his two sisters' husbands, Ibn Taghrī-Birdī enjoyed the status of a second-generation member of the military caste and the income from his father's estates. His brothers-in-law assured him a savant's education, in which the youth excelled. Showing an early flair for history, the young man studied with the eminent chronicler/topographer al-Maqrīzī. Capitalizing on his family connections at court, Ibn Taghrī-Birdī specialized in elucidating intricacies behind regime policies and foreign events. Although the polymath al-Sakhāwī criticized him for chronological, factual, and grammatical errors, Ibn Taghrī-Birdī's opinions reflected sober judgments of crises and shrewd assessments of character. An author of numerous compositions, he concentrated his major efforts on a biographical dictionary of court notables: *al-Manhal al-Ṣafī waʾl-Mustawfī baʿd al-Wāfī (The Pure Spring and Fulfillment after the Completion* [of al-Ṣafadī]); a comprehensive chronicle extending from the origins of Islam to the year 857/1453 and the death of Sultan Jaqmaq; *al-Nujūm al-Zāhira fī Mulūk Miṣr waʾl-Qāhira (Stars that Shine among the Kings of Egypt and Cairo)*; and a continuation of Maqrīzī's history, the *Kitāb al-Sulūk,* beginning in 845/1441 and terminating in 873/1469, several months before the author's death: *Ḥawādith al-Duhūr fī Madā al-Ayyām waʾl-Shuhūr (Episodes of the Epochs which Pass in Days and Months).*

The third work, despite its chronological brevity, contained Ibn Taghrī-Birdī's observations about his own generation. It expresses musings of a mature thinker whose opinions were tinged with the cynicism of old age. A peer of Qāytbāy in years and stature, Ibn Taghrī-Birdī earned the monarch's confidence as a learned adviser. Qāytbāy shared his aspirations, doubts, and fears openly. The historian painstakingly preserved them. Because this chronicler died early in Qāytbāy's reign, while the latter was still quelling opponents intent on deposing him, Ibn Taghrī-Birdī predicted neither Qāytbāy's successful consolidation of power nor his longevity. He therefore dwelled on the monarch's anxieties and greed, in marked contrast with the adulation of his colleagues—who lived to see the end of a glorious reign in which largesse was copiously distributed. His interpretations of Qāytbāy's actions offer a rare critical view of the deportment of an otherwise venerated figure.

The second chronicler exhibited a markedly different class background. Al-Ṣayrafī's father served as a moneychanger in the royal dīwāns. He supplemented an embarassingly meager income by trading in the Jeweler's Market of Cairo.[6] Al-Ṣayrafī remained acutely conscious of his father's penury and mediocre status as a minor bureaucrat. Yet his father supervised his early education personally before sending him off to the care of more eminent authorities. Al-Ṣayrafī attracted the notice of Cairo's learned luminary, Ibn Ḥajar al-ʿAsqalānī. With the esteemed shaykh's encouragement, al-Ṣayrafī tried his hand at historical writing, producing the first works of the so-called "Cairo narrative style," a blending of colloquial and formal usages unique to the second half of the ninth/fifteenth century.[7] Prestige eluded al-Ṣayrafī all his days. Coveting appointment to a senior Ḥanafī judgeship, he never received more than a deputy's bench—and this in his fiftieth year at a colleague's behest. Al-Ṣayrafī took up manuscript copying to support his growing family, selling editions of his famous mentor's works with his own appendices and commentaries (dismissed by al-Sakhāwī as a blight on the great sage's treatises). But al-Ṣayrafī's judicial marginality served his journalistic bent well. Attending sessions of both the religious (*Sharīʿa*) and appeals (*Maẓālim*) courts with few magisterial duties, he took copious notes on proceedings. These he recorded for posterity in his second chronicle.

Al-Ṣayrafī produced two significant historical tracts: *Nuzhat al-Nufūs waʾl-Abdān fī Tawārīkh al-Zamān* (*A Diversion Spiritual and Corporeal in the Annals of Time*) and *Inbāʾ al-Haṣr fī Abnāʾ al-ʿAṣr* (*Informing the Lion about Scions of the Age*). The first surveyed Egyptian politics from 786/1384 to 879/1475, following a hagiographic depiction of the Prophetic era in Madīna (of which only fragments remain). The latter was conceived as a celebration of Qāytbāy's reign (the "Lion" in its title). The author hoped to secure a place in the sultan's entourage by presenting his work as a gift, but no record of its completion has survived. The extant section covers only the years 873–877/1468–1473, albeit in minute detail. Portions of the years 885 and 886/1480–1481 are appended. Nonetheless, the four annals offer insights to judicial controversies available in few contemporary works. Since al-Ṣayrafī never deviated from his endorsement of the "court line," Qāytbāy emerges from his folios as a hero without blemish. Yet the sultan's judicial avocation is praised in the setting of its ambivalent reception among legal authorities compelled to abide the monarch's interference. Al-Ṣayrafī's remarks about their discomfiture are illuminating.

The third author claimed descent from a Mamlūk house, but one rung further down than Ibn Taghrī-Birdī.[8] Al-Malaṭī's father occupied the vizierate in Egypt and served as a provincial governor in Syria. Although his son excelled in Ḥanafī studies, he never aspired to the legal profession. He became an eminent physician and travelled to North Africa on a Genoese galley in the 1460s. Active in Cairo's Ṣūfī orders, al-Malaṭī "enjoyed wide influence among the Turks and amīrs," having translated numerous works into their language. In his later years, he won al-Ghawrī's favor. When he fell ill of consumption, the latter saw to his family's needs. Al-Malaṭī compiled a handbook on scriptural devotions he bestowed on his patron in gratitude: *Majmūʿ al-Bustān al-Nūrī li-Ḥadrat Mawlānā Sulṭān al-Ghūrī* (*Anthology of the Enlightened Arbor Presented to Our Lord Sulṭān al-Ghūrī*). Yet his historical corpus addressed the reign of al-Ghawrī's predecessor. Al-Malaṭī's large chronicle on affairs in Egypt, *al-Rawḍ al-Bāsim fī Ḥawādith al-ʿUmr waʾl-Tarājim* (*Gardens Smiling upon Events of Lifetimes and Lifestories*), deals with the period between 872/1468 and 890/1485. Unedited at present and complete in a single autograph, the work charts a middle course between Ibn Taghrī-Birdī's skepticism and al-Ṣayrafī's effusion.

The last member of this primary group casts a long shadow in Islamic historiography. Ibn Iyās also belonged to the third generation of the Mamlūk elite.[9] His grandfather held several viceroyships in Syria and left his progeny rights to his fief (*iqṭāʿ*). When Sultan al-Ghawrī attempted its expropriation, Ibn Iyās fought a grueling battle in court to reclaim his patrimony. While he succeeded, his brush with destitution scarred him. He never forgave al-Ghawrī and fulminated against him repeatedly for his spoliation of the propertied classes in Egypt. But despite his bias, Ibn Iyās stands as a towering figure among chroniclers of the later Middle Ages in Egypt. His vast tract: *Badāʾiʿ al-Zuhūr fī Waqāʾiʿ al-Duhūr* (*Marvels Blossoming among Incidents of the Epochs*) commences with the pre-Islamic Age but addresses specific events upon Qāytbāy's enthronement. Extending to the year 928/1522, the *Badāʾiʿ* remains the sole firsthand survey of al-Ghawrī's reign.

Our dependence on one author for an informed assessment of this controversial figure is acknowledged.[10] While Ibn Iyās wrote from personal observations, his hostility toward al-Ghawrī cannot be ignored. Dwelling at length on the sultan's altercations with his troops and counselors, Ibn Iyās consistently depicted al-Ghawrī as a schemer who amply merited his subordinates' rancor and suspicion. Yet Ibn Iyās never dismissed this man as a crude tyrant. The image that emerges from his castigations of al-Ghawrī's behavior is one of astute perception rather than callous brutality. Ibn Iyās readily admitted al-Ghawrī's intelligence and acknowledged his capacity to innovate as often as he decried his oppression. That the chronicler found this latter propensity disturbing is apparent in the intensity of his rebukes. But the acumen of a ruler confronting, with new stratagems, dilemmas that his precursors glossed over with timeworn ploys shows throughout Ibn Iyās's writing. The risks in depending on one man's point of view must qualify post hoc assessments of al-Ghawrī's reign. And yet this last chronicler to uphold an august tradition of factual objectivity during the independent Mamlūk period, at least by his own standards, did provide a foundation on which such assessments may be based.[11]

Several other writers complement the perspectives of these chroniclers. While the names of some elude us, their works offer summations composed after the passage of decades and reflect judgments of later generations. An on-site commentator in this secondary category was Aḥmad ibn Muḥammad al-Anṣārī, known as Ibn al-Ḥimṣī.[12] Resident in Damascus during Qāytbāy's early years, Ibn al-Ḥimṣī joined the train of the sultan's ambassador returning from negotiations with the Ottomans and relocated to Cairo. The recipient of a stipend from a trust endowed to free scholars for composition, he wrote his *Ḥawādith al-Zamān wa-Wafayāt al-Shuyūkh wa'l-Aqrān* (*Events of the Age with Necrologies of Elders and Peers*) in 900/1495. Conceived as an extension of Ibn Ḥajar's *Inbā' al-Ghumr,* the chronicle is compiled in an exceedingly colloquial style bordering on the vulgar. But Ibn al-Ḥimṣī captured the ethos of Qāytbāy's viceregal establishment in Damascus, and commented at length on the monarch's visits. The *Ḥawādith* is a goldmine of bureaucratic carpetbaggery in this second city of the empire.

Of greater stature but comparable relevance to our topic is the polymath Muḥammad ibn ʿAbd al-Raḥmān al-Sakhāwī (d. 902/1497).[13] Author of the huge biographical dictionary *al-Ḍaw' al-Lāmiʿ,* al-Sakhāwī wrote a continuation of al-Dhahabī's history during his retirement in Mecca: *al-Dhayl al-Tāmm ʿalā Duwal al-Islām* (*The Consummate Appendix to the Nations of Islam*). While hardly duplicating the former historian's breadth, Sakhāwī's *Appendix* is valuable for its portrayal of elite doings in the holy cities of the Ḥijāz. The interminable rebellions of Bedouin chiefs are reported with details omitted by chronicles using secondary evidence in Cairo. Sakhāwī's descriptions of pilgrimage rites and arrivals of eminent personages from the capital read like a gossip column and recover the festive atmosphere of the Ḥajj season.

A member of the wealthy Cairene house of Jīʿān, Badr al-Dīn Abū'l-Baqā' ibn Yaḥyā (fl. 899/1494), who served as deputy to Qāytbāy's confidential secretary, Zayn al-Dīn ibn Muzhir, participated in the sultan's trip through Syria to the Euphrates frontier in 882/1477.[14] His log of the journey describes conditions of rural life as well as receptions accorded the royal guests by provincial officials: *al-Qawl al-Mustaẓraf fī Safar Mawlānā al-Malik al-Ashraf* (*The Elegant Report Recounting the Voyage of Our Lord the Esteemed Monarch*). Among the swarms of admirers eulogizing Qāytbāy was Muḥammad ibn Yūsuf al-Bāʾūnī, who wrote in rajaz metre *al-Lamḥa al-Ashrafīya wa'l-Bahja al-Sanīya* (*The Noble Glow, the Sublime Resplendence*).[15] Amidst its flowery verses, one can discern the pious beneficence that so endeared Qāytbāy to the ʿulamā' and masked his avarice. Two anonymous authors wrote précis of Qāytbāy's reign: *Ta'rīkh al-Malik al-Ashraf Qāytbāy* (*History of the Honored Sovereign Qāytbāy*)[16] and *Jawāhir al-Sulūk fī'l-Khulafā' wa'l-Mulūk* (*Gems of Deportment about Caliphs and Kings*).[17] While neither yields any original information, each tallies up Qāytbāy's military expenses according to campaigns. Their focus on vast sums bespeaks the favorable impression made by the sultan's defensive stance and his willingness to pay for it long after the Ottoman Conquest.

Al-Ghawrī received nothing comparable to the multiple coverage granted Qāytbāy. But one tenth/sixteenth-century Syrian necrologist penned an intriguing obituary of him. Muḥammad ibn Ibrāhīm al-Ḥalabī al-Ḥanbalī wrote *Durr al-Ḥabab fī Taʾrīkh Aʿyān Ḥalab* (*Loving Pearls Embellishing the History of Aleppo Notables*), which included his savage denunciation of al-Ghawrī's greed and love of luxury.[18] An unnamed courtier left a history of Qāytbāy's hapless heir, al-Nāṣir Muḥammad, which elaborates on his shabby treatment as powerful amīrs maneuvered for power up to al-Ghawrī's succession: *Kitāb Ithbāt Dalālāt Muḥammad ibn al-Marḥūm al-Malik al-Ashraf Qāytbāy* (*A Tome Confirming Tokens of Muḥammad, Son of the Deceased Monarch al-Ashraf Qāytbāy*).[19] The biography of al-Ghawrī composed by the necrologist Abū'l-Makārim Muḥammad al-Ghazzī (977–1061/1570–1651) in his *al-Kawākib al-Sāʾira bi-Manāqib ʿUlamāʾ al-Miʾa al-ʿĀshira* (*Lingering Luminaries among the Virtues of Tenth-Century Savants*) relies on earlier evidence and reveals nothing new.[20] Nor does the Damascene chronicler, Shams al-Dīn Muḥammad ibn Ṭūlūn (884–935/1479–1529), appreciably expand upon Ibn Iyās' comments. His *Iʿlām al-Warā bi-man wulliya Nāʾiban min al-Atrāk bi-Dimashq* (*Men of Distinction among the Turks Appointed Viceroys in Damascus*) focuses primarily on imbroglios confronting governors in that city.[21] His episodic tract *Mufākahat al-Khillān fī Ḥawādith al-Zamān* (*Boon Banter over Anecdotes of the Age*) qualifies few facets of the sultan's image as Ibn Iyās left it.[22]

Archival documents analyzed as a component of the regime's private fiscal preserve consist of several hundred trust (*waqf*) deeds. Investment in charitable trusts proliferated during the later Mamlūk period because of abiding fiscal dilemmas discussed in chapters 6 and 7. These pious endowments are widely recognized as one of the most important cultural institutions of the Muslim community. Waqf donations provided much of the welfare extended to the needy and supported activities of the scholastic elite in a sophisticated academic setting. Their benefits to Islamic societies are incalculable.[23] Equally important but less publicized was the trust's function as an instrument of estate preservation.

This study utilizes data garnered from the large waqfs granted by sultans Qāytbāy and al-Ghawrī, the former's spouse, their close associates, and shorter sale deeds taken over by al-Ghawrī. The massive endowments, each amended several times during their donors' careers, list rural and urban properties yielding revenue for charities described in the other half of the writs. Such properties embraced hundreds of individual agrarian plots, shops, inns, caravansarays, manufactories, rental apartments, and so forth. The rural tracts extended from Aswān to the Delta, while the urban holdings were concentrated in Cairo. Sections outlining the charities describe the sultan's mausoleum complex, comprised of his tomb (*qubba* or "dome"), college of law (*madrasa*), library (*khizānat al-kutub*), mystic hospice (*khānqāh*), orphanage (*ribāṭ al-aytām*) and related institutions, plus his other foundations in Cairo or the provinces. Teaching and custodial staffs, student stipends and rations, pensions for Ṣūfī residents, and related cash benefices are minutely detailed, with salary rates and operating budgets precisely tallied. These figures, when compared against sums generated by the endowments' productive properties, support speculative analysis of the charitable trust as the source of a personal fisc subject solely to its donor's manipulation.

These and related materials issued in Egypt during the Middle Ages (primarily the Ayyūbid and Mamlūk periods) are housed in two Cairo repositories: the National Archives (Dār al-Wathāʾiq al-Qawmīya), classified within the Canonical Tribunal (*Maḥkama Sharʿīya*), with jurisdiction over familial and estate affairs and abbreviated as DW; and the Ministry of Pious Endowments (Wizārat al-Awqāf), classified within the Medieval (pre-Ottoman) Repository (*Daftarkhānah*), abbreviated as AW. Documents in AW marked "old" (*qadīm*) indicate deeds classified before 1967, when a collection of some three hundred sale, substitution, and transfer writs was discovered. The latter were designated "new" (*jadīd*). The great majority of these were appropriated by Sultan al-Ghawrī. Muḥammad Amīn of Cairo University inventoried all surviving pre-Ottoman deeds in his *Catalogue des documents d'archives du Caire de 239/853 à 922/1516* (Cairo: IFAO, 1981), and assigned each a reference number, which accompanies all subsequent notations in chapter 7.

Notes

1. Philip Hitti, *The History of the Arabs*, 8th ed. (London, 1963), 683.

2. To date, this era has yet to be analyzed as a distinctive period. Neither Qāytbāy nor Qānṣūh al-Ghawrī has been the subject of monographs. Brief articles in the *Encyclopaedia of Islam* remain essential sources of reference. See *EI*[1] 2: M. Sobernheim, "Ḳāʾitbey," 663–64 and "Ḳānṣūh," 720–21; *EI*[2] 4: E. Ashtor, "Ḳāʾit Bāy," 462–63 and P. M. Holt, "Ḳānṣawh al-Ghawrī," 552–53. Gaston Wiet's remarks in his survey of Islamic Egypt are still the most coherent statement after five decades. See *L'Égypte arabe,* vol. 4 of G. Hanotaux' *L'histoire de la nation égyptienne* (Paris, 1937), 589–636. For a brief overview of Mamlūk institutions and politics, consult P. M. Holt, *The Age of the Crusades: The near East from the Eleventh Century to 1517* (London, 1986).

3. These summaries outline only prominent events in the regimes of the two sultans. For more in-depth biographies see *Twilight of Majesty,* as per n. 1 in the acknowledgments.

4. E. Ashtor, *A Social and Economic History of the Near East in the Middle Ages* (Berkeley, 1976), 309.

5. *GAL* 2, p. 41, no. 10; *Ḍawʾ* 10, p. 305, no. 1178; *Badāʾiʿ* 3, p. 45, 1. 23.

6. *GAL* Suppl. 2, p. 41, no. 12; *Ḍawʾ* 5, p. 217, no. 738; *Badāʾiʿ* 3, p. 309, 1. 23.

7. Ḥasan Ḥabashī, introduction to *Inbāʾ*, pp. 18–19.

8. *GAL* 2, p. 54, no. 17; Suppl. 2, p. 52, no. 17; *Badāʾiʿ* 4, p. 373, 1. 23.

9. *GAL* 2, p. 295, no. 1; Suppl. 2, p. 405, no. 1; *Badāʾiʿ* 4, p. 47, 1. 11 (obituary of author's father).

10. Ibn Iyās acknowledged Qānṣūh al-Ghawrī's sustained interest in literature. He mentioned the sultan's compositions in Turkish, which remained the language of the military elite in Cairo even when many of its members originated in Circassia. Al-Ghawrī compiled an anthology of Turkish poetry to which he contributed several pieces himself: *Dīvān-i Qānṣawh al-Ghawrī* (ms.: Berlin, Staatsbibliothek: Or. oct. 3744), edited and translated by Mehmet Yalsin, *Dīvān-i Qanṣawh al-Ghawrī: A Critical Edition of an Anthology of Turkish Poetry Commissioned by Sultan Qanṣawh al-Ghawrī (1501–1516)* (Ph. D. diss., Harvard University [Inner Asian and Altaic Studies], 1993). While a work such as the *Dīvān* attests to al-Ghawrī's poetic competence, its contents reflect on literary conventions in the Mamlūk court rather than on the regime's economic or political policies as interpreted by those compelled to endure them. Accordingly, the unique perspective of a close observer like Ibn Iyās remains indispensable.

11. Ibn Iyās' comments on the defensive posture adopted by al-Ghawrī's successor, Ṭūmānbāy, and policies of incorporation imposed by Selim I's governors occupy the bulk of volume five in the *Badāʾiʿ*. There is little evidence that Ibn Iyās recast his assessment of al-Ghawrī's actions to any significant degree either to vent his pent-up spleen with even more intensity or to curry favor with Egypt's new authorities. See Michael Winter, *Society and Religion in Early Ottoman Egypt: Studies in the Writings of ʿAbd al-Wahhāb at-Shaʿrānī* (New Brunswick, 1982), 5–6, 13–14, 18. Winter notes that the chronicler's dismay over the Ottoman Conquest disposed him neither to disparage deceased rulers unduly nor to exaggerate disruptions accompanying the change of government. Annemarie Schimmel focuses on Ibn Iyās' depiction of postconquest changes in judicial proceedings but not his castigation of al-Ghawrī. See "Kalif und Kadi im spätmittelalterlichen Ägypten," *Die Welt des Islams* 24 (1942): 84–93.

12. *GAL* Suppl. 2, p. 41, no. 12a.

13. *GAL* 2, p. 43, no. 1; Suppl. 2, pp. 31–32.

14. *GAL* 2, p. 38, no. 1; Suppl. 2, p. 26, no. 1; *Ḍawʾ* 11, p. 8, no. 21, Not perused for this study but noted here is the account of the amīr Yashbak al-Ẓāhirī's embassy to Uzun Ḥasan in 880/1475, penned by Shams al-Dīn Muḥammad ibn Ajā, edited by ʿAbd al-Qādir Aḥmad Tulaymāt (Cairo, 1973).

15. *GAL* 2, p. 54, no. 18; Suppl. 2, p. 67, no. 3; *Ḍawʾ* 10, p. 89, no. 290.

16. *GAL* 2, p. 38; Suppl. 2, p. 26.

17. *GAL* 2, p. 42; Suppl. 2, p. 53.

18. *GAL* 2, p. 368; M. Sobernheim, "Ḳānṣūh," *EI*[1] 2: 721. The work is dated 11 Dhū'l-Qaʿda 972/10 June 1565 on the colophon.

19. Not listed in *GAL;* Istanbul: Topkapi Saray, no. 2960.

20. *GAL* 2, p. 291, no. 8.

21. Edited by ʿAbd al-ʿAẓīm Ḥāmid Khaṭṭāb (Cairo, 1973).

22. Edited by Muḥammad Muṣṭafā, 2 vols. (Cairo, 1962, 1964). Another noteworthy work not utilized in this monograph bears mention. Aḥmad ibn ʿAlī ibn Zunbul al-Shāfiʿī (d. 926/1520) wrote *Taʾrīkh al-Sulṭān Salīm al-ʿUthmānī maʿa al-Sulṭān Qānṣūh al-Ghūrī (History of Sultan Selim the Ottoman and Sultan Qānṣūh al-Ghūrī),* a detailed log of the latter's last campaign culminating in his defeat and death at Marj Dābiq (*GAL* 2, p. 43, no. 19; Suppl. 2, p. 298, no. 1). Exploiting his post in the (Ottoman?) war office, Ibn Zunbul perused eyewitness versions of the dramatic battle. Because the analysis addresses al-Ghawrī's domestic policies, it omits this manuscript. Whether Ibn Iyās knew of it remains indeterminate since he makes no mention of it.

23. For the significance of charitble trusts in traditional Muslim societies, see Muḥammad M. Amīn, *Al-Awqāf wa'l-Ḥayāt al-Ijtimāʿīya fī Miṣr* (Cairo, 1980); George Makdisi, *The Rise of Colleges: Institutions of Higher Learning in Islam and the West* (Edinburgh, 1981), 35–74; Carl F. Petry, "A Paradox of Patronage during the Later Mamlūk Period," *The Muslim World* 53 (1983): 190–95.

2

THE REIGNS OF AL-ASHRAF QĀYTBĀY AND QĀNṢŪH AL-GHAWRĪ

For two men whose vision was shaped by identical values of caste, their ruling styles could not have diverged more sharply. Qāytbāy (r. 872–901/1468–1496) identified heart and soul with the regime he entered as a purchased slave in his early twenties. Never prone to making enemies for the sake of ambition, he was respected early on as a stalwart who did not betray his comrades. By contrast, Qānṣūh al-Ghawrī (r. 906–922/1501–1516) was respected for his ruthless soldiery but rarely inspired the kind of trust from his peers that Qāytbāy enjoyed for so many decades. Qāytbāy dedicated his adult life to shoring up a ruling institution and imperial edifice riven with corruption and decay. Finding his sovereign office progressively untenable in such an edifice, al-Ghawrī prepared to match his contemporaries, deceit for guile, as he experimented with novel means of relieving the dilemmas he faced. The reigns of these polar opposites thus reveal divergent ways of coping with unremitting crisis.

Qāytbāy: Esteemed Custodian

Al-Malik al-Ashraf Qāytbāy al-Maḥmūdī was born in the Circassian regions of the Caucasus between 818 and 821/1416 and 1418.[1] While no details on his adolescent life were reported in contemporary sources, the mature characteristics they did extol certainly evolved over previous decades. Already an accomplished horseman when he arrived in Cairo, Qāytbāy had caught the eye of his purchaser, Maḥmūd ibn Rustam, in Circassia because of his talents as a mounted archer and lance caster. The young cadet so excelled as a cavalier that he was immediately assigned duties as an instructor of other recruits in the equestrian arts. Qāytbāy's reputation spread rapidly to the royal court in the Citadel, and he was taken on as a palace attendant by Sultan Barsbāy (r. 825–841/1422–1437). Upon the latter's death, his eventual successor, Jaqmaq (r. 842–857/1438–1453) advanced Qāytbāy to the rank of bodyguard (*khāṣṣakī*) and then promoted him to several junior-grade offices. Having already acquired a reputation for trustworthiness, Qāytbāy rose steadily if not spectacularly through the Mamlūk hierarchy during the reigns of Jaqmaq, Īnāl (r. 857–865/1453–1460), and Khushqadam (r. 865–872/1461–1467). He attained a senior officer's summit posting when he received the command of one thousand Mamlūks (*taqdimat alf*) midway through Īnāl's administration.

More than thirty years intervened between Qāytbāy's induction as a recruit and his inclusion within the oligarchy of grand amīrs. These were turbulent times replete with intrigues at court. Yet Qāytbāy stood aloof from involvement in coup plots. Not a single allegation of collusion was lodged against him throughout these decades, nor any report of arrest or exile.[2] This grand amīr therefore enjoyed a special kind of respect in the Mamlūk power structure. He was a competent officer capable of compelling obedience, yet one driven neither by ambition nor greed. Such men were prized as stalwart adjutants by other more impetuous figures who, playing for high stakes prematurely, were toppled from office because of haphazardly organized coalitions of supporters. Thus, although known primarily as a self-effacing lieutenant during the enthronement crisis that ensued upon Sultan Khushqadam's death in 872/1467, Qāytbāy was, in fact, ideally suited to assume the monarchy following the reigns of Khushqadam's ephemeral successors, Yilbāy and Timurbughā.

    Khushqadam's demise plunged the Mamlūk sultanate into the kind of acrimony that had sapped its energies throughout the ninth/fifteenth century. Neither of these two officers commanded sufficient sentiments of loyalty from otherwise contentious factions to retain the autocracy more than a few months. Qāytbāy was a close colleague of the second contender, Timurbughā. When his comrade (*khushdāsh*) was dethroned by Sultan Īnāl's amīrs, who saw their superior status in the military hierarchy threatened by this man, Qāytbāy refused the monarchy they proffered him. Yet his enthronement was a virtual certainty since no other candidate posed less menace to the various disgruntled factions.[3] Thus, for all his protests, Qāytbāy ascended to the sultanate on 6 Rajab 872/31 January 1468. He succumbed to pleas that his cooperation was necessary for the regime's survival. But he insisted that his predecessor, Timurbughā, who now sat under close guard pondering his fate, be treated with all respect due a former monarch and be allowed to retire in honored exile.[4] Only then did Qāytbāy shoulder the burdens of a fractious regime and face the inevitable struggle for consolidation.

Once acclaimed, Qāytbāy wasted no time placating sensitivities of probable rivals. He arrested Timurbughā's chief aides and exiled many of the officers who had accepted his succession only as an interim expedient while they pursued their own schemes for yet another round of revolts.[5] Throughout his remorseless dispatch of detention warrants, Qāytbāy disdained special escorts but rode about the Citadel precinct fearlessly reprimanding haughty amīrs or obstreperous recruits to their faces. In some sixty days after his accession, Qāytbāy had scattered his opposition. This he accomplished without recourse to executions or torture, a tactic that had stained his precursors' successions. Qāytbāy also built up a close-knit coterie of senior associates who, over the coming years, would jointly set the regime's policy and direct its bureaucracy. That these individuals, whose personalities differed markedly, worked together with a modicum of civility testified to the admiration they shared for their colleague-patron.

Prominent within this inner circle were two individuals who wielded powers subordinate only to the sultan's own. Each one's sphere of influence countered the other's, enabling Qāytbāy to maintain his own stance as final arbiter. These were the grand amīrs Yashbak min Mahdī and Azbak[6] min Ṭuṭukh, made executive secretary (*dawādār*) and marshal of the army (*atābak*) respectively. The former, already a legend for his bravery and cruelty when Qāytbāy was enthroned, served as the sultan's hatchet man.[7] Yashbak min Mahdī intimidated every official in the imperial bureaucracy, major or minor. He was invaluable to Qāytbāy as an enforcer who cowed rebellious troopers and squeezed copious revenues from property holders. Yashbak respected the rank of no Mamlūk peer save that of his royal colleague. When he could no longer repress his own ambition for sovereign power, he gambled on a foreign venture, which proved to be his undoing.

The latter, Azbak, succeeded one Jānibak Qulaqsīz, a plotter in the coup that had elevated Qāytbāy but who suffered the misfortune of capture during a campaign against the Dhū'l-Qādrid rebel Shāh Sūwār in 873/1468.[8] Qāytbāy granted Azbak min Ṭuṭukh supreme command over the military because he enjoyed the troops' heartfelt loyalty, in contrast with their dread of Yashbak. Azbak presided over most long-range military planning, advising his royal associate about pragmatic courses of action to contain foreign imbroglios. Qāytbāy could rely upon Yashbak to rescue a campaign from defeat, while he entrusted Azbak with defining parameters of long-range policy. Each performed his ordained function ably, until the former embarked upon his ill-fated attempt at kingdom-building, and the latter submitted to exile for complicity in a revolt almost three decades later, when Qāytbāy's own faculties had waned.

With such adjutants Qāytbāy consolidated his regime. His governing apparatus successfully weathered the escape of Timurbughā, Qāytbāy's predecessor, in Dhū'l-Qaʿda 872/June 1468.[9] Timurbughā was apprehended near Ghazza and returned to his cell in Alexandria. While the sultan spared his former khushdāh, he deported those who had abetted his escape—thereby scattering residual malcontents. Thus, by the end of that year, Qāytbāy had laid durable foundations for his long reign and restored public confidence in the regime's viability after an interregnum of debilitating tumult.

Qāytbāy could not rest on his laurels, however. For an ambitious prince in Southeastern Anatolia, whose family had served as the Mamlūk sultanate's watchmen over its northern marches for generations, exploited this interregnum to rebel. Shāh Sūwār the Dhū'l-Qādrid renounced his vassalage oath, supplanted his brother, and set about entrenching himself as autonomous chieftain in Little Armenia (*Ilbistīn*).[10] Fearing the ripple effect of such a revolt on other allies should Sūwār sustain his secession, Qāytbāy dispatched several expeditions to bring this miscreant to heel. But Sūwār showed himself a skilled strategist, luring his numerically superior opponents into ambush on several occasions. Qāytbāy was compelled to spend large sums on requisitioning supplies for subsequent campaigns. The reputation of the Mamlūk sultanate as a bastion of stability in the tense arena of Southwest Asian politics was dealt a humiliating blow.

When Qāytbāy called upon Yashbak to retrieve the situation, his dawādār captured the Dhū'l-Qādrid rebel, but only after a war that had dragged on until 876/1472.[11] Yashbak conveyed Shāh Sūwār back to Cairo as a treasonous prisoner in 877/1473. There he was publicly rebuked by Qāytbāy and subsequently gibbeted from hooks at the Bāb Zuwayla. Only then could Qāytbāy credibly proclaim the restoration of Mamlūk suzerainty in Southeastern Anatolia—but at a steep cost in men and money. Shāh Sūwār's revolt was a harbinger of future challenges from ambitious rivals to Cairo's supremacy in the central Muslim world. They would pose threats of even greater magnitude, which taxed the regime's resources to its limits.

Yet for the following decade and a half, Qāytbāy savored his reaffirmation as the principal monarch of Sunnī Islam. Throughout these years, the sultan radiated an aura of majesty that inspired many of his subjects to revere their overlord as a conservator of grandeur they recalled from days when Egypt's primacy was uncontested. Qāytbāy inaugurated his lavish program of patronage, which embellished the capital with a host of charitable institutions, several memorable for their architecture. The sultan reveled in progressions through the Delta, Fayyūm, and Middle Valley during which thousands of peasants beheld his royal presence among them.[12] Qāytbāy made trips to Alexandria and Damietta on the Mediterranean coast to inspect their fortifications against frequent Italian piracy. He commissioned construction of an imposing guard tower at the site of the ancient Pharos Lighthouse in Alexandria.[13] He undertook a tour of Damascus and Aleppo Provinces to apprise himself of conditions in these regions hitherto unvisited during his reign.[14]

And despite the time required for these sojourns, Qāytbāy did not shirk his duties as final arbiter of his realm. Not content with hearing magistrates summarize appeals cases, this sultan intervened personally to resolve disputes among judges emerging from complicated suits. He thereby acquired a renown for justice unsurpassed by any of his royal counterparts, past or future. It was Qāytbāy's sincere commitment to the formal responsibilities of kingship—so often neglected by rulers—that mitigated against the weight of his fiscal extractions and the perennial disruption caused by his Mamlūk praetorians. In epochs to come, historians would choose to dwell on Qāytbāy's record as a paragon of charity and justice, an image of him they cherished.

But ideal harmony eludes even esteemed rulers. Qāytbāy's closest aide, Yashbak al-Dawādār, despite his power and eminence, chafed over the prospect of indefinite subordination to a liege-lord who was also his intimate comrade. So long as Qāytbāy reigned, Yashbak could not contemplate any attempt to seize the sultanate for himself. He thus was receptive to rumors circulated at the Citadel by a delegation from the court of Uzun Ḥasan's son, Yaʿqūb, Aqquyunlū prince of the two Iraqs, in 885/1480.[15] The emissaries reported widespread dissatisfaction with this heir's erratic leadership before his officers, who might well swear allegiance to an abler patron willing to supplant him. Qāytbāy, sensitive to the dilemma burdening his khushdāsh, sanctioned Yashbak's request to attempt such a venture, so long as he chose his troops from among the disaffected Īnālīya Mamlūks whose loyalty at home remained suspect.

Yashbak's expedition seemed assured of success because of his military record. Yet when he assaulted the border fortress of al-Ruhā (Urfa) in Ramaḍān 885/November 1480, its prefect, a vassal of Yaʿqūb, inflicted a stunning defeat. Yashbak was imprisoned and executed soon thereafter, his head sent on to Mardīn, where Yaʿqūb was residing, to verify this extraordinary reversal of fortunes.[16] When Qāytbāy received initial reports about the disaster, he was incredulous. But upon inspection of Yashbak's decapitated corpse, returned to Cairo by Yaʿqūb who was now alarmed over possible reprisals by the sultan, Qāytbāy accepted the loss of his comrade. Their joint plans for creation of an allied buffer principality in Iraq and western Iran, which, in consort with Egypt, would assure order in the Dār al-Islām, had come to naught. But Qāytbāy stoically accepted this verdict of fate and ordered no vendetta against the Aqquyunlū regime. Ever disposed to preserve the status quo, Qāytbāy and the marshal Azbak may have interpreted Yashbak's fate as a warning from the All-High decrying such an assault upon the established order of states. No subsequent attempt at conquest abroad would be undertaken by the Mamlūk sultanate in its twilight years.

Foreign affairs were not tranquil despite Qāytbāy's commitment to bolstering the status quo. Trouble was now brewing from a different quarter to the north in the Ottoman State. Throughout the seventies and eighties of the ninth/fifteenth century, the Ottoman and Mamlūk Empires maintained a stance of cordial coexistence neither had any cause to violate. Until his death in 886/1481, the Ottoman Sultan Mehmet II, conqueror of Constantinople, was largely preoccupied with his European adversaries. Only once had he undertaken a campaign troubling to Cairo, when he sent an expedition against the still autonomous Qaramān Principality (*Beylik*) of Southeastern Anatolia in 872/1469.[17] When the Qaramānid Bey repelled the invader, Mehmet elected to accept the consequences for the time being. His successor, Bāyazīd II (r. 886–918/1481–1512), was inclined toward resolving international disputes through diplomacy rather than by force.

Bāyazīd maintained positive relations with Qāytbāy until 889/1484 when, under pressure at home to renew the empire's expansive drive eastward, he began harassing Shāh Suwār's successor, ʿAlāʾ al-Dawla (ʿAlī Dawlāt in Egyptian sources).[18] Reacting with alarm over this threat to the clientship of the Dhū'l-Qādrids, restored at such cost years earlier, Qāytbāy organized a series of expeditions to check the Ottomans that continued to 896/1490. Because of their size, these campaigns were enormously expensive and placed unprecedented demands on the Mamlūk sultanate's resources. Qāytbāy may indeed have done lethal damage to the formal system of supply requisition and revenue collection that had evolved from the Ayyūbid sultan Saladin's reign (567–589/1171–1193). Qāytbāy's eventual successor, Qānṣūh al-Ghawrī, would contemplate the dismal prospect of imminent bankruptcy throughout his troubled regime. Yet despite their costs, these expeditions impeded the Ottomans' designs on the east. Bāyazīd's emissaries were eventually willing to negotiate treaties, which, in effect, acknowledged all the Mamlūk sultan's claims as paramount suzerain in Syria and Southeastern Anatolia. Not until Bāyazīd was succeeded by his aggressive son, Selim, would the balance of power Qāytbāy had so assiduously defended be jeopardized once again.

Upon conclusion of the Ottoman Wars, Qāytbāy enjoyed a primacy of place among Muslim monarchs uncontested by any foreign counterpart. At home, he had become an awe-inspiring institution whose stature among both military peers and civilian subjects had not been equalled since the days of al-Ẓāhir Baybars (r. 658–676/1260–1277) or al-Nāṣir Muḥammad (third reign: 709–741/1309–1340). Nonetheless, no prestige could slow the passage of time, and by the end of the ninth/fifteenth century, Qāytbāy had begun to show his advanced age. Following the fracture of his leg in Rabīʿ I 891/March 1486 during a riding accident, Qāytbāy's brush with death prompted several ambitious adjutants to maneuver for the advantage in a succession struggle.[19] Their plotting, although set aside when Qāytbāy's stamina pulled him through, revealed their growing frustration over so long a wait for a try at the autocracy themselves. As the nineties progressed, the junior Mamlūk recruits became ever more unruly as Qāytbāy's personal force slowly ebbed. Yet no one thought to depose so venerated a figure while he lived. Still, few among the sultan's inner circle expected his son and heir, al-Nāṣir Muḥammad, born late in the reign from a royal concubine, to win the inevitable power contest after his father's demise. At best, this adolescent might briefly survive as the puppet of senior amīrs who exploited his figurehead sultanate until they were prepared to attempt supplanting their rivals. Prominent among these ambitious officers was one Qānṣūh Khamsmi'a min Ṭarābāy (not to be confused with Qānṣūh al-Ghawrī). Emerging to prominence as an aide to Yashbak min Mahdī, this Qānṣūh became a divisive presence in the Citadel following the dawādar's debacle at al-Ruhā.[20] As the years passed and Qāytbāy weakened, this amīr's plans for taking over became more blatant.

The tension his posturing provoked in the Citadel was exacerbated by external factors beyond the regime's control. The most devastating of these was the plague (*ṭāʿūn*), which erupted once again in Egypt during 897/1492.[21] This pestilence ravaged both the urban and rural populace, with casualties estimated at many thousands until it abated after several months. It left behind a ruling apparatus decimated and a monarch depressed by feelings of isolation. Yet Qāytbāy persevered with his typical resolve. He continued to perform his duties as before, disdaining a rising tide of troop unrest and impatience from would-be successors eager to test their leadership skills. Even Qāytbāy's last remaining khushdāsh from earlier glory days, the atābak Azbak, was caught up in the momentum of conspiracy. He sided with Qānṣūh Khamsmi'a, who sought to defeat a hated rival, the current dawādar Aqbirdī, in open combat.[22] Following Qānṣūh's failure to rally support for his coup, Azbak appealed to his old comrade for clemency. Qāytbāy permitted his disgraced marshal to leave Cairo for the Ḥijāz, thus terminating an impressive career of twenty-eight years.

Qāytbāy could no longer suppress the quarrels that now flared up incessantly between his senior associates. He finally died on 27 Dhū'l-Qaʿda 901/8 August 1496 after having convened one last muster of troops to keep the peace.[23] Ironically, neither of the two prime contestants competing to seize the sultanate, Aqbirdī or Qānṣūh Khamsmi'a, were destined to duplicate Qāytbāy's achievement at consolidation nearly three decades earlier. Several years would elapse before the hitherto obscure Qānṣūh al-Ghawrī would preside over a unified military hierarchy and bureaucratic structure.

No one held Qāytbāy responsible for the dissolution of his ruling apparatus immediately following his death. Such struggles for power were a predictable manifestation of the Mamlūk concept of upward mobility. Qāytbāy, as a champion of the old order, never sought to reform the institution he had defended for so long. Nor would this man be remembered for any significant innovations in foreign policy, administrative style, or economic production. Rather he would be admired as custodian of a military tradition that had evolved from its beginning in the Ayyūbid period centuries before. This tradition had kept Egypt a great power for more than three hundred years. Qāytbāy could lay just claim to its rejuvenation under adverse circumstances. Historians would thus idealize the accomplishments of this sultan, the last great military leader in their country's history as an independent state. They would gratefully overlook the legacy of bankruptcy, confiscation, and oppression he left his eventual successor, al-Ghawrī.

Qānsūh al-Ghawrī: Reviled Innovator

Although the sultanate's penultimate ruler came to power as a compromise candidate, he shared little else with his predecessor, Qāytbāy. Before his enthronement, the chroniclers mentioned this obscure officer only in passing as a provincial governor who crushed local insurgents and repelled invaders from outside. A dark horse, Qānsūh al-Ghawrī's character or goals did not impress historians. They provided only a skeletal outline of this private man's career prior to his elevation to the autocracy.[24] Al-Ghawrī, who took his agnomen from the Ghawr Barracks of Cairo where he was trained, was designated an amīr of ten in 889/1484 upon his completion of service in the Ottoman campaign of that year.

The quality of al-Ghawrī's provincial service eventually merited his entry into the oligarchy of grand amīrs who commanded brigades of a thousand Mamlūks.[25] During the feuds that erupted the interregnum following Qāytbāy's death, al-Ghawrī emerged from the coterie of contenders for the imperial office. The removal of Qāytbāy's heir, al-Nāsir Muḥammad, in 904/ 1498 was followed by several fleeting reigns and attempted coups, during which al-Ghawrī became the confidant to al-ʿĀdil Ṭūmānbāy (deposed on 30 Ramaḍān 906/19 April 1501) [not to be confused with al-Ghawrī's nephew of the same name]. After al-ʿĀdil's elimination and the failure of two other plotters to make good their bids for power, al-Ghawrī's colleagues nominated him for the sultanate.[26]

Al-Ghawrī protested his candidacy since at best he would preside over an oligarchy riven by an acrimony and frustrated ambition daunting even by the fractious standards of the later Mamlūk era. At worst, he faced high odds of arrest and execution. Yet al-Ghawrī was no untried novice when he yielded to his backers' coercion. Having already reached the age of sixty, this man was intimately familiar with a conspirator's route to high office in the Mamlūk elite. Only those who trod it adroitly were deemed competent to hold the sultanate. Survival became al-Ghawrī's prime objective from the day of his acclamation (1 Shawwāl 906/20 April 1501) to his death on the battlefield in Syria fifteen years hence. But he responded to the unsavory conditions of his accession with stratagems diverging markedly from Qāytbāy's more traditional policies. Unlike his predecessor, Qānṣūh al-Ghawrī was prepared to alter the power structure rather than to shore it up.

Al-Ghawrī's efforts at consolidating his position superficially paralleled Qāytbāy's tactics of dispersing potential rivals by exiling them—but with less success. Even his closest aides, the atābak Qāyt al-Rajabī and the dawādār Miṣirbāy, exhibited none of the camaraderie with him that Yashbak or Azbak had shown Qāytbāy. From the hour of his enthronement, al-Ghawrī suspected both of treason, and began planning for their elimination as they plotted to get rid of him when the opportunity arose.[27] Qānṣūh al-Ghawrī never overcame such paranoia during his reign. Nor did any of his colleagues, save for the sultan's nephew, Ṭūmānbāy. Al-Ghawrī's former khushdāsh, al-ʿĀdil, was executed after a foiled escape attempt. No honored retirement awaited those who schemed against this autocrat.

Al-Ghawrī did manage to secure his position; a new oligarchy of officers coalesced who were at least willing to bide their time in his service. But the specter of rebellion, tainted by peer assassination, hovered over al-Ghawrī's reign. Al-Ghawrī would remain obsessed with the threat of deposition and resort to public rites of solidarity to bolster his confidence.[28] The historian Ibn Iyās estimated the passage of two years before al-Ghawrī finally purged his ruling oligarchy of malcontents, real or imagined.[29] Not until 908/1502–03 did the chronicler see fit to inventory the roster of prominent executive office holders. Previously, conditions had been too unsettled to forecast that a ruling cabinet would last even one year. Al-Ghawrī did not rest easy until 910/1505, when he arrested his key henchman, Qāyt al-Rajabī, for conspiring with the viceroy of Aleppo, Sībāy, to overthrow him.[30] Only when Qāyt had been locked away in Alexandria did al-Ghawrī feel confident enough to transfer his wife from their private residence in town to the Citadel.[31]

While al-Ghawrī shunned personal ties to most of his subordinates, civilian or military, he did cement bonds with three individuals in these hazardous early years. These he would value for much of his career. The three individuals were themselves studies in contrasts, their diverse backgrounds suggestive of the wide range of personnel who gained prominence in the sultan's inner circle. They were al-Ghawrī's aforementioned nephew, Ṭūmānbāy; his adviser in legal affairs, Sarī al-Dīn ʿAbd al-Barr ibn al-Shiḥna; and his inquisitor, Zayn al-Dīn Barakāt ibn Mūsā. The first was a son of al-Ghawrī's otherwise unidentified brother, who may never have departed from Circassia.[32] But despite his father's obscurity, Ṭūmānbāy already shared a close association with his uncle when the latter was enthroned. Embodying qualities of honor and integrity subordinates found appealing, Ṭūmānbāy served his uncle-patron as a front man. Appointed dawādār several years after al-Ghawrī's accession, Ṭūmānbāy would hold the executive secretaryship until his uncle's defeat at Marj Dābiq by the Ottomans. Whether Ṭūmānbāy questioned al-Ghawrī's innovative designs or sustained abuse of clients we cannot know, for whatever his personal thoughts he never deviated from his loyalty. Al-Ghawrī rewarded his nephew with the offices Qāytbāy had bestowed upon Yashbak min Mahdī. When al-Ghawrī departed to Syria for his confrontation with Selim I in 922/1516, his choice of Ṭūmānbāy as regent was a foregone conclusion. He trusted no one else with the reins of power in his absence.

The second confidant hailed from one of Cairo's prominent 'ulamā' families whose reputation as scholastics was respected in Syria decades before their resettlement in Cairo.[33] Sarī al-Dīn ibn al-Shiḥna had shown himself a precocious jurist during the latter years of Qāytbāy's reign when he manipulated for his own profit academic sinecures of scholars whose death was imminent. Sarī al-Dīn embarrassed his father and angered his sovereign through his legal chicanery, and was sent off to the provincial court circuit in Syria. But he resurfaced in Cairo soon after al-Ghawrī's accession, receiving the Ḥanafī qāḍīship of the capital in 906/1501.[34] Sarī al-Dīn assured himself of a place among the architects of al-Ghawrī's clandestine fiscal strategies when he finessed his patron's first try at waqf confiscation early in 907/July-August 1501.[35]

From that episode until his own fall from grace more than a decade later, Ibn al-Shiḥna helped his patron concoct a variety of techniques aimed at the creation of a private fisc reserved solely for the autocrat's use. Glossing over violations of codes issued to protect the sanctity of charitable trusts from such tampering, Ibn al-Shiḥna won a peculiar kind of prestige among the judicial establishment in Cairo. Both respected and detested by his colleagues, Sarī al-Dīn, with the instinct of a natural sycophant, realized whom he must appease to secure his position. None of the chroniclers who described Ibn al-Shiḥna's special relationship with al-Ghawrī extolled their personal affection. Yet they intimated their mutual dexterity in conspiracy and double-dealing, talents both found intrinsically appealing.

The last participant in this troika first caught al-Ghawrī's eye as a minor Citadel attendant who had earlier served in Qāytbāy's retinue as a falconer's page.[36] The son of a Bedouin groom in the royal stables, al-Zaynī Barakāt ibn Mūsā seems to have possessed a knack for intimidation and spying. When al-Ghawrī made him his bailiff (*bardādār*) in 908/1503, he sensed Barakāt's unique skills as an enforcer and fact gatherer. Zaynī Barakāt assumed the bailiffship upon the fall of a greedy precursor, Ibn Abī'l-Jūd, who had overstepped the bounds of tolerable graft in imperial service. Barakāt proved himself a master of tightrope walking throughout his sponsor's reign. Never forgetting his humble origins, Barakāt carefully nurtured myriad contacts with people in all walks of life. His ability to ferret out plots and point the finger at the most adept schemers rendered him invaluable to al-Ghawrī. Even stiff-backed fortune hoarders succumbed to his skills as a torturer.

Yet the sultan himself eventually worried about the far-reaching influence his inquisitor wielded among the masses. But when he sought to fire his enforcer, Barakāt brought commercial dealings in the capital to a standstill, leaving his patron with no choice but to reinstate him. Al-Zaynī Barakāt therefore overcame the very schemes he helped promote during al-Ghawrī's reign. Upon the sultan's demise in 922/1516, his successor, Ṭūmānbāy, would have no option but to augment the inquisitor's powers, proclaiming him senior market inspector (*muḥtasib*) of Cairo. Along among these three associates of Qānṣūh al-Ghawrī therefore, al-Zaynī Barakāt would live on into the new regime of Ottoman conquerors.

With the assistance of such diverse adjutants al-Ghawrī thus charted his own imaginative path toward unassailable authority, which few disputed by 910/1505. From that time until 918/1512, when Selim I displaced his father Bāyazīd II as Ottoman sultan, al-Ghawrī indulged himself in the luxury of supreme power. Ever paranoid over the threat of rebellion by troops who continued to regard him as a selfish curmudgeon withholding bonuses they regarded as their right of caste to squander on his cronies or grand living, al-Ghawrī responded with a blend of fatalistic insouciance and tentative innovation. Throughout this interval between internal consolidation and foreign catastrophe, al-Ghawrī savored the pleasures of banquets, soirées, leisurely progressions through the provinces, and public spectacles in Cairo. Simultaneously, and with less fanfare, he began experimenting with new kinds of weaponry, military cadres, and financial resources. Because these experiments are considered in subsequent chapters, they are not elaborated upon here. Suffice to note that Qānṣūh al-Ghawrī's brief interlude of unfettered hegemony received none of the accolades showered upon Qāytbāy's reign. Yet for all the denunciation he evoked, al-Ghawrī proved himself a sagacious autocrat whose methods cannot be dismissed as simple despotism. Under the scrutiny hindsight allows, they emerge as perceptive responses to perplexities that Qāytbāy aggravated but never resolved.

Ominous tidings from Asia Minor prefaced Sultan Bāyazīd's passing on 2 Jumādā II 918/15 August 1512. His youngest son, Selim, had effectively taken over the military institution of the Ottoman Empire before his father's death. His brothers had already fled Constantinople, so ominous was the prospect of their sibling's enthronement. Al-Ghawrī accordingly had ample cause for alarm over the demise of a sovereign who had acknowledged his fellow monarchs as peers and respected the balance of power abroad. Selim's behavior during the first year of his rule did little to dispel al-Ghawrī's unease. Slaughtering those blood relatives who remained within his reach, Selim began harrying Muslim principalities on his eastern frontiers once again.[37] But fate and the ambition of a meteoric new dynast in Iran, Ismāʿīl Ṣafawī, intervened to place the Mamlūk and Ottoman sultanates on a collision course.

Selim I reacted with hostility to the charismatic arrogance of the Ṣafavid shāh for strategic and personal reasons. Ismāʿīl was flaunting his own hegemonic goals, violating treaties and pressuring his neighbors when conditions were favorable. His expansionist objectives were bound to clash with Selim's at some future time. The longer Ismāʿīl was allowed to strengthen his army, the more dangerous an obstacle he posed to Ottoman designs on the eastern Islamic world. Selim found Ismāʿīl's élan an affront to his own stature that he tolerated less and less as the Ṣafavid proclaimed his mission of conquest ever more brazenly.[38]

For his part, Qānṣūh al-Ghawrī looked upon Ismāʿīl's designs with some bemusement once he concluded that the Ṣafavid regime could be contained within the former Aqquyunlū sphere of influence. But when Selim began dispatching to Cairo emissaries who initially demanded Egyptian neutrality and then a humiliating alliance while the Ottoman prepared to crush his Persian rival, al-Ghawrī found himself in a tight spot. Al-Ghawrī could not stall indefinitely, finding Selim inhospitable to demurrals he made while seeking to maneuver himself into the best position possible as the Ottomans and Ṣafavids squared off. When Selim inflicted a shattering defeat against Ismāʿīl at the site of Chaldirān near Tabrīz in Rajab 920/August 1514, al-Ghawrī recognized the precariousness of his own position.[39] He had stationed troops in Aleppo, his northern garrison, to take advantage of the battle's outcome. But the disaster he had anticipated for both sides had not materialized. Rather, al-Ghawrī now had to deal with Selim's conviction that his southern neighbor was an opportunist prepared to profit from his fellow monarch's adversity.[40] Selim lost no time venting his antipathy for al-Ghawrī in acts of aggression against allies of the Mamlūk regime. Throughout 921/1515, he beleaguered al-Ghawrī's longsuffering vassal, ʿAlī Dawlāt, stirring up trouble in the Dhū'l-Qādrid march yet another time.[41] Ultimately, the Dhū'l-Qādrids went down to defeat. When Selim's ambassador disdainfully held up the severed heads of ʿAlī Dawlāt and his sons before al-Ghawrī and his courtiers at the Citadel in Cairo, the latter realized his options for evading conflict were now closed. Nothing remained but to confront this most formidable of Muslim rulers face-to-face in combat. Yet once Al-Ghawrī accepted the inevitable, he held his nerve before intimidating odds with the courage that had won so many of the Mamlūk caste grudging admiration even from their remorseless detractors. Al-Ghawrī began mustering his house troops for a march to Aleppo that he would personally lead. But he closed no door to diplomacy even in this last hour before the fateful encounter. Despite Ismāʿīl's defeat, the shāh had managed to escape and rebuild his forces in central Iran. As al-Ghawrī presided over his muster, squeezing emergency funds from his ambivalent subjects, he clung to hopes that Ismāʿīl might yet force Selim's hand a second time. If al-Ghawrī was poised at Aleppo to attack the weakened victor, chance might favor his ploy and salvage his regime.[42]

Al-Ghawrī marched out of Cairo for Aleppo in Rabīʿ II 922/Mary 1516. The warmth of his feelings for colleagues who remained at home to guard the realm was shown by his decision to convey the entire state treasury to Aleppo, in which impregnable fortress he could keep it under close watch.[43] Al-Ghawrī feared that such a sum could become a potent weapon against him in someone else's hands. But with his success to it ensured, he might buy his way out of defeat if fate turned on him in Syria. Al-Ghawrī enlisted the reluctant aid of Sībāy, his long-standing governor in Damascus, and proceeded rapidly to Aleppo, arriving there in Jumādā II/July.[44] When Selim apprehended couriers al-Ghawrī had sent off to reconnoiter with Shah Ismāʿīl's agents, the Ottoman threw an explosive tantrum and resolved to deal with the Mamlūk before confronting the Ṣafavid. The Egyptian and Ottoman armies thus met at the plain of Marj Dābiq, north of Aleppo, on Sunday, 25 Rajab/24 August.[45] Despite their numeric disadvantage, al-Ghawrī's troops inflicted heavy casualties on Selim's host at the outset. But al-Ghawrī's own stratagems combined with the secret designs of a senior commandant to produce his downfall. Al-Ghawrī first sent into the fray his veteran Mamlūks, whose status was already lowered by their service to previous sultans, while he held his younger recruits in abeyance. The veterans, harboring little loyalty to this man, interpreted their deployment on the front line as a sign of their expendability and began bolting from the field. At the same time, al-Ghawrī's viceroy of Aleppo, Khayrbak, broke ranks and led his squadrons off toward the town of Ḥamā. Having negotiated mutually attractive terms with Selim, who pledged to reward his treachery, Khayrbak saw only continued relegation to provincial oblivion if his sovereign pulled out a victory.

Betrayed by his local lieutenant and abandoned by his most seasoned soldiers, Qānṣūh al-Ghawrī recognized the hopelessness of his situation. Desparately rallying those wavering troopers who still stood by him, he promised them his share of any battle spoils. A heart spasm seized him as he called for water, and he fell from his horse into the choking clouds of dust. His retainers secreted his body away during the ensuing mêlée, for no trace of it was ever found. Possibly, it suffered such mutilation at the hands of the random vengeance seekers who galloped around the battlesite slashing at corpses that no identification was possible.

Thus, machinations of his opponent's subordinates aided Selim in the victory that opened the gateway to Egypt. When survivors of the Mamlūk army sought sanctuary in Aleppo and other Syrian towns, local inhabitants took their own revenge for the misery they had endured at their protectors' hands. As lurid descriptions of the defeat began trickling into Cairo, the regent Tūmānbāy resolutely rallied the spirits of his downcast followers and laid preparations for the invasion that would follow.[46] The Mamlūk sultanate was fated to survive into the coming year before Selim arrived to terminate it.

But al-Ghawrī's career ceased abruptly in death at Marj Dābiq. Historians of his generation penned no fond eulogy that compared with the praise they heaped upon Qāytbāy—who never took command of a military campaign abroad during his reign. They held al-Ghawrī accountable for the Ottoman triumph, interpreting his terrible end as divine retribution for a career noteworthy for its avarice and oppression, an affront to the probity of the Dār al-Islām. Were their criticisms justified? Did Qānṣūh al-Ghawrī deserve their rancor? The following analyses will pose this question in the comparative context of Qāytbāy's policies, which, for all the accolades they inspired, restricted the choices available to his successor.

Notes

1. Al-Sakhāwī, *Al-Ḍaw⁾ al-Lāmiʿ fī Aʿyān al-Qarn al-Tāsiʿ* (Cairo: 1943), vol. 6, p. 201, no. 697, who places his birth during the initial years of the third decade of the ninth Hijrī century. Ibn Iyās in his *Badā⁾iʿ* (vol. 3, p. 324, 1. 16) gives Qāytbāy's age as approaching 84 when he expired (27 Dhū'l-Qaʿda 901/8 August 1496).

2. *Badā⁾iʿ* 3, p. 325, 1. 7.

3. *Rawḍ,* f. 166, 1, 4–11; 166-b, 1. 8; E. Ashtor, "Ḳāit Bāy," *EI²* 2; 462; Wiet, *L'Égypte arabe,* 589.

4. *Rawḍ,* f. 170, 1. 7, 19; *Ḥawādith* 4, p. 617, 1. 19; Ibn al-Ḥimṣī, *Ḥawādith al-Zamān wa-Wafayāt al-Shuyūkh wa'l-Aqrān,* ms. (Istanbul: Feizullah, 1438), f. 52, 1. 5.

5. *Ḥawādith* 4, p. 618, 1. 1; *Rawḍ,* f. 174, 1. 18, 27; *Ḥawādith* 4, p. 627, 1. 6; *Badā⁾iʿ* 3, pp. 10, 1. 24; *Rawḍ,* f. 175-b, 1. 28.

6. This name is alternately rendered "Ezbak" or "Uzbak" in Arabic sources. The "u" is closest to the Turkish original. (See J. Sauvaget, "Noms et surnoms des Mamlouks," *JA* 238 [1950]: 36, # 9). However, "a" appears most commonly in Egyptian usage, and is adopted consistently here.

7. *Ḍaw⁾* 10, p. 272, no. 1077; *Rawḍ,* f. 175, 1. 21, 26; *Badā⁾iʿ* 3, p. 173, 1. 6.

8. *Ḍaw⁾* 2, p. 270, no. 844; *Ḥawādith* 4, p. 676, 1. 10; *Rawḍ,* f. 203, 1. 14, 21; *Badā⁾iʿ* 3, p. 20, 1. 7.

9. *Badāʾiʿ* 3, p. 15, 1. 4.

10. J. Mordtmann and V. Menage, "Dhū'l-Ḳadr," *EI*² 2:239.

11. *Inbāʾ*, p. 439, 1. 20; *Badāʾiʿ* 3, p. 72, 1. 23; *ʿUqūd*, f. 225, 1. 2.

12. *Inbāʾ*, p. 419, 1. 21.

13. *Badāʾiʿ* 3, p. 130, 1. 10.

14. Ibn al-Jīʿān, *Al-Qawl al-Mustaẓraf fī Mawlānā al-Malik al-Ashraf*, French translation by H. Devonshire, *IFAO Bulletin* 20 (1922): 2–40; *Badāʾiʿ* 3, p. 134, 1. 16.

15. On Mamlūk relations with the Aqquyunlū, see chapter 3.

16. *Badāʾiʿ* 3, p. 170, 1. 19; *ʿUqūd*, f. 213-b, 1. 19.

17. *Ḥawādith* 4, p. 650, 1. 19, 23; *Rawḍ*, f. 186-b, 1. 31.

18. *Badāʾiʿ* 3, p. 205, 1. 21.

19. Ibid., pp. 227, 1. 3; 228, 1. 10; 229, 1. 3.

20. Ibid., pp. 91, 1. 22 (he briefly preceded Qānṣūh al-Ghawrī as sultan after al-Nāṣir Muḥammad was deposed); 158, 1. 17.

21. Ibid., pp. 286, 1. 5; 289, 1. 10; 292, 1. 3.

22. Ibn al-Ḥimṣī, *Ḥawādith*, ff. 158-b, 1. 4; 159, 1.7; *Jawāhir*, f. 397, 1. 14; *Badāʾiʿ* 3, p. 310, 1. 21; *ʿUqūd*, f. 237, 1. 18; al-Sakhāwī, *Dhayl*, f. 278-b, 1. 5; *Badāʾiʿ* 3, p. 314, 1. 6.

23. *Badāʾiʿ* 3, pp. 323, 1. 13; 324, 1. 16; *ʿUqūd*, ff. 239, 1. 15; 239-b, 1. 14.

24. *Badāʾiʿ* 3, p. 190, 1. 20; 4, p. 2, 1. 3; al-Ḥalabī, *Durr al-Ḥabab*, ff. 177-b, 1. 5–179-b, 1. 13.

25. *Badāʾiʿ* 3, pp. 264, 1. 21; 284, 1. 18.

26. *Badāʾiʿ* 4, p. 3, 1. 12; ʿAbd al-Bāsiṭ, *Al-Risāla al-Laṭīfa tashtamilu ʿalā Dhikri man waliya Miṣr min al-Salaṭīn* (Istanbul: Laleli, 2044), ff. 8-b, 1. 20; 9, 1. 8.

27. *Badāʾiʿ* 4, pp. 6, 1. 10; 8, 1. 6; 11, 1. 4; 17, 1. 21.

28. Ibid., p. 18, 1. 11 (al-Ghawrī compels mass oath swearing on ʿUthmānī copy of Koran held in Citadel Mosque).

29. Ibid., p. 30, 1. 6.

30. Ibid., p. 73, 1. 1; 74, 1. 8.

31. Ibid., p. 81, l. 1.

32. Ibid., pp. 93, l. 10; 99, l. 23; 107, l. 1.

33. K. S. Salibi, "Listes chronologiques des grands cadis de l'Égypte sous les Mamlouks," *REI* 25 (1957): 108–09, nos. 51, 53.

34. *Badā'iʿ* 4, p. 7, l. 3.

35. Ibid. p. 14. l. 13.

36. Ibid., p. 50, l. 7; in recent fiction: Jamāl al-Ghaytānī, *Al-Zaynī Barakāt,* 3d ed. (Cairo: Dār al-Mustaqbil al-ʿArabī, 1985); English translation by Farouk Mustafa (New York: Penguin Books, 1989).

37. *Badā'iʿ* 4, p. 269, l. 18, 22.

38. See Adel Allouche, *The Origins and Development of the Ottoman-Ṣafavid Conflict (906–962/1500–1555)* (Berlin, 1983), 100–30 for the background to Selim's hostility.

39. *Badā'iʿ* 4, pp. 396, l. 3; 398, l. 1; 400, l. 15; 402, l. 6.

40. Ibid., pp. 400, l. 1; 432, l. 3.

41. Ibid., p. 435, l. 11.

42. al-Ḥalabī, *Durr,* f. 178-b, l. 13; *Badā'iʿ* 5, p. 35, l. 13.

43. *Badā'iʿ* 5, p. 42, l. 2.

44. *Badā'iʿ* 4, p. 60, l. 5; al-Ḥalabī, *Durr,* f. 177-b, l. 22.

45. *Badā'iʿ* 5, pp. 69, l. 9; 72, l. 18.

46. Ibid., pp. 81, l. 18; 85, l. 1.

3

Beleaguered Bulwark: The Mamlūk State and International Politics

Egyptian chroniclers of the later Middle Ages routinely included annual lists of kings or potentates who held sway over the central Islamic lands and even further afield. A common leitmotif, interminable strife, was discernible in their remarks about such rulers.[1] These princes or chieftains threatened to disrupt the harmony favored by God for the prosperity of His commonwealth on Earth. In marked contrast, the historians lauded the sultan of Egypt who defended the established order among nations. While presiding over an imposing military establishment, he eschewed warfare, pursuing instead negotiated solutions to disputes and nurturing alliances that would deter bellicose impulses of unruly neighbors. The Mamlūk State inherited a centuries-old world view and chancery bureaucracy from its Fāṭimid and Ayyūbid predecessors, to which it added an obsession with preservation of the status quo in international affairs. Since the officers who assumed power by coup after the death of al-Malik al-Ṣāliḥ Ayyūb in 647/1249 claimed to uphold his dynasty's legitimating principles of stability and orthodoxy, they saw no reason to engage in deviations from time-honored traditions. The founding generation of amīrs, and in particular Baybars and Qalāwūn (collectively: 658–689/1260–1290), occupied themselves with construction of a cohesive territorial union on the remnants of the Fāṭimid and Ayyūbid Empires. Their hegemonic vision was thus focused by strategic imperatives for supremacy in the Eastern Mediterranean and Southwest Asia prevalent three centuries earlier: dominion over the Palestinian corridor, the Upper Euphrates marches, the Nile Valley, and the Red Sea.

Historically, foreign enemies had passed through Syria to menace Egypt. Accordingly, no alien power could be allowed political influence in this region. Southeastern Anatolia and the Jazīra between the Mesopotamian rivers served as buffers separating volatile regimes that were endemically fractious. Only a great power's presence could nullify their incessant bickering. The Delta and Ṣaʿīd proper generated the agrarian produce on which the military system relied. Protected by surrounding deserts, they were accessible to armies only from the south via Aswān, the east from Sinai and the west along the coast. The Mamlūk regime placed a high priority on barring these sites of entry to any hostile polity. Finally, the Red Sea linked the Mediterranean to India and East Asia, sources of the most lucrative foreign commodities passing through the regime's customs houses. Until the navigational revolution at the end of the fifteenth century, Egypt straddled the most important commercial artery of international trade during the Middle Ages. Her ministries extracted handsome profits from the spices, textiles, and other luxury items transiting her Red Sea entrepôts on their way to consumers on both sides of the Mediterranean. Of different but equal significance, the holiest cities of Islam were accessed from Red Sea ports. As destinations for thousands of devout pilgrims seeking spiritual fulfillment every year, Mecca and Madīna lent an aura of legitimacy to the regime ensuring their safety. From its inception, the Mamlūk sultanate acted as guardian of the holy cities. Since Jerusalem and Hebron also lay within its domain, this government enjoyed a status unique among Muslim empires. No other state was so well placed for rendering equivalent service to God's community. Safeguarding the passage of pilgrims and promoting their harmonious fulfillment of religious obligations represented fundamental contributions of the sultanate to the Ummah's unity. Successive autocrats emphasized their custodianship over the holy places in titles, inscriptions and proclamations.[2]

Yet all these strategic and symbolic principles dated from epochs long past. The early Mamlūk sultans built their reputations as warrior-kings of international stature by defeating enemies of bygone eras. They had repelled Mongol invaders from Central Asia and Crusader zealots from Western Europe, both representatives of ideologies or incentives outmoded by the dawn of the modern age. Sweeping changes in military technology and maritime practice were limiting the capacity of nomadic tribal confederations from the Asian outback to overrun sedentary peoples or monopolize trade routes. The predations of Timur Lenk (r. 771–807/1369–1405), intimidating as they were, marked the end of an era rather than portending a future one. The peculiar combination of commercial pragmatism, religious fervor, and territorial ambition that produced the Crusader movement in the eleventh century could no longer be resurrected in the Europe of 1500. The crude mercantilism that had motivated Italian trading states to lend the Crusader enterprise money and ships had now been replaced by far more sophisticated concepts of international markets, integrated currencies, and negotiated relations with governments regardless of their religion. These republics viewed the Mamlūk Empire, along with other Islamic regimes, as a partner with which one did business. Its capitulation mattered far more than its dissolution.[3]

Throughout the eighth/fourteenth and ninth/fifteenth centuries, the Mamlūk sultanate preserved hegemony over its bailiwick by maintaining the status quo it assumed from the Crusader and Mongol eras. For one hundred and fifty years the regime succeeded reasonably well. Certainly during the reigns of powerful sultans such as al-Nāṣir Muḥammad or al-Ashraf Barsbāy, one could acknowledge an effective *Pax Mamlūkia* guaranteeing a viable balance of power if not total peace throughout this turbulent region. But after 1450, shifts in the world order manifested themselves rather disturbingly. In Iraq and Iran, a new kind of overlord was forging aggressive confederacies from the patchwork of nomadic tribes and market towns that emerged in the aftermath of the Timurid episode. At the very end of the fifteenth century, this region produced a charismatic leader in the person of Ismāʿīl Ṣafawī who exploited religious dogma and imperialist drive to create an ideologically cohesive kingdom in the Persian heartland for the first time since the Mongol invasions. Further west, the frontier Beylik of ʿUthmān, perched on the threshold of Europe, had rapidly expanded into a formidable military power with dominion over both Christian and Muslim subjects. By 872/1468, Qāytbāy's accession year, the Ottomans' conquests had brought them disturbingly close to the Mamlūk frontiers. They thus constituted a potential rival who showed little respect for the status quo. Finally, the Europeans had become shapers of commercial dealings in the international marketplace. Their societies were in the process of creating economic institutions unprecedented in world history. Mamlūk bureaucrats and merchants minimally sensed their own growing dependence on European crafts and currency sources, but they found the new European presence in both the central and southern seas a tangible menace.[4] Therefore, by our period the Mamlūk sultanate was facing the emergence of a new world system. How equipped was it to cope?

Mamlūk foreign policy aimed, as its primary objective, at preserving stasis. While such a goal may seem uninspiring to modern strategists, it was rooted in practical experience with interstate relations in the central Islamic lands and idiosyncracies of the Mamlūk institution. The superficial fragility of ties between sovereign states and their clients masked a set of concepts all shared to varying degrees. While many competed for suzerainty, regional prominence, or control over strategic routes, few envisioned realigning the profile of international politics they inherited from the high medieval period.

Principles of universal empire under the Prophet's caliph-successor now found their expression primarily in cultural and religious patterns mutually shared by most polities in the area. Until the latter fifteenth century, local rivalries posed few challenges to these patterns, since the temporary dominance of one regime over its neighbors rarely resulted in profound cultural or religious discontinuity.[5] Indeed, following disruptions wrought by the invasions, resurgent regimes laid considerable store on preservation of venerable traditions from the classical era. Since change was far more likely to disturb or disorient than to invigorate or renew, most sophisticated governments looked back to achievements of an idealized golden age rather than forward to an uncertain future. Maintenance of stasis assured continuance of political systems that enabled these traditions to survive. The Mamlūk sultanate, as caretaker of the ʿAbbāsid caliphate, posed as champion of religious orthodoxy in the manner of Saladin. Although the caliph possessed no executive authority, his presence sanctified the sultan's office, originally usurped from his Ayyūbid predecessors, and gave Cairo a clear primacy of diplomatic protocol over other Muslim capitals.[6] Princes or chieftains recently enthroned by coup often requested formal confirmation of their positions from the caliph in Cairo. His unique authority to grant such endorsements (*taqālīd*) lent the sultan who protected him a prestige no other Muslim commander could claim.[7] During the fourteenth and fifteenth centuries, Cairo was acknowledged as the preeminent seat of authority among Sunnī Muslims. Envoys continuously ascended to the Citadel to pay their respects and present the sultan with entreaties for support, proposals for regulating trade, requests for safe transit, and pleas for sanctuary from rivals or hostile kin. When al-Ghawrī received fourteen emissaries in Rabīʿ II 918/May-June 1512, he no longer presided over a power with unchallenged sway throughout Southwest Asia. Yet so deeply entrenched was Cairo's diplomatic seniority that these representatives, ranging from couriers sent by worried Turkmān aghās to the French king's splendidly arrayed ambassador, automatically accorded its ruler the highest rank among Muslim lords.[8] Mamlūk sultans, many of whom had seized their thrones by force, cherished the status they enjoyed in consequence of patronizing the "Commander of Believers." His presence in their capital symbolized all the venerated customs from the golden age they sought to enshrine.

The military hierarchy controlling Egypt and Syria was composed of slave-soldiers imported from foreign lands and trained arduously for years before performing their allotted duties. Since their purchase and schooling were costly, the government husbanded its investment by avoiding losses on the battlefront. Although the performance record of Mamlūk armies is impressive, the relative paucity of their engagements after Qalāwūn's death in 689/1290 bespeaks the regime's reluctance to squander its precious reserve of skilled troops. The Mamlūk sultanate routinely brandished its martial clout by displaying its military apparatus before visiting dignitaries. But it invariably exhausted all diplomatic measures in its chancery's arsenal before resorting to armed conflict. The parallel with the professional army of Prussia after 1648 is striking. Few doubted the combat ability of either force if compelled, but carefully engineered shows of strength usually sufficed to dampen a rival's enthusiasm for open confrontation.[9] It is in light of these motives for caution and restraint that axioms of Mamlūk statecraft reveal their rationale.

These may be summarized as follows: commitment to coexistence, reliance on negotiation to resolve disputes, recognition of mutually defined spheres of influence, and acknowledgment of strategic and commercial interests superseding political or religious differences between states. Like policymakers in modern times, officials in the Mamlūk bureaucracy noted subtle distinctions between coexistence and peace. The former implied resignation to the reality of a potentially hostile rival's presence without according it formal recognition. This flexibility of approach enabled the Mamlūk chancery to deal with any state whose objectives coincided with its own interests while wasting little time soul-searching over that state's behavior or confession. Above all, a commitment to coexistence provided the regime a convenient way of bypassing declaration of Jihād, or holy war, against an enemy of Islam. As self-proclaimed defenders of orthodoxy, sultans paid lip service to this ancient principle of communal defense. In practice, they and their ministers devised countless excuses to avoid it. Implementation of Jihād would compromise the regime's fundamental imperative of upholding the status quo.

By the time of its late maturity, the Mamlūk State had refined its diplomatic procedures. Receptions for emissaries were staged according to procedures initiated hundreds of years earlier and elaborated over the centuries, with some variation. Honors shown a guest, the sultan's degree of intimacy toward him, terms imployed in salutations, and the relative munificence of gifts exchanged all established an ambassador's rank and the weight of his patron's missive before any negotiations began. Although few chroniclers were privy to actual discussions, enough tidbits were leaked through gossip to indicate their substance. These might be superficial if a policy decision had already been made, or significant if an emissary brought with him a detailed treaty formula, outlining privileges of foreign merchants, delimiting borders, encompassing zones of free trade, or resolving a vexing dispute.[10] The frequency of embassies to the Duhaysha Palace during our period underscores the centrality of diplomacy in Mamlūk foreign policy. A decision to organize a military expedition would be reached only after exhaustive discussions failed. And ambassadors purveying last ditch offers of compromise were dispatched even after the military option had been reluctantly adopted.

Although archives of the Mamlūk Chancery (*Dīwān al-Inshā³*) have disappeared, clerical officials copied lengthy tracts from documents they perused in manuals of diplomacy. The most prominent of these from the Mamlūk period is al-Qalqashandī's *Ṣubḥ al-Aᶜshā³*.[11] A secretary of medial rank in the

dīwān, Qalqashandī compiled his voluminous survey as a guide for future
generations to accepted literary style, terminology, and protocol dating from
the ninth century A.D., and even earlier in certain instances. He quoted many
letters, edicts and treaties verbatim to demonstrate usages in context. The
Ṣubḥ is therefore a goldmine of documentation for diplomacy in the Mamlūk
era. The work also suggests the great range of issues ambassadors resolved.
Individuals chosen for service abroad had usually attained fluency in literary
Arabic. Those treating with non-Muslim rulers had mastered languages rele-
vant to their courts or were aided by interpreters who had.[12] While most del-
egations were led by a senior officer, they included the expertise of attendant
clerks, judges, notaries, and even historians familiar with salient events of a
regime's past. These individuals debated with their counterparts in the host
country to set the legal parameters, mutually acknowledged, of their agreements. The range and subtlety of terms Qalqashandī lists, their meanings
painstakingly compared to highlight nuances, shows how refined this art had
become by the later Middle Ages.

The heightened diplomatic exchanges between Cairo and Istanbul during
al-Ghawrī's last years disclosed the vital importance the sultanate attached to
mutual respect for spheres of influence. The contempt Selim Yavūz exhibited
for the autonomy of al-Ghawrī's Dhū'l-Qādrid client in Southeastern Anatolia,
ʿAlī Dawlāt, was regarded in Cairo as a megalomaniac's act. Civilized dis-
course between nations was posited on their reciprocal recognition of territories
lying off limits within a neighbor's suzerainty. Crossing of boundaries without
permission constituted, at the very least, an act of trespass. At worst, it violated the spirit of harmony requisite to continued prosperity of the Muslim
Commonwealth. A regime would draw upon its limited reserves of manpower
and matériel to counter it. Shockwaves emanating from such aggression would
cause undue alarm in courts throughout the region, creating an atmosphere of
tension conducive neither to peace nor solidarity in the face of worse adversity.
Certainly, such acts would jeopardize the last objective: acknowledgment of
interests regarded as vital by foreign states. The roster of treaties Mamlūk sultans negotiated with their contemporaries, Christian or Muslim, discloses their
regime's conception of world order as a network of interlocking interests, each
dependent on the other for efficient transfer of commodities, setting of tariffs,
assurance of safe conduct, and diplomatic immunity, or guarantee of access to
holy places.[13] Only if all parties admitted the value of recognizing common
interests could business be conducted in a profitable fashion. Only if doctrinal
or sectarian differences were laid aside could pilgrims and savants visit shrines
sacred to their beliefs. The Mamlūk sultanate assiduously upheld the principle
of shared interests as an overreaching goal outweighing petty quarrels or religious rivalries.

All these axioms aimed at maintaining the prevailing balance of power.
Officials of the Dīwān al-Inshāʾ sought security by impeding shifts in the es-

tablished order. The extant rank and prerogatives of rulers would be sanctified by every device possible, since the Mamlūk sultan already enjoyed superiority in the hierarchy of monarchs, and could only lose stature in the advent of change. Preservation of equilibrium thus became an ideal fundamental to this regime's welfare, The sultanate abhored deviations from this objective. New ideologies of relations between states, expansive visions of imperialism, or experiments with new styles of diplomacy found minimal receptivity. The climate for their adoption remained ambivalent if not hostile. So long as no other regime initiated such experiments, the sultanate managed to maintain the *Pax Mamlūkia*. But how capable was it of confronting radical changes transforming the region at the end of the Middle Ages?

The Syrian Provinces: Restive Subordinates

When Qāytbāy accepted the sultanate, the Syrian littoral had been linked to Egypt for more than two hundred years. Intermittent Egyptian sovereignty over this variegated region in the Islamic age dated back to Ṭūlūnid and Fāṭimid times.[14] Interrupted by sporadic revolts or foreign incursions, Egyptian authority was inevitably restored when a powerful military oligarchy reasserted itself in Cairo. The strategic necessity of securing Syria from hostile powers ranked before all others in the minds of sultans and their counselors from the reign of Baybars. This architect of the Mamlūk State invested the prime of his career subduing Ayyūbid claimants and ambitious officers in the Syrian towns who profited from a new regime's disarray by declaring their independence. Once they had crushed residual opposition, Baybars and his successor, Qalāwūn, established the peculiar model of dependence and autonomy that would characterize Egypto-Syrian relations until the sultanate's fall.[15]

The region was divided into two paramount provinces: Damascus (*Dimashq, al-Shām*), which exercised military jurisdiction over Palestine (Jerusalem [*al-Quds*], Nāblus, Ṣafad and Hebron [*al-Khalīl*], and al-Karak east of the Jordan River; and Aleppo (*Ḥalab*) with authority over Ḥimṣ, Ḥamā, Ṭarābulus and the march towns of Southeastern Anatolia (prominent among these: ʿAynṭāb, Diyār Bakr, al-Bīra, Adanā, Malaṭya and Ṭarsūṣ). While the sultan appointed governors (*nuwwāb*) selected from medial ranks of his khāṣṣakī corps over all these centers, he delegated the viceroys of Damascus and Aleppo powers second only to his own. Holders of these "deputy sultanates" were chosen from among the autocrat's intimate colleagues. Since most already held the rank of muqaddam, they presided over large households and mini-armies of their own before they assumed their offices in Syria. Placing officers who had matured in Cairo and who, thus, fashioned their own courts after that imperial model was fundamental to inculcating the identity binding the provincial centers to the Egyptian capital. A coterie of officers who emerged to prominence within Cairene factions were assigned supreme authority over this potentially rebellious league of towns. Many longed to return to the seat of supreme power as soon as possible. Several connived to rally armies from their garrisons that might aid them in their bids for the sultanate itself. Others exploited their autonomy to build fiefdoms for themselves that would last their lifetimes. But all imitated the cultural and political milieu they grew up with in Cairo. The resulting unity they imposed, albeit from on high, remains unequalled in the modern age. Never before or since have Egypt and Syria been so interdependent.

The control exercised by viceroys sent from Cairo was paralleled by the influence of a bureaucracy and judiciary also appointed by the imperial government. Similar to a policy prevailing in the capital, four chief justices, one per canonical madhhab, presided over a host of subordinates in both Damascus and Aleppo whose jurisdiction reached to remote villages and outlying districts peopled by Bedouin for the most part.[16] The sultan jealously guarded his prerogative of choosing the senior qāḍīs. Upon the advice of their four counterparts in Cairo, he balanced prominent representatives of local 'ulamā' families against Cairenes whose reputations were well established before they assumed their provincial duties. The Syrian judiciary therefore comprised another component of the imperial system that bound the regional capitals to Cairo in the Mamlūk period. A fraternity of learned jurist-scholars, many of whom had attended lectures in the same madrasas, served as penultimate appellate judges and interpreters of a uniform Shar'ī tradition throughout this fractious zone.

The final decades of this imperial relationship witnessed an intensification of divisive tendencies eroding the ties sketched above. Feuds between executive officers, often within the same town, simmered throughout the latter fifteenth and early sixteenth centuries. When these flared into open conflict, troop factions lined up behind their respective patrons and terrorized the populace.[17] Compounding their vendettas was the growing trend toward corruption on the part of fiscal officials sent from Cairo to collect taxes and monitor trade. As the central regime grappled with mounting insolvency and sought relief via clandestine sources of revenue, it became more tolerant of exploitation in the provinces. Citizens of Syrian towns were more disposed to react violently against such oppression than their Egyptian counterparts, however. Perhaps the most vivid incident of popular outbursts over such oppression occurred during Ṣafar 882/May-June 1477 in Damascus. The sultan's superintendent of military fiefs (*nāẓir al-jaysh*), Shihāb al-Dīn Aḥmad al-Nābulusī, was attacked by the mob for his manipulation of wheat stores.[18] This individual had frequently dabbled in embezzlement. He had speculated in construction licenses, selling building rights to unscrupulous contractors for the highest fees. He had sold myriad offices to greedy incompetents. He had aided selfish heirs in their schemes to alienate religious trusts. He had profited from his hoarding of grain reserved for troop rations, selling it when prices rose precipitously and silencing squadron leaders with bribes. Ensconced by Qāytbāy with orders to supply his quota of tax revenues, no questions asked, he dutifully met his patron's requests. But when the populace's irritation reached its limit, they stoned al-Nābulusī as he left his townhouse. After setting it on fire, they pursued him to the Umayyad Mosque where he sought sanctuary. Al-Nābulusī cowered in the mosque for several weeks until a commission of inquiry arrived from Cairo. When the sultan was apprised of al-Nābulusī's behavior, he ordered his imprisonment and confiscation of his wealth (a sum exceeding one million dīnārs). The commission encountered many acrimonious claims from plaintiffs bickering over amounts al-Nābulusī had swindled from them. The resultant litigation dragged on for years. But al-Nābulusī's case was noteworthy only for its public scandal. Many other officials who bilked their districts of lesser sums lived to retire with their gains. And despite this undercurrent of corruption, the rhythm of official business in the provinces went on unaffected. The narrative sources are replete with references to royal agents traveling from Cairo to the Syrian towns bearing edicts requisitioning supplies, altering tariffs, or setting infantry quotas from local militias.[19]

The specter of conspiracy on the part of viceroys who dreamed of supplanting their colleagues in Cairo haunted every sultan who had reason to suspect his peers' ambitions. But al-Ghawrī was particularly worried over his subordinates' plotting in Syria. He had cause for concern. Syrian partisans of his Machiavellian atābak, Qāyt al-Rajabī, schemed with the marshal to unseat him. The inciter of this rebellion was also an associate of the incarcerated Sultan al-ʿĀdil Ṭūmānbāy. An amīr by the name of Dawlātbāy, he held the governorship of Ṭarābulus when he dissolved his ties of allegiance to al-Ghawrī in Jamādā II 910/November–December 1504.[20] After convincing Sībāy, then viceroy of Aleppo, to join his revolt, Dawlātbāy seized control of northern Syria and proceeded south toward Damascus. He and Qāyt had secretly planned for the effective partition of the Mamlūk Empire. Once the atābak met up with his ally in Damascus, the two would join forces, march on Cairo, rally disaffected officers and dethrone al-Ghawrī. Dawlātbāy and Sībāy would subsequently divide Syria between them while Qāyt assumed power in Egypt. Al-Ghawrī was informed of this plot just before Qāyt was scheduled to depart. We have already recounted the atābak's formal denunciation, disgrace and imprisonment. Al-Ghawrī designated a more reliable subordinate, Azdamur al-Dawādār, to lead the expedition but, true to his character, vacillated until Dawlātbāy's own supporters in Syria rethought the wisdom of sharing his risk.

After Qāyt was removed, enthusiasm for the rebellion diminished precipitously. Sībāy prudently decided that he stood to gain more autonomy in Syria by reconciling with the sultan rather than chancing an open break. In Rabīʿ I 911/August 1505, he sent a mediator professing his repentence and renewed loyalty if a pardon were extended him. He was prepared to submit personally before his liege-lord at the Citadel if protected by a writ of safe conduct (*amāna*).[21] Al-Ghawrī forthwith granted his request and received him at the Duhaysha. The former viceroy ascended carrying his mantle of office over his arm with its blazons torn off, as Qānṣūh Khamsmi'a had done when he begged clemency from Qāytbāy years before. Al-Ghawrī had every reason to forgive an officer of such standing. The current viceroy of Damascus, Arikmās min Ṭarābāy, had succeeded in alienating all factions of civil notables in that city. Having been pelted by an angry mob, he fled ignominiously from its gates. Al-Ghawrī then offered Sībāy the most esteemed governorship in the empire in return for his oath of support. Sībāy swore his fealty on the ʿUthmānī Koran which the caliph held out to him. Following the oath, all four qāḍīs witnessed a written pledge of obedience he signed. Only then did al-Ghawrī confer Sībāy's new robe of honor. Sībāy was allowed free rein, administering his great fief as he saw fit so long as he remained true. This he did. Sībāy exercised unchallenged rule over Damascus Province for the next eleven years, while acknowledging al-Ghawrī's suzerainty.

For his part, the sultan was satisfied with Sībāy's behavior in Damascus. Only when he perceived a renewed threat of dissension accompanying the re-emergence of Ottoman aggression did he attempt to bind Sībāy more closely. In Dhū'l-Qaʿda 919/December 1513-January 1514, al-Ghawrī sent an amīr to Damascus with a betrothal request for the viceroy. Al-Ghawrī wished his son to wed Sībāy's daughter.[22] Sībāy reacted hesitantly to this request, which, in fact, was an ultimatum. A lineage tie would curb his authority. Fate intervened to defer his response temporarily. Before the second delegation arrived with the contract and initial dowry payment in Jumādā I 920/June-July 1515, Sībāy's eldest daughter died of the plague. Uncertain as to how they should proceed, the sultan's negotiators informed al-Ghawrī that the viceroy had a second daughter six years of age. Ever the pragmatist, al-Ghawrī replied that she would do under the circumstances and the documents should be signed over to her. But Sībāy protested the betrothal of a girl so young, who did not know to whom her fate was being consigned. A standoff persisted until Shawwāl/November when Sībāy finally relented. The ante had been raised substantially, for al-Ghawrī agreed to double his first dowry offer of ten thousand dīnārs. And who could foretell what the future held? Neither child was old enough to consummate what the law had sanctioned. The world order was changing rapidly and when the two came of age, their parents' relationship might have altered. But a contract had been signed and Sībāy backed al-Ghawrī, albeit reluctantly, when the latter confronted Selim in 922.

Compounding local unrest over exploitation by officers and threats of sedition against the throne itself was the endemic problem of Bedouin predation. Although Syria had been urbanized for millennia, its desert outback harbored a significant nomadic element. Some districts, such as Nāblus and Ḥawrān, lay under the control of semisedentary shaykhs whose succession Cairo symbolically confirmed. Other tribal confederations roved broad regions, preying upon farmers and townspeople when they perceived weakness within provincial Mamlūk garrisons. During the medial years of Qāytbāy's reign, the tribe of Āl Faḍl, led by its aggressive chief Sayf, ravaged Ḥamā and other north Syrian towns with impunity. Yashbak min Mahdī made his ill-starred decision to seek his fortune ostensibly for the purpose of apprehending this marauder.[23] The wiliest culprits of al-Ghawrī's time were the Banū Lām, who raided Palestine and Trans-Jordan between 912 and 921.[24] Because of their inhospitable terrain, the Banū Lām eked out an existence marginal even by Bedouin standards, and their poverty may explain their perennial raiding. Many stories circulated in Cairo of their proverbial endurance and bravery, but in 896/1491 they allegedly encountered a being who intimidated them. The governor of al-Karak reported their repeated encounters with a demon of human shape but monstrous size who feasted on raw flesh, bones and all.[25] Depleting the Banū Lām's herds, this creature proved impervious to arrow or lance wounds and devoured his attackers alive if he caught them. So cowed were the Banū Lām warriors that they abandoned the territories the creature frequented. He thus achieved what the Mamlūk soldiery could not. Whether such tales were fanciful or posited on some kernel of fact, they underscored the looseness of Mamlūk authority over the Bedouin of Syria-Palestine. As the regime's internal problems worsened, these nomads intensified their spoliation.

Thus, by the end of the fifteenth century, the Syrian provinces were restive within the Mamlūk orbit. Tied to the governing institution in Cairo more than two centuries earlier as a bulwark against invasion, these districts now exhibited persistent resentment over Egyptian rule. Since their own military contingents had whittled away at the sultan's suzerainty, they reacted ambivalently to his calls for support when he planned expeditions against foreign regimes they were prepared to recognize. After al-Ghawrī's army scattered in defeat before Selim Yavūz, survivors found no haven in the garrison towns. Both inhabitants and prescient commanders were ready to shift their allegiance to the more successful warlord with few qualms.

The Ḥijāz: Obstreperous Tribesmen, Isolated Sanctuaries

The Mamlūk sultanate inherited suzerainty over Western Arabia from the Ayyūbids. Although a backwater, the Ḥijāz retained prominence in the Dār al-Islām because of its ports on the Red Sea, critical entrepôts for commodities arriving from South and East Asia, and its shrines, which sheltered the holiest sanctuaries of the faith. Despite its minimal influence over great power politics, this region remained semi-autonomous throughout the Mamlūk period due to stubborn resistance of its tribes against subjugation from Cairo. During the final half century of the Egyptian sultanate, the Ḥijāzī Bedouin grudg-

ingly acknowledged primacy of the sharīf of Mecca, who himself did homage
to the sultan in Cairo. The latter's authority was enforced locally by several
military intendants who bore the title Shādd (inspector) rather than nā'ib (governor). These were installed at the head of Mamlūk garrisons maintained at
Mecca, Jidda, Madīna, and several fortresses along the coast guarding the pilgrimage road and sea routes from ʿAqaba to Yemen. The Egyptian sultan also
reserved the right to appoint judges in Mecca. Since the shrine cities maintained such a large population of mendicants and savants (*mujāwira*) who, arriving from many lands, had retired near the Kaʿba or environs of the Prophet's
Mosque (*Masjid al-Nabī*) to await death on venerated ground, the Mamlūk sultanate posed as their protectors. And finally, custodianship over lucrative pious
foundations supporting the sanctuaries was delegated to prominent servants
(*khuddām*) of the sultan's household—usually retired barracks eunuchs. The
narrative sources abound with references to travels of royal agents and jurists
to and from the holy cities.[26]

But these representatives of the sultan's authority rarely discharged their
duties unchallenged. Throughout Qāytbāy's and al-Ghawrī's reigns, Bedouin
chieftains sought to dispossess rivals from competing tribes and even dared
assault royal officials if the opportunity arose. For more than a decade Qāytbāy
dealt with repeated attempts by mutinous amīrs of the Hujār clan, perennial
raiders of Yanbuʿ port, to topple the sharīf of Mecca.[27] The pace of rebellion
quickened after al-Ghawrī's accession. In early Ṣafar 908/August 1502, when
the pilgrimage caravans returned, their commanders (*umarā' al-Ḥajj*) brought
disturbing news. Following the previous sharīf's demise, his sons had fallen
out over the succession. Although one named Barakāt had received the acclamation of Meccan notables and the sultan's agents, his brother, al-Jāzānī, refused to acknowledge his preference.[28] One of the Ḥajj amīrs, Aṣṭamur,
admitted having whetted al-Jāzānī's ambition by offering him a royal robe of
investiture in return for a bribe of fifty thousand dīnārs. Once al-Jāzānī had
the robe in his possession, he openly declared against Barakāt. But Aṣṭamur
had sent a secret message to Barakāt, urging him to rally loyal tribes and set
upon his upstart sibling. He, Aṣṭamur, would then place his Mamlūk contingent behind the "rightful heir." When al-Jāzānī found out about the Ḥajj
amīr's duplicity, he flew into a rage he would nurse as a hatred of all the sultan's representatives. Fleeing Mecca by night, he gathered malcontents within
the tribe of Banī Ibrāhīm and ravaged the central Ḥijāz. When he encountered
the Syrian pilgrimage caravan proceeding toward Mecca from Damascus, he
slaughtered its guards, despoiled its valuables and allowed his men to rape its
female participants. Al-Jāzānī also harassed the Egyptian caravan under
Aṣṭamur's supervision on its way home and filled wells along the route with
rocks, reminding its protector of treachery's price. When Aṣṭamur finally presented himself at the Citadel, al-Ghawrī rebuked him for his conceit and ordered his descent in disgrace.

Aṣṭamur's error in judgment caused al-Ghawrī problems "fit to grey one's hair." Throughout the following year, al-Jāzānī kept up his mutiny against Barakāt who repeatedly sent appeals for assistance to Cairo.[29] This Jāzānī's ferocity gave even the most redoubtable Mamlūk officers pause. When a previous marshal, Tānibak al-Jamālī, emerged from retirement in Mecca to confront this rebel, al-Jāzānī captured him and trussed his genitals with a cord until he expired. When word of his atrocities reached Cairo in Shaʿbān 908/ January-February 1503, al-Ghawrī dispatched Qāyt al-Rajabī to arrest him. Following his arrival in Mecca, the marshal checked al-Jāzāni's coalition temporarily but failed to apprehend the rebel. Qāyt returned to the Citadel in a pyrrhic triumph with al-Jāzāni's brother in tow but not the criminal himself. The atābak's own behavior in Mecca while he pursued al-Jāzānī hardly endeared him to its inhabitants. He had brutally extracted money and supplies from local notables during his sojourn. So oppressive was this deliverer's presence that many residents secretly hoped for al-Jāzāni's victory over his brother and expulsion of the sultan's hated minion once and for all. Only fortune relieved al-Ghawrī of this thorn his officers could not pluck. When, in Shaʿbān 909/January-February 1504, al-Jāzānī impudently entered the Kaʿba precinct in disguise, an alert officer recognized and killed him.[30]

After news of al-Jāzāni's death spread throughout the region, his coalition wavered but did not dissolve. The Banū Ibrāhīm transferred their allegiance over to Yaḥyā ibn Sabʿ, amīr of Yanbuʿ, who resented the settlement Qāytbāy had foisted on his forebears. Showing less flamboyance but more sagacity than al-Jāzānī, Yaḥyā in two years plunged the Ḥijāz in turmoil once again. By Shawwāl 911/February-March 1506, as preparations for the year's coming pilgrimage progressed, security around the shrine cities had almost totally lapsed. Al-Ghawrī thus took a step "unprecedented in the reigns of all his Turkish predecessors." He ordered the cessation of pilgrimage activities, claiming his government could not assure the safety of even pious worshippers. Ibn Iyās condemned al-Ghawrī's decision as "the height of folly."[31] Caravans from West Africa (*al-Takrūr*) and the Maghrib had already appeared at the Pilgrims' Lake south of Cairo; placing themselves under the sultan's protection for the journey. Now they would turn back with stories of his hollow promises.

By early 912/May 1506, al-Ghawrī's subsequent expeditions belatedly turned the tide against the Ḥijāz rebels.[32] Qāyt's successor, Khayrbak al-Miʿmār, governor of Gharbīya Province in the Delta, inflicted such punishment on the Banī Ibrāhīm that they sundered their alliance with Yaḥyā and reacknowledged Barakāt's primacy. When Khayrbak returned to Cairo in Shawwāl/February-March 1507, al-Ghawrī ordered seven days of festivities to celebrate his victory. The sultan promoted the former governor to an amīrship of forty in gratitude for his exceptional accomplishment. Khayrbak had restored credibility to the regime's claim of custodianship over the revered places, and with far less devastation than Qāyt had inflicted. The order prevailing before 908 was reestablished with Barakāt's position intact, if not unanimously accepted. Over the next decade, Yaḥyā ibn Sabʿ reconciled himself with Cairo and received al-Ghawrī's renewal of his authority over Yanbuʿ.[33] Al-Ghawrī proclaimed the pilgrimage routes open once again.[34] But his satisfaction was short-lived.

Soon after the Ḥajj of 913/1508, in which so many luminaries performed their devotions, reports of incursions by a different enemy ruffled the sultanate's restored tranquility. The Portuguese had passed through the Bāb al-Mandab and were raiding along the Red Sea coast.[35] Al-Ghawrī now confronted an entity whose presence had previously been restricted to the Mediterranean. His administration found its commercial monopoly menaced from a second front. Al-Ghawrī's paranoia over European penetration from the Indian Ocean would lead him toward innovative measures to ward it off. But for the present, his authority had been sustained. The sharīf Barakāt became one of al-Ghawrī's most trustworthy vassals, journeying to Cairo as his sultan's guest in 921/1515.[36] Bedazzling Barakāt with all the ceremonial ploys he had refined, al-Ghawrī impressed upon his ally the benefits of loyalty. The gifts he bestowed, upon the sharīf's departure, dismayed Ibn Iyās by their magnitude. Of course, Barakāt was compelled to swear the predictable fealty oath on the ʿUthmānī Koran in the presence of Ibn Ajā, confidential secretary and foreign minister. For his part, Barakāt remained true to his patron until the following year's events, when all al-Ghawrī's regional clients had to rethink their allegiance.

Provincial Sedition: Sūwār the Dhū'l-Qādrid

Shāh Sūwār's revolt disrupted Qāytbāy's early reign. His success in defying the most respected monarch of the central Muslim world so unsettled Qāytbāy's staff because it was unforeseen. Other march lords had attempted to throw off Cairo's ties in the past but few posed such a threat to the repute of the Mamlūk military institution. Since the regime relied so heavily on its redoubtable image to nip restive impulses in the bud, Sūwār's victories gave other potential rebels food for thought. Whether Sūwār's venture would have fared less well in former times when the Mamlūk Empire's status was unchallenged remains an imponderable question. That he thwarted Qāytbāy's repeated efforts to defeat him at a time of growing unease in Cairo over changes in the international scene was certainly regarded as foreboding. Observers rightly interpreted Sūwār as a warning of things to come.

Sūwār's family had attempted to carve out an autonomous niche in Southeastern Anatolia from its founder's migration in 738/1335.[37] But from his grandson's days, the clan had accustomed itself to Mamlūk suzerainty. The aggression exhibited by the Ottoman sultan, Yilderim Bāyazīd, may have persuaded Dhū'l-Qādrid warriors that Cairo's hand rested on them less heavily. Nonetheless, when Sūwār challenged his brother's submission to the Mamlūk sultanate, he was deliberately mimicking his bellicose ancestors more than a century earlier. Even though Sūwār launched his rebellion as an Ottoman client, he soon made his ulterior intentions clear. He planned to break free from both great powers and set up an independent principality excised from territories long under the claim of one or the other. It was this threat of a power-grasping dynast who quarreled with his own siblings and disrupted the Mamlūks' maintenance of the status quo in their frontier buffer zone that so rattled Qāytbāy.[38] Sūwār's aims dissuaded the Ottomans under Bāyazīd II from risking an all-out confrontation with Qāytbāy over his support. Sūwār obviously entertained no thought of submitting meekly to Istanbul if he nullified Cairo's suzerainty. The Ottomans were thus prepared to accept termination of so wayward a client if he proved incapable of realizing his goals against the Egyptians.

Sūwār's strategic skills, shown to such devastating effect in 872 and 873, severely embarrassed Qāytbāy's council. His first victory cast a pall of gloom over the Citadel after initial reactions of incredulity wore off.[39] Ibn Taghrī-Birdī, who watched Qāytbāy at close range, observed that he "verged on death": "The people were agitated. The catastrophe weighed heavily on them all, even the religious minorities (*ahl al-Dhimma*). . . . The Sultan's depression was magnified since, as a consequence of these disasters, his valor was diminished by Shāh Sūwār—the weakest, the least of the Turkmān tribesmen. Shāh Sūwār did battle against the Egyptian army . . . the vastness of which had been unparalleled. Yet they suffered defeat at the hands of this lowly man, minimal of power, junior in age, distant from authority. But God's will prevailed." As one report succeeded another corroborating the rout, the regime could no longer confidently assume its continued control over Aleppo, its northern garrison. Who could predict the aims of this meteoric figure?[40] When Sūwār released aides of Qāytbāy's first atābak Jānibak Qulaqsīz, who had suffered the humiliation of capture, to convey his ransom demand, the court suffered a loss of face. It is noteworthy that Qāytbāy refused to extract the money, leaving Qulaqsīz's subordinates to face the unappealing task. For a sultan to accept such a demand was tantamount to attribution of peer status, a gesture Qāytbāy disavowed. Once his regime perceived the gravity of Sūwār's threat, all offers of adjudication were rebuffed.[41] Acceptance of a mediator's credentials symbolized acknowledgment of his master's legitimacy and Qāytbāy was now resolved to discredit Sūwār as a rebel who held stability in contempt. He who behaved as an outlaw must expect the treatment a criminal deserved. In subsequent proclamations, the regime routinely referred to Sūwār as "the Forsaken" (*al-Makhdhūl*) or "the Dissident" (*al-Khārijī*).[42] The renegade who dissolved his allegiance would find himself abandoned on his own day of judgment.

But despite Qāytbāy's dogged will, Sūwār's triumphs gave many pause for reflection over the sultan's seeming incapacity to sustain his authority abroad. So unsettling were they that rumors of supernatural forces converging against the regime proliferated.[43] And after Yashbak min Mahdī finally brought Sūwār to bay, his dramatic briefings thrilled the capital, sorely in need of a miracle. Decorations festooning the streets included caricatures of Sūwār, depicting him as a monster with superhuman, if not fiendish, qualities. Al-Ṣayrafī marveled, "We are not aware that such a spectacle occurred in any previous epoch, neither for the Maḥmal nor for the arrival of the ambassador of Timur Lenk."[44]

The military hierarchy had come to loathe this affair. Sūwār seemed invincible and efforts against him led only to ignominious defeats and retreats back to Egypt. Yet other client princes were closely watching Qāytbāy's handling of the revolt. If he failed to eliminate such a rebel from a minor house, how profitable was their own fealty? Suzerain loyalty in the medieval Muslim world was tenuous. Subject chieftains respected a powerful overlord who dealt swiftly with opposition. But ties to a monarch whose authority was eroding could only diminish a client's own stature at home. Subordinates would seek out other patrons or pursue their own autonomy. Shāh Sūwār therefore posed a far greater threat than the fear he planted among Qāytbāy's soldiers. These regarded him merely as a stain on their reputations, a Turkmān upstart driven by ambition. If fate destined his secession from the empire, their lot might improve. But Qāytbāy and his colleagues saw the broader implications of Sūwār's uprising. Unopposed, this man might initiate a domino effect culminating in the empire's disintegration. It is in this light that Qāytbāy's perseverence and expenditures must be understood. His lucky designation of Yashbak finally resuscitated the faltering enterprise and brought Sūwār to execution as a traitor. But Sūwār's legacy could not be so easily undone. Even though Sūwār's rival brother, ʿAlāʾ al-Dawla (ʿAlī Dawlāt), was installed as a docile puppet, he could not duplicate his sibling's charisma. Mamlūk control over Southeastern Anatolia had been restored but at inordinate cost. And Sūwār's example was not lost on more powerful rulers who contemplated violating the *Pax Mamlūkia* for their own purposes.

Ḥasan the Tall: Opportunistic Imperialist

In the seventh and eighth decades of the ninth/fifteenth century, a warlord molded his White Sheep Turkmān (Aqquyunlū) of Central Iran into an imperial confederation that disrupted the balance of power in Southwest Asia.[45]

This man, known in Arabic as Ḥasan al-Ṭawīl, nurtured dreams of authority more grandiose then Sūwār's passion for dominion over a discrete region. Uzun Ḥasan's vision was limited by no perimeter of fixed boundaries. He sought to extend his power as far as his cavalrymen and agents provacateurs could reach. His sudden emergence on the international stage therefore provoked guarded worry if not profound alarm in the chancery at Cairo. Although Uzun Ḥasan menaced the status quo, he could not be dismissed as a simple rustic. Uzun Ḥasan proved himself a shrewd diplomat who attempted to assuage regimes, which, for the present, he had no wish to cross. But while professing his heart-felt sentiments of respect or even submission, he sought out their rivals in far-off places such as Western Europe—offering them alliances in return for their connivance. Paying lip service to religious solidarity and royal protocol, Uzun Ḥasan violated both in his drive for imperial supremacy. Ruthlessness does not invariably prejudice subtlety, however, and Uzun Ḥasan rarely indulged in needless rival baiting. His contacts with Qāytbāy's court reveal a clever grasp of Mamlūk sensibilities on matters of territorial integrity and monarchic preference.

Egyptian chroniclers first took note of Uzun Ḥasan as a shaper of events in Southwest Asia at the end of 872/1468, when he scored a victory over his longtime enemy Jahān Shāh, chieftain of the Black Sheep Turkmān (Qarāquyyunlū) and ruler of Iraq and Adhirbayjān.[46] Preoccupied with Sūwār's rebellion, Qāytbāy and his associates paid this development little heed. But Ibn Taghrī-Birdī appreciated its significance. Jahān Shāh lost his life in the mêlée, assuring the incorporation of his lands into the Aqquyunlū domain. The defeat destabilized the entire Iranian zone, promoting "numerous battles and disputes in the eastern regions between a host of Turkmān and others—requiring a month to relate. A vast throng were killed." Qāytbāy and his adjutants may be excused for their distraction in part because Uzun Ḥasan initially deported himself as the model vassal. In the months following his triumph, Ḥasan approached the Egyptian sultan as a deferential ally. First came an emissary bearing congratulations for Qāytbāy's accession. He was soon followed by others who pledged their patron's obedience.[47] Ḥasan exhibited his inexperience in the art of diplomacy at first when his messengers arrived bearing "paltry gifts, as was the custom of Turkmān princes." He soon learned what tradition deemed a sultan's due and increased subsequent offerings. But throughout 873, he sent the same reassuring missive. "Overjoyed at the sultan's enthronement, he regarded himself as his Mamlūk and pledged his service. The sultan's wishes were his commands." Ḥasan kept up the flow of ambassadors conveying promises of his fidelity, while he eliminated residual opponents in Iran and Central Asia. Qāytbāy received conflicting reports about the outcome of a confrontation between Uzun Ḥasan and Jahān Shāh's son, Ḥasan ʿAlī, who had rallied surviving elements of his father's shattered forces in a last ditch counterstroke against the Aqquyunlū.[48] But ultimately,

Uzun Ḥasan's success was confirmed. Qāytbāy now weighed the prospects of treating with a new regime which had consolidated its authority over much of Iran. But he continued to regard Sūwār as his pressing issue. After all, the Aqquyunlū were farther away and as yet showed no signs of hostility.

As 873 drew to a close, news of Ḥasan's broadening military adventures reached the Citadel. Even though he focused his attention on opponents east and north, his seeming invincibility finally persuaded the oligarchy in Cairo that his activities should be monitored and his emissaries reprimanded when appropriate. In Dhū'l-Ḥijja/June-July 1469, one such representative arrived bearing the severed head of Sulṭān Abū Saʿīd, Timurid ruler of Bukhāra and Samarqānd in Central Asia.[49] Upon its offering to the sultan, rumors about the circumstances behind the defeat of this powerful monarch spread into the city. Uzun Ḥasan had allegedly attacked him in revenge for his previous assistance to Jahān Shāh. Since Sulṭān Abū Saʿīd's armies were among the most formidable of the eastern Islamic world, Ḥasan's victory bespoke the ferocity of his own host. The emissary had asked Qāytbāy's permission to have the head impaled on a lance and paraded through Cairo's streets, preceded by heralds and torchbearers. The sultan refused this request on grounds that such a barbaric display violated Sulṭān Abū Saʿīd's rights as a believer. Instead, Qāytbāy took possession of his remains and had them interred. One speculates that Qāytbāy had no wish to augment Ḥasan's stature in his own capital. The Timurid prince had enjoyed a great chieftain's standing. His untimely end enhanced Ḥasan's own reputation as a commander whom the mighty could no longer dismiss. Qāytbāy reminded the emissary of his own precedence as a monarch among princes. He ordered a formal procession of his Mamlūk squadrons from the Bāb al-Naṣr to the Rumayla Square.[50] Participants wore their battle regalia with full complement of arms while the sultan himself donned his most elaborate turban, usually reserved for troop reviews. "Finding the emissary somewhat presumptuous, he decided to impress him with a display of grandeur his master could not match."

Qāytbāy's ceremonial ploy seemingly had an effect on the Aqquyunlū leader, for 874 passed without further incident. But the next year witnessed a shift in his forays westward. In Muḥarram/July 1470, a messenger from Istanbul produced reports that Uzun Ḥasan had seized several strongholds the Venetians held on the Black Sea coast.[51] Heretofore, the Aqquyunlū had behaved as their tribal predecessors during earlier expansive phases of their existence, reducing rival confederations to client status or eliminating them outright. But now the regime showed inclinations toward grander designs. By occupying entrepôts of commercial powers with which it had no record of hostility, the Aqquyunlū were fishing in uncharted waters. The Ottomans, who had established a profitable modus vivendi with the Italians, perceived this move as a threat to their share of the Black Sea trade. Yet Uzun Ḥasan had offered them no open challenge and the Ottoman government thus decided to inform the

Egyptians of this incident while awaiting subsequent developments. They were not long in coming.

In Rabī͑ II/September-October, the viceroy of Aleppo sent a courier post-haste with a dispatch describing Ḥasan's entry into the sultan's northern marches.[52] Encouraged by Sūwār's unexpected rout of the Egyptians, Ḥasan made his own move. The contingent he sent was not equipped to attempt a siege of either al-Bīra or al-Ruhā at this time, however. Conflicts with the Timurid rulers of Herāt and Samarqānd diverted his main forces back east.[53] Nonetheless, Ḥasan had challenged Qāytbāy by trespassing on Mamlūk territory. In Dhū'l-Qa͑da 876/April-May 1472, he sent an emissary with a lengthy letter "touching on important matters."[54] Since Qāytbāy refused a public reading of this missive, al-Ṣayrafī could only transmit rumors of its contents. Ḥasan allegedly demanded the right to send a mantle (*kiswa*) for the Ka͑ba shrine at Mecca, as the Timurid Shāh Rukh had done during Jaqmaq's reign. He also vouched for Sūwār's good behavior, offering to pay bond money in return for the sultan's formal pardon. Qāytbāy found this quid pro quo outrageous since Ḥasan was, in effect, interceding for Sūwār's conduct as the latter's true suzerain. And the Cairo regime jealously guarded its traditional privilege of presenting the annual Ka͑ba mantle during the Ḥajj ceremonials in Mecca. Ḥasan was daring to compare his parvenu confederacy with the Mamlūk sultanate. But since the Aqquyunlū contingent had retreated, Qāytbāy still opted for caution. No expedition was dispatched that year.

Uzun Ḥasan waited until Yashbak captured Sūwār before taking the initiative once again. In Jumādā II 877/November-December 1472, word arrived from Aleppo of an Aqquyunlū force commanded by Ḥasan's son, Ughurlū Muḥammad, having placed al-Ruhā under siege.[55] Qāytbāy and his colleagues decided that military action was now warranted. Two units were mobilized. The first departed immediately under the atābak's direction to reinforce Aleppo. The second left the next month. Qāytbāy wished to show Ḥasan his muscle and conscripted a thousand Sulṭānī Mamlūks for the latter contingent. Yashbak agreed to lead it since his relentless harassment of Sūwār was certain to daunt Ḥasan's troops. Ḥasan's behavior toward his former "esteemed suzerain" had undergone a complete transformation. Previously humbling himself as Qāytbāy's Mamlūk, he now sent missives throughout Eastern Anatolia and Northern Syria replete with verses from the Koran asserting his stature as God's legitimate agent on earth before whom righteous believers duly submitted.[56] As Yashbak made his way toward Aleppo, reports both positive and negative arrived at the Citadel. The governor of al-Bīra had driven off Ḥasan's troops from the town's environs. Yet in Sha͑bān, the viceroy of Aleppo apprehended some forty persons who had secretly entered the gates, fomented opposition to the sultan's rule, and sent their master intelligence about divisions among barracks factions.[57] All the suspects had been hanged without further review of charges against them but the situation clearly had deteriorated. Yashbak, who reached Aleppo in Shawwāl/March 1473, wasted no time dallying but set out for the Euphrates. Having now assumed command over his cavalrymen camped near al-Bīra, Ḥasan confronted Qāytbāy's most formidable adjutant in Dhū'l-Qaʿda/April.[58] After a violent battle, he met defeat and fled from the scene. One of his sons had been killed; another lost an eye. Ḥasan retreated with such haste that he abandoned his portable archives. Upon their inventory, Yashbak found several letters Ḥasan had addressed to European courts offering collusion with them against the sultans of Cairo and Istanbul. Brandishing these documents in the Aleppo Mosque, Yashbak condemned Uzun Ḥasan as an opportunist who betrayed his coreligionaries to the infidel. Qāytbāy had received further confirmation of Ḥasan's duplicity directly from the Ottoman ruler. Suspecting Ḥasan's schemes, the latter had arrested his ambassador who was crossing Anatolia on his way to Europe.[59] In his pouch were discovered more letters urging Frankish princes to attack Egypt and Asia Minor by sea while he, Ḥasan, invaded their realms by land. Accepting this information from the Ottoman courier, Qāytbāy savored Yashbak's triumph with particular relish.

After his embarrassing failure at al-Bīra, Uzun Ḥasan attempted no further military adventures against the Mamlūk State. But plots undermining the sultan's authority were still uncovered in unexpected quarters, revealing how far Ḥasan's web of conspiracy had extended. At the end of 877/May 1473, the intendant (*mubāshir*) of the pilgrimage arrived in Cairo with news of an incident involving the Iraqi Ḥajj caravan.[60] Two of Ḥasan's agents, an officer and a judge, had intimidated the imāms of Medina. They had pressured them to preach the khuṭba at the Prophet's Mosque with Uzun Ḥasan's title: al-Malik al-ʿĀdil "the Just Monarch, True Servant of the Two Sanctuaries." Upon their departure, the alarmed clerics had written to Barakāt, amīr of Mecca, informing him of this event. Barakāt apprehended the two provacateurs outside of Mecca, clapped them in irons and sent them to Cairo for questioning. When they were interrogated, they disclosed Ḥasan's intent to pose himself as the new guardian of the holy places once he had supplanted the Egyptian sultan. Since the Iraqi caravan had departed for the Ḥijāz before Ḥasan's dream was shattered at al-Bīra, his agents' plot now seemed ludicrous. Qāytbāy ultimately released them both "as a sign of his good will, upon Yashbak's recommendation." Early in 879/May-June 1474, Uzun Ḥasan mended his fences with Cairo, claiming his behavior had been impelled by "circumstances not of his own choosing."[61] Qāytbāy played the magnanimous victor who prized tranquility over spoils and pledged not to pursue any further retribution. In his final years, Ḥasan faced insurrection much closer to home from members of his own family. His son, Ughurlū Muḥammad, who had led the first expedition against al-Birā, fell out with his father and requested aid from the viceroy of Aleppo.[62] The prince's mother presented herself before the sultan at the Citadel and requested his service as an intermediary between her son and husband. Although Qāytbāy received her with honors befitting her station and lodged her in the harem under his wife's care, he remained noncommittal on the matter of her son's claims. He did welcome Ughurlū Muḥammad's heir, whom he retained as his ward in Cairo. Since Ḥasan was quarreling with his brother Uways during these sorties, his empire, recently assembled, now faced possible disintegration.

In Shaʿbān 883/October-November 1478, word of Ḥasan's death reached the Citadel.[63] In light of his own regicidal tactics, the fate of Ḥasan's succession seemed to hang in the balance. His eldest surviving son, Khalīl, had been acclaimed as leader of the confederation but was deposed after little more than a year by disgruntled amīrs.[64] The next son who followed him, Yaʿqūb, reconsolidated his father's power base and reigned for more than a decade. It was during his tenure that Yashbak attempted his ill-fated bid for kingship in the border zone between the Mamlūk and Aqquyunlū Empires.

Uzun Ḥasan's brief skirmish with imperial dominion caused minimal difficulty for Qāytbāy's administration, when compared with challenges elsewhere. Yet Ḥasan's pragmatic approach to both conspiracy and diplomacy set him apart from other ephemeral conquerors. Ḥasan was not the first ambitious warlord who ignored principles of Islamic solidarity to strike deals with Christian rulers if they shared a common interest. But in Qāytbāy's day, he alone entertained such schemes while portraying himself simultaneously as a better defender of the faith than his rival. Yet his greatest crime remained his disregard for the status quo. Had Uzun Ḥasan willingly acknowledged the prerogatives of his fellow monarchs and confined himself to solidifying his own region, Qāytbāy would have found no fault with him, regardless of his posturing. But when Ḥasan violated the established order, preemptive action was necessary. His antics set an example for subsequent dynasts in Iran, who combined charisma with doctrine to inspire their followers in a different kind of imperial venture.

Ismāʿīl Ṣafawī: Sectarian Enigma

The Mamlūk sultanate enjoyed a respite of three decades from eastern invaders. But in Ṣafar 908/August-September 1502, reports of yet another transgressor crossing the frontier of Aleppo province unsettled the sultan's entourage.[65] His identity was obscure at this early date. In 908, Ibn Iyās referred to him simply as Shāh Ismāʿīl Al-Ṣūfī ("the Mystic"), with no details on his genealogy, ideological inclinations or motives for conquest. The historian's only descriptive term was illustrative, however. He labeled Ismāʿīl a "dissident" (*khārijīyan*), although solely in the context of digression from tranquility rather than departure from doctrinal conformity. Throughout their comments about Ismāʿīl's frenetic activities until his shattering defeat at Chaldirān,

Egyptian narrators took little note of his Shī'ī revival or its exploitation for state building. To the end Ismā'īl remained merely the Ṣūfī, depicted as a reincarnation of Uzun Ḥasan and his predecessors who periodically emerged from the Iranian plateau to disrupt the status quo. But Ismā'īl certainly amounted to more than another warlord who welded tribes into a transitory imperial unit, collapsing as rapidly as it had coalesced. Although his own mission, so intimately bound to his charisma, never recovered from Chaldirān, the regime he founded and the doctrine he shaped long outlasted him.[66]

None of these portents could have been envisioned in Cairo when the first Ṣafavid raid was reported in 908. Yet in light of Uzun Ḥasan's precedent, al-Ghawrī took it seriously enough to mobilize troops. When news arrived of the Ṣafavid's departure, al-Ghawrī released from duty the Mamlūks he had designated, much to their relief. Despite his continuing unease, Ismā'īl's Kizilbāsh (literally "Red Heads," from their distinctive headgear) never duplicated Sūwār's or Ḥasan's menace. Indeed, their tactical behavior was unfathomable. When they lost initial skirmishes, they showed no staying power but abandoned the field for the east. Ultimately, their feints conformed to an identifiable pattern of rapid forays that took advantage of surprise to inflict widespread destruction with few losses. Yet the marauders rarely tarried long, avoiding the risk of reprisal. Fading away quickly, they left a wake of fear behind them. No one knew when or where they would pounce again. These raiders seemed more interested in agitating a region than in systematically incorporating it into an imperial domain. Until Chaldirān, the Ṣafavids remained more inclined in the west toward spreading their propaganda of invincibility than in substantive conquest. The latter enterprise might, after all, result in setbacks or outright defeats. Neither enhanced the charismatic mission of their leader.

The heightened frequency of al-Ghawrī's dealings with Ismā'īl after 918 have been mentioned previously. Although no consensus of opinion emerges from statements offered by chroniclers, several alluded to al-Ghawrī's collusion with the shah against Selim. In Rabī' I of 920/April-May 1514, Ibn Iyās noted the sultan's stalling when the Ottoman urged him to join his crusade against Ismā'īl.[67] Even though both Selim and al-Ghawrī championed the cause of Sunnism, the latter saw no chance of Shī'ism corroding the spiritual integrity of his realm, while the former regarded Ismā'īl's agents as a serious challenge to his authority over Eastern Anatolia. The Syrian biographer al-Ḥalabī, who spared al-Ghawrī no censure, openly accused him of "secret friendship" with Ismā'īl, that fomenter of "abominable Shī'ism."[68] Of course, this denunciation, written after Selim's victory, reflected a judgment *post quem*. Nonetheless, the collective impression left by these deprecations and rumors implies al-Ghawrī's indifference to Ismā'īl's doctrinal deviance. True to his predecessors' concepts of foreign policy, he kept his options open until the final hour, cherishing the prospect of his rivals destroying each other. Fully prepared to deal with whoever emerged the victor, al-Ghawrī was the pragmatist protecting his position rather than the purist defending orthodoxy. In the prevailing religious climate of Egypt, Shīʿism posed little palpable threat. But given the crumbling foundations of his authority at home, the sultan had every reason to fear a foreign conqueror who promised salvation from his own oppression. Ismāʿīl's ulterior purpose remained an enigma that al-Ghawrī took lightly. Selim, on the other hand, flagrantly brandished his imperialist designs, and he clearly possessed the means of transforming them into reality. Under such circumstances, al-Ghawrī's alleged deviousness acquires a logic that conformed with practical experience if not spiritual idealism.

The Ottomans: Institutionalized Aggression

In contrast with the preceding figures, the Ottoman sultan enjoyed parity with his Egyptian counterpart. From the time of their recovery following Yilderin Bāyazīd's debacle before Timur Lenk's horde, the Ottomans had retained their hold over Southeastern Europe while reextending their rule throughout Western and Central Anatolia. By the time of Qāytbāy's accession, they had restored their status as a world power. Their dominion now rested on much firmer institutional foundations than during Bāyazīd's reign.[69] Certainly from the time of Mehmet II Fātiḥ ("the Conqueror") (855–886/1451–1481), Cairo's imperial dīwān accorded the Ottoman sultan peer rank as a monarch whose prerogatives equalled those devolving upon the Egyptian ruler. When Mehmet died, Ibn Iyās extolled him as "the glorious and omnipotent sultan, indomitable warrior, master of Anatolia, custodian of Constantinople. An illustrious esteemed sovereign, superior to all his forebears in the House of ʿUthmān. All the universe acknowledged his justice. He exhibited morality, wisdom, rectitude, generosity. He possessed a vast fortune, commanded invincible armies. He expanded his domain at the expense of infidel nations."[70] Ibn Iyās extended no such accolades to parvenus such as Shāh Sūwār, Uzun Ḥasan, or Ismāʿīl Ṣafawī. The historian touched on all the ideals of monarchy according to Islamic law when he eulogized the Conqueror. His concluding epithet lauding Mehmet for venting his aggression on Christian states rather than fellow Muslims was placed for pointed effect. Ibn Iyās looked back whimsically to Mehmet's reign as a happier time of mutually accorded respect between the two bastions of Sunnism, in contrast with the threat of impending invasion posed by Selim I during al-Ghawrī's tenure. In those former days, both empires shared common goals with minimal friction. Above all, each cherished the prevailing political order and cooperated to see it bolstered. Of course, Ibn Iyās' obsequies conveniently glossed over telltale signs of Ottoman hostility. During Qāytbāy's early years, he was bombarded with entreaties from the Bey of Qaramān in the southern corner of Anatolia for aid against his aggressive neighbor.[71] Once this vestige of princely resistance to Ottoman imperialism was absorbed, the two empires would share a common frontier. History had shown the misfortunes heaped upon those who contested with the house of 'Uthmān over adjacent spheres of influence. The Ottomans always found distant allies better friends than regimes next door.

From Qāytbāy's enthronement, Mamlūk-Ottoman relations ran the gamut from amicable coexistence to escalating rivalry, wary stand off, and, finally, outright confrontation. These phases in the two states' interaction bespeak a fundamental contrast in imperial ideologies. We have noted objectives hallowed by the Mamlūk regime. Cairo attached no particular weight to a doctrinaire stance. Imperialism represented the best means of ensuring harmony among potentially acrimonious populations. Although the Mamlūk sultanate paid defense of Sunnism profuse lip service, in practice it was prepared to coexist with governments pledged to divergent views of Islam, or even non-Muslim creeds. A benefit of imperialism was its sustenance of the ruling elite in grand style. While the military caste behaved profligately, draining assets from productive elements of society and consuming them in ostentatious ways, it recognized the relationship between undisputed territorial control and maximal extractions. Maintenance of its patrimony was essential to its continued survival as the dominant economic group. Confrontations with foreign competitors over ideological matters would result in this patrimony's diminution. Time-honored stratagems aimed at upholding equilibrium coincided most positively with the Mamlūk's concept of their role as an entrenched elite.

The Ottoman sultanate had evolved under radically different circumstances. Born on the northwestern fringe of the Muslim world and poised at the threshold of Europe, the Ottoman State began as a minor principality. Committed from its inception to the principle of *ghazwa,* or raiding against the infidel, Ottoman warlords and their followers conceived of their goal and defined their legitimacy through conquest.[72] For them, expansion represented an overriding objective. The Ottoman ruling establishment was not obsessed with preservation of a fixed patrimony but rather with enlargement of a territorial network until it encompassed the known world. Heady visions of universal dominion captivated most autocrats who presided over the expansionist period of Ottoman history (to the death of Sulaymān Qānūnī in 974/1566). Given attitudes inspired by such a worldview, the Ottoman ruling elite was bound to look upon Mamlūk veneration of the status quo with ambivalence, if not contempt. They would regard its defenders as an impediment to their own mission, even in the context of their common faith. To the Mamlūks, peace was synonymous with preservation of the prevailing international order. To their Ottoman rivals, peace was equated with unified authority not merely over the Dār al-Islām but all regions beyond it. The ideal international system envisioned in Istanbul, at least until the mid-tenth/sixteenth century, was a single imperial confederacy, possessing resources sufficient to prevent discord, subdue recalcitrant clients, and integrate agriculturalists, merchants, or artisans into one cohesive whole. The Ottoman concept of religious solidarity fitted intimately into their view of universal sway. Not content with protecting holy places, the Ottomans sought to impose Sunnism over all Muslim peoples. Tolerant of other monotheists, they vehemently rejected claims of sectarian rivals within their own faith. Given these opposing views, antipathy between the two military elites was inevitable. Their sporadic cordiality is noteworthy because it signalled crises both recognized as greater threats. When their interests no longer coincided, conflict was resumed.

Qāytbāy's staff adapted their strategies to accost the Ottomans as they moved into Anatolia. Yet their ultimate goal of restoring the status quo was apparent in all of their strategies. While Mehmet II still lived, relations remained positive. The Ottoman's worry over Uzun Ḥasan's hegemonistic ambitions disposed him toward a tacit alliance with Cairo.[73] Since the Aqquyunlū warlord challenged both powers, Cairo overlooked Ottoman overtures toward Qāytbāy's Christian vassal in Cyprus, who chafed under Egyptian suzerainty,[74] and the Ottoman siege of Rhodes, held by the Templar Knights.[75] The Egyptian Chancery discerned signs of creeping Ottoman aggression in these developments. But they could be endured as minimally disruptive of the existing balance. When Mehmet's successor, Bāyazīd II, began pressuring Sūwār's successors in Southeastern Anatolia, however, Qāytbāy responded vigorously. Having already expended copious resources to subdue a client who refused to keep his place, the Egyptian sultan would permit no further tampering with his settlement for the Dhū'l-Qādrids. The Ottomans first enticed Sūwār's displaced brother, Shāh Budāq, into declaring his bid for autonomy. When he proved too wayward, they applied similar inducements to Qāytbāy's own puppet, ʿAlī Dawlāt.[76] The massive expeditions Qāytbāy sent against both of them in 889–896/1484–1491 reminded the Ottoman hierarchy rather jarringly that their southern neighbors had not yet surrendered martial primacy. After his successive defeats, Bāyazīd desisted from any further designs against Mamlūk holdings in Dhū'l-Qādrid regions. His preference for coexistence did not please restive factions at home. Bāyazīd's youngest son, Selim, regarded his father's lack of belligerence as effete passivity, deleterious to the Ottomans' image abroad.

Al-Ghawrī's attempts at containing this choleric man drew upon tactics devised over the preceding two centuries. His failure may be interpreted in part as a consequence of Selim's relentless commitment to his rivals' subjugation. But the strategies al-Ghawrī's predecessors had conceived for neutralizing foreign competitors were proven woefully inadequate when applied against a militarist who refused playing by old rules. Al-Ghawrī's decision to take the field himself, reluctant as it may have been, emerged from his own proclivity for innovation and duplicity. Recognizing that further diplomatic ploys were futile, al-Ghawrī marched toward Aleppo hoping that Ismāʿīl might solve his dilemma for him. Whether Selim's contempt derived significantly from al-Ghawrī's collusion with the shāh remains a moot question. Selim accepted the legitimacy of no state as ordained by either divine providence or time-honored tradition. Selim's behavior must be understood as a harbinger of pragmatic aggressiveness that has troubled international affairs all too frequently in modern times. Ever ready to muddy the waters, seek out weaknesses in his enemies' defenses or hurl threats they were ill-prepared to counter, Selim's tactics represent the epitome of Ottoman encroachment expressed with an intensity new to the central Muslim world.[77]

Specific circumstances that drew the two empires toward irrepressible conflict following Chaldirān involved renewal of Ottoman pressure upon the Dhū'l-Qādrid march. After one of Sūwār's sons revolted against his uncle, ʿAlī Dawlāt, now an aging client resigned to his lot, Selim backed the prodigal's claim against al-Ghawrī's vassal.[78] When ʿAlī Dawlāt called upon his patron for help, al-Ghawrī was in no position financially or politically to replicate Qāytbāy's massive reprisals. A quarter century earlier, ʿAlī Dawlāt's initial success in subduing his nephew therefore provided Selim with an excuse for a wholesale assault on the Dhū'l-Qādrid Principality. No longer disposed to prop up a vassal of dubious competence, Selim now aimed at annexing the buffer zone outright. When his emissary displayed ʿAlī Dawlāt's head at the Citadel for all to see, al-Ghawrī realized that his devices had been for naught. Whatever his personal estimate of Ismāʿīl's capacity to defeat the Ottoman or at least divert his attention away from Syria, al-Ghawrī had no other wild card left in his deck. That he made a bold show of force in the face of such odds betokens the élan exhibited by his caste at its best, even in times of widespread corruption and demoralization at home.

Selim's victories against his competitors invite a consensus historians have reached in hindsight, sealing al-Ghawrī's doom when Bāyazīd died. The advantages Selim enjoyed in firepower certainly gave him an edge over his Muslim contemporaries.[79] But we have seen that treachery on the part of al-Ghawrī's lieutenants contributed an equally critical factor behind his demise at Marj Dābiq—at least according to the Egyptian perspective. Al-Ghawrī's experiments with his own artillery units had not advanced sufficiently for their employment against the Ottomans in 922. In any case, his troops' adamant rejection of innovations with their weaponry prohibited any chance of such trials at this critical juncture. The Mamlūks' redoubtable performance before sedition divided their ranks qualifies the absolute gain that Selim's firearms provided on that fateful day. But the readiness of Selim's military to incorporate them reveals yet another dimension of Ottoman expediency in good times or bad.

In the long and torturous road to Marj Dābiq, al-Ghawrī exhausted every ploy he drew out from his precursors' examples. Whether his own inventive tactics could have altered the course of events had he found the opportunity to perfect them remains speculation. Al-Ghawrī was fated to preside over a regime uneasy with change. By contrast, the Ottoman sultanate demonstrated its capacity for confronting challenges of a shifting environment. Its commitment to imperialism as a means of transforming the world order overwhelmed the containment policies of its Mamlūk rival.

The Europeans: Heralds of Commercial Decline

The century beginning in 1450 A.D. witnessed a navigational revolution calamitous for the governments of the Mediterranean Basin and Southwest Asia that had dominated global trade for hundreds of years. But important as it was for restructuring the commercial system, this revolution was only an exterior symbol of economic and social changes transforming Western Europe.[80] To potentates of the central Muslim lands, such changes could only be dimly perceived at this early date. But the navigational revolution influenced them in disturbingly tangible ways. Fāṭimid, Ayyūbid and Mamlūk monarchs of Egypt and Syria had profited handsomely from their control over territories straddling the most traversed route between the Orient and Europe in the Middle Ages.[81] Sultans Qāytbāy and al-Ghawrī were fated to reign when Europeans actively contested their monopoly. The two autocrats recognized this new spurt of European energy for what it was: disruption of their comfortable situation. They reacted at first with repeated attempts at deterring aggression, only working at containing it when prevention proved impossible. Yet the historian must inquire whether their stratagems represented a positive plan for outmaneuvering these competitors or were merely reactive devices aimed at coping with a presence that defied eradication. From this perspective, the European question provides a vivid test case of the Mamlūk obsession with upholding the status quo.

Commercial contacts with European governments were a routine aspect of foreign policy in Cairo when Qāytbāy assumed power. Despite escalating provocations he and al-Ghawrī faced in coming decades, neither spurned positive relations. Embassies from Frankish regimes seeking to renew their treaty rights in Cairo arrived regularly throughout the later fifteenth and early sixteenth centuries.[82] Qāytbāy and al-Ghawrī contemplated tactics of reprisal only after Christian armies menaced a vulnerable Muslim state, Europeans connived with rivals nearby, and pirates seized Egyptian vessels. When Qāytbāy received pleas from the amīr of Granada in southern Spain (*al-Andalus*) for aid against the Castilian Reconquista in Jumādā I 884/ July-August 1479, he dispatched no troops but instead impounded assets of the Resurrection Church in Jerusalem.[83] He demanded a letter from its clerics to the prince of Naples, who would dissuade his Spanish colleagues from further attacks. If his request were refused, European access to holy places in Jerusalem would terminate. Qāytbāy's action revealed his awareness of ties between the dynastic houses of Naples and Castile but also underscored his reluctance at committing soldiers on a fool's errand. His diplomatic ploy produced no positive result. Ibn Iyās ruefully observed: "None of this came to anything, for the Franks occupied Granada soon thereafter." When Qānṣūh al-Ghawrī received proof of Ṣafavid overtures to European powers against him in 916/1511, he seized resident consuls of these governments in Cairo and threatened their execution if they facilitated their patrons' schemes.[84] Yet he refrained from closing their hospices in Cairo or Alexandria, preferring the suspects' close supervision by the prefect until Ṣafavid intentions became clearer. Al-Ghawrī suspected espionage from a more personal agent, for early in 917/April 1511 he arrested his own interpreter (*tarjumān*), Taghrī-Birdī, on evidence of the latter's treason.[85] This Taghrī-Birdī, who had returned from an extended European sojourn in 913, had kept up close ties with his former hosts. When the sultan discovered letters the interpreter had sent describing how seriously his regime's authority had eroded, al-Ghawrī reacted spitefully. Taghrī-Birdī had urged the Europeans to send maritime expeditions against Egypt's ports, "since no meaningful defense could be mounted." The outraged ruler might sequester his faithless official's estate and cast him in irons for life but could do little to uproot the seeds his missives had planted. For throughout this trying period when the Mamlūk regime encountered multiple challenges from land-based competitors, Europeans heightened their encroachment on two fronts: in the Mediterranean in the form of piracy and in the Red Sea at the hands of Portuguese navigators seeking dominion over the Indian spice route.

Sporadic harassment of Muslim shipping in Mediterranean waters had occurred ever since the revival of Italian seafaring during the high Middle Ages. But with the apogee of their commercial activity in the later medieval period came a dramatic increase in plundering by corsairs. Qāytbāy apparently enjoyed a brief respite from piracy lasting until the end of 876/1472, although al-Ṣayrafī noted a furtive trip he made to Palestine the year before in response to reports of European raiding.[86] In any case, a series of reports arrived from Rashīd (Rosetta) and al-Ṭīna during Dhū'l-Ḥijja/May-June describing several attacks against Egyptian vessels making for the ports. Their crews had been apprehended and their cargos confiscated. The governor of Alexandria captured one of the Christian pirate ships and sent its sailors to Cairo in irons for ransoming the captured crew and stolen goods.[87] But Qāytbāy realized the inefficacy of such feeble remonstrances and decided upon a major project of deterrence. His plan graphically symbolized Mamlūk concepts of reactive containment rather than assertive retaliation.

The sultan ordered construction of several massive guard towers in Egyptian coastal ports. The first was begun at Rashīd immediately following the Frankish incursion.[88] As the frequency of assaults quickened, Qāytbāy fortified other entrepôts. Heavy chains were strung across harbor entrances. His largest structure still protects Alexandria's inner harbor. In Rabīᶜ I 882/June-July 1477, Qāytbāy chose the site of the ancient Pharos Lighthouse for his most imposing watchtower.[89] Requiring two years to erect, this edifice confronted the Franks with enormous walls to withstand their bombardment. Spaces for cannons were designed behind its external apertures, one of the very few references to artillery from Qāytbāy's reign. The sultan invested more than one hundred thousand dīnārs in his Alexandria burj and endowed waqfs for its upkeep. He regarded the tower as his finest military structure and made several inspection visits during and after construction. Yet Qāytbāy, true to his predecessors' attitudes, conceived of his response solely as an act of restraint. The thought of investing equivalent sums in building new ships, training Egyptian mariners in European techniques, or even hiring Christian renegades to advise them never occurred to him. The conservator entertained no concept of turning the Europeans' game against them in their own element. No plans were laid for a naval counterstroke.

Al-Ghawrī showed himself somewhat more assertive when he dealt with acts of piracy. Raiding became a serious matter in 913–916/1508–1511, warranting some kind of reprisal. Since Qāytbāy's coastal fortresses could not protect Egyptian or Syrian ships offshore, al-Ghawrī outfitted one of the few Mediterranean expeditions of the later Mamlūk period following Barsbāy's invasion of Cyprus.[90] In Dhū'l-Qaᶜda 913/March 1508, al-Ghawrī placed his associate (*qarīb*), Muḥammad Bak, in command of this flotilla. Seeking to avoid any deliberate provocation, the sultan defined Muḥammad's purpose as the collection of naval stores from the Gulf of Ayās (Alexandretta) at the northeast corner of the Mediterranean. But if European corsairs showed signs of hostility, he should pounce on them. Until Jumādā II 916/September-October 1510, al-Ghawrī's ad hoc admiral succeeded remarkably well, capturing scores of European ships despoiling the Delta and Syrian coasts. But in that month, his fortune was reversed. The governor of Ṭarābulus sent a missive relating Muḥammad's defeat and death following his encounter with a European squadron off Ayās.[91] Eighteen Mamlūk vessels had been impounded and their store of munitions expropriated.

Stunned by this catastrophe, al-Ghawrī refused food for two days as he pondered his options. Dismissing any further naval ventures as too risky, he opted for Qāytbāy's Jerusalem tactic. The sultan sent agents to arrest monks (*ruhbān*) at the Resurrection Church. Upon their arrival at the Citadel, they joined merchants and consuls rounded up from Alexandria and Damietta. Al-Ghawrī compelled his assembled hostages to draft letters demanding the release of ships captured by "vile agents" of European kings whose pirates perverted their own agreements sanctioning safe passage.[92] If his ultimatum were refused, the sultan would not merely close the Resurrection Church as his pious predecessor had done but demolish it stone by stone. Sacred though their calling might be, the monks would be hanged along with the factors and merchants. Al-Ghawrī's threat almost certainly exceeded his resolve since he placed the hostages under his financial secretary's confinement pending the Europeans' reply. He and they had to wait almost two years before it arrived.

In Ṣafar 918/April-May 1512, an ambassador from Egypt's closest Italian ally, the doge of Venice, presented himself at the Citadel.[93] Ibn Iyās described the emissary as "an elderly man with a white beard and vast bulk—a commanding presence." He wore a magnificent robe of Chinese silk with gold embroidery. Obviously seeking his host's placation, the ambassador bore splendid gifts. So profuse was his patron's generosity that two hundred bearers were necessary to convey the gifts up the stairs. He offered al-Ghawrī crystal vases, velvet garments embossed with dragons, a great variety of silk and satin cloth, and "other precious items." While the Venetian emissary, with this display of Chinese finery, made his point about the overriding need for both sides to preserve the oriental trade, which no incident of piracy or sequestration of a holy place should hinder, he brought no promise of restitution from the offenders. How al-Ghawrī received his plea for a negotiated settlement is unclear. But Ibn Iyās reported no subsequent acts of execution or demolition. Almost certainly, sultan and emissary reached some mutually acceptable arrangement allowing both parties to save face without direct capitulation. The Resurrection Church was closed for an indefinite period but it did remain intact. Previous commercial treaties were reactivated as well. Whether the Venetians actually curbed piracy in the Mediterranean cannot be ascertained from Arabic sources, yet the latter report no further raids during Al-Ghawrī's final years. The threat of such operations continued nonetheless, since no active steps had been taken to prevent them. The Ottomans would therefore inherit this abiding problem so elusive of Cairo's resolution. ʿAbd al-Bāsiṭ al-Malaṭī, al-Ghawrī's effusive publicist, might well extol his sovereign as the merciless hammerer of Franks, "who despoiled the Muslims' wealth and commodities, violating hallowed covenants."[94] His praise provided scant solace in the face of a rapidly shifting balance of power over the central sea, in which the Muslims would come up woefully short. How they dealt with the Portuguese challenge further south shows their groping attempts at a preemptive response.

The Portuguese penetration of the Indian Ocean heralded direct European access to markets of South and East Asia heretofore served by merchants from central Muslim states. Precisely when Portuguese mariners first entered the Red Sea is unclear in Arabic texts but Ibn Iyās noted their presence in Dhū'l-Ḥijja 912/April-May 1507.[95] Mamlūk authorities had learned of their maneuvers off the Indian littoral several years earlier, presumably from their own agents or local merchants who sent reports of Portuguese aggression. Al-Ghawrī organized his first expedition to strengthen fortifications along the

Red Sea and Yemen coasts in 911/1505. Realizing that tactics aimed solely at containment would not eliminate the Portuguese as dangerous competitors, the sultan ordered his officers to confront the new arrivals by sea.[96] But when the court found out about Portuguese raiding north of the Bāb al-Mandab in waters regarded as secure, rumors spread depicting their devilish yet ingenious methods. Supposedly, the Portuguese had breached a dyke constructed by Alexander the Great (referred to by Ibn Iyās as Iskandar ibn Filībis al-Rūmī) connecting "the Chinese and Roman Seas." The Europeans had worked patiently for years enlarging their rupture until whole fleets could pass it. Now, twenty of their ships had appeared in the Red Sea and were ambushing Indian commercial vessels bound for Sawākin and Jidda. Although the Portuguese presence within the southern maritime front, so sudden and unexpected, provoked alarm in Cairo, the regime did not succumb to paralysis. In 914/1508, the sultan's first retaliatory contingent, commanded by Amīr Ḥusayn al-Mushrif, vanquished several Portuguese squadrons in the Indian Ocean.[97] Galvanized by this victory, al-Ghawrī proceeded with his plan for building a Red Sea fleet capable of standing off the invaders and restoring the Egyptian trade monopoly. Soon after celebrations over Ḥusayn's achievement, al-Ghawrī reviewed a regatta of warships he had commissioned for service in the Mediterranean and Red Seas, the first so constructed in seventy years.

But fortune did not favor al-Ghawrī's efforts. The following year brought reports of Ḥusayn's defeat in several clashes with the Portuguese. Rajahs of Indian states that exported spice to Egypt dispatched messengers with dismal tales of European encroachment and requests for aid al-Ghawrī was hard-pressed to supply.[98] Al-Ghawrī drafted a reply profuse with pledges of solidarity but vague on concrete proposals, which he placed in the hands of a eunuch official. This emissary visited allied Indian princes and urged their cooperation against European interlopers. Although the courier returned safely some months later (Muḥarram 917/March-April 1511), he brought back no comforting word of sustained resistance. For more than twelve months, the court received few tidings from the Indian Ocean. Then, on 30 Ramaḍān 918/9 December 1512, the unlucky Amīr Ḥusayn arrived at the Citadel after an absence of seven years.[99] Despite his sorry showing against Portuguese invaders, he had made contact with several Indian rulers. When the amīr ascended to his audience, he was accompanied by an emissary of Muẓaffar Shāh ibn Maḥmūd, ruler of Kanbāya. This ambassador presumably discussed the Portuguese presence during his briefing, but seemed not at all preoccupied with it since he had come ostensibly to request a certificate from the caliph confirming his patron's succession. One wonders how great a threat the Portuguese really posed from the perspective of Indian potentates concerned primarily about their spice profits. While they might endorse the importance of Egypt's continued trade monopoly, their own interests were minimally compromised regardless of who purchased the commodity.

But al-Ghawrī certainly realized the likelihood of being supplanted by these newcomers. When the Portuguese once again entered the Red Sea, in Rabī‘ II 919/June-July 1513, he planned a second naval expedition.[100] The Europeans had besieged Sawākin after occupying Kamarān Island off the Malabar coast. Al-Ghawrī therefore concentrated his efforts on securing the Red Sea and began enlarging a shipyard in Suez at the southern end of the isthmus between Sinai and the Delta. He chose this campaign as an opportunity to try out his new Fifth Corps, recruited from groups outside the Mamlūk hierarchy who did not oppose new weaponry. All its members received training in the use of muskets (*arquebuses*), weapons Mamlūk regulars scorned. The latter showed an intense lack of enthusiasm for this venture. Serving alongside the Fifth Corpsmen certainly piqued their ire, while the prospect of participation in a desert campaign burdened with armor aroused their rebellious impulses. True to form, al-Ghawrī dallied for months over their demands for additional bonus incentives. He also weighed leading the contingent himself to Suez. For the sultan had accepted the assistance of an officer from his rival's navy, the Ottoman Admiral Salmān al-Ra’īs, and sought a favorable impression when he arrived. Because of extended preparations and wrangling over payments, the expedition did not set out until early in 920/March 1514.[101] Although plagued with unseasonable heat and polluted water supplies (larvae in the transport skins), both cavalry troops and Fifth Corps musketeers reached Suez intact for their rendezvous with Salmān, who had already begun outfitting vessels. The meeting between Mamlūk sultan and Ottoman admiral went off with a cordiality remarkable in light of mounting tensions between Cairo and Istanbul over other diplomatic issues. Both governments shared an interest in blocking further European gains in the Red Sea.

Thus did conviviality of convenience enable the two regimes to mount a final nautical campaign against the Portuguese the next year, 921/1515.[102] Amīr Ḥusayn, having regained his sovereign's favor, shared command with Salmān al-Ra’īs. By Sha‘bān 922/August-September 1516, the two had dislodged the Portuguese from their recent enclaves in the Yemen. They were now preparing their pursuit through the Bāb al-Mandab when Ibn Iyās broke off his narrative to focus on al-Ghawrī's encounter with destiny at Marj Dābiq. But the very fact of this expedition's size and partial success underscores the mutual recognition by powers of the central Muslim world that a new entity challenged their commercial hegemony. More noteworthy was its timing and coordination during a precipitous decline in Mamlūk-Ottoman relations. Since Selim gained the victory, his descendants would face the task of confronting the Europeans. Whether the Ottomans' response in coming centuries merely extended the reactive policy of their predecessors lies beyond the scope of this analysis. For its part, the Cairo regime confined its tactics to thwarting rather than outflanking its European rivals.

Retrospect

The efforts expended on deterrence by the Mamlūk sultanate typified its broader approach to foreign policy. Having scored its greatest triumphs centuries before against Crusaders and Mongols, both anachronistic to international realities by 1500, the regime had perfected many stratagems suited for preserving an order that was rapidly passing away. But it lacked the capacity, or the inclination, to devise tactics aimed at embracing sweeping change. Whether fortifying provincial capitals as bulwarks rather than entrepôts in a volatile commercial milieu, balancing off regional dynasts as warlords instead of revolutionaries who preached new ideologies, or confronting rival powers bent on aggression rather than coexistence, this government sought the maintenance of an environment in which its specialized institutions could survive. When forces converged to alter that environment irrevocably, the Mamlūk sultanate was engulfed. The ingenuity of acts aimed at containment or nullification is countered by the equally striking disinclination of the Mamlūk regime to initiate proactive policies. In none of the preceding interstate relationships did the sultanate show any proclivity for speculation over the long-range implications of its rivals' designs. Stasis was pursued even when all the signs suggested the impossibility of its continuance. Why was the Mamlūk regime so fixated on upholding equilibrium? Was its obsession with factional infighting an impediment to a more creative, outward-looking deployment of its energies? Did its "peculiar institutions" so depend on a static setting that they effectively delimited its options?

Notes

1. See *Rawḍ*, f. 246, l. 17 for a list of "kings of the East" in the year 874, all embroiled in rivalries.

2. In his laudatory introduction to the primer of devotional observance he presented to al-Ghawrī, ʿAbd al-Bāsiṭ al-Malaṭī dwelled on his sovereign's role as defender of the holy places. Pacifier of obstreperous princes, al-Ghawrī was depicted as a wise statesman whose farsightedness ensured the cohesion and integrity of the Muslim community, under constant threat of disruption by rulers who possessed a less encompassing world view. See his *Majmūʿ al-Bustān al-Nūrī li-Ḥaḍrat Mawlāna Sulṭān al-Ghūrī*, ff. 3, l. 7–5, l. 4.

3. Eliyahu Ashtor, *Levant Trade in the Later Middle Ages* (Princeton, 1983), esp. chap. 7; "Medieval Levant Trade at its Height, 1453–1498"; Wilhelm

Heyd, *Histoire du commerce du Levant au moyen-âge,* trans. F. Reynaud (Leipzig, 1885–1886); Subhi Labib, *Handelsgeschichte Ägyptens im Spätmittelalter (1171–1517)* (Wiesbaden, 1965), esp. chap. 4: "Die Verkehrsverbindungen Ägyptens".

4. Ibn Iyās mentioned attacks on coastal towns of North Africa at the end of the fifteenth century as evidence of the new European aggression. This was also the era of the Reconquista when Christian princes subdued the Muslim states of southern Spain. See *Badāʾiʿ* 4, pp. 190, l. 18; 191, l. 9; 201, l. 13; 218, l. 9.

5. Marshall Hodgson has perceptively summarized the cultural unity prevailing in the Middle Period. See *The Venture of Islam* 2 (Chicago, 1974), 329–68, 386–436.

6. P. M. Holt, "Some Observations on the Abbasid Caliphate of Cairo," *BSOAS* 47 (1984); P. Thorau, *Sultan Baibars I. von Ägypten* (Wiesbaden, 1987), 131–42.

7. For example, during Qāytbāy's sultanate, in Jumādā II 876/November-December 1471 an ambassador from the new sultan of Delhi, Ghiyāth al-Dīn, arrived requesting a diploma of confirmation from the caliph. He had succeeded the former sultan of Hind and sought to receive formal confirmation of his claim from the symbolic head of Sunnī Islam. See al-Suyūṭī, *Inbāʾ,* p. 362, l. 14; *Badāʾiʿ* 3, p. 65, l. 16.

8. *Badāʾiʿ* 4, pp. 255, l. 6; 257, l. 15; 268, l. 21.

9. In Rabīʿ I 873/September-October 1468, Qāytbāy invited the emissaries of Uzun Ḥasan, ruler of the Aqquyunlū confederacy, the sultan of Hind and other foreign princes to attend a gala troop review. According to al-Ṣayrafī, "they verged on stupefaction at the spectacle of his armies, their vastness, and the sultan's own courage, demeanor and grandeur." See *Inbāʾ,* p. 18, l. 11.

10. See Ashtor, *Levant Trade,* 122–24 for Venetian embassies sent in the fourteenth century; 451–56 for embassies in the 1460s, references to adjudicated claims from Venetian archives; 457–61 for negotiations in 1476 over ransoming of Egyptian prisoners and resolution of Cyprus tributory status. An interesting incident over gifts during al-Ghawrī's reception of an embassy from Ethiopia (al-Ḥabasha) reveals how precisely records of such exchanges were kept. When the Ethiopian emissary presented his wares, al-Ghawrī found them paltry and produced the inventory of gifts the courrier's predecessors had offered. See *Badāʾiʿ* 5, p. 12, l. 12.

11. Al-Qalqashandī, *Ṣubḥ al-Aʿshāʾ fī Ṣināʿat al-Inshāʾ,* 14 vols. (Cairo, 1914–1928).

12. Ibn Iyās noted language proficiency as a special skill worth including in obituaries of prominent diplomats. See *Badāʾiʿ* 3, p. 206, l. 8 for Yaḥyā ibn Shādbak, known as "Emissary to the Ethiopians" (*Qāsid al-Ḥabasha*), fluent in Ethiopian (presumably Amharic); 246, l. 19 the necrology of Jānibak Ḥabīb al-ʿAlāʾī al-Īnālī, who had treated with the ministers of Uzun Ḥasan. His command of Arabic was considered superb.

13. M. Canard, "Le traité de 1281 entre Michel Paleologue et le Sultan Qalāʾūn," *Byzantion* 10 (1935): 669–80, translated from al-Qalqashandī's *Ṣubḥ*, vol. 14, p. 72; M. Canard, "Un traité entre Byzance et l'Égypte au XIIIᵉ siècle et les relations diplomatiques de Michel VIII Paleologue avec les sultans Mamluks Baibars et Qalāʾūn," *Mélanges Gaudefroy-Demombynes* (Cairo, 1934–1945), 197–224; F. Dölger, "Der Vertrag des Sultans Qālāʾūn von Ägypten mit dem Kaiser Michael Palaiologos," in *Serta Monacensia* (Leiden, 1952), 60; S. Y. Labib, "Ein Brief des Mamluken Sultan Qaitbay an den Dogen von Venedig aus dem Jahre 1473," *Der Islam* 32 (1957): 324–29; P. M. Holt, "Qalawun's Treaty with Genoa in 1290," *Des Islam* 57 (1980): 101–08; P. M. Holt, "The Treaties of the Early Mamluk Sultans with the Frankish States," *BSOAS* 43 (1980): 67–76; J. Wansbrough, "A Mamluk Commercial Treaty concluded with the Republic of Florence," in *Documents from Islamic Chanceries*, ed. S. Stern, (Oxford, 1965), 39–79; J. Wansbrough, "Venice and Florence in the Mamlūk Commercial Privileges," *BSOAS* 28 (1965): 483–523; J. Wansbrough, "The Safe-Conduct in Muslim Chancery Practice," *BSOAS* 34 (1971): 20–35.

14. Wiet, *L'Égypte arabe*, 94–95 (Ibn Ṭūlūn's invasion of Syria) 102–04 (Khumārawayh's accord with Baghdād over Syria) 188–95, 209–12, 220–26 (Fāṭimid claims in Syria); J. L. Bacharach, "Palestine in the Policies of Tulunid and Ikhshidid Governors of Egypt," 51–65, and A. S. Ehrenkreutz, "The Fatimids in Palestine—Unwitting Promoters of the Crusades," 66–72, in *Egypt and Palestine: A Millennium of Association (868–1948)* ed. Amnon Cohen and Gabriel Baer (New York, 1984). For Saladin's campaigns, see A. S. Ehrenkreutz, *Saladin* (Albany, 1972), 155–70; M. C. Lyons and D. E. P. Jackson, *Saladin; the Politics of the Holy War* (New York, 1982).

15. P. M. Holt, *The Age of the Crusades: The Near East from the Eleventh Century to 1517* (New York, 1086), 90–100, 155–66; R. Irwin, *The Middle East in the Middle Ages: The Early Mamluk Sultanate, 1250–1382* (London, 1986), 37–84; H. Rabie, "Ḳalāwūn," *EI 2*, 4: 484–86; Thorau, *Baibars*, chap. 8, 11–15; D. Ayalon, "Egypt as a Dominant Factor in Syria and Palestine during the Islamic Period," 31–37, D. P. Little, "Relations between Jerusalem and Egypt during the Mamluk Period according to Literary and Documentary Sources," 73–93, B. Shoshan, "On the Relations between Egypt and Palestine, 1382–1517 A.D.," 94–101 in *Egypt and Palestine: A Millennium of Association*.

16. J. H. Escovitz, *The Office of Qāḍī al-Quḍāt in Cairo under the Baḥrī Mamlūks* (Berlin, 1984), 94–123; I. M. Lapidus, "Ayyubid Religious Policy and the Development of Schools of Law in Cairo," in *Colloque international sur l'histoire du Caire* (Cairo, 1969), 279–86; I. M. Lapidus, *Muslim Cities in the Later Middle Ages* (Cambridge, 1967); J. Mandaville, "The Muslim Judiciary of Damascus in the Late Mamluk Period," Ph.D. diss., Near Eastern Studies, Princeton University, 1969; C. Petry and S. Mendenhall, "Geographic Origins of the Civil Judiciary of Cairo in the Fifteenth Century," *JESHO* 21 (1978): 52–74; K. S. Salibi, "The Banū Jamāʿa: A Dynasty of Shāfiʿite Jurists in the Mamluk Period," *SI* 9 (1958): 97–109; A. Schimmel, "Kalif und Ḳāḍī im Spätmittelalterlichen Ägypten," *Der Welt des Islams* 24 (1942): 1–128.

17. On the outbreak of factional rivalries in Syrian provincial capitals during Qāytbāy's reign, see *Inbāʾ*, pp. 130, l. 19 (nāʾib of Damascus plotting revolt); 242, l. 16 (nāʾib of Aleppo attacks commander of its garrison); 404, l. 1 (dispute between grand dawādār and nāʾib of Damascus); *Badāʾ* 3, pp. 120, l. 20 (nāʾib of Aleppo reconciled with Qāytbāy after revolt); 132, l. 19 (revolt in Ḥamā against Mamlūk oppression); 177, l. 20 (assassination of commander of Aleppo Citadel by mob due to his fiscal extractions); 231, l. 3 (threat of revolt against the atābak Azbak in Aleppo); 284, l. 18 (Qānṣūh al-Ghawrī intervenes to stave off rebellion in Aleppo against its nāʾib); Ibn Taghrī-Birdī, *Ḥawādith*, f. 131, l. 7; *Badāʾiʿ* 3, p. 296, l. 3 (murder of sultan's dawādār in Damascus by mob angry over requisition); *Ḥawādith*, f. 156-b, l. 6 (sultan sends governors to quell popular revolt in Ḥamā against its nāʾib). For the reign of al-Ghawrī: *Badāʾiʿ* 4, pp. 23, l. 10 (Damascenes stone nāʾib when he imposes seven-months property tax); 94, l. 2 (populace of al-Karak rebel against new governor); 105, l. 1 (dispute between governors of Ghazza and al-Quds); 118, l. 3; 125, l. 21 (commandant of Aleppo Citadel disputes with city's nāʾib); 168, l. 18 (governor of Ṭarābulus quarrels with populace, recalled by sultan); 210, l.7 (sultan sends agent to mediate feud between governors of Damascus and Ṣafad); 400, l. 1; 401, l. 14; 432, l. 3 (sultan's Mamlūk recruits sent to Aleppo despoil city).

18. *Badāʾiʿ* 3, pp. 110, l. 9, 21; 115, l. 17; Ibn al-Ḥimṣī, *Ḥawādith*, ff. 66-b, l. 4–68, l. 3; 70, l. 11.

19. Examples from Qāytbāy's reign: *Inbāʾ*, pp. 9, l. 6 (new viceroy of Damascus receives royal decrees before assuming office); 150, l. 16; *Rawḍ*, f. 248, l. 28 (Syndic of Prophet's Descendants [Nāqīb al-Ashrāf] departs for Syria on royal business); *Inbāʾ*, pp. 270 l. 8 (Nāqīb al-Ashrāf travels to Syria to inspect trust properties); p. 403, l. 8; *Badāʾiʿ* 3, p. 68, l. 12 (amīr departs for Syrian garrisons with robes of honor for officers and troops); *Inbāʾ*, pp. 417, l. 10 (qāḍī sent to al-Karak to oversee repairs of spring and aqueduct); 483, l. 1 (sultan sends weaponry chief to inspect local fortifications); *Badāʾiʿ*

3, p. 201, l. 4 (retired amīr restores water source in Jerusalem); Ibn al-Ḥimṣī, *Ḥawādith*, f. 112-b, l. 8 (sultan's agent arrives in Damascus with arrest warrants); *Badāʾiʿ* 3, pp. 275, l. 11 (amīr departs for Nāblus to requisition water-bearing camels for Ottoman expedition); 280, l. 8 (sultan sends officer to Damascus to collect special five-month property tax).

20. *Badāʾiʿ* 4, pp. 70, l. 18; 71, l. 22; 76, l. 6.

21. Ibid., pp. 81, l. 15; 88, l. 20.

22. Ibin Ṭūlūn, *Iʿlām*, pp. 228, l. 3; 230, l. 13; *Badāʾiʿ* 4, pp. 379, l. 15; 399, l. 14; 406, l. 7; 407, l. 15.

23. *Inbāʾ*, p. 484, l. 11; *Badāʿiʿ* 3, pp. 147, l. 1; 164, l. 17; 165, l. 19; Ibn al-Ḥimṣī, *Ḥawādith*, f. 81-b, l. 4.

24. *Badāʾiʿ* 4, pp. 99, l. 7; 105, l. 20; 108, l. 11; 117, l. 3; 193, l. 5; 245, l. 23; 468, l. 11.

25. *Badāʾiʿ* 3, p. 281, l. 8.

26. On arrival of royal officials in the Ḥijāz, Qāytbāy's reign, see: *Inbāʾ*, pp. 244, l. 10 (shadd of Jidda sets out from Cairo with Mamlūks who declined service in Sūwār expedition); 292, l. 7 (qāḍī of Mecca protests his dismissal by Qāytbāy on charges of embezzling orphan fund of Kaʿba Mosque; requests audience in Cairo); *Badāʾiʿ* 3, p. 62, l. 3 (qāḍī's brother arrives in Cairo to arrange audience); 93, l. 12 (sultan receives qāḍī of Mecca along with the sharīf Barakāt); 132, l. 23 (courier arrives from Mecca announcing lightning damage to the Gate of Peace, civil strife between the sharīf and tribe of Banī Jāzān); 145, l. 1 (assassination of qāḍī and khaṭīb of Madīna over demolition of zealot's house; commission of inquiry); al-Sakhāwī, *Dhayl*, ff. 221, l. 21 (mendicant in Mecca claims to behold Prophet in vision); 226-b, l. 38 (commander of Mecca garrison shows affection for retired savants); 236-b, l. 7 (commandant of Mecca tries two merchants disputing over debts); 241, 4 (arrest of Ḥājib of Ghazza in Mecca for waqf abuse); *Badāʾiʿ* 3, p. 318, l. 5 (Bedouin amīr of Madīna steals from pious fund and flees to Iraq); *Dhayl*, f. 276, l. 25 (edict from Cairo ordering amīr of Mecca to restore order in Madīna). Reign of al-Ghawrī: *Badāʾiʿ* 4, pp. 80, l. 6 (Ḥajj courier reports capture of royal messenger by Bedouin); 116, l. 3 (sultan sends financial secretary to investigate dispute between garrison commanders); 151, l. 19 (pilgrims report on sultan's restorations of the ʿAqaba-Mecca road); 157, l. 17; 158, l. 23 (sultan sends troops for year's duty at Ṭīna garrison); 209, l. 21 (eunuch sends armorers and musketeers to Jidda to defend against Portuguese).

27. *Ḥawādith* 4, p. 640, l. 19 (pilgrims at Yanbuʿ seized by Bedouin); *Badāʾiʿ* 3, p. 15, l. 15 (Hujār's sons, Sabʿ and Sabbāʿ, attack sharīf of Mecca's brother at Yanbuʿ); *Ḥawādith* 4, p. 650, l. 3; *Rawḍ*, f. 186-b, l. 11 (shaykh of

Yanbuʿ attacks Hujār's sons); *Inbāʾ*, p. 289, l. 1 (Qāytbāy compels his Bedouin vassals to drop titles glorifying his stature); *Badāʾiʿ* 3, p. 60, l. 14 (sultan acknowledges succession of Yanbuʿ shaykh's son); *Inbāʾ*, p. 322, l. 13 (revival of discord over control of Yanbuʿ); *Badāʾiʿ* 3, pp. 122, l. 20 (amīr of Mecca's brother arrives in Cairo seeking Qāytbāy's mediation in sibling dispute); 147, l. 23 (Qāytbāy confirms the sharīf Sabʿ as amīr of Yanbuʿ).

28. *Badāʾiʿ* 4, pp. 36, l. 18; 47, l. 22.

29. Ibid., pp. 47, l. 22; 48, l. 12; 54, l. 6; 56, l. 21.

30. Ibid., p. 62, l. 2.

31. Ibid., p. 89, l. 7.

32. Ibid., pp. 94, l. 19; 95, l. 16; 99, l. 17; 101, l. 3; 104, l. 1; 105, l. 9; 106, l. 1.

33. Ibid., pp. 138, l. 8; 211, l. 8.

34. Ibid., p. 128, l. 10

35. Ibid., p. 109, l. 2.

36. Ibid., pp. 437, l. 15; 442, l. 2; 448, l. 18; 453, l. 10; 455, l. 17; 456, l. 8; 457, l. 6; 459, l. 13.

37. J. Mordtmann and L. Menage, "Dhū'l-Ḳadr," *EI*[2] I; 239.

38. *ʿUqūd*, f. 223, l. 22 (who dwells on Sūwār's impudence at the end of Khushqadam's reign); *Rawḍ*, f. 175-b, l. 16 (refers to Sūwār's growing influence perceived as menace in Cairo); *Ḥawādith* 4, p. 629, l. 21 (alarm in Cairo over reports that Sūwār seized ʿAynṭāb, major garrison town); *Inbāʾ*, p. 44, l. 1; *Rawḍ*, f. 211-b, l. 28 (greater alarm when confirmed reports arrive that Sūwār has occupied Darnada, which guards trade routes).

39. *Ḥawādith* 4, pp. 633, l. 21; *Rawḍ*, ff. 182, l. 3; 184, l. 29; *Badāʾiʿ* 3, p. 13, l. 12.

40. *Ḥawādith* 4, p. 641, l. 6; *Rawḍ*, ff. 185, l. 30; 186, l. 3.

41. *Ḥawādith* 4, p. 697, l. 5; *Inbāʾ*, p. 47, l. 3; *Rawḍ*, f. 212-b, l. 21. Protocol-shattering as Qāytbāy's refusal might seem, he had substantive reasons for rejecting the emissary. Recall Sūwār's letter addressed to all the people of Syria, promising them autonomy and prosperity if they clove to him. See *Ḥawādith* 4, p. 686, l. 7; *Inbāʾ*, p. 29, l. 14; *Rawḍ*, f. 207, l. 19.

42. *Rawḍ*, f. 215-b, l. 21; *Badāʾiʿ* 3, p. 28, l. 2.

43. *Inbāʾ*, p. 138, l. 11; *Rawḍ*, f. 247-b, l. 6.

44. *Inbāʾ*, p. 319, l. 8.

45. V. Minorsky, "The Aq-quyunlu and Land Reforms," *BSOAS* 17 (1955): 449–62; J. Woods, *The Aqqoyunlu; Clan, Confederation, Empire* (Chicago, 1976).

46. *Ḥawādith* 4, p. 652, l. 19.

47. *Ḥawādith* 4, pp. 675, l. 1; 699, l. 12; *Inbāʾ*, pp. 12, l. 4; 51, l. 11; 52, l. 8; *Rawḍ*, ff. 202, l. 26; 214-b, l. 20; 215, l. 8; *Badāʾiʿ* 3, pp. 19, l. 12; 27, l. 17.

48. *Inbāʾ*, pp. 27, l. 21; 29, l. 3; *Ḥawādith* 4, p. 685, l. 1; *Rawḍ*, f. 207, l. 11; *Badāʾiʿ* 3, p. 24, l. 2.

49. *Badāʾiʿ* 3, pp. 32, l. 4; 34, l. 11; *Ḥawādith* 4, pp. 712, l. 17; 713, l. 23; *Inbāʾ*, p. 74, l. 19; *Rawḍ*, f. 222-b, l. 18.

50. *Rawḍ*, f. 223, l. 7; *Inbāʾ*, p. 77, l. 5.

51. *Badāʾiʿ* 3, p. 52, l. 4.

52. *Inbāʾ*, p. 219, l. 12; *Rawḍ*, f. 248, l. 4; *Badāʾiʿ* 3, p. 53, l. 24.

53. *Badāʾiʿ* 3, p. 72, l. 13.

54. *Inbāʾ*, p. 428, l. 15; *Badāʾiʿ* 3, p. 70, l. 21.

55. *Badāʾiʿ* 3, pp. 80, l. 5; 81, l. 2.

56. Ibid., pp. 81, l. 19; 82, l. 12.

57. Ibid., p. 82, l. 12.

58. Ibid., p. 86, l. 3.

59. Ibid., p. 87, l. 13.

60. Ibid., pp. 88, l. 5; 90, l. 1; 91, l. 14.

61. Ibid., p. 95, l. 21.

62. Ibid., pp. 108, l. 21; 110, l. 13; 111, l. 9.

63. Ibid., p. 148, l. 18.

64. Ibid., pp. 148, l. 18; 161, l. 10.

65. *Badāʾiʿ* 4, p. 39, l. 7.

66. Allouche, *The Origins and Development of the Ottoman-Ṣafavid Conflict*, 30–60; Hodgson, *Venture* 3: 16–58; H. Rabie, "Political Relations between the Safavids of Persia and Mamluks of Egypt and Syria in the early Sixteenth

Century," *JARCE* 15 (1978): 75–81; H. R. Roemer, "The Ṣafavid Period" in
P. Jackson, ed., *The Cambridge History of Iran* (New York, 1986), 6: 189–232.

67. *Badāʾiʿ* 4, pp. 372, l. 21; 373, l. 11.

68. Al-Ḥalabī, *Durr*, ff. 177, l. 23; 178-b, l. 13.

69. H. Inalcik, *The Ottoman Empire; The Classical Age, 1300–1600* (New
York, 1973), 17–34.

70. *Badāʾiʿ* 3, p. 181, l. 11.

71. *Ḥawādith* 4, pp. 650, l. 19; 709, l. 22; *Inbāʾ*, pp. 69, l. 16; 162, l.
21; 199, l. 4; 214, l. 21; *Rawḍ*, ff. 221-b, l. 2; 250-b, l. 7.

72. On the Ghazwa tradition and early Ottoman expansionism, see:
Hodgson, *Venture* 2: 424–36; Inalcik, *Ottoman Empire*, 5–22, 55–69; P. Wittek, *The Rise of the Ottoman Empire* (London, 1938).

73. *Badāʾiʿ* 3, pp. 86, l. 7 (Ottoman sultan offers assistance to Yashbak
against Uzun Ḥasan); 87, l. 13 (Ottoman ambassador discloses Uzun Ḥasan's
overtures to the Europeans); 91, l. 4 (Ottomans defeat Uzun Ḥasan's troops).

74. *Inbāʾ*, p. 441, l. 12; *Badāʾiʿ* 3, p. 150, l. 11.

75. *Inbāʾ*, p. 482, l. 5. Although Rhodes was ruled by a Christian regime, the Mamlūk sultanate did not welcome an expansion of Ottoman power
in the Mediterranean. The Templars of Rhodes sought no alteration of the status quo or disruption of prevailing trade agreements.

76. *Inbāʾ*, pp. 493, l. 20; 496, l. 4 (Shāh Budāq flees to Syria from his
brother ʿAlī Dawlat); *Badāʾiʿ* 3, p. 196, l. 8 (Qāytbāy orders al-Bīra's walls
strengthened); *Inbāʾ*, pp. 505, l. 12 (Atābak Azbak reports about clashes between Dhūʾ-l-Qādrid rivals); 516, l. 6 (ʿAlī Dawlāt honored at Ḥalab as loyal
vassal); *Badāʾiʿ* 3, pp. 202, l. 14 (Jumādā II 888/July-August 1483: ʿAlī
Dawlāt seizes Malaṭya from its Mamlūk governor at Ottoman inducement);
Ibn al-Ḥimṣī, *Ḥawādith*, f. 103, l. 7 (Qāytbāy prepares expedition at immense
cost); *Badāʾiʿ* 3, pp. 205, l. 21 (Qāytbāy plans another expedition in
Muḥarram 889/January-February 1484 after learning of more Ottoman support for ʿAlī Dawlāt); pp. 210, l. 18 (Egyptian defeat of ʿAlī Dawlāt. Ibn Iyās
notes "subliminal" Ottoman hostility toward Egypt); 213, l. 12 (Qāytbāy
sends ambassador skilled at reconciliation to Istanbul); 216, l. 6 (Rabīʿ I 890/
March-April 1485; Qāytbāy prepares third expedition against ʿAlī Dawlāt);
220, l. 10 (high cost of expedition); 221, l. 12 (Qāytbāy's ambassador returns
from Istanbul; reports Ottoman duplicity); 221, l. 24 (ʿAlī Dawlāt's first
peace overtures as contrite vassal); 244, l.8 (Shāh Budāq escapes to Istanbul);
250, l. 8 (Ottoman host reaches Adana early in 893; Egyptian response); Ibn
al-Ḥimṣī, *Ḥawādith*, f. 116-b, l. 5 (Ottoman defeat); *Badāʾiʿ* 3, 264, l. 16

(Rabīʿ II 894/March-April 1489; Shāh Budāq captures Ilbistīn with Ottoman help); 265, l. 24 (Jumādā II 894/May 1489: Qāytbāy flays alive two Aleppans caught spying for Ottomans); 266, l. 9 (same month: Ottoman emissary inquires about peace; Qāytbāy demands restoration of status quo *ante bellum*); 268, l. 8; *Ḥawādith*, f. 121-b, l. 1 (Budāq returns to Egyptian custody after falling out with Ottomans); *Badāʾiʿ* 3, p. 281, l. 21; *Ḥawādith*, f. 123-b, l. 3 (final Ottoman peace negotiations in Jumādā II 896/April-may 1491).

77. Ibn Iyās often referred to Selim's lack of scruples when he dealt with opposition, real or imagined. While describing the autocrat's fratricide, the historian fatalistically observed: "there is no power other than God Almighty." (*Badāʾiʿ* 4, 306, l. 16). Early in 921/February-March 1515, after Selim insulted al-Ghawrī with terms denigrating his status, Ibn Iyās described the Ottoman as "an ignoramus who delighted in disputes. He reveled in bloodshed, murdering off his own brothers and their children—even those still breastfeeding." (*Badāʾiʿ* 4, p. 435, l. 19). With due allowance for hyperbole, Ibn Iyās' depiction of Selim as a monster also implied, by allusion to his successes, how effective draconian measures were in the world of realpolitik.

78. *Badāʾiʿ* 4, pp. 435, l. 11 (Muḥarram 921/February-March 1515: al-Ghawrī rejects Selim's request that he support his claimant over ʿAlī Dawlat); 436, l. 4 (al-Ghawrī holds council after ʿAlī Dawlat's first defeat); 438, l. 8 (al-Ghawrī sends noncommittal response to Selim's demand); 446, l. 12 (Rabīʿ I 921/April-May: Al-Ghawrī learns of Selim's impending invasion of Dhūʾl-Qādrid March); 458, l. 11 (Jumādā I/June-July: ʿAlī Dawlāt defeated again by Ottoman contingent; next month: al-Ghawrī shown ʿAlī Dawlāt's head); 465, l. 23 (Rajab/August-September: al-Ghawrī learns that Selim has occupied Dhūʾl-Qādrid March); 470, l. 20 (Shaʿbān/September-October: al-Ghawrī hears of Selim's plans to attack him by land and sea); 482, l. 23 (Shawwāl/November-December: Impending Ottoman invasion of Aleppo Province); *vol. 5:* pp. 8, l. 2 (Muḥarram 922/February-March 1516: Sūwār's son sends emissary to Cairo with paltry gift; demands recognition); 33, l. 3 (Rabīʿ I/April-May: al-Ghawrī displays his field tent, signalling intent to depart).

79. David Ayalon has commented on the contrast in receptivity between the Mamlūk and Ottoman regimes over the use of artillery and gunpowder. See *Gunpowder and Firearms in the Mamluk Kingdom* (London, 1956), 86–112, 141–44.

80. Ashtor, *Levant Trade*, 200–10; I. Wallerstein, *The Modern World System; Capitalist Agriculture and the Origins of the European World-Economy in the Sixteenth Century* (New York, 1976).

81. Labib, *Handelsgeschichte*, 337–440.

82. For example, al-Ghawrī lavishly welcomed the French king's ambassador in Muḥarram 918/March-April 1512 (*Badāʾiʿ* 4, pp. 255, l. 7; 257, l. 15; 268, l. 13). Ibn Iyās dwelt on the emissary's retinue and luxurious tapestries they bore as representations of textiles they could manufacture. The sultan rightly regarded the French as commercial allies who posed no maritime threat, unlike several Italian republics or the Portuguese. But the historian's marveling over the quality of their wares bespoke the long-term superiority French and Flemish craftsmen would attain in textile processing over the short-term aggression by corsairs off Alexandria or Damietta.

83. *Badāʾiʿ* 3, pp. 244, l. 18; 252, l. 8; 276, l. 2. Qāytbāy had no wish to disrupt profitable trade relations with Spanish regimes. See Mark D. Meyerson, *The Muslims of Valencia in the Age of Fernando and Isabel* (Berkeley, 1991), 66 for Egyptian reliance on grain from Castile.

84. *Badāʾiʿ* 4, p. 205, l. 7.

85. Ibid., pp. 120, l. 5; 209, l. 23.

86. Ibnāʾ, p. 236, l. 14.

87. Ibid., pp. 441, l. 17; 444, l. 6, 21.

88. *Badāʾiʿ* 3, pp. 71, l. 17; 75, l. 13; 79, l. 12; 89, l. 13.

89. Ibid., pp. 132, l. 12; 155, l. 11.

90. *Badāʾiʿ* 4, pp. 129, l. 9; 130, l. 11; 146, l. 3; 163, l. 19; 164, l. 16; 183, l. 21.

91. Ibid., p. 191, l. 21.

92. Ibid., pp. 192, l. 15; 195, l. 8; 196, l. 2; 199, l. 3.

93. Ibid., p. 259, l. 4.

94. ʿAbd al-Bāsiṭ, *Majmūʿ al-Bustān al-Nūrī li-Ḥaḍrat Malwānā Sulṭān al-Ghūrī* (Istanbul: Aya Sofya, 4793), ff. 2-b, l.2; 3-b, l. 6.

95. *Badāʾiʿ* 4, p. 109, l. 2; R. B. Serjeant, *The Portuguese off the South Arabian Coast* (London, 1963), 13–21.

96. *Badāʾiʿ* 4, pp. 82, l. 11; 84, l. 10; 85, l. 1; 95, l. 16; 99, l. 17; 101, l. 3.

97. *Badāʾiʿ* 4, pp. 142, l. 7; 150, l. 23; A. Kammerer, *La mer rouge, l'Abyssinie et l'Arabie depuis l'antiquité* (Cairo, 1935) 2: 153, 155.

98. *Badāʾiʿ* 4, pp. 156, l. 8; 182, l. 20; 185, l. 10; 209, l. 21. Ibn Iyās' geographic references are contradictory when he discusses al-Ghawrī's embassies to "Indian rulers." He seems to use the terms "Hind" and "Yaman" in-

terchangeably. When he mentions specific towns or ports, however, most are located in the Yemen.

99. *Badāʾiʿ* 4, pp. 286, l. 20; 287, l. 10.

100. Ibid., pp. 307, l. 14; 308, l. 3; 310, l. 16; 320, l. 8; 331, l. 7; 335, l. 7; 337, l. 6.

101. Ibid., pp. 362, l. 2; 364, l. 7; 365, l. 6.

102. *Badāʾiʿ* 4, pp. 435, l. 7; 458, l. 1; 460, l. 2; 466, l. 15; 472, l. 16; *vol.* 5, pp. 83, l. 1.

$$4$$

The Mamlūk Institution: A Victim of Success

When Qāytbāy accepted the sultanate, he acquired a military apparatus only minimally altered since its inception. Moreover, the ruling elite in Cairo had assumed many of its characteristics during the Ayyūbid period (567–647/1171–1249). Although Saladin and his descendants relied on an army of free-born cavalrymen primarily, their values and, more significantly, their views of proprietorship over Egypt and Syria differed little from those of the slave-soldiers who followed them. The last Ayyūbid sultan in Cairo, al-Malik al-Ṣāliḥ, introduced the Mamlūk system for his own security, which he felt a wayward coterie of freemen jeopardized.[1] The officers who created the autonomous Mamlūk State after al-Ṣāliḥ's death had grown to maturity in his service. They initially conceived of their position as custodial, aimed at protecting their own status from Ayyūbid claimants or any other rivals.[2] Inchoate as their ideas about statecraft were at this early date, the founders recognized their vulnerability. Installed as instruments of a paranoid monarch, they saw their tenuous future if a successor jealous of privileges their patron had granted them won out. Thus, from the beginning of the Mamlūk era, even before its architects began fashioning a positive ideology of autocracy, these officers were obsessed with their own self-interest. Over subsequent decades political circumstances and strategies to cope with them varied, but this preoccupation never wavered. The Mamlūk institution ultimately pursued its survival through an elaborate system of troop procurement from distant regions and a posture of absolute control over the society it guarded. The former enabled the regime to sustain itself with successive generations cloned in its own image. The latter guaranteed the elite's primacy in the social hierarchy, along with a level of economic privilege sufficient for inculcating its soldiers' loyalty to a system that nurtured them so generously.

Born as the device of slaves, the Mamlūk sultanate eschewed dynastic succession as its transfer of authority. The founders spent vast sums reduplicating the host of recruits (*julbān*) from Central Asia their patron has first molded into a formidable army.[3] Their objective in importing adolescents from alien regions was to instill allegiance through isolation. Encouraged from their arrival to prize ethnic distinction, these youths might grow up as praetorians apt to intrigue, sedition, and murder against their fellows if they saw a chance for advancement. But their training succeeded well in implanting their sense of group solidarity. By Qalāwūn's death, his regime had created a self-sustaining military caste respected for its combat prowess but also feared for its arrogance. To the military elite, imperial welfare was synonymous with their economic and social primacy. The elite owned the state as a patrimony. Laying their lives on the line for its defense, they assumed the right to tap its resources for their benefit—before anyone else's. Although Qalāwūn's descendants installed several princes on the throne in the eighth/fourteenth century, their inheritance rights were never sanctioned. When an officer of Circassian origin seized power in 784/1382, the ad hoc Qalāwūnid experiment with lineage succession was abandoned.[4] As our period commenced in 872/1468, first-generation recruits who clawed their way up the hazardous ladder to fellowship in the supreme oligarchy of grand amīrs had dominated the sultanate for some eighty years.

Such a method of promotion, merciless though it might seem, emphasized personal adroitness, impeccable courage, and absolute belief in one's own worth. It also encouraged the pervasive feeling of caste awareness so critical to the regime's identity. By 872, this consciousness has assumed the finality of eternity, for no living member had considered any alternative. The rationale of survival in the face of adversity, manifested by the founding generation, had now disappeared. Not since Timur Lenk emerged on the international stage early in the century had a foreigner threatened the Mamlūks' dominion over Egypt or the Levant. Nor did any element challenge them from within. Therefore, self-interest and group solidarity had become entrenched values with little sense of further justification—at least in the realm of temporal politics. The Mamlūks certainly showered their beneficence on devout scholars or believers in need. But such generosity was offered for God's glory in beseechment of His salvation—sorely required by these men, but not for feelings of guilt over savagery meted out to comrades or oppression burdening the masses.

Enduring the Praetorians: Beyond Fatalism's Limits

Tales of hardship abound in narrative depictions of civilian life under militarist governments in the central Islamic lands during the Middle Ages. Modern analysts of medieval Muslim societies must approach these myriad descriptions with a grain of salt, alert to the possibilty of exaggeration and with an eye for setting tales of spectacular cruelty in their indigenous setting of resilience before arbitrary rule. In a turbulent age when state security could never be taken for granted, the masses realized they had to pay a price for safety. Whatever their excesses, the militarists they knew posed less of a threat than those they did not—and whose ulterior intentions could not be fathomed. Familiar predators meted out predictable oppression, around which the populace could adjust their survival tactics.

Chroniclers of our period, nonetheless, are lurid when they discuss hardships inflicted on civilians by their Mamlūk overlords. Were their comments voiced in the abstract, as part and parcel of broader summaries of difficult years, they might be suspect as "poetic lament." The remarks offered by Ibn Taghrī-Birdī, al-Ṣayrafī and ʿAbd al-Bāsiṭ al-Malaṭī at the end of 873 parallel the others so closely that such an interpretation seems plausible[5]:

> The year ended as the people were burdened with severe suffering due to the intensity of famine, the frequency of riots, the terrorizing of roadways, general wickedness, oppression, pestilence and other calumnies—all generating rumors of even worse to come. What God wills occurs.
>
> Thus did the year conclude, the people enduring hardship as they suffered from severe inflation, uncontrolled riots, lawlessness on the roadways. False rumors were on every tongue!
>
> This year closed after incessant rioting, public disorders, the ravage of plague, widespread marauding and plundering of the masses, the countryside's ruin. Brigandage ran rampant!

Anyone familiar with narrative literature relating conditions of life for those saddled with their rulers' support is well aware of this generic depiction. But the chroniclers' more detailed accounts of specific incidents take up a substantial portion of their compendia. These comments provide tangible examples of violence or extractions that the chroniclers themselves condemned as symptomatic of the decay they saw around them. A modern historian may read more into even these statements than the observers intended. As members of the lettered classes who mediated between the civilian masses and their overlords, they shared the former's fatalistic acceptance of Mamlūk spoliation as inescapable. Yet their pessimistic assessments, offered soberly with minimal bombast, convey quite graphically their conviction that the militarists' conduct had gotten out of hand. If it continued, society would suffer wounds slow to heal. Occasional acts of assault, rape, or pilfering had always accompanied the soldier caste's presence. But malaise over their unceasing strife and devices concocted to appease them could warp the long-term attitude of the masses toward government itself and their stake in the economy. It is significant, moreover, that neither Qāytbāy nor Qānṣūh al-Ghawrī was spared the historians' castigation for his extortion. Both loomed over the requisitions and seizures so prominent in the regime's policies during these final decades of the empire's existence. Pious gentleman though he may have been, Qāytbāy matched his successor's rapacity when his coffers ran dry. Both men presided over a rising tide of disorder that taxed their subjects' endurance.

Riots erupting throughout Qāytbāy's reign revealed which elements of the military were most prone toward violent behavior, and how vulnerable the unarmed masses remained. Perpetrators almost invariably belonged to the ranks of julbān. As the youngest Mamlūk soldiers, their exuberance was tolerable. But their impudence and frustration grew as the regime's capacity to punish their waywardness and satisfy their aspirations declined. During Qāytbāy's ascendant period, he reined in the recruits' predations. But he was loath to match his chastisement to their insolence. At the end of 872, the sultan's prefect of police (*wālī al-shurṭa*) arrested many of the recruits' black slaves and grooms who had been insulting civilians and tearing their turbans off.[6] Several were brought up to the Citadel where they were flogged or dismembered as a warning to their owners. But the latter themselves escaped such treatment, even though they winked at their retainers' assaults.

Three years later, when Qāytbāy ordered the departure of an expedition against Sūwār, he admonished the Sulṭānī Mamlūks against "striking any civilian. Whoever did so would be drawn and quartered without a hearing of his case."[7] Despite his severity, whether Qāytbāy intended it primarily to focus his warriors' attention on the object of their muster or to protect his subjects remains unclear. Certainly his readiness to remove any valuable soldier from the ranks at this critical juncture merely because of infringements against the masses must be questioned. When he had finished with his enemy, Qāytbāy did show his opposition to lawlessness, even if his own recruits were guilty. In Ṣafar 877/July 1472, he ordered three julbān flogged for public disturbances.[8] But none were executed and thus dissuaded from future violence.

Julbān found ample incentives for their assaults in their superiors' contempt for the masses. In that year the armaments minister, Jānibak Qulaqsīz, resented the presence of civilian spectators at a polo match in which he hosted his rival, Yashbak.[9] Irate over his defeat, he ordered his retainers "to remove any observers watching from their doors and houses. If they did not depart, they would suffer beatings on the spot. Truly a dreadful hour!" One example of such arrogance on an officer's part occurred during al-Ghawrī's middle years. In Rajab 915/October–November 1509, Qurqmās al-Muqriʾ, an amīr of ten, was robbed of a thousand dīnārs he kept stashed in his townhouse at the Alley of Kuḥl Dealers.[10] Enraged at the theft, the amīr rounded up all his neighbors and conducted them before the prefect for interrogation. They were compelled to yield up a sum greater than Qurqmās' loss. No further inquiry into the theft was initiated. But less than a year later, one of Qurqmās' own Mamlūks was discovered to be the culprit. He had escaped with his loot and fled to Mecca by sea were he "indulged himself with his ill-gotten gains." Although the thief was duly returned to Cairo by the pilgrimage commander, he claimed to have spent all the money and could make no restitution. "When Qurqmās' aggrieved neighbors found out about this, they ascended to the sultan and presented him with a petition protesting their injustice. The sultan summoned Qurqmās and castigated the amīr, forcing him to compensate his neighbors." But Ibn Iyās emphasized his amazement over al-Ghawrī's sternness. "The ruling was exceptional, since Qurqmās earned his sovereign's rancor solely because of his trifling misdeed."

Although Qāytbāy showed only marginally more solicitude than al-Ghawrī for his subjects' safety in the face of Mamlūk rioting, he apparently inhibited them from responding in self-defense. Under al-Ghawrī's unraveling administration, predation reached a level inducing civilians toward desperate reprisals, albeit with little chance of success. In 915 and 916, he forbade his subjects "to bear weapons after dark, but urged their attendance of all five daily prayer services," apparently in hopes of assuaging their anger.[11] The masses found al-Ghawrī's admonition cynical since he offered them no hope of relief. Yet even passing mention of civil resistance is noteworthy because of its paucity.

During most of this era, the sources make few references to armed vigilantism. Militarist regimes in the central Islamic lands uniformly prohibited such a recourse for the populace on pain of death. The resignation of Cairo's inhabitants to abuse at their guardians' hands showed a stoic endurance. Throughout all these harrowing events, no counterprotest took place on a scale comparable to the recruits' provocations. Only in Syria, as Ottoman power grew in the north, did the masses openly threaten their occupiers. In Dhū'l-Ḥijja 920/January–February 1515, al-Ghawrī summoned home a band of Sulṭānī Mamlūks garrisoned in Aleppo to monitor Selim's doings. Suffering themselves from the city's famine, they had sold all they possessed, even their mounts and weapons, to buy food. Despairing of their survival, these disciplined veterans, the best of al-Ghawrī's assault forces, abandoned all restraint and set upon the populace whom they regarded as hoarders who withheld rations until prices "pierced the Heavens." "The troops descended on their houses, pillaged their clothing, violated their harems, plundered their markets, and seized their goods. It was even rumored that several rampaging soldiers raped a three-year old child, who died of the crime—but this cannot be verified. It was alleged that troopers repeatedly attacked women in the baths and stripped them nude. The Mamlūks committed numerous deeds of this kind never before perpetrated by Sulṭānīs. They stained their own cadre by such acts."[12] When the populace rose up against their protectors, al-Ghawrī ordered them back before the situation worsened. He might as well open the city's gates to the son of ʿUthmān personally if such upheavals continued. Ibn Iyās commented on the failure of al-Ghawrī's attempts at safeguarding his northern bastion. "Their (the Mamlūks') presence inflicted severe damage but produced no benefit. It would have been preferable never to have sent them!"

Civilian vulnerability to crimes inflicted by troops may have been a ubiquitous aspect of Mamlūk oppression unaffected by the regime's incapacity to restrain them. Unlike collective acts of dissidence, individual felonies were inflicted by soldiers from various ranks. But the chroniclers indicated the government's increasing reluctance to prosecute such behavior vigorously. Often a show of investigation was exposed as a mockery of justice after charges were summarily dropped. When an eminent jurist, a Ḥanbalī deputy judge, was murdered in broad daylight as he sat at his bench in the Aydamur Square, Qāytbāy's authorities could not ignore the affair. But after a Mamlūk and his groom were accused, the sultan merely ordered an inquiry into their guilt. Al-Ṣayrafī, who recounted dealings in Sharīʿa courts minutely, reported no conviction of either offender.[13] Of course, those who earned popular hatred because of their cruelty ran the risk of covert reprisals. Bodies of known murderers often turned up on the Citadel steps, their corpses riddled with stab wounds.[14] Whether their killers were rival soldiers paying off a vendetta or civilians taking revenge could not be ascertained. The latter had ample cause, especially when the honor of women was at stake. How frequently men of any class punished allegations of infidelity with no recourse to legal procedures can only be guessed. But only Mamlūks who did so appeared in the chronicles. Al-Ṣayrafī and Ibn Iyās both noted the ferocity of a reservist who murdered an estranged intimate solely on grounds of hearsay.[15] "On the ninth of Rajab, one of the Turks' sons demanded a sum from a woman of a Mālikī house in compensation for his shame, which she denied. He had searched her residence . . . and accused her of consorting with a servant there. Upon her rebuttal, he struck the woman in her abdomen with his dagger. She fell dead immediately. The man went out in plain sight with the knife in his hand, spattered with her blood—which was wasted. There is no power but in God." Ibn Iyās claimed the incident occurred "in the public street." But each author concurred that the killer went free.

Unsettling as such vindications may have been, they did not transcend popular outrage over Mamlūk assaults against the humble for trifling insults. The sources teem with accounts of troopers abusing persons of low rank for the least sign of stubbornness. Few cases were elaborated on unless the fracas resulted in a homicide. While such extreme consequences of a heated argument occurred rarely, their details bespeak mass resentment over the militarists' power of life and death, which they might unleash at the least provocation. One such case took place late in al-Ghawrī's reign, after he had departed for Aleppo.[16]:

> In Jumādā I 922/June 1516, a recruit bought some wheat from a grain ship lying at anchor on the river shore. Upon his purchase, he could locate no porter to transport it. So he waylaid a peasant from Upper Egypt leading a donkey with a sack. He seized the donkey and bag, but the peasant fought back. The Mamlūk then struck him a violent blow on the head, causing blood to flow. The peasant fell into the river where he fainted and drowned. The populace thereupon attacked the recruit and conveyed him to the dawādār's residence. The recruit was placed in irons and sent to the prefect's custody. The latter imprisoned him pending the sultan's return. When the recruit's comrades learned of the affair, they marched on the dawādār's house. They found him absent, overseeing repairs of dykes damaged by the flood, but were told the prefect had arrested their colleague. The recruits then descended upon the prefect's house and forcibly released the Mamlūk accused of the peasant's murder. They threatened to burn the prefect's residence if the case were prosecuted. The dawādār dismissed the charges and tension subsided.

A callous waiving of justice by the regent bound to uphold God's law. Yet was one peasant's death worth another revolt, especially now that the sultan was away? Ṭūmānbāy, widely respected for his staunch defense of Sharīʿa, may well have acted for the overall welfare of his subjects, more of whom would have suffered if a full-scale rebellion had erupted. Still, his summary annulment of an indictment against a soldier who struck down a fellow believer for political expedience left a bad taste in the mouth of Ibn Iyās. Himself an aristocrat who rarely fraternized with fallāḥīn from the Ṣaʿīdī outback, the historian found this incident deplorable.

The regime showed more concern over violations of merchants' rights. Thievery on the part of soldiers angered by their poverty occurred rampantly as noted. But when merchants, especially those from states whose trade the sultanate valued, were targeted, the government made efforts to curb their losses.[17] Local craftsmen rarely fared so well, especially when they were pressured to fulfill the sultan's or a grand amīr's requisitions for a campaign. Al-Ṣayrafī provides a glimpse into adversities borne by bootmakers and clothiers forced to supply Yashbak's quotas on short notice as he prepared for his march against Sūwār in 875.[18] But even though they were pressed ruthlessly to hasten their work, these artisans were paid—to the tune of a thousand dīnārs per day. In cases of the government's deficit, when it could not provide bonuses or sacrifice animals for religious festivals, marketeers and stockmen often lost their commodities or herds with no compensation whatsoever.[19] Chroniclers rarely dwelled on these misfortunes. Men of commerce were no more immune from the breakdown in public order plaguing the sultanate in its final decades

than any other property holders. But the historians were well aware of the stymying effect such seizures had on economic growth. None touted the empire's
prosperity during these troubled times. The regime gave few incentives for
productive deployment of capital resources as it fought off bankruptcy. Why
the Mamlūk caste exhibited such a propensity for predation must be sought in
its class values and fiscal demands.

Endemic Dilemma: Camaraderie versus Ambition

In retrospect, the Mamlūk elite exhibits a striking case of tension between conflicting allegiances. A military caste that imbued recruits with an abiding collective identity and trained its members to form tightly knit factions as cadets,
the institution simultaneously laid great store on personal adroitness. Trainees
were induced to regard their milieu as both dangerous and lucrative: dangerous because one's fellows could never be fully trusted and lucrative because the
stakes behind a power bid were so high. In a system that granted a minority
group such exceptional advantages, personal ambition was curbed primarily
by caution and limitations—secondarily by scruples. Mamlūks of all ranks:
novices, line troopers, junior officers, and senior amīrs who competed for the
sultanate, regarded their group integrity as sacred but rarely allowed personal
bonds to inhibit an opportunity for gain through treachery. Every member
understood this trade-off between cohesion and self-interest. No factional tie
was absolute. Few amīrs would miss a chance for aggrandizement when a coterie of peers, even from rival cliques, coalesced behind an objective for the
moment. Factional ties were thus inherently fluid and short-lived. Close allies
of one day might become implacable enemies the next.

The fickleness of peer relations and dubious loyalties of soldiers behind
even respected autocrats abound in narrative sources. When Qāytbāy suffered
a serious illness in Ramaḍān 882/December 1477–January 1478, while on sojourn in Aleppo, his hierarchy of officers began to disband immediately. Ibn
Iyās reported rumors dispersing "rapidly among the people, for every day new
stories that he had died and been buried reached Cairo. The amīrs became
agitated, each plotting how to win the sultanate for himself."[20] When missives
confirming Qāytbāy's recovery arrived, they were addressed to "the caliph, the
four qāḍīs, the atābak Azbak and all other officers without exception." By confirming the sultan's revival among both civil and military staff, the couriers
could counter conflicting stories at once and head off a coup attempt. Nine
years later, after Qāytbāy fractured his leg in the Citadel courtyard, he put off
the bonesetters to dictate letters that very day assuring his survival for dispatch
to the Syrian provinces—again checking rumors of his demise.[21]

So commonplace were hints of sedition for al-Ghawrī that he occasionally
attempted entrapment of rebellious subordinates by planting such ruses him-

self. When the dawādār Miṣirbāy escaped from Alexandria, Ibn Iyās reported
his proceeding to Cairo in disguise. "As news of his return spread, anxiety
seized the amīrs, who took special precautions." Al-Ghawrī ordered his troops
to declare a sham revolt as "a subterfuge to force Miṣirbāy's hand. But he was
not deceived and remained out of sight."[22] Quarrels erupted frequently between amīrs at al-Ghawrī's councils, bespeaking the antagonism lurking behind the facade of unity. In Shawwāl 909/March–April 1504, after the sharīf
of Mecca escaped from the marshal Qāyt's house with his brothers, al-Ghawrī
summoned his atābak for a reprimand. The armaments minister (*amīr silāḥ*),
Qurqmās, interrupted his sovereign to insult Qāyt by insinuating his ineptitude if not his treason. "All of this derives from your incompetence, for
you simply allowed them to walk out free! So heated was their exchange that
the sultan intervened to prevent a brawl. But their truce hardly laid the dispute to rest."[23]

Several years later in Dhū'l-Ḥijja 914/March–April 1509, an imbroglio
erupted over quite a different cause. The chamberlain Anaṣbāy accused another amīr, Nawrūz, of operating a profitable house of prostitution in a structure he ostensibly rented to transients.[24] When Nawrūz ignored Anaṣbāy's
closure order, the chamberlain sent his own staff to arrest the offending women
and bring them before a tribunal. But Nawrūz set his own grooms and black
slaves upon Anaṣbāy's agents, who were soundly thrashed and sent packing
"with nary a whore." Incensed at Nawrūz's cheek, Anaṣbāy rode personally to
the house of ill-repute with his armed henchmen. He had the prostitutes
stripped, beaten and paraded nude through the streets. Whether the chamberlain found Nawrūz's dealings so odious from moral indignation or lack of
a bribe to overlook the affair Ibn Iyās did not specify. Given the corruption
pervading al-Ghawrī's administration, the latter was likely. For avarice was
equally ubiquitous among al-Ghawrī's adjutants.

In Rajab 920/August–September 1514, the sultan reluctantly arrested his
acting major-domo, Jānibak, only after denunciations from colleagues he insulted portended a genuine revolt.[25] This Jānibak had charged his fellow
amīrs "protection money" (*ḥimāya*) from their estate yields in return for his
safeguarding their urban properties. "He sent brutal agents even to houses of
muqqadamīn, brigands who demanded the illegal tax in a rude manner. All
the amīrs united in their outrage at this offense—a rare concurrence. The sultan had held Jānibak in high esteem, initially heeding no complaints against
him. But when his enemies intensified their maledictions, he shifted his opinion." Following the major-domo's arrest, al-Ghawrī's accountants went over
his books and found his kickbacks to the Special Fund thirty-three thousand
dīnārs in arrears.

The foregoing incidents highlight issues of acrimony and greed not peculiar to this regime. But one must ponder their long-term consequences at
this time and place. Were tensions between caste cohesion and personal rivalry

dysfunctional in their propensity for channeling the Mamlūks' creative energies in unproductive directions? Did such tensions promote an effective, if brutal, system of mobility by merit that rewarded the adroit? Or did they compel members of the elite to preoccupy themselves with intrigue? In short, was the Mamlūk institution viable by its own standards in the late Circassian era? If viability is defined as self-preservation, probably—so long as no challenge from without disrupted the equilibrium enabling all contenders to focus on their rivalries at the expense of other duties. But if measured by receptivity to innovation, or capacity for devising positive initiatives in the face of change, the military elite came up short. While reasons behind their myopia seem clear in hindsight, they acquire an air of inevitability when assessed in context with other problems.

Financing the Praetorians: Demands versus Resources

No issue figured more prominently in chronicles treating the later Circassian period than the regime's shortfalls of cash in the face of unremitting demands by its troops for pay increases. As an interest group aware of their indispensability in a world ever less secure, the military caste had become astute at pressuring the sultan for bonuses he was straitened to pay. We must recall that the autocrat remained the social equal of even the rawest of his imported novices. His status sanctioned neither by principle of dynastic succession nor concept of divine right, the sultan was compelled to win his soldiers' loyalty by his personal force and his guarantee of their privileged position. The former posed fewer dilemmas than the latter but ultimately counted for less. Qāytbāy and al-Ghawrī inherited a time-honored propensity toward lavish expenditures on expanding the corps through purchase and ensuring its allegiance with generous salaries. But neither could routinely assume a supply of revenue sufficient for the needs of even their own imported troops, not to mention those their predecessors had acquired. Qāytbāy's enormous expenditures, in light of diminishing funds culled from licit sources, remain a paradox of his administration. Committed to maintaining a cohort of reliable importees that equalled the hosts his most eminent predecessors had assembled, Qāytbāy spent more than three million dīnārs on troop recruitment.[26] Consonant with his overall program of neutralizing factional rivalries, he also purchased Mamlūks of his immediate precursors, thereby granting them first-rank status rather than relegating them to the unenviable, and restive, position of outcasts with reduced bonus or iqtāʿ claims.[27]

For their part, both officers and recruits fully appreciated their influence over their peer-sovereign. They preyed upon his attendant fears of being supplanted at home, or confronting a foreign enemy with an army whose willingness for battle could not be assumed. The sources comment frequently on the troops' ambivalence over summons for mobilization against a formidable opponent. Their recalcitrance stemmed from irritation at delays in stipends rather than cowardice. When, in Ṣafar 873/August–September 1461, Qāytbāy's soldiers realized that quelling Sūwār's rebellion might claim their lives, they reacted bitterly against Qāytbāy's pleading of an empty purse.[28] Heeding their fulminations, the sultan stopped all stipends to reservists (*awlād al-nās*) or civil notables (*aʿyān*) for the month. The resultant savings enabled him to grant Sulṭānī Mamlūks assigned to active duty advances on their salaries and inducement bonuses. Dismissing the clamor raised by reservists and scholars over their losses, Qāytbāy recounted his difficulties—"steep commodity prices, the river's rapid descent, a consequent decrease in irrigated land and reduced harvest, the burden posed by the war against Sūwār, and the treasury's previous depletion." He promised a deferred payment in Rabīʿ I while stressing the primacy of his line soldiers' needs in these trying times.

Even Qāytbāy's highest ranking officers exploited this ploy of penury to enhance their fortunes. When Qāytbāy appointed Azbak commander of the Sūwār campaign in Rajab, the grand marshal decided on a calculated demurral.[29] The atābak "caviled, stressing his depleted means. He recounted his losses in horses and equipment during his previous encounter with Sūwār. The sultan argued with him at length, until he reluctantly agreed. But when he descended to his house, rumors spread of a pending riot (presumably by Azbak's retainers)." The marshal tarried for several weeks before the sultan finally granted his vast bonus. After Qāytbāy tapped Ibn Taghrī-Birdī's skills as a mediator, the historian persuaded Azbak to accept. But although the marshal bowed and consented, saying: "to hear is to obey," he pointedly stressed his delayed gratuity. Upon Ibn Taghrī-Birdī's confirmation, Qāytbāy sent Azbak twelve thousand dīnārs. Equivalent grants were required to line up other officers behind the cause. When Qāytbāy mustered the troops themselves, he admonished them "to keep their spirits high, unite in agreement, eschew divisiveness and focus their efforts against the enemy."[30] But they gave no pledge until he promised them four-months' stipend prior to departure. And following their initial defeats by Sūwār, surviving soldiers ignored Qāytbāy's express order that they remain in Aleppo until further notice. They straggled back to Egypt "covertly and hid in their homes. Upon learning of their stealth, the sultan concealed his distress behind a mien of serenity. Unable to forbid their return, he feigned ignorance of it."[31]

These asides bespeak the delicate balance between the sultan's authority and his troops' leverage. They underscore the Mamlūks' concept of their mission as warriors for hire. Few contemporaries rivaled their military skill. None contested their bravery. But their service was never offered for free. They expected fiscal rewards commensurate with the vital function they performed, and aggressively negotiated with their sovereign over remuneration— brandishing the threat of revolt if he balked. These interminable reports of sedition must therefore be interpreted as collective bargaining on conditions of service and its compensation. But by the later Circassian period, the sultan's own options had decreased. Even purchases of new cadres could not counter the presence of so many soldiers surviving from previous reigns. These veterans had honed their skills at coalition building too well, thereby nullifying the sultan's attempts at exploiting internecine rivalries.

The sultan's arbitrary extractions from all productive elements of society loom so vividly in the narrative sources that they warrant assessment as a cause of the regime's decline. Here we note that most cases of confiscation followed upon troop pressure for pay raises. From a superficial perspective, the root of this dilemma might be attributed to uncompromising greed. But how well-off were various ranks of the Mamlūk elite? Their assumption of preference in society was, after all, a natural consequence of conditioning imposed on them by a military hierarchy dominant for some three hundred years. Comparisons offered by Ibn Iyās may highlight contrasts in the behavior of Qāytbāy and al-Ghawrī when each confronted this problem of inflating demands. But neither could avoid it and hope to survive:

> He (Qāytbāy) was obsessed with a lust for money, scheming to squeeze it from the populace. . . . In part, his greed was excusable. During his sultanate, he had to deal with Shāh Sūwār, Ḥasan al-Ṭawīl, Ibn ʿUthmān and other monarchs of the East. In all, he organized sixteen campaigns against them. Yet his grip on the throne was unshakable. It was stated that the total of his expenditures for military expeditions amounted to some 7,065,000 dīnārs, excluding bonuses to Mamlūks upon their return. This sum was unprecedented. . . . He was also a prodigious purchaser of Mamlūks, so that had the plagues not ravaged his reign, he would have accumulated eight thousand troopers.[32]

For al-Ghawrī's disbursements in the final months of his rule, Ibn Iyās stressed outlays far lower than those of Qāytbāy, even though al-Ghawrī's need was surely as pressing:

> On Saturday the twenty-third of Rabīʿ I (922)/25 April 1516, the sultan paid his senior officers their bonuses before they set out to confront the Ottoman. To the atābak . . . he sent five thousand dīnārs; to the amīr of Council, captain of the guard and grand chamberlain—four thousand each. The remaining muqaddamūn each received three thousand. How indeed would these paltry figures compare with al-Ashraf Qāytbāy's lavish bestowals on his commanders upon their departure against the Son of ʿUthmān? He had sent his atābak alone thirty thousand dīnārs. To the armaments amīr twenty thousand, the same to the council amīr. Each of the remaining muqaddamīn holding office received fifteen thousand; while all the other commanders got ten thousand.[33]

Whether al-Ghawrī really possessed less money for grants or was covertly reducing stipends from levels prevalent in Qāytbāy's days remains speculative.

Both monarchs reacted to demands for increases soon after their accessions with elaborate shows of anger. Although Qāytbāy gave out immense sums, he scrutinized the entire payment procedure, announcing new reductions and standards of performance as measure by public tests of competence.

The most vivid case of his reign occurred on 16 Rabīᶜ II 873/4 October 1468.[34] After examining accounts in the Army Bureau from the time of al-Muʾayyad Shaykh (815–824/1412–1421), he convened the four qāḍīs and sought their advice on reforming corrupt procedures. Qāytbāy produced ledgers showing a steady rise in troop salary totals from Shaykh's reign when they stood at ten thousand dīnārs a month, to Khushqadam's death when they had topped forty-six thousand. The sultan threw something of a tantrum after disclosing the increase, claiming the troops provided no extra service for this inflation. While they differed on trivial points, all three historians discussing the incident, Ibn Taghrī-Birdī, al-Ṣayrafī and ᶜAbd al-Bāsiṭ, concurred about the origin of this phenomenon. When Sultan Jaqmaq (842–857/1438–1453) had entrusted fiscal affairs of the military to his adjutant, Zayn al-Dīn al-Ustādār, the latter had usurped functions previously devolving upon the wazīr, paymasters and rations purveyors. He had actually removed several salaried slots reserved for officers and royal bodyguards from the Special Fund (*Dīwān al-Mufrad*), simultaneously laundering its monthly budget. He and staff associates had pocketed the resulting difference between income and outlay. His successors and other fiscal officials had taken their cue from his behavior. Since both Īnāl and Khushqadam had feared for their safety, they relied excessively on their respective major-domos, who continued these practices. Qāytbāy stormed over the irony between reduced salaried slots for frontline soldiers and the drain on his treasury this scheme caused. When he brought up the possibility of funding his Sūwār expedition by tapping endowed trusts, the qāḍīs unanimously rejected the expedient. Qāytbāy then threatened abdication and revival of the chaos preceding his accession.

But eventually he decided upon reform of the distribution process itself. All claimants, including second-generation reservists, were compelled to demonstrate their physical prowess by drawing three bows of increasing resistance. If they failed at any of these tests, their stipend was revoked. Recruits and Royal Mamlūks who could not pass muster were demoted to out-of-service (*ṭarkhān*) status and forfeited their iqṭāᶜs. All claimants also had to present a valid registry card and receipt form, individually validated by the sultan's own notaries before they tried their bows. Since Qāytbāy personally oversaw each trial, the allotment process was drawn out over several days. One can envision the dour demeanor Qāytbāy assumed as he presided over this review. A seasoned warrior in his mid-fifties sat on the dais and glared at each man as he mounted the steps to present his affidavit and pull his bow. Young recruits cocksure in their youthful prime or grizzled veterans secure in their field experience must have quailed alike before their lord's baleful gaze, knowing their futures depended on a single tug at an arrowstring before all their comrades to see. For soldiers on active call, the test was intimidating but at least weeded out weaklings and restored a measure of merit to pay rosters. Qāytbāy repeated this test periodically. Because he made a sincere effort at curbing corrupt practices in which noncombatants drew campaigners' salaries, the army grudgingly respected him. Yet in his waning phase after 894, recruits and older Mamlūks reasserted their claims.[35]

Al-Ghawrī's relationship with his troops can best be described as ambivalent: mutual distrust interspersed with the sultan's sporadic attempts at buying loyalty with pay raises. Al-Ghawrī tried out the abdication ploy soon after his accession when the Royal Mamlūks demanded a reshuffling of fief allotments and provision of high-paying sinecures in Shawwāl 906/April–May 1501.[36] The following month they called for a homage gift (*nafaqat al-bayʿa*) al-Ghawrī accepted only with reluctance. Although he would hold out the warning of withdrawal from the sultanate again, al-Ghawrī exploited this stratagem less frequently than Qāytbāy—possibly because he recognized the tenuousness of his own position. Rather, he incorporated a peculiar blend of carrot-and-stick incentives into his amalgam of bribes and extractions. It is difficult to disentangle al-Ghawrī's web of schemes, even if these embrace only his manipulation of stipends. We behold his simultaneous profiteering from the private sale of meat, fodder, and cloth allotments destined for his own soldiers, and arrest of the very agents he connived with to implement the deals.[37]

Such tactics became readily apparent to his soldiers, who found his ploy irksome less for its illegality than the destitution it caused them. On 11 Muḥarram 916/20 April 1510, several units of recruits, youths with the fewest worries over raising a disturbance and the least tolerance of insult, showed their displeasure over short rations by pelting civilians with stones from their barracks. They then marched down to the atābak's residence, where they compelled his personal request to the sultan for their allotments or a cash supplement for purchases of supplies on the open market. When al-Ghawrī refused even his marshal's plea, the recruits donned their sheepskin assault gear and fell upon the public sūqs. A mêlée of looting ensued that ended only after more than five hundred shops had been pilfered of goods worth twenty thousand dīnārs.[38] When the outraged merchants presented al-Ghawrī with bills for their losses, he paid out more in compensation than his original rations budget. The actions of these soldiers suggest more a sense of frustration over their lack of staples than their heartless ravaging of civilians.

In al-Ghawrī's later years, when his penchant for opulence contrasted sharply with his soldier's deteriorating living standard, the recruits often interrupted his soirées. An amusing incident occurred in Rabīʿ I 920/April–May 1514 as the sultan hosted companions at a banquet by his Citadel pool on a stifling evening.[39] The recruits interrupted the meal, snatched delicacies from diners' hands, shattered the beautiful porcelain ware, and doused guests with rose water reserved for postrepast laving. Al-Ghawrī was furious over their rowdiness but retreated to the Duhaysha Palace instead of punishing any culprits. He might spark another riot and incur truly serious opposition. However annoying this affair was, he had suffered only a minor disruption of his pleasures.

Both Qāytbāy and al-Ghawrī thus wrestled with a dilemma neither could resolve with their extant resources. Each parried persistent requests for increased compensation from their troops precisely when external crises necessitated a reliable military apparatus. Neither dared allow a decline in combat fitness. But no other issue created such nagging problems for the two monarchs. Despite disparities in response, each ultimately met his soldiers' requirements. The strain this burden imposed on them was readily apparent in their behavior toward reservists.

Second- or third-generation reservists of the Ḥalqa Corps "sons of the (elite) people" (*awlād al-nās*), suffered the humiliation of scapegoats whenever either ruler faced demands from his regular troops. The awlād al-nās occupied a precarious position in the military hierarchy. Since first-generation men performed most vital combat or policing duties, the reservists' functions remained marginal. Sultans frequently neglected their training altogether, and froze their stipends at levels prevailing in their forefathers' time. Ravaged by the price inflation of the fifteenth century, the awlād al-nās seemingly enjoyed more social prestige than fiscal advantage because of their fixed incomes.[40] Yet they persisted as a distinct, self-conscious interest group, clinging to their peripheral status at the lower fringes of the ruling elite. The continuation of their summonses before both Qāytbāy and al-Ghawrī when either sought bonus money suggests that their own salaries *in toto* amounted to more than negligible sums.

During the fiscal crisis of 873/1468 that precipitated Qāytbāy's fitness trials, the sultan subjected reservists to the same bow-drawing tests he imposed on his recruits and veterans. Fully realizing how few of them could pass, Qāytbāy imposed the exercise for an ulterior purpose. Any walad al-nās who failed was cut from the expedition roster *if* he paid one hundred dīnārs for a replacement in lieu of his monthly allowance fixed at two thousand dirhams.[41] Those receiving a mere one thousand monthly (a figure worth little more than a few Ashrafī dīnārs due to debasement) were let off. All chroniclers agreed this tactic imposed hardships on the reservists, but we should recall that both ʿAbd al-Bāsiṭ and Ibn Iyās belonged to the Ḥalqa themselves and did not offer impartial opinions. In fact, Qāytbāy showed this perception of reality when he insisted on every man, high or low, who drew a combatant's salary contributing some tangible service. The awlād al-nās provided little reliable utility for the war effort and therefore represented a drain on the regime's resources. And Qāytbāy was no ogre, even in his dealings with partisan cadre like the reservists. The following year, 874, when the Sūwār crisis had eased somewhat, he returned some of the money he had taken from them.[42] But Qāytbāy never abandoned his contempt for the awlād al-nās. To the end of his reign he held the specter of stipend deprivation over them.

Al-Ghawrī exhibited his precursors' scorn for the Ḥalqa but, consistent with his aversion to pay musters, he simply wrung substitute money from them with no pretext of fitness check.[43] Yet the reservists' successful retention of at least some vestiges of their inherited estates is indicated by the regime's persistent pressuring of them when it faced shortfalls for regulars' bonuses. From the sultan's point of view, the awlād al-nās posed an ominous threat, however latent. If they succeeded in retaining their forefathers' fiefs, they might alienate a significant portion of the state's land reservoir available for redistribution to future generations of troops on whom it would rely for combat duty. But regardless of measures devised for extracting funds from reservists, or limiting their inheritance of estates, the awlād al-nās clearly did not hoard enough assets to resolve the regime's deficit.

Reservists were hardly the sole element of the military hierarchy adept at surreptitiously diverting properties from the royal domain. By the late Circassian period, manipulation of iqṭāʿs had become widespread at every level of the military institution. Both Qāytbāy and al-Ghawrī incurred intense agitation among their officers when they juggled iqṭāʿ assignments, or reallocated estates freed by deaths of amīrs in battle in favor of their own followers. Soon after his enthronement, Qāytbāy issued an edict demanding the return of all troopers to Syria if they drew their income from iqṭāʿs located there.[44] Absenteeism posed a weighty problem for the regime since fiefholders continuously shirked their provincial duties, preferring life in the capital where they might stir up trouble in a rival's faction. Two years later, in Rabīʿ I 874/ September–October 1469, Qāytbāy lost his temper when two junior officers brought their dispute over the same fief before him.[45] Qāytbāy had secretly arranged for his second dawādar to arrest one of the two contestants, he who belonged to the suspect Ināliya corps. When this officer, one Qānṣūh al-Ishāqī, presented himself, Qāytbāy exploded in rage and struck the dawādar with his fist. Then, in a rare loss of composure, he drew his dagger, forcing a defensive posture from his own subordinate. Qāytbāy subsequently withdrew from the assembly to brood in his private apartments until several of his colleagues restored calm in the audience hall. The assembled Ināli amīrs ran amok through the Citadel courtyards, proclaiming mutiny if their insult were not atoned. Qāytbāy's tantrum revealed his wrath when a ploy for bestowing land grants on his own partisans was disclosed in an embarrassing fashion.

This kind of tension over distribution of iqṭāʿs erupted repeatedly throughout the two reigns. Its frequency suggests the centrality of land allotments in the regime's system of finance, and the efforts of both autocrat and troopers to manipulate them. More heated exchanges between officers occurred over conflicting iqṭāʿ suits than any other aspect of their remuneration.

Ibn Iyās reported several incidents of suicide when the sultan rejected an amīr's petition for a land grant.[46] In the face of such pressure on its pool of fiefdoms, steadily dwindling because of alienation, each sultan strove above all to ensure grants for his personal retainers regardless of how many individuals with legitimate claims he dispossessed. If this discord is considered against the backdrop of embezzlement affecting all fiscal transactions involving the Mamlūk soldiery, their abiding discontent may be fathomed.[47] Their interminable revolts cannot be assessed outside this context of self-perceived abuse.

Revolt: Tactic or Protest?

Mutiny dated from the origins of the Mamlūk sultanate. Baybars and his colleagues denied the Syrian Ayyūbid Tūrān Shāh's claims to the succession after al-Ṣāliḥ's death and seized power. As self-proclaimed guardians of legitimacy, they therefore set a precedent for subsequent generations of officers and troops. To those men, the distinction between public responsibility and personal interest remained inconsequent; one equalled the other. The incidence of revolt thus matters less than its motives. If rebellion is examined as a process, its frequency may be understood as the result of frustrated factional ambitions or the regime's failure at maintaining the standard of living the elite expected as a right of caste.

Revolts erupting from factional conflicts reflect endemic tension between officers or troopers who had risen in a previous sultan's service and the current monarch's attempt at neutralizing their influence by retirement or exile. Qāytbāy confronted coteries hostile toward him from the beginnings of his reign. Veteran Mamlūks (*qarānisa*) purchased by al-Ẓāhir Jaqmaq and al-Ashraf Īnāl regarded the accession of an outsider, one who harbored no loyalty to a common patron, as a challenge to their favored position in the hierarchy. They accordingly staged an elaborate show of mutiny.[48] Since their posturing fit into a durable pattern of ritualized opposition, its occurrence at this phase of Qāytbāy's career is not surprising. More indicative of its symbolic significance was Qāytbāy's disdain. His departure from the Citadel's safety under minimal escort implies more a lack of any serious danger from these malcontents than the sultan's own bravery. No violent insurrection broke out, even when Qāytbāy rendered himself personally vulnerable. Yet though he treated former sultans, who still lived, with courtesy, he took rumors of sedition by their partisans more seriously.

As 872 drew to a close, after Qāytbāy had weathered his first critical months, he imposed curfews on parties supportive of the exiled Timurbughā. Subsequently, he allowed his adjutant Yashbak free rein in arranging their deportation from Cairo to provincial posts where they could do little to facilitate their sponsor's restoration.[49] Qāytbāy faced no further overt challenges from clients of former rulers for more than a decade after 872. Yet these certainly persisted as latent opposition groups because the sultan decided upon their systematic exile in 884, when he concluded their presence augured trouble if he planned an excursion. Throughout this year, Qāytbāy sent off small units of Ināliya officers and troops for duty in either Upper Egypt or Syria.[50] Because he now planned trips requiring his prolonged absence, he took steps at dissolving coalitions of Ināliya officers who nurtured hopes of supplanting him.

The visible weakening of an autocrat's faculties invariably aroused insurrectionary tendencies among even those officers whose loyalty had been unquestioned. The plotting of Qānṣūh Khamsmi'a late in 900, ostensibly focused against his old enemy Aqbirdī, in fact signalled his maneuvering for royal succession.[51] Every astute observer realized that Qānṣūh's ambitions were matched only by his aggression. Elimination of rivals like Aqbirdī would further his claim on the sultanate when Qāytbāy finally expired. But Qānṣūh failed utterly in his bid for power. Aqbirdī retained his office while Qānṣūh's rallies of other ambitious soldiers ended in mockeries of imperial reviews, with only token appearances by officers demoted by Qāytbāy. Qānṣūh's lack of success contrasted with his continued prominence in the highest oligarchy of the military elite. His actions were consistent with the expected behavior of an adept officer, whose suitability for the succession was blocked by fear of his ferocity toward fellow competitors rather than by doubts over his competence. The sultanate eluded Qānṣūh because he won over no close allies. His fomenting of revolt itself was predictable. Such an act represented a process of succession every militarist acknowledged.

Factional strife during al-Ghawrī's reign was less prominent but nonetheless highlighted his obsessive doubts over loyalty from the ranks. Al-Ghawrī's failure at building collegial ties with adjutants who enjoyed comparable stature was obvious when Miṣirbāy, an architect of his own accession, plotted his overthrow.[52] Ibn Iyās' musings over Miṣirbāy's revolt, which flared up and sputtered out in only two days, reveal the tenuousness of bondings at the loftiest level of the Mamlūk hierarchy:

> This incident was both lamentable and ridiculous. Miṣirbāy had imagined he could kill the amīr and occupy the Citadel with but a petty band of Mamlūks backing him—less than twenty! It was the height of stupidity, even though Miṣirbāy hardly lacked intelligence. . . . But this man had caused the death of al-ʿĀdil Ṭūmānbāy. He had lured him out by ruse and decapitated him. After al-ʿĀdil's execution, his head was displayed on a tray in the Rumayla. For this abomination, Miṣirbāy was widely condemned. Soon thereafter, Miṣirbāy was himself captured and subjected to horrendous treatment. His mangled corpse was carried up to the Citadel on a horse ridden by his guardian for all to see. Truly does the punishment fit the crime. This incident

gave many pause for thought. When Miṣirbāy was killed, the revolt terminated. His elimination is yet another example of the sultan's good fortune.

Ibn Iyās castigated the dawādār for his flawed planning and his betrayal of a
former monarch rather than for the act of sedition itself. His ineptitude played
into al-Ghawrī's hands. Three years later, when al-Ghawrī intercepted Qāyt
al-Rajabī's treason, he uncovered a more dangerous plot meticulously
calculated.[53] Al-Ghawrī's most vehement advocate back in 906 had obviously
endorsed his enthronement solely for the marshalship. As atābak, Qāyt could
bide his time until circumstances were ripe for his own coup. Once again, Ibn
Iyās decried Qāyt's cruelty but found nothing amiss about this scheme. Instead, he marveled at its audacity.

Factional acrimony under al-Ghawrī was confined primarily to partisans of
amīrs like Miṣirbāy and Qāyt. Qāytbāy had effectively disbanded cliques
bound to earlier sultans. Yet so haunted was al-Ghawrī by the wraith of sedition that he subjected his men to public oath swearings. These ceremonies
were ritualized reaffirmations of contractual agreements implicit in the enthronement of every autocrat. Al-Ghawrī would pledge respect for his subordinates' rights, in particular sanctity of their persons from arbitrary arrest. In
return, they vowed abstinence from revolt.[54] The long lines of troopers, shifting from foot to foot while they waited to press their hands against an
ʿUthmānī copy of the Koran, presented a scene Ibn Iyās regarded as an affront
to the holy relic, since he inferred that no one but the sultan harbored any
belief in its efficacy. The historian regarded this tactic as superstition, a maud-
lin sign of the sultan's shortcomings. While his disparagement of the ceremony may be excessive, he was correct about its failure to compensate for
perceived abuses. All ranks of the military held al-Ghawrī responsible for their
degradation—the more foreboding source of their outbursts.

The Mamlūks' perception of their deteriorating status during the later
Circassian period evolved from both genuine grievances and a sharpened
awareness of their power. The line between injury and self-interest is often difficult to draw, however, because of the militarists' indifference over the burden
their lifestyle imposed on the civil population. Nonetheless, dissatisfaction
over salary payments had become a ubiquitous theme of Mamlūk politics
when Qāytbāy was installed. Most references to revolt evoked by anger over
pay or rations delays during his reign laid stress on the growing obduracy of the
recruits. During Qāytbāy's later years these trainees, ideally the most trustworthy because of their status as the sultan's purchases, exhibited an unruli-
ness that threatened to disrupt the balance between personal ambition and
group solidarity.

Ibn Iyās first mentioned trouble from the julbān in Shaʿbān 877/January
1473, and the circumstances were prophetic[55]: "Several Mamlūk recruits rioted against Sharaf al-Dīn ibn Kātib Gharīb (a Muslim of Coptic ancestry),

who combined duties of the vizierate and the major-domoship on behalf of the amīr Yashbak. The julbān marched on his house and broke down the front gate. Ibn Kātib Gharīb fled into seclusion. This was the first disorder the recruits committed (under Qāytbāy), but their misdeeds increased—as will be noted." The recruits usually vented their wrath on a fiscal official responsible for paying their stipends or distributing their supplies rather than the sultan who assigned him this task. The official may thus be interpreted as a buffer deliberately installed by the monarch to deflect his recruits' anger from his own person, even though *he* decided how much they would receive. Also, this particular minister had his office at Yashbak's behest. The sultan had ordered his dawādār to bring the wildly fluctuating payment system of the Mamlūk corps under control, and the devices of this Ibn Kātib Gharīb must be regarded as one aspect of Yashbak's draconian methods. But the recruits' disruption over coming years seems to have exceeded either Qāytbāy's or Yashbak's expectations. The dawādār's measures apparently created precisely what his colleague most feared: a highly politicized element at the base of the military hierarchy whose activism would infect every other cadre above them. From 877, the julbān rioted periodically until Qāytbāy's decline after 900 when senior amīrs began plotting to succeed him.[56] While causes varied, they paralleled issues of the first case: ire over pay delays, demands for increases following calls to service, and hatred of Yashbak min Mahdī.

By the 880s, the recruits had refined their refractory skills and insisted on audiences with the sultan. Qāytbāy's own prestige was so august that he called their bluff when they presented unreasonable claims. In Jumādā I 883/August 1478, the julbān came to blows during their stipend review. "Furious at them, the sultan laid aside his emblems of authority: the dagger (*najma*) and shield (*turs*), and descended from the Citadel in a livid rage. He proceeded toward Shaṭanūf. Terrified by his outburst, the recruits ceased quarreling. The atābak and kātib al-sirr went to join the sultan so that they might calm his temper and urge his return. Initially, he was not so disposed, but the two persisted until he relented."[57] While the histrionics of Qāytbāy's ploy are obvious, the julbān's submission was revealing. Although they incessantly pressured their master for more money and rations, they never envisioned his loss. He remained, after all, the instrument of their favored status. If he resigned, their position would plummet.

But by the nineties, as the sultan's vigor ebbed, even this device lost some of its restraint over the recruits "whose greed now knew no limits."[58] In Dhū'l-Ḥijja 892/November-December 1487, as word spread of new julbān demands for pay hikes, the senior amīrs bolted themselves behind their townhouse doors and refused their liege-lord's call for assistance in admonishing the troopers. "As rumors became more alarming, the sultan presided over Friday prayer. Upon its conclusion, he entered the courtyard and sat on the dais. He then summoned the barracks guards (*aghāwāt al-ṭibāq*) and notable julbān, rebuking them as follows: "If you intend my assassination, do so now!" The assembled troops apologized to the sultan and made their submission. But after they departed from him, they resumed their previous squabbles and requests for raises." Qāytbāy therefore left al-Ghawrī a legacy of militancy on the part of the regime's trainees, who held their patron hostage to their demands.

Riots by julbān over stipends flared up during al-Ghawrī's middle years, persisting until the sultan's preparations for his showdown with Selim. Al-Ghawrī's response contrasted significantly from his precursor's. A studied obstinacy on his part is apparent as he confronted the recruits' insistence for pay raises. Al-Ghawrī would initially reject their requests out of hand, rarely defending his action with pleas of an empty treasury. Both recruits and veterans were thus convinced of their master's duplicity. He intended to accentuate their degradation while fattening his private coffers and indulging his experimental regiments. Their rebellions consequently intensified after 913/1508. The first incident, occurring in Shawwāl/February, was illustrative of both the sultan's recalcitrance and the recruits' ire.[59] "The julbān descended from their barracks wearing their sheepskin tunics inside out. They shouted their intention to rebel and committed outrages all through the day. They sought to accost the sultan while he sat in the Duhaysha and voice their complaints. Several amīrs went out to address them, but the recruits rebuffed them, stating they would not disband until each received a bonus of one hundred dīnārs. Their riot persisted through the night and into the following day. No amīr could ascend to the Citadel. The sultan himself dared not venture forth, nor could he take his official meal in public. He considered fleeing the Citadel in disguise and so escape his own Mamlūks' wrath, but his nephew Ṭūmānbāy prevented him. The revolt endured three days with the Citadel closed down. Calm was gradually restored but without gain for the recruits, since the sultan had not relented." Lapsing control, humiliation to the royal dignity—neither daunted al-Ghawrī. Only when he detected a heightening of tensions beyond ritual protests to support for rivals would the sultan capitulate.

Yet all his settlements were in practice ad hoc, despite formal reaffirmations of mutual loyalty. Within a year of an agreement, or following the sultan's call to muster, recruits and veterans would once again protest their poverty while the sultan scorned their demonstrations. Throughout these replaying stand-offs, al-Ghawrī was currying the allegiance of his closest dependents, the khāṣṣakīya bodyguards and members of the new Fifth Corps.[60] After 920, as relations with the Ottomans deteriorated, both julbān and qarānisa, seeing a cardinal opportunity for salary enhancements, stepped up their disturbances.[61] When the sultan departed on a trip in Ramaḍān 921/ October 1515, the recruits showed their audacity by stealing from his arms stocks hoarded for his favorites.[62] "Casting iron grappling hooks attached to ropes over the arsenal gate, they crawled up the wall and entered the courtyard. They found precious items inlaid with silver and pilfered them. At daybreak, the arsenal master arrived. When informed of the break-in, he beheld the ropes suspended from a window and wrote a report. But nothing was recovered nor any recruit apprehended." Al-Ghawrī found this thievery by trainees he had purchased annoying but not dangerous. No policy changes ensued. But one affair in that tumultuous year shook his complacency and induced him to abandon a valued client.

At the end of Jumādā II/August 1515, Sunbul, the eunuch tutor (*lālā*) of al-Ghawrī's son, struck one of the prince's novice pages with a whip "because of his impertinence."[63] The young man died after a few days and his barracks mates vowed the tutor's murder in revenge. When al-Ghawrī forbade any hostile action against his son's mentor, all the recruits united in their passion of besmirched honor. Over the following week, the julbān tried repeatedly to seize the eunuch, who had taken refuge in the Duhaysha Palace under the sultan's protection. They then rose in full-scale mutiny, donned their assault sheepskins and shut down Cairo's markets. Belatedly, al-Ghawrī consented to hear their terms for a settlement. "Hand over Sunbul or pay us an indemnity of one hundred dīnārs per man. Also, respect our honor. The merchants grab our horse bridles in the markets and belittle us. Throughout your reign, we have received no respect form the masses." Now convinced of the recruits' fury, al-Ghawrī forsook the unfortunate lālā rather than part with any money. He consigned his eunuch to the prefect, who dressed him in a penitent's white tunic and shoved him out the palace gate where the julbān awaited him. "When he exited the door, the Mamlūks pounced on him, intending to slash him with their swords on the spot. He promised to pay his victim's relatives a thousand dīnārs but in vain, since the Mamlūks refused this compensation, saying, 'Only his life!' They dragged him down the steps and over to the cistern where they disemboweled him. They then procured a coffin for his body, which they washed and buried. Thus Sunbul ceased to exist, as if he never had." For his part, al-Ghawrī issued the following proclamation: "No shopkeeper or merchant shall insult the sultan's Mamlūks nor touch their horse bridles. He who does will lose his hand and enjoy no security for his life." Ibn Iyās found al-Ghawrī's rejoinder a misuse of the populace, who suffered for an internal dispute between his own lackeys and trainees. From this time, "the people lived under the threat of terror and oppression by the julbān. But for now, the Mamlūks were satisfied with Sunbul's execution and the sultan's edict. They demanded no further bonus." An enlightening commentary on al-Ghawrī's handling of revolt crises. By his last years, the regular troops of the army had evolved into a tightly organized pressure group over which the autocrat's control was eroding. He could no longer set a campaign agenda or oppose demands for pay hikes without expecting full-scale mutinies instead of token duty stoppages. By the end of the Mamlūk regime, its vaunted soldiery had become a heavy burden.

Although many officers' rapacity typified the burden imposed on civil society by the Mamlūk caste at the sultanate's end, a necrology of one Qānībāy Qarā, chief fodderer (*amīr akhūr*) and commander (*bāsh*) of the sultan's ill-fated Aleppo expedition in 920, illustrates the peculiar interplay of valor and tyranny that rendered these men so effective yet so predacious[64]:

On Thursday the twenty-sixth (of Rabī' I 921)/10 May 1515, the amīr Qānībāy Qarā died. . . . His death was sudden and unexpected since he had been ill only five days. Indeed, foul play was rumored. Only God knows. He was one of Al-Ashraf Qāytbāy's purchased Mamlūks. Qāytbāy manumitted him, granted him horses and a uniform, and appointed him to the ranks of his wardrobe pages (*jamdārīya*). He then became an armaments supervisor (*silāḥdār*), and was subsequently promoted to an amīrship of ten in 898. He was soon appointed prefect of Sahyūn, which office he allegedly bought with a bribe. . . . Some time later, the grand amīrship of Aleppo was conferred upon him. He returned to Cairo during the reign of al-Nāṣir Muḥammad ibn Qāytbāy to assume a commandership of one thousand. He took over the chief fodderer's post from Kurtbāy (Qāytbāy's relative) after the fall of Aqbirdī al-Dawādār, when he struck down the amīr (Kurtbāy) in the madrasa of Sultan Ḥasan. He then held office for sixteen years and three months.

In truth, he was a gallant officer with distinctive abilities, possessed of a vast fortune, maintaining a huge arsenal. . . . He controlled an army of Mamlūk retainers. He owned everything in abundance. He founded the mosque next to the cistern of the Horse Market, and the shrine near the Mahāra Square on the Naṣirīya Lake shore. He was approaching sixty at his death. He was tall and broad, of swarthy complexion which darkened as he aged. He was renowned for his bravery and horsemanship, with exceptional skills at lance casting, so that he was called "the Lancer" (*al-Rammāḥ*).

But he was avaricious and cruel. His dealings were odious and he devoured the people's wealth without remorse. He placed his hand on both pious trusts and inheritances—seizing all their proceeds. If he purchased a commodity, he expropriated its price. If he employed anyone to perform a service or fashion some item, or if he hired an agent, he denied the individual his fee. No one left his gate satisfied. The sultan appointed him commander of the Aleppo expedition, and en route he inflicted the grossest injustices while in Damascus and Aleppo Provinces. He extracted large sums of money from each district, using gleaners who preceded the army. He harassed the populace and took from farmers some thirty thousand head of sheep—maybe more. At one time, the sultan had designated him to protect Sharqīya province from Bedouin marauding. When he arrested a hapless peasant there, he either disemboweled him or flayed him from head to foot. He treated even persons of higher status the same way. He claimed they were Bedouin sympathizers on the basis of hearsay. Thus did his defects outweigh his positive qualities. A dour person, very ignorant, from whom God delivered the people. When he died, none attributed the least good to him.

I ask God's pardon for this denunciation but by airing these iniquities,
I have sought to remind others that they may ameliorate their deportment.
     For his part, the sultan (al-Ghawrī) greatly admired this amīr. . . .
When he recommended Qānībāy for the senior stewardship of armaments
several times, the latter refused and the sultan acquiesced. But when the sultan sought to place one of his own colleagues in the stewardship, Qānībāy
resisted and won. When this Qānībāy fell ill, he continued residing at the
Chain Gate for five days. He expired there on the eve of Friday (Thursday
night) after evening prayer. The sultan then ordered his corpse conveyed to
his house in a casket (*tābūt*). . . . He was married to the amīr Yashbak's
daughter. Upon his death, she ordered the drums sounded for three days
straight (an unseemly sign of rejoicing). The sultan found her delight dis-
pleasing. It was whispered among Qānībāy's family that he had been poi-
soned, and the sultan suspected the amīr Yashbak's daughter. He fined her
more than thirty thousand dīnārs and claimed that Qānībāy had hidden away
larger sums under her care. She was obliged to sell her wedding trousseau to
meet his demand.

After describing Qānibāy's funeral, Ibn Iyās concluded with the following:
"knowledge of him faded rapidly; his career was forgotten." Perhaps Qānibāy
the individual was forgotten but not the legacy of his actions. Ibn Iyās set an
example of this amīr to show the imbalance of worthy qualities outweighed by
greed made possible by unchecked power. The message in this obituary is
clear. Praetorians who fear no one save peers of equal stature are certain to
pillage society. Their demands, once justified at least in part by their service
as protectors, could no longer warrant that quid pro quo. For now the guardians themselves disrupted the stability they had been pledged to uphold. This
obituary is thus a metaphor for the breakdown of order in society, a dilemma
incurable from within.

Notes

1. On al-Ṣāliḥ's creation of a Mamlūk praetorian guard, see: D. Ayalon,
"Aspects of the Mamlūk Phenomenon, B. Ayyūbids, Kurds and Turks," *Der
Islam* 55 (1977): 24–28; U. Haarmann, "Miṣr: 5. The Mamlūk Period," *EI*²
8: 165–67; R. S. Humphreys, *"The Emergence of the Mamlūk Army,"* SI 45
(1977): 94–99; R. S. Humphreys, "Mamluk Dynasty," *Dictionary of the Middle Ages,* ed. J. R. Strayer (New York, 1987) 8: 73–74; Robert Irwin, *The
Middle East in the Middle Ages: The Early Mamluk Sultanate, 1250–1382* (London, 1986), 19–23; Peter Thorau, *Sultan Baibars I. von Ägypten* (Wiesbaden,
1987), 31–42; Wiet, *L'Égypte arabe,* 365–67, 369–72, 377–79.

2. For ad hoc procedures of administration by the founding generation,
see J.-C. Garcin, "The Mamlūk Military System and the Blocking of Medieval

Muslim Society," in J. Baechler, J. A. Hall, and M. Mann, eds. *Europe and the Rise of Capitalism* (Oxford, 1988), 119–23; Irwin, *Middle East,* 26–36; Thorau, *Baibars,* 109–30.

3. On the recruitment of Mamlūk slave-soldiers see: D. Ayalon, "Aspects of the Mamlūk Phenomenon, A. The Importance of the Mamlūk Institution," *Der Islam* 53 (1976): 205–18; D. Ayalon, "L'esclavage du Mamlouk," *Oriental Notes and Studies* 1 (Jerusalem, 1951); D. Ayalon, "Le régiment Baḥrīya dans l'armée memelouk," *REI* (1951): 133–41; D. Ayalon, "The Wafidīya in the Mamlūk Kingdom," *IC* 25 (1951): 89–109.

4. See D. Ayalon, "The Circassians in the Mamlūk Kingdom," *JAOS* 69 (1939): 135–42; Haarmann, "Miṣr," 171–72; Irwin, *Middle East,* 143–51; Wiet, *Égypte,* 508–20.

5. *Ḥawādith* 4, p. 716, l. 4; *Inbāʾ,* p. 79, l. 14; *Rawḍ,* f. 224–b, l. 23.

6. *Rawḍ,* f. 186–b, l. 24.

7. *Inbāʾ,* p. 193, l. 9.

8. *Badāʾiʿ* 3, p. 75, l. 10. Later on, Qāytbāy did inflict drastic penalties on soldiers whose rapacity proved incurable. In Jumādā II 890/June–July 1485, he ordered a repeating thief's hand severed (*Badāʾiʿ* 3, p. 218, l. 11). Such a reprisal was rare since most offenders got off with verbal reprimands or temporary exile.

9. *Inbāʾ,* p. 473, l. 9. Senior amīrs often encouraged rioting by their support of civilian gangs in Cairo, who defended their patrons' interests in the streets. When two such groups, mutually hostile and competing for protection rights over Būlāq, came to blows in Jumādā II 913/October–November 1507, al-Ghawrī did nothing to punish them. One gang enjoyed the atābak's patronage while the other held the chief fodderer's. "Neither officer would permit any reprimands of his clients. Accordingly, the sultan could not assign fault. Thus did the masses suffer from their ravages." (*Badāʾiʿ* 4, p. 122, l. 17).

10. *Badāʾiʿ* 4, pp. 162, l. 4; 180, l. 12.

11. Ibid., pp. 161, l. 7; 208, l. 5.

12. Ibid., p. 432, l. 3.

13. *Inbāʾ,* p. 149, l. 2.

14. *Badāʾiʿ* 3, p. 217, l. 8.

15. *Inbāʾ,* p. 379, l. 4; *Badāʾiʿ* 3, p. 67, l. 4.

16. *Badāʾiʿ* 5, p. 50, l. 12. The peasant's courage is typical of farmers from the Upper Valley. Widely feared for their sensitivity over insults, Ṣaʿīdīs

had a reputation for avenging vendettas or matters of honor no matter the risk. This individual paid his life for his defense of property. To him, the affront merited the response.

17. For incidents of Anatolian merchants robbed while under the sultanate's protection, see *Badā'i*ᶜ 4, p. 98, l. 1 (Rabīᶜ II 912/August–September 1506: Sultan exiles Mamlūk who strikes Greek [Rūmī] merchant); 5, p. 82, l. 10 (Shaᶜbān 922/August–September 1516: Regent heads off reprisal of recruits against Anatolian merchants in the Khān al-Khalīlī suspected of spying for the Ottoman ruler).

18. *Inbā'*, p. 261, l. 3.

19. For cases of the government, or its soldiery, seizing merchants' or stockmen's property, see Ibn al-Ḥimṣī, *Ḥawādith*, f. 102, l. 5 (Jumādā I 888/June–July 1483: julbān riot in Cairo over recruits' refusal to pay merchant for bolt of cloth); *Badā'i*ᶜ 4, pp. 177, l. 8 (Muḥarram 916/April–May 1510: riot by recruits over rations delays; 570 shops pillaged); 295, l. 1 (Dhū'l-Ḥijja 918/February–March 1513: livestock rare due to Mamlūk seizures from farmers; latter hide remaining animals and cause scarcity); 431, l. 6 (Dhū'l-Ḥijja 920/January–February 1515: recruits plunder Ṣalība Street markets); 442, l. 17 (Ṣafar 921/March–April 1515: Sultan pressures merchants to buy commodities hoarded by regime at high prices; procedure causes abrupt price drop on open market); 466, l. 4 (Rajab/August–September: Sultan angrily rejects merchants' grievances over Mamlūk spoliation); *vol. 5*, p. 28, l. 13 (Rabīᶜ I 922/April–May 1516: Sultan rushes supply requisitions for Ottoman campaign; shops and mills close in protest). The issue of confiscation by the regime is not treated here. It is examined in chapter 6 as part of the government's schemes for fiscal solvency.

20. *Badā'i*ᶜ 3, pp. 136, l. 12; 137, l. 12.

21. Ibid., p. 227, l. 3.

22. *Badā'i*ᶜ 4, pp. 21, l. 7; 22, l. 8.

23. Ibid., p. 62, l. 13.

24. Ibid., p. 148, l. 13.

25. Ibid., p. 390, l. 13.

26. *Ta'rīkh Qāytbāy*, f. 15. The anonymous author gives figures of one thousand Mamlūks purchased at a cost of 3,770,000 dīnārs, not counting equipment prices.

27. *Ḥawādith* 4, p. 672, l. 12; *Inbā'*, p. 7, l. 17; *Badā'i*ᶜ 3, pp. 18, l. 12; 37, l. 18. Qāytbāy bought five hundred of Khushqadam's Mamlūks in Muḥarram 873/July–August 1468 to assuage their despair over falling from

most-favored status in the army. All three authors agreed, however, on the ex-orbitant expense, even though they praised the sultan as a conciliator.

28. *Inbāʾ*, p. 16, l. 10; *Rawḍ*, ff. 203–b, l. 22; 214, l. 12.

29. *Hawādith* 4, pp. 699, l. 3; 702, l. 3; *Inbāʾ*, p. 50, l. 16; *Rawḍ*, ff. 214–b, l. 9; 216–b, l. 30; *Badāʾiʿ* 3, p. 27, l. 15.

30. *Rawḍ*, f. 215, l. 30; *Hawādith* r, 701, l. 4.

31. *Hawādith* 4, p. 672. l. 20; *Inbāʾ*, pp. 8, l. 16; 122, l. 11; *Rawḍ*, f. 246–b, l. 22.

32. *Badāʾiʿ* 3, p. 325, l. 14.

33. *Badāʾiʿ* 5, p. 29, l. 9.

34. *Hawādith* 4, p. 689, l. 1; 692, l. 23; 693, l. 6; *Rawḍ*, f. 209, l. 6; *Inbāʾ*, pp. 33, l. 13; 34, l. 10; 36, l. 19; 39, l. 14; Badāʾiʿ 3, p. 24, l. 13.

35. *Badāʾiʿ* 3, p. 261, l. 12 (Rabīʿ I 894/February–March 1489: Mamlūks demand bonus of one hundred dīnārs beyond salary); 261, l. 16 (Rabīʿ II/March–April: sultan threatens abdication; bonus demand reduced to fifty, in payments two months apart; veterans receive only twenty-five each); 276, l. 20 (Muḥarram 896/November–December 1490: Mamlūks demand bonus; sultan threatens retirement in Mecca); 280, l. 6 (Rabīʿ II 896/ February–March 1491: following revolt, sultan grants bonus); 295, l. 11 (Rajab 898/April–May 1493: recruits insist on bonus; block Citadel gates; markets close in expectation of looting). Mean figures for the basic monthly stipend (jāmakīya) paid to a Royal Mamlūk are evasive. The most frequently quoted amount is one hundred Ashrafī dīnārs, before bonus. But higher and lower sums were reported, often spread over broader intervals.

36. *Badāʾiʿ* 4, pp. 7, l. 6; 8, l. 18.

37. *Badāʾiʿ* 4, pp. 22, l. 12 (Jumādā I 907/November–December 1501: Nāẓir al-dawla complains of meat rations shortage caused by sultan's own agents); 130, l. 7 (Dhūʾl-Ḥijja 913/April–May 1508: Sultan denies civil officials sacrifice animals for ʿĪd, having sold many himself); 207, l. 2 (Dhūʾl-Ḥijja 916/March 1511: similar situation but now Mamlūk troopers pillage animals); 230, l. 18 (Jumādā I 917/July–August 1512: Sultan arrests his meat purveyors after three-month delay in supplying rations); 237, l. 13 (Jumādā II/August–September: he flogs them when they protest); 241, l. 8 (Rajab/September–October: recruits pillage royal granary due to sultan's hoarding for higher market prices); 242, l. 22; 243, l. 8 (Shaʿbān/October–November: meat rations shortage because of sultan's abuse of butchers who flee their jobs); 359, l. 6; 371, l. 12 (Muḥarram 920/February–March 1514: six-month delay in meat rations, due in part to dīwān cash shortfall, in part to sultan's

speculation); 480, l. 3 (Shawwāl 921/November–December 1515: Sultan arrests his meat purveyor, confines him until he releases rations, presumably held for private sale); *vol. 5*, pp. 8, l. 12; 13, l. 7 (Muḥarram 922/February–March 1516: in preparation for Ottoman expedition, sultan announces cash payment for delayed meat rations; cost: forty thousand dīnārs; money collected from funds accumulating in vacant vizier department, presumably hoarded by al-Ghawrī as secret reserve).

38. *Badā'i'* 4, pp. 177, l. 8.

39. Ibid., p. 373, l. 13.

40. Al-Ṣayrafī (*Inbā'*, 490, l. 4) observed their pitiful appearance when Qāytbāy summoned them for muster in Dhū'l-Ḥijja of 885/February 1481: "They were reviewed in great shame, meekness, degradation and contempt—for they owned neither their raiment nor mounts (presumably renting both for the occasion). For most, their iqṭā's yielded them no protection money (*ḥimāya*) nor cultivated produce. . . . Indeed, some (officials) sought to deprive from some of them their fiefs since they no longer yielded any (tax). The accountants (*mubāshirīn*) did not know whether their land was producing or fallow. Even if some owned estates, they still resembled these wretched (landless) types. . . . The sultan enjoined the Muqaddam al-Mamālīk . . . to order their battle readiness in case of a summons. This obliged them to ascend with sword, lance, bow and headgear. They had no choice but to obey, even though most who did had to borrow their equipage—even their kerchiefs (*manādīl*)!" See also p. 501, l. 9. Ulrich Haarmann has dealt with the issue of social prestige but fiscal decline of the awlād al-nās. See "The Sons of Mamluks as Fiefholders in Late Medieval Egypt," in *Land Tenure and Social Transformation in the Middle East*, ed. Tarif Khalidi (Beirut, 1984), 141–43. Haarmann's discovery of a sharp diminution in iqṭā's held by awlād al-nās after the accession of Barqūq (784–801/1382–1398), the first Circassian sultan, complements remarks made by ninth/fifteenth-century chroniclers.

41. *Ḥawādith* 4, p. 681, l. 7; *Inbā'*, pp. 20, l. 19; 22, l. 4; 23, l. 5; *Rawḍ*, f. 205, l. 6, 29; *Badā'i'* 3, pp. 22, l. 1; 26, l. 17.

42. *Inbā'*, p. 162, l. 6; *Rawḍ*, f. 250–b, l. 8.

43. *Badā'i'* 4, pp. 25, l. 7; 285, l. 17; vol. 5, p. 28, l. 8. Ibn Iyās dwelt on the personal hardship he suffered in Jumādā II 914/September–October 1508, when al-Ghawrī expropriated his own iqṭā', passed down from a military forebear. But he also expressed his relief when the estate was restored to him, his case indicating the ability of the awlād al-nās to recover their losses either through influence at court or bribes. See vol. 4, p. 136, l. 5.

44. *Rawḍ*, f. 177, l. 28.

45. *Inbā²*, p. 137, l. 8.

46. *Badā²i°* 3, pp. 212, l. 21 (Dhū'l-Qa°da 889/November–December 1485; Amīr and skilled archer requests deceased officer's allotment; cuts his own throat when rejected); 258, l. 14 (Dhū'l-Ḥijja 893/November–December 1488: impoverished amīr of ten, whose iqṭā° no longer produces its stated yield, pleads poverty of his family and retainers in request for new grant; hangs himself upon refusal); 321, l. 8 (Shawwāl 901/June–July 1496: Amīr of ten hangs himself "from intensity of despair" when sultan denies his appeal for iqṭā° of fellow Ẓāhirī [Jaqmaq] colleague of same rank).

47. For incidents of corruption recorded during al-Ghawrī's reign, see *Badā²i°* 4, pp. 123, l. 11 (Rajab 913/November–December 1507: Sultan fines moneychanger for issuing counterfeit money to troops); 134, l. 21 (Rabī° II 914/July–August 1508: Sultan fines his arsenal director for distributing defective weapons); 146, l. 22 (Dhū'l-Qa°da 914/February 1509: arsenal director's case reconsidered; new fines demanded as gravity of affair explored); 179, l. 4 (Muḥarram 916/April–May 1510: nāẓir al-dawla goes into hiding when accused of pilfering meat rations); 185, l. 15 (Rabī° I/June–July: major-domo flogged for embezzling troop stipends); 199, l. 14 (Shawwāl/January 1511: arsenal director turned over to amīr whom the former unjustly implicated in weaponry scandal); 242, l. 10 (Rajab 917/September–October 1511: Sultan forces senior officers to implement food purchases of staple commodities among merchants for raising bonus money); 330, l. 4 (Rajab 919/September 1513: sultan's bailiff forced to make up bonus shortfall from his own purse).

48. *Ḥawādith* 4, p. 621, l. 1; *Rawḍ*, ff. 176–b, l. 30; 177, l. 1; *Badā²i°* 3, p. 8, l. 3.

49. *Rawḍ*, f. 184, l. 18, 23; *Ḥawādith* 4, p. 643, l. 8.

50. *Badā²i°* 3, pp. 152, l. 9; 157, l. 9; 158, l. 5; 159, l. 10.

51. *Badā²i°* 3, pp. 310, l. 21—313, l. 18; 314, l. 6; 321, l. 20; 322, l. 6; Ibn al-Ḥimṣī, *Ḥawādith*, ff. 158–b, l. 4; 159, l. 7; 160, l. 1.

52. *Badā²i°* 4, p. 26, l. 14.

53. Ibid., p. 73, l. 1.

54. Ibid., pp. 18, l. 20; 49, l. 19; 65, l. 20; 98, l. 21; 103, l. 15; 123, l. 18; 180, l. 5; 313, l. 6; 428, l. 11.

55. *Badā²i°* 3, p. 82, l. 9.

56. The pattern of revolts linked directly to pay grievances or anger over Yashbak's policies is as follows: *Badā²i°* 3, pp. 92, l. 3 (Jumādā II 878/October–November 1473); l. 13 (Rajab/November–December); l. 22

(Shaʿbān/December 1413–January 1414); 94, l. 5 (Dhū'l-Qaʿda/March–April); l. 13 (Dhū'l-Ḥijja 878/April–May); 96, l. 14 (Rabīʿ I 879/July–August 1474); 97, l. 3 (same month); 97, l. 23 (Rabīʿ II/August–September); 136, l. 18 (Ramaḍān 882/December–January 1478); 195, l. 14 (Jumādā I 887/June–July 1482); 217, l. 5 (Rabīʿ I 890/March–April 1485); 235, l. 21 (Dhū'l-Qaʿda 891/October–November 1486); 245, l. 21 (Dhū'l-Ḥijja 892/November–December 1487); 261, l. 12 (Rabīʿ I 894/February–March 1488); 266, l. 19 (Shaʿbān/July); 276, l. 20 (Muḥarram 896/November–December 1490); al-Sakhāwī, *Dhayl*, f. 205, l. 4 (same month); *Badāʾiʿ* 3, p. 295, l. 11 (Rajab 898/April–May 1493); *Dhayl*, f. 259, l. 30 (Shawwāl 900/June–July 1495). Note that incidents occurred least frequently during the 880s when Qāytbāy was at the height of his powers.

57. *Badāʾiʿ* 3, p. 147, l. 5.

58. Ibid., p. 245, l. 21.

59. *Badāʾiʿ* 4, p. 127, l. 13.

60. Ibid., pp. 358, l. 11: Muḥarram 920/February–March 1514, "On Tuesday, the third, the sultan sat in the Hippodrome and distributed to his khāṣṣakīs lustrous armaments from his own stock. Some time previously, he had granted them silver-embossed swords, coats of mail, and bows. Unlike his predecessors, the sultan lavished on them money, estates, rich raiment;" 359, l. 19: "Wednesday, the eleventh, the sultan sat in the courtyard reviewing his khāṣṣakīs—only. He granted them eight hundred helmets (*khūdhan*). He also bestowed six hundred mail tunics in multicolored velour. All these arms came from the imperial arsenal, from supplies of Mamlūks deceased during the plague epidemic of the preceding year. The sultan reserved them for distribution (to his favorites) this month."

61. On riots from 920: *Badāʾiʿ* 4, pp. 368, l. 10 (Ṣafar 920/March–April 1514: julbān revolt over pay, delayed rations); 424, l. 21 (Dhū'l-Ḥijja/January–February 1515: Sultan's khāṣṣakīs demand bonus from governor of Alexandria); 427, l. 14 (same month: recruits and veterans revolt over travel advance); 430, l. 9 (same month: Sultan threatens abdication if bonus demand not dropped); 446, l. 2 (Ṣafar 921/March–April 1515: Sultan orders troops receiving stipend to prepare for duty in Aleppo; revolt rumored); 474, l. 4 (Shaʿbān 921/September–October 1515: Mamlūks rampage when informed of expedition to Aleppo).

62. *Badāʾiʿ* 4, p. 475, l. 18.

63. Ibid., pp. 463, l. 13; 465, l. 16.

64. Ibid., p. 450, l. 13.

5

ECONOMIC DILEMMAS: HEIGHTENED DEMAND, STATIC RESOURCES

"As for the commons, they could be divided in three groups by (descending) need: the rich who became impoverished; the earner who languished on his wage's remnant; and the poor who previously had requested a whole loaf, but now begged for a morsel or scrap."[1] With such words did the chronicler al-Ṣayrafī sum up the masses' lot in Cairo at the start of 875/June–July 1470. Such offhand comments about fiscal malaise by contemporary observers far outweigh either their forecasts of prosperity or assessments of causes behind recession. What motivated statements of this ilk and why did they occur so frequently? Certainly a facade of grandeur still enveloped the Mamlūk sultanate even in its latter decades when the ruling caste was wracked by factionalism. For all its apparent disarray, the regime managed to extract sums adequate for its own expenses and campaign costs. The revenues it tapped required an economic foundation sufficiently fruitful to yield them without irreparably damaging that foundation's infrastructure. Analysis of any economic system is complicated when contemporary sources touch marginally on its mundane functions. Yet despite their lacunae, these texts do depict a fisc crippled by an intense exploitation that dissuaded the open productive investment of assets. This leitmotif of oppression emerges so ubiquitously in the narratives that we can speculate about, if not definitively plot, its long-term consequences.

Although chroniclers refer repeatedly to alterations in crop or commodity prices, usually linked with their reports of the Nile's annual innundation, they rarely offer commentary about substantive change in the economy.[2] Despite this lack of sources, several historians have, over the last century, constructed models of forces driving economic change in the Mamlūk State. So far, none has presented a definitive explanation for the alleged decline that sapped the energies of cultivators, artisans, and merchants who yielded up the monies bolstering their regime's finances. No consensus at present prevails among those who ponder the Mamlūk's role in Egypt's retreat from her medieval status as the economic colossus of the Eastern Mediterranean.[3] Some historians have questioned any significant weakening of Egypt's productive capacity, even under unremitting pressure from ruling authorities. They interpret the Mamlūk State's dilemma as primarily a challenge imposed from without. Alterations in European patterns of investment, capital accumulation, and manipulation of markets unprecedented in world history would confront the Mamlūk regime, along with all its Afro-Asiatic contemporaries, with techniques beyond their conceptual powers. Before such an alien challenge, no polity from Egypt to China could compete—at least in the short run.[4]

With due respect for such claims, the sustained opinion of chroniclers that Egypt and Syria presided over a deteriorating financial system warrants scrutiny of their assertions. The Mamlūk Empire inherited a rich agrarian base, which had yielded surpluses capable of replenishing grain stores in such capitals as Alexandria, Rome, and Constantinople in bygone days. The craft industries of its cities had fashioned commodities of such quality that foreign consumers paid dearly for them. And its network of merchants marketed these wares, in addition to luxury items and spices from South and East Asia, at prices generating lucrative profits for the regime's tax collectors. By the fifteenth century, these revenue generators had settled comfortably into time-honored modes of production no longer attuned to a changing environment. None of the sources discussing economic activities in the later medieval period depict adaptability to profound alterations in the commercial process. On the contrary, they suggest an economy locked in stasis with little proclivity for innovation or reform. Yet it was this atrophied foundation that carried a military institution conditioned to living beyond its means. In the twilight of its influence as a world power, the Mamlūk sultanate reaped the harvest of excessive bureaucratic sophistication, which refined schemes of extraction while ignoring new ways of enhancing its revenue producers' output. Finite assets few expected to grow were strained as the regime inflated its demands. Regarding these tendencies in our period, how were the sultanate's income providers faring during its last half century? Were they producing less effusively or exploited more stringently?[5] The chroniclers' record implies less a precipitous decline in agrarian output (albeit one compromised by Bedouin marauding), crafting of commodities, or commercial marketing than a growing resignation to harassment which discouraged experimentation but promoted languor.

Agriculture: Between Nature's Vagaries and Government Mulctings

All surveys of Egypt, regardless of era, allude to the Nile flood for her proverbial crops. When statistics on innundations are compared against crop prices (see appendices 1–4), their generalities are transformed into a stark depiction of the slim margin separating abundance from famine. The chroniclers' tallying of these statistics stands as testimony to the annual flood as Egypt's crucial event. While Qāytbāy's lengthy reign witnessed fluctuations in flood crests, no catastrophic troughs resulted from monsoon failures in the Ethiopian Highlands. Yet these alterations, rarely varying more than three cubits in any given year, sufficed to inflate or depress crop prices sharply and on occasion forced the regime to quell panicked speculation by selling its own stores. Qāytbāy's initial year began inauspiciously with a sluggish Nile crest several days late.[6] Although the surge's peak ultimately attained a level of average height, the delay alarmed jittery grain dealers who, by hoarding their stocks of wheat, fūl beans and rice, drove prices up.[7] Once a price rise was triggered, its momentum defied quick remedy. Prices for the above staples increased steadily throughout 873, even though the crest slightly exceeded the preceding season's. Crop blights in the Delta, temporary lapses in surges necessary to fill catch basins and Bedouin raids throughout the Upper Valley combined to ensure shortages well into 874. Wheat that had sold for six hundred dirhams an irdabb two years earlier now brought double that amount.[8]

Two more weak flood seasons prefaced scant harvests, but from 876 to the mid-eighties a series of high Niles gradually reduced staple prices.[9] No dramatic relief accompanied abundant yields in the field, however, because of hoarding by amīrs who kept huge stores from their iqtā's off the market. Having become accustomed to revenues generated by price increases over the preceding period of scarcity, they saw no gain from a drop. Also, Cairo's market inspectors either belonged to the fraternity of senior officers or owed their appointments to the latter's pervasive whispers in the sultan's ear. Under pressure to hold up staple prices even in the face of occasional overstocks, they connived to delay their distribution. Only when consumers rioted over the artificially steep cost of bread did the sultan intervene by setting prices himself or firing the current incumbent. Throughout the remainder of Qāytbāy's tenure, staple prices fluctuated up and down but no catastrophic shortages occurred. His reign terminated with agrarian prosperity.[10] In sum, such increases as did appear reflected the perennial problems of weather shifts, Bedouin spoliation, stockpiling by amīrs or manipulation on the part of market officials. No significant disruption in agrarian output plagued Egypt during these otherwise turbulent decades.

Riven by internal acrimony and beset with foreign threats as his reign was, al-Ghawrī confronted no worse agrarian conditions than had Qāytbāy. The Nile behaved beneficently for the most part, and crests between 906 and 922 never fell below seventeen cubits.[11] In fact, through the later years of al-Ghawrī's rule, the river surged with excess power, its treacherous currents gouging out dykes and soaking the alluvium excessively. Seeds were often so waterlogged they failed to germinate. As the sultan had earlier summoned his qāḍīs and Ṣūfī prayer reciters to the Nilometer where they evoked divine clemency when the surge fell behind, he now called upon them to implore God's slowing of the flood.[12] Although Ibn Iyās' price data for these years was meager compared with the multiple details provided by historians of Qāytbāy's time, the figures he does report suggest no serious shortfalls in staples or inordinate market tampering.[13] We therefore may not attribute the general malaise afflicting the chroniclers' view of economic stasis during al-Ghawrī's reign to a diminution in crop production. Paralleling its earlier performance, Egypt's agrarian system under al-Ghawrī functioned at levels comparable with former eras of plenty.[14]

Yet the specter of calamity haunted both farmers and consumers in even the best of times. So closely dependent upon minor changes in the river's movement or shifts in the region's climate was Egypt's agriculture that any alteration could spark fear and hoarding—each often more damaging than the elements themselves. The texts abound with descriptions of alarm when the Nile surge was delayed even a few days, or occurred off-season.[15] Specialists in flood projection, using methods developed over millennia of observation, estimated the height and duration of the annual crest on the basis of surge intervals and density of alluvium deposits measured at stations throughout the Nile Valley.[16] When their forecasts fell short, the public reacted with fear of God's wrath. And no group was more likely to have provoked His ire than the ruling caste itself.

In Jumādā II 916/September–October 1510, after Coptic clerics weighed the alluvium during St. Michael's Festival and forecast a high flood, their predictions proved false. As rumors spread over this evil omen, a Muslim woman's dream was widely repeated throughout the city: "It was said that she beheld in a vision two angels descending from Heaven. They proceeded to the river, and after one of them touched its surface with his foot, it sank rapidly. The angel than addressed his companion: 'Truly, God the All-High did order the Nile to reach a level of twenty cubits. But when tyranny prevailed in Egypt, he caused its sinkage after only eighteen!' Upon the woman's awakening the next morning, the Nile had indeed fallen over the night by the foretold measure."[17] Such tales unsettled al-Ghawrī and his colleagues as could no formal protest over their expropriations. Al-Ghawrī certainly brooded over these signs of God's displeasure. When the river's crest was again delayed the following year, he drove all revelers who had convened to celebrate it away from the Nilometer precinct. Fearing God's anger over their "libertinage," he nipped any affront in the bud, however trivial.[18] Similar to his scoffing at the sultan's Koranic oath swearings, Ibn Iyās chided al-Ghawrī's alarm since the crest deficit was minor. Nonetheless, the sultan visited the Nilometer personally and led the Koran readings he had ordered nonstop until the surge resumed. To the end of his days, al-Ghawrī continued his program of prayer vigils at the Nilometer, followed predictably by public banquets when the river peaked. Ibn Iyās' skepticism over the efficacy of al-Ghawrī efforts notwithstanding, the floods of these final years were among the highest on record. Despite his excesses, al-Ghawrī remained the legitimate sovereign over Egypt. The masses did not take his intercession lightly and credited his visits with at least some softening of God's rancor.[19]

Whatever the cycles of prosperity and scarcity in their villages, Egypt's farmers knew all too well the regime would tap much of their bounty. By the later Middle Ages, most tillable land in the Upper Valley and Delta belonged to absentee agencies: the Royal Preserve (*Khāṣṣ* and *Dīwān al-Mufrad*), the Army Bureau (*Dīwān al-Jaysh*), which allotted fiefs (*iqṭāʿs*) to officers and their retainers, or trusts (*awqāf*) maintaining the charitable and religious foundations in Cairo and elsewhere. Heinz Halm, in his summation of cadastral (*rawq*) surveys commissioned during al-Nāṣir Muḥammad's third reign (709–741/1309–1340) or earlier, lists more than 3300 villages or harvest districts (*nāḥiya*) throughout the country, annual yields of which were tallied in several currencies of account.[20] Only a minute percentage of croplands in Upper or Lower Egypt appeared under the designation "*milk*" or private freeholdings. And when an owner could be ascertained, he usually derived from the military caste. Few civilians are included among rural landlords in the rawq surveys. Since virtually all fallāḥīn were tenants, they gave up the majority of their crops to collectors of one or more bureaus in Cairo. Even in years when harvests were lean, these agencies demanded fulfillment of quotas set long before in cadastral registers.[21]

Most expeditions sent out by the regime into the provinces collected rents, seized arrears and hoardings, or quelled Bedouin raids. But rare are chroniclers' remarks about reclamation or repairs, and the few we have describe the government's belated responses to dyke ruptures that jeopardized an entire district's harvest.[22] By contrast, the sources often mentioned the departure of a senior officer, usually the atābak or dawādār if either were not abroad, to gather up the several dīwāns' shares of crops, draft animals or rations herds. When the requisitioners encountered no resistance, these entries report few singular details. But if local cultivators were caught withholding part of what they owed, or if they dared protest when a corrupt officer seized more than his allotment, the chroniclers mention severe reprisals. Even al-Ghawrī's nephew Ṭūmānbāy, renowned for his equity, dealt harshly with recalcitrant peasants who had concealed grain due the sultan's Special Bureau:

On Thursday the twenty-third (of Jumādā II 919/26 August 1513), the
dawādār returned from a tour of Upper Egypt. He had in tow a large number
of Bedouin shaykhs, as well as local reconnaissance agents (*mudarrikīn*) and
a host of peasants (*fallāḥīn*) and farmers (*muzāriʿīn*) in chains. He had arrested them because of their arrears in crop payments, which dated back to
the days of Ibn Thaʿlab and other officials. It was rumored that they owed the
bureau seventy thousand irdabbs of wheat. When the dawādār ascended to
the Citadel, the sultan draped him with a splendid robe and he descended in
formal procession. . . . After the peasants and tillers were brought before
the sultan in their shackles, he exclaimed: "What crime have these committed?" They (the dawādār's staff) replied: "They are liable for crops due from
previous years—all the way back to Ibn Thaʿlab and before. They owe seventy thousand irdabbs!" Upon reflecting a moment, the sultan said: "Release
them all; I absolve them of their debt, by God's will!" Voices were raised to
His Majesty in praise, for within the group were elderly men, ill and infirm
persons, and young children. They were freed from their irons while the sultan looked on. An extraordinary event.[23]

Extraordinary indeed, for al-Ghawrī's heart was rarely softened even when the
regime's harvest requisitions imposed starvation on his subjects. More typical
were the methods he employed in Syria to finance his Aleppo expedition of
Shawwāl 920/November–December 1515.[24]

On Friday the fourteenth, Māmāy al-Khāṣṣakī, designated by the sultan to
proceed to the Jabal Nāblus and elsewhere, set out. He was to collect the
monies charged these districts by the monarch to defray the expedition's infantry costs. . . . It was alleged that the inhabitants of the Jabal Nāblus
were taxed one hundred thousand dīnārs and had to yield up an additional
twenty-four thousand to pay the marchers. The local populace had never before faced taxes like these. By contrast, al-Ashraf Qāytbāy, to support the
expeditions he sent out, paid the infantrymen from his own purse, giving
each a fixed stipend. But al-Ghawrī departed from this precedent, imposing
his costs on shaykhs of the Jabal Nāblus. They in turn bled these sums from
local tribesmen. But they failed in their attempts, for many inhabitants mi-
grated away to avoid mulcting. Residents of Damascus were also charged a
heavy amount to pay the infantry, as were the people of Ghazza, Ṣafad,
Ṭarābulus. Edicts spelling out their obligations were carried by the proven-
der officer, commander of the expedition, for proclamation in Aleppo and
Ḥamā. It was claimed that every soul in these towns had to furnish twenty
dīnārs, no less. These measures brought on the region's ruin, promoted disorder, encouraged the troops' disloyalty and weakened the realm. Syria was
reduced to chaos.

Oppression of similar vein proliferated throughout all the agrarian districts of the sultanate when fiscal needs in the face of mounting hostility
abroad exceeded the capacity of formal sources of revenue.[25] The evidence,
such as it is, depicts an inordinate heightening of demand rather than a decline

in output. These intensifying pressures on fixed resources were further complicated by the regime's failures at curbing Bedouin nomads who roamed, seemingly at will, the settled areas.

The Bedouin: Harbingers of Lapsing Authority

By the later Mamlūk period, entire districts of Upper and Lower Egypt had fallen under the shadow of Bedouin predation. Qāytbāy and al-Ghawrī inherited a situation of de facto autonomy on the part of several impetuous tribes who spread disorder and gleaned a substantial portion of local crop yields from several of Egypt's wealthiest provinces. Hardly confined to the desert fringes of the Nile Valley or Delta, these tribes moved with impunity throughout the fertile central districts, often disrupting commerce, impounding rivercraft and occasionally launching forays into the capital itself. Upon Qāytbāy's accession, the narrative sources noted increased Bedouin raiding. The chroniclers acknowledged Qāytbāy's preoccupation with his own tenuous position, of which tribal shaykhs were well aware. But they differed as to the effectiveness of the sultan's response. Ibn Taghrī-Birdī, whose ambivalence over Qāytbāy's leadership appeared in several contexts, openly criticized the monarch's indifference to rural safety or his capacity to ensure it. In Dhū'l-Qaʿda 872/May–June 1468, couriers brought news of Bedouin raids in the western Delta that were ominous because of their coordination. An officer sent to patrol Buḥayra Province reported that he was immobilized "as if he were under siege."[26] Ibn Taghrī-Birdī chose this occasion to speculate on causes underlying the carefully planned attack: "We have known no time nor moment when the Bedouin divulged their stratagems in the Egyptian realm. Yet their ravages have intensified in these days and they have infested all the Delta districts." Having alluded to the Bedouin's endemic threat, the historian placed its blame on the military authorities:

> This (predation) is due to the lack of solicitude by the government over their (Bedouin) affairs, not to mention the regime's inconstancy, especially during this particular year. For in 872, four sultans reigned, as we have recounted at length in our history, *Al-Nujūm al-Zāhira*. . . . The people could have expected some modest protection from the Bedouin menace until Yashbak min Mahdī the dawādār summoned the Hazanbul tribe from Upper Egypt and settled them in Jīza Province. Once there, they plundered the district severely. They then spread their marauding to al-Minūfīya and elsewhere. Their ravaging engulfed all the villages and towns, for they subjected the whole countryside to adversity with no thought of disobedience, since they were Yashbak's creatures. They rose to prominence by his sanction, having been appointed inspectors (*kashshāf*) in Upper Egypt by him. No one knew the reason why Yashbak had called them and then turned them loose so close

by him, with the sultan's cognizance of their arrival and heinous behavior. But some persons were rumored to claim that the monarch so feared the Ināliya Mamlūks whom he had coopted by promotions to high office that he secretly ordered Yashbak to call in his Bedouin clients to ward off the Ināliya's plots against him. . . . If this allegation be true, it is among the Turks' most disgraceful acts—their seeking Bedouin aid against others of their caste.

Even though Ibn Taghrī-Birdī's own father had enjoyed a distinguished career as a senior officer, the historian found duplicitous the contrast between the new sultan's formal proclamations and his covert ploys. Ibn Taghrī-Birdī went on to accuse Qāytbāy of connivance with the Bedouin marauders once he had entrenched himself and could risk excursions from the capital. A year after the previous entry, the chronicler described one of the sultan's first progressions through the Delta.[27] Remarking about Qāytbāy's obvious pleasure at being free of the Citadel's confines, Ibn Taghrī-Birdī regarded his rapid pace (outdistancing his own escort) as a sign of recklessness rather than courage. Once Qāytbāy reached the Delta towns, he disclosed no constructive purpose for his trip:

> Rather, the excursion, in effect, endorsed pillaging in most places. Pilfering was not curbed nor blockage of roads prohibited. Indeed, the sultan's real objective was apparent in his eager acceptance of gifts from the villages (which presumably paid for his "protection" from the raiding his presence had encouraged). When the bandits learned of his purpose, they fed off the populace, intensified their barbarity, and terrorized the roadways, even those close upon the sultan's bivouac. . . . The sultan thus promoted chaos in his realm. The people despaired over the Bedouin ravaging they suffered and said, "If the sultan continues to inflict this on us, those who survive will surely endure its like.

Ibn Taghrī-Birdī's contemporary, al-Ṣayrafī, sharply differed with his colleague's version, claiming that Qāytbāy's presence intimidated the raiders: "When he (Qāytbāy) proceeded by himself to a town or village, the bandits fled before him. . . . His sojourn pacified the region and relieved the populace. When his officers sent couriers to Cairo, they requested reinforcements since the sultan intended to lengthen his stay until order was assured."[28] Which author's depiction more accurately describes Qāytbāy's intentions during his Delta venture of 873 evades resolution. But their controversy itself implies both the ubiquitousness of this problem and the regime's readiness to exploit it for short-term gain. Throughout the seventies, Bedouin bands continued their operations with little worry over the regime's responses. Whatever the veracity of either Ibn Taghrī-Birdī's or al-Ṣayrafī's interpretations, Qāytbāy made a public show of inhibiting subsequent raids. Every significant outbreak of violence spurred an armed reprisal from Cairo. Yet the pattern of marauding remained so consistent over the years that the sincerity of the administration's responses must be questioned. They may actually have exacerbated rebelliousness the government ostensibly sought to quench. But the regime confined its most intense reprisals, whatever their efficacy, to those raids that threatened its revenue sources or crop supplies. Endemic raiding as a phenomenon troubling its rural subjects was accepted as an irremedial condition which might suit an amīr's own schemes if the circumstances were right.

The regime was genuinely alarmed when Bedouin tribes set aside their perpetual bickering to coordinate their forays, violate ad hoc agreements with regional prefects, or overstep tolerable levels of harassment. In the troubled months of 872, several Bedouin bands who normally spent themselves in bloody feuds called a truce for mutual profit when they learned of Qāytbāy's obsession with Sūwār's rebellion in Anatolia.[29] By the time Qāytbāy reacted, the level of predation already exceeded his expedition's capacity to quell it. During 873, reports arrived at the Citadel detailing repeated failures on the part of officers who either chased after Bedouin gleefully evading their pursuit or suffered humiliating defeats when they caught up with them. Late that year, Qāytbāy charged Yashbak, who had made his reputation intimidating Bedouin in Upper Egypt, with restoring order in the Delta.[30] Yashbak was so successful in quelling raids that his grateful sovereign granted him a hero's welcome when he returned to Cairo in Muḥarram 874/July–August 1469. Al-Ṣayrafī's comments about the reception are suggestive of the dawādār's tactics. He observed the large number of Bedouin notables in Yashbak's procession, quite possibly individuals he had coopted, Hazanbul style, to end their pillaging— for the time being. Qāytbāy dispatched Yashbak back to Upper Egypt the very same month.[31] In the course of this second expedition, al-Ṣayrafī mentioned one of Yashbak's rare altercations with Qāytbāy over the latter's priorities. The dawādār chided his sovereign for wasting men or money on Sūwār, "against whom Your Majesty's soldiers have won nothing!" Yashbak urged an immediate dispatch of fresh troops "and royal gifts" to his own service so that he could put down the rebels quickly and then turn his own attention against Sūwār. "The sultan responded with respect, honor and gratitude, saying: 'Indeed, you shall decide your needs which we shall meet as God wishes.' " But despite Yashbak's brilliant counterraids in the south and his ferocious reprisals for subsequent ruptures of obedience oaths, Bedouin marauding resumed after his departure. For all its efforts, the regime never curbed the plague of Bedouin revolt conclusively. To the sultanate's end, tribes "withdrew from obedience" whenever they sensed an opportune moment.[32]

Although the sultanate discovered no successful means of subduing the Bedouin, it alternated between attempts at coopting tribal leaders with offices, largely symbolic honoraria, and savage acts of retribution often worse than the Bedouin's atrocities. The former are reported less frequently in the narrative texts, but appear often enough to indicate an uneasy suzerain relationship. Obstreperous Bedouin shaykhs were cast into dungeons for life on the rare occasions when their lives were spared after capture. But in even fewer cases, they might receive clemency if they promised good conduct. During his Ṣaʿīdī expedition of 874, Yashbak received an eminent divine (*faqīr*) who pleaded for release of a local chieftain's son, whom the dawādār kept confined in wooden stocks for public ridicule.[33] Yashbak acknowledged the ascetic's entreaty and let the youth go. This incident may reveal a bond between spiritual figures of the Upper Valley and Bedouin headmen which the dawādār chose to honor, possibly as a means of enhancing his own status as a guarantor of order in the region.

The sultan normally acted as titular overlord before all the tribal shaykhs. The chroniclers report several instances of Qāytbāy reconfirming chieftains in their positions, or formally acclaiming the succession of sons in the absence of any routine procedure of transition.[34] Al-Ghawrī made similar gestures, and his leniency toward one prominent figure from Sharqīya, Baybars ibn Aḥmad, discloses his own style of persuasion. This Baybars had been supreme chief (*shaykh al-ʿArab*) of the province. Al-Ghawrī restored him to his post in Rabīʿ I 910/August–September 1504, reconfirmed his title several months later, and finally received him at the Citadel in 918/1512 for ritual homage following a period of revolt.[35] While Baybars accepted al-Ghawrī's invitation only upon receipt of a safe conduct writ (*amāna*), mutual suspicions did not prevent either shaykh or sultan from reaching a mutually convenient settlement. Such acts of reconciliation occurred in the aftermath of a stalemate all parties found onerous. In light of foreign difficulties looming on the horizon by 918, al-Ghawrī was willing to forgive old insults.

Qāytbāy was himself amenable to offers of truce from former Bedouin rebels. In Shaʿbān 876/January–February 1472, he accepted the Yasar tribe's invitation to share their hospitality at a lavish tent feast on the desert fringe.[36] Having previously raided through al-Jīza, this band now placed itself under the sultan's authority. The incident reveals the mutual pragmatism of tribal leaders and the military elite when local circumstances favored reconciliation. Yet accounts of reprisals so outnumber such settlements that they must be considered a sign of the regime's failure at checking Bedouin excesses. Ibn Iyās provides an interesting anecdote of a stay of execution toward the end of al-Ghawrī's reign. In Rabīʿ I 920/April–May 1515, his adjutant Ṭūmānbāy captured several leaders of the Ghazāla tribe who had been ravaging Jīza Province.[37] Frustrated by the intensity of their resistance and skill at eluding his forays, Ṭūmānbāy ordered their slow deaths by suspension from iron hooks at the Bāb Zuwayla: "But several amīrs dissuaded him, saying: 'If you execute these warriors, the entire tribe will devastate the district.' Reluctantly rescinding his order, the dawādār instead imprisoned the culprits in the Maqshara

Dungeon." Prudence, even in the face of insult, was characteristic of
Ṭūmānbāy's behavior. His predecessor, Yashbak, exhibited less restraint in his
dealings with Bedouin who had broken troth.

With due regard for Yashbak's sporadic magnaminity, Qāytbāy's stalwart
meted out punishments to Bedouin who crossed him that were disturbing even
by contemporary standards of cruelty. His most unconscionable act, which
evoked denunciations from all four chroniclers, occurred in Jumādā I 873/
November–December 1468. On the twenty-second of that month, Yashbak
returned from an arduous journey through Upper Egypt. He had pursued one
tribe, the Halba, whose leaders had especially galled him with their evasive
tactics.[38] Presumably executing all the men he could lay his hands on, the
dawādār reserved their dependents for a fate he hoped would give other bands
pause before indulging rebellious sentiments. Yashbak conveyed these unfortunate women and children, some four hundred in number, back to Cairo in
ships. Since no food or water was offered them during the interval, when they
arrived at the Būlāq wharfs their wretched condition appalled "all people of
decency." Yashbak herded the piteous mob into a warehouse (*wakāla*) in the
port, locked the gates and left them there to starve. Only the charitable feelings of local residents, few of whom bore any love for Bedouin thieves, rescued
them from death. Several irdabbs of broad beans (*fūl ṣaḥīḥ*) were smuggled to
them. One can envision the wild snatching of these morsels since "they disappeared in an instant!" The ultimate fate of these women and children, whom
custom normally spared from abuse suffered by adult males in warfare, remains unknown. Although they received sporadic donations of food, none of
the historians mentioned their release. "Yashbak confined them there, and
they so remained until this day of ours."

If Yashbak intended his brutal treatment of helpless persons as an impediment to further raiding in Upper Egypt, his act provoked the opposite
response. When surviving members of the Banī Halba learned of their relatives' suffering, they inflicted devastation "even worse than before, plundering
grain vessels on their way to Cairo and driving up the price of wheat." Ibn
Taghrī-Birdī and al-Ṣayrafī admitted a positive result of Yashbak's expedition.
He waylaid Ibn Jummāʿ, one of the worst Bedouin bandits in the Upper Valley, and flayed him alive—thus ridding the area of an incorrigible rogue.
Nonetheless, both condemned Yashbak for his torture of the wives and progeny of the Banī Halba. Whether the dawādār's ferocity was motivated by a
clandestine arrangement their chiefs had concluded with him earlier and now
violated they did not say. Certainly a breach of agreement remains a possibility
since Yashbak had forged many ties with tribesmen during his tour of duty as
inspector in Upper Egypt. Following their example, he had initiated his own
dabblings in grain speculation.

But whatever the provocation, Yashbak's tactics produced no reduction in
Bedouin predation. The dawādār led several more expeditions to the Ṣaʿīd

while his colleague, the atābak Azbak, headed progressions through the Delta. Following Yashbak's foiled attempt at kingdom building, his successor Aqbirdī assumed responsibility for the regime's efforts at quelling Bedouin violence. Neither his campaigns nor those of adjutants who served al-Ghawrī brought any lasting success. And while the sources recounted no further abuse of noncombatants, they yielded a lengthy list of executions. Chieftains who spurned the sultan's calls for order were beheaded, burned alive, crucified, flayed, drawn and quartered, and impaled.[39] These measures clearly aimed at impressing the local populace with the regime's vehemence, even if they did little to restrain their victims' comrades. The barbarity of these executions may have betokened the government's grudging admiration of the troublesome nomads' toughness. Mamlūk officers brought home tales of amazing, even supernatural, endurance shown by Bedouin marauders whom they attempted to terminate.[40] The desert warrior, who recklessly flaunted his disdain of authority from anyone, always cut a vivid figure in the imaginations of his sedentary neighbors. Perhaps his waywardness, beyond the regime's control, could be more stoically borne if it were explained by his larger-than-life stamina. Bedouin predation thus lingered as an omnipresent threat, a further symbol of the sultanate's waning power over its hinterlands. To what extent spoliation disrupted agriculture in the Nile Valley eludes precise assessment. The attendant level of anxiety on the regime's part, however, implies its significance as another factor debilitating the economy.

Egypt's Crafts: The Liability of Profit

The later Mamlūk regime maintained an ambivalent truce with artisans and marketeers who fashioned the commodities purchased domestically or exported abroad. Among the empire's prominent accumulators of wealth, they paid the military authorities a plethora of taxes in return, theoretically, for its guarantee of credible market standards, uniform weights and measures, prohibition of price gouging and support of equitable business practices. In reality, these assetholders lived in constant fear of the regime's expropriation. Later Mamlūk sultans were not the first autocrats in Egyptian history to seize their artisans' profits in times of crisis. Certainly commodity producers and traders had learned to cope with this inescapable condition of their commercial existence. But one must inquire whether measures imposed under the straitened circumstances prevalent during Qāytbāy's and al-Ghawrī's reigns encouraged their predisposition to hoard rather than to enlarge output or to experiment with what they fashioned. Any conclusions offered on this issue remain hypothetical in light of limitations imposed by surviving sources. Biases of chroniclers who pondered the government's tactics must be taken into account. Yet the uniformity of their negative appraisals cannot be ignored either. Any claim that their censure merely bespeaks routine doom saying discards the hard facts they provide, often at length.

Craft industries flourishing in Egypt and Syria during the high Middle Ages had evolved from aggregate techniques devised since Pharaonic times. But growth-oriented policies aggressively pursued from the early Fāṭimid period (ca. 969–1094 C.E.) had given them an impetus for innovation and refinement. Between 1000 and 1400 C.E., artisans achieved standards of quality and expertise enabling them to compete aggressively with rivals in the Mediterranean Basin or Southwest Asia. Egyptian and Syrian craftsmen manufactured textiles of great diversity, ceramics that approached Persian or Chinese wares in beauty, metallurgy prized even by feudatories in Western Europe, aromatics that enhanced effects of perfume, glassware incorporating complex mineral compounds to attain subtle tints and shades, chemicals distilled for a wide array of manufacturing processes, soaps and detergents ranging from delicate skin balms to powerful cleansers of raw materials, and paper products of high gloss and durability.[41] Improvements in food processing accompanied these technical accomplishments, especially with regard to sugar and oil.[42] Nonetheless, the sources describing these advances date overwhelmingly from the earlier decades of this era. The later Mamlūk period witnessed few changes in methods of production applied to any commodity or staple crop.

The narrative texts of Qāytbāy's and al-Ghawrī's time are tellingly reticent about artisanal activities. Their remarks are confined for the most part to large-scale restoration projects such as bridge and dyke repair, requiring unskilled labor, or construction of edifices commissioned by the regime for public charity or personal profit. The former often involved conscripts or forced payments from local residents to relieve the government of their costs. Both sultans charged their adjutants with ensnaring workers and coercing funds from fiefholders or shopkeepers. The ever caustic Ibn Taghrī-Birdī mentioned Qāytbāy's first efforts at canal dredging in the setting of his general rural neglect:

> On Sunday the eleventh of Muḥarram (873)/1 August 1468, the sultan descended from the Citadel and rode along the dyke canal. When he found it obstructed, he became angry and summoned the dawādār, Yashbak, to clear it. The latter proceeded there posthaste, accompanied by a swarm of conscripts. He gave this project his highest priority since the sultan assigned it to him. He ordered a group of notables to complete it (without compensation). The people had been aghast at the sultan's neglect of the Upper and Lower Egyptian provinces. . . . But now he became preoccupied with this one dyke, which in fact warranted no such concern. You may rest assured the importance he attached to its repair resulted solely from the inability of his muqaddamayn Ṣūdūn al-Qaṣrawī and Lājīn al-Ẓāhirī to cross the dyke with their cohorts.[43]

In the decades that followed, both autocrats responded to reports of clogged canals, broken bridges, or ruptured barrages with compulsory repairs. Rarely did either initiate such projects before disaster impended. When they so decreed, residents who bore the brunt of their expense often preferred decrepitude to restoration. While Qāytbāy occasionally lavished money on highly visible constructions around Cairo, such as bridges over the Jīza and Abū'l-Munajja Canals, al-Ghawrī refused outlays of state funds for public restorations.[44] When debris accumulated on city streets or canals filled in to levels impeding flow, the sultan ordered propertyholders to rectify the situation. In one such case of canal dredging, "the task of removing the earth was exceedingly onerous, and when the costs became prohibitive, many landlords sold their plots along the canal at cheap prices and left."[45]

Since both rulers indulged in construction of monumental buildings, architects and artisans surely found employment in large numbers. (See chapter 7, notes 28 and 41.) These skilled craftsmen received at the very least prevailing wage levels for their work and were never compelled to labor without remuneration. Eager to insure high standards of quality, neither monarch would risk shoddiness from surly artisans. The chroniclers' descriptions of their palaces, pavillions, belvederes, caravansarays, hospices, mosques, and madrasas provide ample evidence that the building trades upheld sophisticated methods of design and decoration. But particularly in al-Ghawrī's programs, confiscating existing adornments rather than purchasing new materials or commissioning original motifs was common.

When al-Ghawrī resolved upon his massive renovation of the Hippodrome Square below the Citadel in Ṣafar 909/July–August 1503, he ordered new work.[46] But less than a year later, the sultan remodeled the Citadel reception halls with marbles stripped from homes of imprisoned rivals or fallen favorites.[47] Al-Ghawrī's penchant for seizing expensive construction materials already in place can be seen as symptomatic of the regime's declining role as a prime patron of the building trade. Decreasing sponsorship of original artisanship was a measure of an overall diminution in demand for the intricate, and expensive, skills of craftsmen in many fields. Of course, few of these industries ceased functioning, since most were present in the Ottoman period.[48] But their malaise under the burdensome excises imposed by the military class is consistently affirmed in the narratives.

The chroniclers allude to commercial activities most frequently in the backdrop of expropriations and ad hoc tariffs, hardly a positive indicator of the government's promotion of new ventures. Through all of al-Ghawrī's tenure, Ibn Iyās mentioned a novel discovery only once: He cites the location of hitherto unknown sources of saltpeter, marble, and porphyry in Dhū'l-Qaʿda 916/January–February 1511.[49] While the sultan rejoiced at the finds, he paid the informant a mere ten dīnars for his report. If this pittance is compared with the enormous sums garnered by clients involved in al-Ghawrī's extortion network, the regime's fiscal priorties are readily apparent.

The sources provide an impression of vulnerability by incessant references to regime interference—keenly felt by artificers. The chroniclers exude a sense of their poignant resignation to the inevitability of exploitation. If this conviction that extraction was inescapable is coupled with the military caste's disdain for involvement in commerce, an attitude toward production may be discerned, which gave few incentives for innovation or risk investment to either party. Indeed, the prevailing milieu of confiscation promoted the opposite: confining efforts to time-tested methods, closeting assets instead of experimenting with new ventures, and focusing creative energies on concealing profits rather than enhancing them. Although the Mamlūk regime was aware of its legacy as guardian of the strategic advantage in external trade, it exhibited little identity with the welfare of craftsmen whose wares had once competed so successfully with goods of their foreign counterparts. Although chroniclers elaborate on the fundamental role of Mamlūk demand for commodities generated by the artisan economy, they provide no examples of partnership with an artisan's enterprise. There are few cases of militarists ploughing back any portion of their enormous wealth into commercial ventures.[50] Speculation in trade of staple crops on the part of amīrs holding large iqṭāʿs occurred frequently to be sure, but only for the purpose of manipulating prices for profit gouging. Compulsion of merchants to purchase such staples at rates set arbitrarily high would induce few of them to think positively about new investment options. The Mamlūk's relationship with craftspersons was symbiotic because they bought such large quantities of producers' goods. Yet it was simultaneously abusive, an interaction with scant incentives for invention but many for self-protection.

The historian al-Ṣayrafī reported an incident which illustrates the tensions underlying contacts between the regime's agents and commodity producers. On 16 Ṣafar 875/14 August 1470, the market inspector of Cairo, a Mamlūk officer, arrested a fig merchant accused of selling his crop at prices determined by popular demand rather than by government fiat[51]: "He received three thrashings, once on his buttocks, once on his legs and once on his shoulders. His was paraded through the city dressed in a thief's smock and suspended before his own shop, his hands tied behind his back. His body was then daubed in honey and left hanging in the sun. Bees, flies and wasps swarmed around him inflicting torment beyond description. Missives pleading clemency on his behalf were sent (to the muḥtasib) but to no avail, until the realm's guide (*raʾīs al-dunyā*) Ibn Muzhir al-Anṣārī, the confidential secretary, passed by and witnessed the dealer's affliction. He then arranged his release after sunset prayer." Al-Ṣayrafī went on to decry the muḥtasib's behavior. An officer whose greed was proverbial inflicted torture on a marketeer who was caught trying to maximize his gain—presumably without a prior agreement with the inspector over sharing his profit.

Such chastisement would be lamentable even if confined to exceptional circumstances. But, in fact, similar measures were routinely applied to artisans and merchants in these times of fiscal crisis and ministerial corruption.

The implications of such treatment for the warping of commercial morality probably matter less than their consequences for its productive capacity. Whatever the scruples of a commodity fashioner or dealer might be, he had little incentive to increase his output if he faced the certainty of its expropriation. If security of fortune was found in clandestine clientship, technical experimentation offered no advantage and might indeed attract even further exploitation with minimal concern for growth potential. It is in this milieu of cynicism and defensiveness that the behavior of merchants themselves must be assessed.

Commerce: Local Stagnation, Foreign Rivalry

Upon its formation, the Mamlūk sultanate presided over a monopoly in trade between the Mediterranean and South Asia. Precious commodities cultivated or crafted in the Orient found a seemingly insatiable demand in the expanding consumer economy of Western Europe. Profits garnered from the transiting of spices, luxury textiles, aromatic gums, fine woods, porcelains, and a host of exotic wares brought mutual profits to the governments of all states involved from India to Spain. Accordingly, no impediments raised by ideological differences or religious animosities were allowed to hamper this lucrative trade. Conflicts erupting from interdicts proclaimed by spiritual leaders or clashes over acts of aggression inevitably found some pragmatic means of resolution.[52] The Mamlūk government consistently subordinated rigid principles to practical necessity in its dealings with both European and Asian potentates.

Yet by the second half of the fifteenth century, this commerce—and its mercantile purveyors—exhibited signs of languor while they confronted growing challenges to the monopoly they had enjoyed from abroad. Consonant with their brevity of detail on artisanship, the narrative sources rarely elaborate on the substance of commerce, foreign or domestic. Yet asides to embassies, reconnaissance excursions, ship arrivals or departures, and the construction of port facilities abound.[53] The bits of data they present in sum enable us to discern broader trends affecting patterns of trade in the regime's final years.

Spices clearly remained the most lucrative items of international trade. Economic historians relying primarily on statements in chronicles of the early fifteenth century, which summarize edicts from the Citadel, saw the decline of free market passage of spices as the sultanate placed them under state control.[54] The elite group of kārimī merchants who amassed vast fortunes and acquired expertise in foreign affairs from their dealings in spices allegedly lost their privileged status, their laissez-faire operations replaced by regime dominance. But the later chronicles list obituaries of numerous merchants who bore the title *"kārimī."* All drew profits from their callings, admittedly at high risk of confiscation when they died.[55] On the other hand, the narratives make little mention of the regime intervening directly in their enterprise. Indeed, these necrologies suggest the merchants' continued function as free agents, while the government limited its harassment to special taxes and contests with heirs over a share of their patrimonies. Prominent merchants certainly faced the same pressures for funds their counterparts in craft industries or superintendancies of endowments endured when dīwāns ran short of cash. But the sultanate's sporadic attempts at imposing its own monopolies over foreign trade seem to have been short-lived, primarily because of their minimal return. The take skimmed from such measures did not warrant the effort.[56]

The diversity of local crafts supported an active domestic trade in Cairo and other urban centers—not to mention rural markets to which the sources only vaguely allude. Although not generating the spectacular fortunes of eminent khawājas who handled exotic goods, local commerce embraced a broader range of customers and counted for a larger share of the overall economy. Ibn Iyās twice mentioned a trade fair along the shore of Jazīra Island across from Būlāq on the eve of a saint's mawlid, that of Sīdī Ismāʿīl al-Anbābī.[57] He described a raucous festival attracting a vast host "who rejoiced to the limit" the entire night. Shopkeepers from all over the Cairo area and beyond set up some five hundred tents where participants "bought and sold a great array of merchandise." One may assume that fairs of this kind occurred in most towns or villages fortunate enough to maintain a venerated shrine. The frequency of holy days, birth festivals, and rituals dating from the pre-Islamic period provided ample opportunity for buyers and sellers to do business. The rhythm of domestic commerce was less susceptible to either foreign vagaries or regime tampering. Commodities fashioned locally for sale in their immediate vicinity reached consumers with only modest fluctuations in price. Their exchange usually escaped the notice of the ruling elite, which tapped profits from more lucrative ventures. Nonetheless, the chroniclers do not omit even this aspect of parochial trade from their statements about economic stagnation. Bound by traditions of production, distribution, and consumption dating back more than a millennium, domestic commerce showed no indications of innovation. If the regime largely spared small dealers the extractions it squeezed from wealthier merchants, it provided them few incentives for growth.

Despite its own predation, the Mamlūk sultanate reacted with alarm to the Portuguese's sudden appearance in the Indian Ocean as we have seen. But the threat posed by their arrival should not be interpreted as a terminal blow to the sultanate's European trade. The Mediterranean continued as an important medium linking Alexandria and Damietta with European ports. Frankish merchants still docked their vessels in these harbors, and embassies wound their way up the Citadel steps laden with gifts offered as pledges of their patrons' desire to uphold long-standing agreements.[58] Qāytbāy and al-Ghawrī received them with no less courtesy than the precursors who drafted the original treaties.

One of the chroniclers' rare comments about the monarch taking responsibility for revitalizing commerce addressed a valuable export crop, cultivation of which had lapsed. In Dhū'l-Ḥijja 914/March–April 1509, al-Ghawrī ordered the replanting of balsam shrubs in plots at al-Maṭarīya, north of Cairo, where the plant had previously been harvested[59]:

> Its husbandry had ceased from the first of the year. Egypt had been unique among all lands for its balsam production. European kings had purchased it at high prices, even paying its weight in gold. To them, baptism was invalid unless they poured some oil of balsam in the font water before an initiate's immersion. This essence was customarily extracted during the spring, in the Coptic month of Barmahāt (April). When the sultan learned of this lapse in balsam cultivation, he made an inquiry as to its location elsewhere. He pursued the matter until some seeds from wild bushes were brought from the Ḥijāz. They were planted in the same plots where the crop had previously been sown. Their revival was successful after watering from a well in their vicinity. This was one of al-Ghawrī's finer acts.

A refreshing interlude in the midst of so many reports of hardship and decline. But as we contemplate the evidence Egypt's historians offer about the economy in the sultanate's final decades, sentiments of pessimism outnumber isolated cases of initiative. Both Qāytbāy and al-Ghawrī received poor marks from the chroniclers for their responses to adversity. When Ibn Iyās mused over prospects for the new year 892/1488, he penned the following: "Prices of commodities rose sharply, . . . and the populace suffered uncertainty because of the (sultan's) new currency. The half faḍḍa now exchanged for twenty-four dirhams of debased money. Foodstuffs sold for two prices, the official and the real. . . . All of this along with the Mamlūks' oppression of the people, Bedouin spoliation on the rise in both Sharqīya and the Delta. . . . The sultan himself became tyrannical, bleeding the masses to finance his second Ottoman expedition. The army's morale was deplorable."[60] This is a typical entry for the state of economic affairs during the reign of this champion of Muslim welfare. As for al-Ghawrī, Ibn Iyās was even more despondent. When the sultan visited Alexandria in Dhū'l-Ḥijja 920/January–February 1515, he toured a sad remnant of a once vital international entrepôt[61]:

> The sultan crossed the city in formal procession. A few Venetian merchants threw gold and silver pieces over his head as he passed. When the sultan traversed the town, it had been decorated for his reception in crude fashion, for at this time Alexandria was in decline—whole tracts vacant. . . . In these days there were no eminent traders, either Muslim or European, left in Alexandria. The city was desolate because of the regime's oppression, the greed of the sultan's fiscal agents. They had bled the merchants of the tithe ten times over. Frankish and Maghribī dealers therefore ceased entering the (port) district. The town waned gradually and became increasingly aban-

doned. It was said that he who sought bread there could now buy none, nor any other food. Only a few meager stalls could be found open, while the rest were deserted. Alexandria had been one of the proudest cities of the world. When ʿAmr ibn al-ʿĀṣ conquered it, four thousand houses solidly built were located there, paneled with multicolored marble. Every house contained a private bath. The city maintained twelve thousand greengrocers who sold produce from noon to nightfall. Forty thousand Jews resided there—each paying the jizya (capitation tax). Six hundred thousand persons of Greek or Coptic origin dwelled within. The city commanded a fleet of one hundred thousand vessels of Byzantine style and imposing proportions. How poorly does the town's present condition compare!

Poor indeed. With due allowance for Ibn Iyās' nostalgic hyperbole about Alexandria's fabled past, his description of its lamentable condition when al-Ghawrī chose to visit was hardly happpenstance. Alexandria had symbolized Egypt's commercial hegemony in the high Middle Ages. Its decline signalled the passing of her preeminence in international trade, for which the historian held the sultanate accountable. Whether Ibn Iyās' censure was justified depends on perspective. Was the Mamlūk regime struggling with crises beyond its control, or implementing policies detrimental to commercial prosperity and thus augmenting an already egregious situation? However one inclines on this issue, the historians' consensus on stasis instead of growth must be acknowledged. The sultanate's efforts at preserving its solvency encouraged few positive measures but numerous survival strategies from those burdened with its support.

Notes

1. *Inbāʾ*, p. 188, l. 3.

2. Economic data appear regularly in chronicles or handbooks charting events in Egypt and Syria from the establishment of the Fāṭimid caliphate. Noteworthy representatives from the Mamlūk era, exclusive of those quoted in the text, are: Ibn Duqmāq, *Al-Jawhar al-Thamīn fī Siyār al-Mulūk wa'l-Salāṭīn* (ms., Cairo: Dār al-Kutub, 1522 Taʾrīkh); *Nuzhat al-Anām fī Taʾrīkh al-Islām* (ms., Cairo: Dār al-Kutub, 1740 Taʾrīkh); al-Maqrīzī, *Al-Mawāʿiẓ wa'l-Iʿtibār bi-Dhikr al-Khiṭaṭ wa'l-Āthār*, 2 vols. (Cairo, 1853–1854); *Kitāb al-Sulūk li-Maʿrifat Duwal al-Mulūk*, 4 vols., 3 parts each (Cairo, 1934–1973); *Ighāthat al-Umma bi-Kashf al-Ghumma* (Cairo, 1940); Ibn Ḥajar al-ʿAsqalānī, *Inbāʾ al-Ghumr bi-Anbāʾ al-ʿUmr*, 3 vols. (Cairo, 1969–1972); al-ʿAynī, *ʿIqd al-Jumān fī Taʾrīkh Ahl al-Zamān* (ms., Pairs, B.N., 1842–1844; in process of publication, Cairo, 1987–); Ibn Taghrī-Birdī, *Al-Nujūm al-Zāhira fī Mulūk Miṣr wa'l-Qāhira*, 9 vols. (Berkeley, 1915–1916). Yet the only Arab historian

to have created a theory of political economy remains Ibn Khaldūn, *Al-Muqaddima* (English translation by Franz Rosenthal, 3 vols., New York, 1958).

3. Prominent among modern authors who have speculated over the rise and decline of Egypt's medieval economy are: Wilhelm Heyd, *Histoire du commerce du Levant au Moyen-Age* (2nd ed., translated and enlarged from the German original by F. Reynaud, Leipzig, 1885–1886); Claude Cahen, numerous articles, several compiled in *Makhzūmiyyāt, études sur l'historie économique et financière de l'Égypte médiévale* (Leiden, 1977); Subhi Y. Labib, *Handelsgeschichte Ägyptens im Spätmittelalter (1171–1517)* (Wiesbaden, 1965); Ira Lapidus, *Muslim Cities in the Later Middle Ages* (Cambridge, 1967); Eliyahu Ashtor, *L'histoire des prix et des salaires dans l'orient médiévale* (Paris, 1969), 267–382; *Levant Trade in the Later Middle Ages* (Princeton, 1983).

4. The proponent of this thesis is, most notably, Immanuel Wallerstein, *The Modern World System*, vols. 1 and 2 (New York, 1974, 1979). But Janet L. Abu-Lughod had recently refined Wallerstein's concepts of commercial interaction in her *Before European Hegemony, The World System A.D. 1250–1350* (Oxford, 1989), which presents the most innovative, yet carefully reasoned, analysis of the medieval world economy to date.

5. The following remarks are submitted hypothetically. Replete as references to price inflation, Nile innundations, or commercial transactions may be, they do not furnish a basis for a definitive analysis of the Egyptian economy between 1468 and 1517. Any conclusion, no matter how persuasive, represents an educated guess. Contemporary sources provide neither the proportions of productive land allotted to military grants or private use, nor comprehensive tax registers. To date, no reliable figures for tax yields from any major source of revenue are available. Surviving endowment (*waqf*) deeds may contribute fiscal data heretofore untapped, and writs granted or appropriated by Qāytbāy and al-Ghawrī are studied in chapter 7. But even these sources, promising as they are, cannot compensate for tax inventories—of which only fragments survive. The analyst is therefore compelled to interpret reported shortfalls in revenue to project inadequate yields from formal revenue sources.

6. The Nile crest, marking its primary surge, was measured annually at the Nilometer (*Miqyās*) located at the southern tip of Rawḍā Island, according to the solar calendar devised during the Pharaonic period and maintained by the Coptic Church. The crest usually occurred in mid-Misūrī (early August). But in Dhū'l-Ḥijja 875/May–June 1471, it came three days late. See *Ḥawādith* 4, p. 641, l. 18; *Rawḍ*, f. 185, l. 7 (preflood level of six cubits, fourteen fingers); *Ḥawādith* 4, p. 651, l. 7; *Rawḍ*, f. 187, l. 7; *Badāʾiʿ* 3, p. 17, l. 5 (three days delay); *Ḥawādith* 4, p. 656, l. 4 (peak flood level at eighteen cubits, six fingers). One Egyptian cubit (*dhirāʿ*) equals 66.5 cm.;

one Egyptian finger (*isba*ᶜ) equals 3.125 cm. See H. Rabie, "Some Technical Aspects of Agriculture in Medieval Egypt," in *The Middle East, 700–1900; Studies in Economic and Social History,* ed. A. L. Udovitch (Princeton, 1981), 59–60.

7. For 872 crop prices, see *Ḥawādith* 4, p. 628, l. 16; *Rawḍ,* f. 180-b, l. 22; *Badā'iᶜ* 3, p. 11, l. 20: wheat: 600 dirhams/irdabb (198 liters in Egypt); barley: 240 dr/irdabb; fūl beans; 200 dr/irdabb; rice: 1500 dr/irdabb.

8. In light of staple grain shortfalls throughout 873, the narrative sources quoted price increases every few months. While the flood peaked slightly higher than in 872 (*Rawḍ,* f. 203, l. 32), it stalled several times. Monitors who predicted its behavior based on past precedent had forecast a strong surge with a depth exceeding twenty cubits. But a premature drop resulted in a modest peak. See *Ḥawādith* 4, p. 677, l. 1; *Inbā',* p. 15, l. 1. On price rises for the year, see appendix 2. In Rabīᶜ I 873, wheat brought nine hundred dirhams on the open market. In Rajab 874, it sold for twelve hundred.

9. Ibn Iyās noted a temporary drop in grain prices during Rajab 875/ December 1470–January 1471 (*Badā'iᶜ* 3, p. 55, l. 22). When they began to climb again at year's end (*Inbā',* p. 431, l. 1), Qāytbāy suspended his muḥtasib's prerogative of price fixing, reducing all prices to a level commensurate with supply. 878/1473–1474 witnessed a bumper crop with correspondingly low prices (*Inbā',* p. 477, l. 9), while violent hail storms and an erratic surge diminished the harvest of 879 (*Badā'iᶜ* 3, pp. 97, l. 4; 100, l. 5). Between 879 and 888, Ibn Iyās (now the sole narrative writer for Qāytbāy's reign) reported no price data whatsoever. Allowing for his marginal interest in commodity tariffs, this nine-year lapse suggests by its void the lack of spectacular changes up or down. Only once in this interval did Ibn Iyās report a crest below nineteen cubits (*Badā'iᶜ* 3, p. 146, l. 17).

10. See appendices 1–2 for Nile crests and staple prices from 888 to 901.

11. See appendix 3 for Nile surges and peaks for the years between 906 and 922.

12. *Badā'iᶜ* 4, p. 477, l. 23.

13. See appendix 4. Only ten references to prices appear among Ibn Iyās' myriad entries. They indicate moderate crop scarcities to 917, a situation due as much to abnormally cold winters as to erratic floods. But between 918 and 922, harvests were bountiful and prices low.

14. U. Haarmann refers to the "wholesale collapse of Egyptian agriculture" during the Circassian period ("Miṣr: 5. The Mamlūk Period," *EI*² 8: 174–75), basing his claim on interpretations of cadasters (*rawāq*) surveying iqṭāᶜ allotments from the royal fisc. Yet these estimates should be compared against comments about relative agrarian prosperity by contemporary historians.

15. References to alarm over minor delays in flood surges: *Ḥawādith* 4, p. 651, l. 7; *Rawḍ,* f. 187, l. 7; *Badāʾiʿ* 3, 17, l. 5 (Dhū'l-Ḥijja 872/June–July 1468: Nile rise ceases for three says; widespread anxiety); *Rawḍ,* f. 247-b, l. 21 (Rabīʿ I 874/September–October 1469: Nile crest low, leaves much land dry); *Inbāʾ,* pp. 203, l. 9; 205, l. 4 (Ṣafar 875/July–August 1470: crest lower than predicted; when rise resumes, populace rush to measuring stations and behave "in heinous and sinful ways, committing acts of fornication, imbibery and hashīsh smoking."); *Badāʾiʿ* 3, pp. 97, l. 14 (Rabīʿ I 879/July–August 1474: overdue crest, widespread concern); 134, l. 11 (Jumādā I 882/August–September 1477: excessively high crest, more than twenty-one cubits; dykes breached, widespread field damage); 146, l. 17 (Rabīʿ II 883/July 1478: peculiar flood profile; erratic surges but steady levels; populace agitated); 155, l. 4 (Jumādā I 884/July–August 1479: Nile crests early on twenty-ninth of Coptic month, Abīb, very rare); 208, l. 4 (Jumādā II 889/June–July 1484: rapid Nile rise causes alarm; when river reached normal flood stage, calm returns); 209, l. 20 (Shaʿbān 889/August–September: flood recedes rapidly leaving much land untouched; grain prices rise); 211, l. 3 (Ramaḍān 889/September–October: river rises out of season, but too late for crop benefit); 241, l. 20 (Rajab 892/June–July 1486: Nile rise halts temporarily; widespread alarm); 304, l. 7 (Dhū'l-Qaʿda 899/August–September 1494: River ceases rising for several days; grain hoarding); *vol. 4,* p. 66, l. 2 (Ṣafar 910/July–August 1504: Nile stops rising for six days; grain hoarding); 117, l. 15 (Rabīʿ I 913/July–August 1507: Nile rises in rapid surges); 133, l. 17 (Rabīʿ II 914/July–August 1508: second high flood; surges of fifty fingers in a single day; only two equivalent surges recorded since the Arab conquest); 188, l. 8 (Jumādā I 916/August–September 1510: crest late; sultan orders complete reading of Koran at Nilometer); *vol. 5,* p. 52, l. 3 (Jumādā I 922/June–July 1516: Nile rises too slowly off-season; fear of low flood).

16. In Ṣafar 873/August–September 1468, the river failed to reach a projected crest of twenty cubits and fell rapidly. Nile officials had calculated the high level on the basis of alluvium deposits observed and compared with former patterns of silting. Such a miscalculation had never occurred before since records were kept of the river's behavior. See *Ḥawādith* 4, p. 677, l. 1; *Inbāʾ,* p. 15, l. 1; *Rawḍ,* f. 203, l. 32.

17. *Badāʾiʿ,* 4 p. 193, l. 19.

18. Ibid., p. 230, l. 22.

19. The regime's ceremonials to celebrate the crest are described in detail. These rituals involved the opening of dykes feeding canals surrounding the city. Descending from customs that evolved during the Pharaonic era, these observances annually renewed the government's mediation between God and the mass of cultivators. By tradition, the sultan and caliph ordered the marshal (*atābak*) to breach the dyke with a golden spade and perfume the Nilometer

scale with saffron. For examples during the period: *Ḥawādith* 4, 674, l. 13; *Inbāʾ*, 11, l. 2; *Rawḍ*, f. 202, l. 1 (Muḥarram 873/July–August 1468: the atābak Qurqmās breaches the dyke and annoints the scale); *Inbāʾ*, 205, l. 20; *Badāʾiʿ* 3, pp. 52, l. 15 (Ṣafar 875/July–August 1470: Sultan orders lavish dyke-breaching ceremony to distract masses from Sūwār rebellion); 267, l. 6 (Ramaḍān 894/July–August 1489: during breaching ritual, many spectators, including religious dignitaries, break their fast due to extreme heat); 284, l. 9 (Shawwāl 896/August–September 1491: Nile crests on eve of ʿĪd al-Fiṭr; breaching is thus scheduled to follow immediately; two days of festivities); al-Sakhāwī, *Dhayl*, f. 250-b, l. 5 (Ramaḍān 899/June–July 1494: Sultan debuts his son's coming of age during breaching ceremony); *Badāʾiʿ* 3, p. 310, l. 6 (Dhū'l-Qaʿda 900 (July–August 1496: Atābak Azbak presides over his final dyke breaching); 323, l. 9 (Dhūʾl-Qaʿda 901/July–August 1496: Atābak Timrāz supervises breaching while plotting mounts during sultan's coma); *vol.* 4, p. 18, l. 18 (Muḥarram 907/July–August 1501: Atābak Qāyt al-Rajabī refuses to attend breaching due to rival's assassination threat); 96, l. 22 (Rabīʿ I 912/July–August 1506: Atābak Qurqmās thrown from his horse into canal during ceremony; forced to preside in soaked uniform); 325, l. 9 (Jumādā II 919/August–September 1513: Atābak Ṣūdūn al-ʿAjamī organizes spectacular procession for dyke breaching; entourage preceded by elephants bearing his standards); 389, l. 13 (Jumādā II 920/July–August 1514: Nile rises again after dyke breaching; bad omen); 396, l. 14 (Shaʿbān 920/September–October 1514: Boats carrying caterers for breaching ceremony sink, festival tainted).

20. Heinz Halm, *Ägypten nach den mamlukischen Lehenregistern* (Wiesbaden, vol. 1: Oberägypten und das Fayyūm [1979], vol. 2: Das Delta [1982]). Halm's primary sources are Ibn al-Jīʿān, *Al-Tuḥfat al-Sanīya bi-Asmāʾ al-Bilād al-Miṣrīya* (Cairo, 1898, reprint, 1974) and Ibn Duqmāq, *Kitāb al-Intiṣār li-Wāsiṭat ʿIqd al-Amṣār* (Cairo, 1892, 1896). See vol. 1, pp. 30–34.

21. By Qāytbāy's time, many iqṭāʿs no longer yielded the sums recorded in cadasteral registers decades earlier. So many had been subdivided to provide allotments for new officers that they now produced insufficient income for an amīr's needs, not to mention his retainers'. In Ramaḍān 897/June–July 1492, Ibn Iyās stated that even allotments freed by plague deaths and held in reserve could not satisfy the recruits, since their maximum annual output now rarely exceeded thirty thousand dirhams (roughly twenty-four silver dirhams to one dīnār, but three hundred debased copper dirhams per gold coin) (Badāʾiʿ 2, p. 292, l. 12, 22). Qāytbāy deprived retired Inālī veterans of their estates to guarantee that none of his own trainees did without.

22. On dyke repair missions: *Inbāʾ*, p. 43, l. 16; *Badāʾiʿ* 3, p. 25, l. 7 (Jumādā I 873/November–December 1468: Timrāz al-Shamsī sets out for

western Delta to repair dykes breached by Bedouin); *Inbāʾ*, p. 221, l. 16 (Rabīʿ II 875/September–October 1470: Timrāz returns from al-Gharbīya); *Badāʾiʿ* 4, p. 159, l. 2 (Rabīʿ II 915/July–August 1509: Dyke in al-Jīza Province ruptures, field damage; major restoration expedition but inept repairs); *vol. 5*, pp. 8, l. 7; 12, l. 23 (Muḥarram 922/February–March 1516: Sultan sends Ṭūmānbāy to inspect Fayyūm dyke); 19, l. 18 (Ṣafar 922/March–April 1516: Sultan dissatisfied with progress of Fayyūm dyke restoration, which has run over thirty thousand dīnārs; inspects it personally); 55, l. 20 (Jumādā II 922/July 1516: Viceroy inspects work on Fayyūm dyke). Only one reference to any other reclamation project occurred during either reign: *vol. 4*, p. 104, l. 20 (Shawwāl 1507/February–March 1507: Sultan orders iqṭāʿ holders to restore fallow land).

23. *Badāʾiʿ* 4, p. 327, l. 5.

24. Ibid., p. 408, l. 8.

25. Ibn Iyās described the harrowing consequences of al-Ghawrī's planned levy of five thousand Bedouin cavalrymen who would precede his expedition to Aleppo in Rabīʿ II 922/May–June 1516 (*Badāʾiʿ* 5, 31, l. 19): "They (the Bedouin) descended upon all the villages and demanded from each a sum equivalent to two horsemen's stipend—some one hundred dīnārs. Larger towns were required to yield four riders' stipends—two hundred dīnārs. When the populace of these districts: Sharqīya, Gharbīya, and Upper Egypt, learned of this, they abandoned their lands with the crops in the ground and took flight. Some fields reverted to waste after this mobilization. When the officers ascertained the disaster, they complained to the sultan. The amīrs rebuked him, saying: 'We agreed to travel with you, and now our lands are ruined. On what shall we live, and how shall we pay our debts when we depart?' Heeding their charge, the sultan canceled the levy. . . . If his first order had been carried out, all Egypt would have been devastated and dreadful famine would have resulted from land reverting to fallow. Praise be to God for this reversal!"

26. *Ḥawādith* 4, p. 631, l. 6.

27. Ibid., p. 710, l. 22.

28. *Inbāʾ*, p. 72, l. 14.

29. *Rawḍ*, ff. 181-b, l. 19; 184, l. 6. Ibn Taghrī-Birdī once again attributed their increasing predation to government indifference. See *Ḥawādith* 4, p. 653, l. 13.

30. *Rawḍ*, f. 220, l. 21; *Inbāʾ*, p. 119, l. 10.

31. *Rawḍ*, ff. 240-b, l. 29; 247, l. 7; *Inbāʾ*, pp. 123, l. 16; 126, l. 8; 131, l. 1.

32. On Bedouin revolts through Qāytbāy's and al-Ghawrī's reigns: *Inbāʾ*, pp. 153, l. 8 (Jumādā I 874/November–December 1469: officer ambushed in Buḥayra); 192, l. 12 (Muḥarram 875/July 1470: Bedouin plunder Buḥayra; resident prefect requests reinforcements); 195, l. 9 (same month: Atābak Azbak leads expedition to Buḥayra); 291, l. 3; *Badāʾiʿ* 3, p. 60, l. 20 (Dhū'l-Ḥijja 875/May–June 1471: Chamberlain leads contingent to Sharqīya after reports of severe plundering by Saʿd and Wāʾil tribes); *Inbāʾ*, pp. 427, l. 15; 433, l. 9 (Dhū'l-Qaʿda 876/April–May 1472: Banū Ḥarām ravage vicinity of al-Khānkāh; local residents vent their outrage against sultan's tax collector); 443, l. 6; *Badāʾiʿ* 3, pp. 71, l. 18 (Dhū'l-Ḥijja 876/May–June 1472: Saʿd and Wāʾil feuding resumes; Cairo threatened); 102, l. 12 (Shaʿbān 879/December 1474–January 1475: Bedouin raiders capture and strip Mamlūk officer in vicinity of Cairo); 105, l. 6 (Dhū'l-Qaʿda 879/March–April 1475: ʿAzāla tribesmen invade Jīza and steal horses from royal herd; reprisal detachment finds no culprits); 119, l. 2 (Muḥarram 881/April–May 1476: Atābak pursues brigands of Labīdh tribe into desert where his soldiers suffer terribly); 120, l. 18 (Jumādā I 881/August–September 1476: Yashbak returns from Upper Egypt after futile expedition against Ibn ʿUmar tribe); 232, l. 12 (Shawwāl 891/October 1486: Expedition sent to Buḥayra retreats without scoring victory); 253, l. 5 (Rajab 893/June–July 1488: Sultan hears rumors of Bedouin plotting revolt to topple him); *vol. 4*, pp. 25, l. 18 (Shaʿbān 907/February–March 1502: al-Ghawrī's prefect of Gharbīya frustrated by Bedouin; received contemptuous title of "Milk Bearer"); 51, l. 18 (Dhū'l-Qaʿda 908/April–May 1503: Bedouin marauding in Delta and Valley becomes endemic; iqṭāʿ holders fear for their estates); 96, l. 18 (Rabīʿ I 912/July–August 1506: Bedouin rupture dykes in Buḥayra, flood granaries); 104, l. 22 (Shawwāl 912/February–March 1507: Sharqīya Bedouin capture caravan conveying sultan's assets); 115, l. 16 (Ṣafar 913/June–July 1507: Cairo alarmed over escape of Bedouin criminals from prison; no inquiry by regime); 180, l. 2 (Muḥarram 916/April–May 1510: Ṭūmānbāy leads expedition to Upper Egypt to prevent feuding during harvest); 217, l. 6 (Ṣafar 917/May 1511: Ṭūmānbāy returns after failing to capture any Bedouin).

33. *Inbāʾ*, p. 122, l. 5.

34. On sultan reconfirming shaykhs or acknowledging a son's assumption of authority: *Badāʾiʿ* 2, pp. 60, 3. 18 (Dhū'l-Ḥijja 875/May–June 1471: Sultan appoints new shaykh of Sharqīya Province); 148, l. 12 (Shaʿbān 883/October–November 1478: Shaykh's reinstatement after ten years's imprisonment); 297, l. 2 (Dhū'l-Qaʿda 898/August–September 1493: Sultan confirms shaykh of Huwāra tribe in Upper Egypt).

35. *Badāʾiʿ* 4, pp. 66, l. 21; 72, l. 21; 270, l. 21.

36. *Badāʾiʿ* 3, p. 68, l. 17.

37. *Badāʾiʿ* 4, p. 371, l. 21.

38. *Ḥawādith* 4, p. 695, l. 16; *Inbāʾ*, p. 44, l. 16; *Rawḍ*, f. 212, l. 8; *Badāʾiʿ* 3, p. 25, l. 19.

39. On executions: *Inbāʾ*, pp. 119, l. 1 (Muḥarram 874/July–August 1469: beheadings); 139, l. 17 (Rabīʿ I 874/September–October 1468: threat of burning alive); 326, l. 17 (Ṣafar 876/July–August 1471: scourging and nailing in Cairo); 330, l. 13; *Badāʾiʿ* 3, p. 62, l. 18 (same month: bisection; vengeance by relatives); *Inbāʾ*, p. 445, l. 12 (Dhū'l-Ḥijja 876/May–June 1472: crucifixion); *Badāʾiʿ* 3, pp. 106, l. 11 (Muḥarram 880/May–June 1475: drawing and quartering); 146, l. 10 (Rabīʿ II 883/July 1478: decapitation and parading of head); 147, l. 15 (Jumāda II 883/August–September 1478: suspension from hooks); 234, l. 12 (Dhū'l-Qaʿda 891/October–November 1486: bisection); 240, l. 4 (Jumāda I 892/April–May 1487: mass execution, sale of survivors into slavery "at prices below those of blacks"); *vol. 4*, pp. 46, l. 11 (Jumāda II 908/December 1502: suspension); 52, l. 8 (Dhū'l-Qaʿda 908/April–May 1503: flaying and burning); 63, l. 7 (Dhū'l-Qaʿda 909/April–May 1504: suspension); 116, l. 8 (Rabīʿ I 913/July–August 1507: suspension); 121, l. 9 (Jumāda II 913/October–November 1507: bisection; 186, l. 6 (Rabīʿ I 916/June–July 1510: decapitation); 194, l. 14 (Jumāda II 916/September–October 1510: suspension); 229, l. 18 (Rabīʿ II 917/June–July 1511: flaying, stuffing of skin as trophy for display in Cairo); 238, l. 12 (Jumāda II 917/August–September 1511: bisection of escapees from prison); 324, l. 20 (Jumāda II 919/August–September 1513: flaying and stuffing); *vol. 5*, p. 8, l. 21 (Muḥarram 922/February–March 1516: bisection).

40. Al-Ṣayrafī related a fascinating anecdote reported during Yashbak's Saʿīd expedition of 874 (*Inbāʾ*, p. 130, l. 11). In Ṣafar of that month, a captured Bedouin named Ibn Zaʿāziʿ earned the dawādār's particular ire for his "crimes and marauding." Yashbak ordered his death by bisection, but the executioner could not cut his skin even after seventeen sword strokes. The blade was miraculously deflected. The dawādār angrily admonished his swordsman for incompetence but the latter replied: "He possesses some power that wards off my slashes!" When the Bedouin was examined, his arm was found protected by a peculiar metal shield (*khūdha*). Upon its removal, the Bedouin warned the dawādār to restore it since it resisted blows by a spell in his name only and brought death to those who touched it. Paying no heed, Yashbak ordered the executioner to complete his task.

41. For inventories of commodities crafted in Egypt, see: Solomon D. Goitein, *A Mediterranean Society: The Jewish Communities of the Arab World as Portrayed in the Cairo Geniza* (Berkeley, 1967), 1: *Economic Foundations*, 80–91; 4: *Daily Life*, 150–200 (1983) (description of textiles); Claude Cahen,

"Douanes et commerce dans les ports méditerranéens de l'Égypte médiévale d'après le *Minhadj* d'al-Makhzūmī," in *Makhzūmiyyat,* 57–154; Labib, *Handelsgeschichte,* 286–336; Ashtor, *Levant Trade* (primarily lists of spices, cotton and raw materials); see ix–x for lists of ship cargos; George Scanlon, "Fusṭāṭ Expedition Preliminary Report, 1968," pt 1, *JARCE* 11 (1974): 81–92; pt 2, 12 (1975): 69–90; "1971," pt 1, 13 (1975); pt 2, 17 (1980): 77–96; "1972," pt 1, 18 (1981): 57–84; pt 2, 19 (1982): 119–30; "1978," 21 (1984): 1–38.

42. See Labib, *Handelsgeschichte,* for sugar processing: 186, 219, 251–55, 298, 319, 323, 421–23; oil production: 39, 45, 77, 101, 206, 239, 255, 292, 318–22, 340, 478.

43. *Ḥawādith* 4, p. 673, l. 9. See also *Inbāʾ,* pp. 9, l. 13; 483, l. 12. Al-Ṣayrafī described Yashbak's stratagem for pressing laborers into service on his dyke repair projects. In Rabīʿ I 877/August–September 1472, he ensnared persons from the street rabble in Būlāq who came to watch public floggings and ordered them to work or suffer the same fate. Two thousand conscripts were rounded up in this way.

44. *Badāʾiʿ* 3, pp. 150, l. 1; 160, l. 19; 169, l. 23; 240, l. 18; 277, l. 23.

45. *Badāʾiʿ* 4, p. 63, l. 15. Other examples of al-Ghawrī's oppressive restoration policies: pp. 59, l. 13 (Jumādā I 909/October–November 1503: Sultan orders shopkeepers to pay for street debris removal); 110, l. 5 (Dhū'l-Ḥijja 912/April–May 1507: Citadel aqueduct funded illegally); 211, l. 3 (Muḥarram 917/April 1511: canal dredging to be undertaken by local iqṭāʿ holders; threat of foreclosure upon refusal); 228, l. 14 (Rabīʿ II 917/June–July 1511: dredging funded by ad hoc taxes); *vol. 5,* p. 14, l. 4 (Muḥarram 922/February–March 1516: shopkeepers again forced to pay for debris removal).

46. *Badāʾiʿ* 4, p. 56, l. 3.

47. Ibid., pp. 67, l. 23 (Rabīʿ II 910/September–October 1504: Sultan remodels Citadel halls with confiscated marbles); 80, l. 2 (Muḥarram 911/June–July 1505: Sultan redecorates Duhaysha Palace with marbles from Ibn Muzhir residence).

48. André Raymond, *Artisans et commerçants au Caire au XVIIᵉ siècle* (Damascus, 1973), 1:129–36, 160, 173–83, 203–43, 229–36; Nelly Hanna, *An Urban History of Būlāq in the Mamlūk and Ottoman Periods* (Cairo, 1983), 7–32.

49. *Badāʾiʿ* 4, p. 204, l. 8.

50. Qāytbāy's widely publicized investments in caravansarays were motivated in part by his financial interest in long-term trade, where profits could still support high rents and tariffs. Al-Ghawrī rennovated the Khān al-Khalīlī

Bazaar, although only after he had assumed legal ownership over the land it occupied with rights to shopkeepers' rent. He also commissioned construction of a new slave market, an indicator of continued large revenues from this trade. See *Badāʾiʿ* 4, pp. 230, l. 7; 237, l. 7; 243, l. 15; 404, l. 23.

51. *Inbāʾ*, p. 203, l. 21.

52. Ashtor, *Levant Trade*, 9–14, 17–25, 44–46, 64–77.

53. On international commerce: *Inbāʾ*, p. 428, l. 4; *Badāʾiʿ* 3, p. 70, l. 17 (Dhū'l-Qaʿda 876/April–May 1472: Ship with European merchants and their black slaves sinks in Nile); *Inbāʾ*, p. 481, l. 8 (Rabīʿ I 877/August–September 1472: Europeans attack vessel bearing merchants from Maghrib); Ibn al-Ḥimṣī, *Ḥawādith*, f. 72, l. 15 (Ramaḍān 883/November–December 1478: European merchants held liable for one thousand loads of spice); al-Sakhāwī, *Dhayl*, ff. 210-b, l. 18 (Shawwāl 896/August–September 1491: Royal merchant leads trade delegation to India); 231-b, l. 19 (Shaʿbān 898/May–June 1493: arrival of ships from Kālikūt at Jidda); 249, l. 28 (Rajab 899/April–May 1494: arrival of Indian ships at Jidda); 242-b, l. 25 (Shawwāl 899/July–August 1494: Sultan's eunuch agent returns to Jidda from India); 267, l. 30 (Rajab 900/March–April 1495: ships at Jidda from Kālikūt); *Badāʾiʿ* 4, pp. 103, l. 2 (Shaʿbān 912/December 1506–January 1507: Ships from Egypt sink in Red Sea); 139, l. 3 (Rajab 914/October–November 1508: Nāẓir al-khāṣṣ returns home from fleet inspection in Rashīd); 160, l. 16 (Jumādā I 915/August–September 1509: same official returns from inspection in Alexandria); 193, l. 8; 194, l. 19 (Jumādā II 916/September–October 1510: Sultan, then atābak prepare to examine port defenses in Alexandria); 196, l. 19 (Shaʿbān 916/November–December 1510: Sultan surveys scale model of Alexandria harbor, plans rennovations).

54. See Ahmad Darraj, *L'Égypte sous le règne de Barsbay* (Damascus, 1961), 222–37; Ashtor, *Levant Trade*, 278–83; Labib, *Handelsgeschichte*, 355–61.

55. On the fiscal status of deceased merchants: *Inbāʾ*, pp. 211, l. 1 (Rabīʿ I 875/August–September 1470: obituary of Khawāja kārimī merchant Shams al-Dīn Muḥammad ibn Kursūn who leaves his children substantial assets; sultan waives some claims due to his charity); 478, l. 4 (Rabīʿ I 877/August–September 1472: obituary of spice trader; leaves vast fortune; owes sultan thirty thousand dīnārs); *Badāʾiʿ* 3, pp. 113, l. 6 (Shaʿbān 880/December 1475: death of royal trader in Mamlūks; large estate); 207, l. 16 (Jumādā I 889/May–June 1484; obituary of kārimī merchant who holds royal patent); 208, l. 1 (same month: death of merchant who leaves large estate; no mention of confiscation); Ibn al-Ḥimṣī, *Ḥawādith*, f. 150-b, l. 14 (Ṣafar 900/November 1494: death of Khawāja merchant; sultan refuses to pilfer his estate—in excess of one hundred thousand dīnārs); *Badāʾiʿ* 4, pp. 108, l. 4 (Dhū'l-Qaʿda 912/

March–April 1507: obituary of silk merchant who stashes four thousand dīnārs below his shop floor); 169, l. 22 (Dhū'l-Qaᶜda 915/February–March 1510: death of merchant well endowed with money and mass, "one of the fattest of God's creatures"; very miserly); 373, l. 4 (Rabīᶜ I 920/April–May 1514: obituary of Khawāja Shams al-Dīn al-Ḥalabī, possessor of vast fortune; arrested by al-Ghawrī for impiety as excuse to seize estate).

56. The pepper monopoly was abolished by Sultan Jaqmaq in 1449. See Ashtor, *Levant Trade*, 308.

57. *Badāʾiᶜ* 4, pp. 214, l. 7 (Ṣafar 917/May 1511); 375, l. 10 (Rabīᶜ I 920/April–May 1514).

58. On European merchants and embassies in the later periods of both reigns: *Badāʾiᶜ* 3, p. 150, l. 10 (Dhū'l-Ḥijja 883/February–March 1479: Qāytbāy sends khawāja to ruler of Catalonia with gift); al-Sakhāwī, *Dhayl*, f. 248, l. 39 (Rajab 899/April–May 1494: Genoese merchants arrive at Alexandria); *Badāʾiᶜ* 4, pp. 255, l. 7 (Muḥarram 918/March–April 1512: Ambassador from king of France arrives); 257, l. 15 (same month: Al-Ghawrī receives French ambassador's gifts); 268, l. 13 (Rabīᶜ I 918/May–June 1512: al-Ghawrī drapes French ambassador with robe of honor).

59. *Badāʾiᶜ* 4, p. 149, l. 8.

60. *Badāʾiᶜ* 3, p. 237, l. 2.

61. *Badāʾiᶜ* 4, p. 423, l. 21.

6

COPING WITH CRISIS:
OVERT INERTIA

The dilemmas confronting the Mamlūk sultanate may well have defied substantive remedy. Because of its peculiar evolution as an elite focused on static perpetuation, the military caste was ill-disposed for implementing change. And since its subordinate groups endured regime extractions by concentrating their creative efforts on concealment or deception, they too had little incentive for altering their deployment of capital or techniques of production. Accordingly, the sultanate in its final decades exhibited the external signs of a state mired in the inertia of its own devices. Evoking minimal loyalty from its subjects, such a regime would seem ripe for conquest by a foreign power. Certainly, Ibn Iyās interpreted the sultanate's decay in this fashion as he summed up events leading to Marj Dābiq as the final act of a drama whose outcome was foregone.[1]

Yet had foreign affairs taken a different course, there is little tangible evidence for the imminent demise of the Mamlūk Empire. The regime had adapted to the now-incessant rhythm of troop insurrections and ultimatums. No civilian element of society possessed the means or the will to overthrow it. We must therefore juxtapose Ibn Iyās' opinion against the ploys all parties involved in either the economy or politics devised to survive, and even prosper. For many did prosper in the face of adversity.

How then did both the elite and its subjects cope with their respective dilemmas, and what implications did their tactics have for the future evolution of society in Egypt? The following proposals are conjectural. While they rest on evidence culled from narrative and archival sources, any hypotheses offered about clandestine survival strategies can only speculate on ulterior motives or hidden agendas. No chronicler who observed these issues firsthand penned a formal treatise summarizing the regime's covert means of countering its problems. Nowhere are the masses' attempts at diffusing exploitation described as a coherent response. The modern historian must therefore assume either an insensitivity of contemporary observers to these stratagems or a deliberate refusal to acknowledge their existence. How shrewdly these writers perceived the workings of an intricate design that staved off disaster with a bewildering array of adroit ploys remains an unresolved mystery of Islamic historiography. This chapter does not purport to settle the enigma in any definitive way. But it will identify these ploys lurking within the chronicles' myriad references to procurement and confiscation, beneficence and cruelty, hoarding and sheltering of assets. If the chronicles' silence about hidden agendas at best heightens debate on these hypotheses, they nonetheless provide a rationale for the behavior of all parties engrossed in this process that heretofore has eluded any commentator, medieval or modern. Such a rationale may have indelibly imprinted attitudes toward regime intervention, deployment of assets, dependency versus self-sufficiency, and security of person and property on the Egyptian popular mind.

The Context of Clientage: Primacy of Hidden Service

Mamlūk sultans presided over a hierarchy of officials they inherited from their Fāṭimid and Ayyūbid predecessors. During the Circassian period, several offices, in particular those involved with finances, were substantially modified, reduced in authority, or eliminated outright.[2] The titles senior executives or bureaucrats received grandiosely proclaimed their formal callings. But by the fifteenth century, stated charges rarely embraced the vital services a sultan's "trusted men" performed. Bureaucracies of states in the central Muslim regions were composed of informal and highly fluid networks of retainers connected to their employers by either fraternal ties if they were military peers or patronage bonds if they were learned civilians. The relationships underlying such ties never attained the legal stature they enjoyed in medieval Europe since Islamic law recognized no corporate ties between members of the Muslim Commonwealth.[3] Our use of terms such as "peer" or "liege" must be applied with caution as the inexact approximations they are. But nonetheless, the imperial bureaucracy of the later Mamlūk State had clearly developed an administrative style unique to itself. This style rested on intimate interaction of the ruler, his powerful colleagues of the military caste, and swarms of civil clerks who translated their edicts into policy, gathered the intelligence they required and garnered revenues they expected.

The network that brought the autocrat and his great men into a symbiotic relationship with their officialdom relied on bonds forged through years of personal contact. Individuals of proven accounting, legal, or scholarly skills, frequently from humble origins, assumed positions of considerable influence. The relationship they nurtured with their patrons was often remarkably close and qualifies the formal barriers of caste dividing the military and civil elites of the Mamlūk State. Yet this relationship remained one of dependence in an apanage system that granted the militarists proprietorship over the realm. Such power as a civil bureaucrat wielded, substantial as it might appear, rarely departed from the aegis of his patron's authority. Existing as his employer's creature, a bureaucrat was not allowed to forget that those who rose high at a sponsor's behest might fall low indeed when his ire was aroused—or if his special needs were not addressed to his liking.

Creation of client networks by Qāytbāy and al-Ghawrī during the early phases of their reigns was a critical aspect of their consolidation. Individuals who gained prominence in their respective circles derived from a broad range of callings. The talents they brought with them provided their sovereigns with expertise in both formal matters such as supervision of protocol or collection of taxes, and unofficial tasks such as embezzlement or spying. Persons whose stature as orthodox Muslims might raise eyebrows because of their Coptic heritage or deviant beliefs often attained influential ministerial posts because of their dependence on the sultan's favor. But regardless of career tracks, all bureaucrats who emerged prominently in the chronicles owed their advancement to a patron's personal endorsement.

Qāytbāy's dealings with officials exhibited tension between the sultan's public piety and his covert requirements. This tension manifested itself early when he chastised one of his more trusted dīwān ministers, ʿAlam al-Dīn Abū'l-Ḥasan ibn al-Ḥayṣam, a convert and senior accountant of the Privy Fund (*Musṭawfī al-khāṣṣ*).[4] Although adept in laundering monies diverted into this fund, Ibn al-Ḥayṣam persisted with his "inclinations toward the Christian religion." Similar to many Copts who abandoned their church for political advantage, Ibn al-Ḥayṣam shunned Islamic observances whenever possible. He ultimately was summoned before his sovereign who upbraided him for stealing away from Friday prayer sessions at the Citadel mosque while his colleagues in other bureaus dutifully attended. When Ibn al-Ḥayṣam refused to mend his ways, he was flogged. Yet Qāytbāy made no move to dismiss him from his accountancy. Whatever Ibn al-Ḥayṣam's devotional lapses, his skills at fattening the Privy Fund necessitated his retention. When he died, possibly of diabetes due to his "love of sugar" in Jumādā I 874/November-December 1469, he was buried among other Muslims, over protests of several shaykhs who disputed his convictions.

Bureaucrats and judges recognized early in their careers that security of post and freedom of speech rested on their patrons' whims rather than on de-

nunciation of rivals. When, in Ṣafar 875/July-August 1470, a quarrel erupted
between two jurists over a madrasa oration, both enlisted their Mamlūk sponsor's support.[5] The lecture, presumably touching on a controversial interpretation of jurisprudence, was delivered by one Abū Bakr al-Abshīhī, a Shāfiʿī
deputy judge who held a chair in the Jānibakīya College. When his oration,
preached at another institution, aroused the wrath of the sultan's personal
imām, Burhān al-Dīn al-Karakī, al-Abshīhī wasted no time on righteous defense of his tenets. He forthwith sought out Yashbak min Mahdī, "who was
favorably disposed toward him." When Yashbak interceded, he "ordered his
restoration to duties. Whoever opposed al-Abshīhī was the dawādār's antago-
nist." Qāytbāy, who had initially sided with his imām in the dispute, now
dropped all charges. His adjutant's good will counted too highly to be risked
on an argument over trifling details by two civil subordinates. For all his posturing as a champion of orthodoxy, Qāytbāy never lost sight of his first priority: retention of his own office. Yashbak's good will was indispensable to that
end, while a jurist's petty deviance was not.

The symbiotic relationship between military and civil notables was vividly apparent in ceremonials held at the court. Following his confirmation as
governor of Damascus at Qāytbāy's hands on 12 Rabīʿ II 875/8 October 1470,
the amīr Barqūq al-Nāṣirī prepared to depart Cairo in an elaborate procession.[6] After he accepted his gold saddle of office and strapped it on his
charger, Barqūq received the acclamation of his fellow officers. Yet when he
swore his oath of fealty, he did so not before Qāytbāy but the latter's chancellor, Zayn al-Dīn ibn Muzhir, the most esteemed civilian on the sultan's
staff. Ibn Muzhir enjoyed Qāytbāy's absolute confidence throughout his
lengthy tenure. In this case, Qāytbāy entrusted his kātib al-sirr with the cau-
tionary homily to a new "vice-sultan" of Damascus. If any provincial officer
were prone toward revolt, it was this second-ranked executive of the realm. Ibn
Muzhir met Barqūq at al-Raydānīya, north of Cairo, and "advised him . . .
that he had not departed from obedience to his great Imām." Ibn Muzhir's
reiteration of Barqūq's homage to his peer-sovereign carried no enforcement
power whatsoever. But his moral authority, matched by no other ʿālim, underscored the importance of harmonious interactions between militarists and
bureaucrats. Obedience mattered even for someone at the zenith of the military
hierarchy because if a viceroy violated his investiture oath, he set a precedent
for backstabbing among all his own civil dependents, not to mention his
Mamlūk adjutants. The kātib al-sirr personified the security gained from unquestioned compliance. Even so bold an amīr as Barqūq would be well-
advised to remember it.

Zayn al-Dīn's son, Badr, rode his father's gownhems to high office. Dem-
onstrating all the ambition and delight in pomp al-Zaynī spurned, this man
exploited his father's reputation to attain offices otherwise destined for a man
of greater experience. In Rajab 876/January 1472, Qāytbāy honored his es-

teemed secretary by granting his son the lucrative superintendency of the Privy Fund (*Niẓārat al-khāṣṣ*).[7] The association of loyalty with filial respect clearly influenced Qāytbāy in his choice for an official essential to his own fiscal aggrandizement. This son would prove a dubious successor to his father, however. Zayn al-Dīn later ruefully acknowledged his offspring's machinations. Yet so long as he lived, Qāytbāy never revoked the son's appointment—despite numerous charges of his graft. In Rabīʿ II 877/August 1472, Qāytbāy bestowed the market inspectorship of Cairo upon Badr al-Dīn, even when he referred "complaints about your son" to his kātib al-sirr.[8] Zayn al-Dīn reacted ambivalently to Qāytbāy's choice, apparently dubious over his son's deportment when installed in a post riddled with so many enticements. Still, Qāytbāy resolutely confirmed Badr al-Dīn in the ḥisba, convinced that the father's authority sufficed to insure the son's timely sharing of bribe money. After Qāytbāy and Zayn al-Dīn had died, Badr would discover how risky his schemes were when a sultan who respected none of his predecessors' clients was enthroned.

Qāytbāy drew upon talents of other savants who gained renown as members of his inner circle. The House of Jīʿān, prospering off the fortune its forebears had amassed in commerce and real estate, engendered several individuals whose wealth negated any need to pilfer monies their patron coveted.[9] Zayn al-Dīn ibn Muzhir was ably served by an assistant from this family, one Abū'l-Barakāt Aḥmad ibn Yaḥyā al-Shāfiʿī.[10] Having first attracted al-Zaynī's notice for his scholastic erudition, Abū'l-Barakāt won Qāytbāy's respect as a bureaucrat whose opinion he valued because "his intellect was exceeded only by his loyalty." "This Abū'l-Barakāt was unswervingly devoted to the sultan's interests." Such a credit is telling in its brevity. Abū'l-Barakāt's acumen assuredly enhanced his stature in his contemporaries' eyes. But it was his reliability as a client that earned him Qāytbāy's heartfelt eulogy at his funeral: "If I could redeem his life for any amount of money, I would have spared no sum." By implication, revenue was ephemeral while devotion waxed eternal. Only the latter guaranteed steady supplies of the former.

Al-Ghawrī evinced less concern about the moral scruples of men he gathered around him and sought more pragmatic means of coercion. His appointment patterns counterbalanced any official placed within reach of lucrative funds by placement of someone else to watch him. In Rajab 910/December 1504, the rectorship of the venerated Badawīya Shrine in the Delta came vacant when al-Ghawrī acceded to complaints over malfeasance and arrested its incumbent.[11] The sultan invested the former rector's son with his father's post, eschewing any inquiries into the former's past record of fiscal dealings. But he also installed a Mamlūk amīr, an assistant guard captain, as supervisor charged with monitoring the rector's dispensation of the shrine's substantial endowment. Presumably, this officer could be relied on to collect a portion of any funds secreted from his master in Cairo. Al-Ghawrī often dispensed with interviews of potential candidates for dīwān or scholarly posts. Indifferent to matters of professional propriety, he chose the more efficient method of installing a guardian who exercised shadow authority over the formal appointee. Accordingly, in his reign sons often succeeded to their parents' sinecures in the dīwāns and madrases as a matter of convenience (and profit, since a fee was often required) with little regard for their qualifications. So long as they fulfilled their covert functions, impelled by fear of reprisal, they were left installed.

Because of his aversion to tedious interrogations, al-Ghawrī readily reconfirmed individuals who had previously served his senior adjutants. In Rabīᶜ II 911/August 1505, the sultan granted the superintendency of waqfs in the affluent Zimāmīya College to the qāḍī Ibrāhīm al-Sharābīshī.[12] This appointment might have seemed routine since the judge's skills as a manager of endowments were widely acknowledged. But this individual had formerly worked for al-Ghawrī's previous marshal, Qāyt al-Rajabī, now disgraced and exiled. Al-Ghawrī's decision may have reflected his awareness that civil clients transferred their allegiance fickly according to circumstance. His own beneficence might well ensure devoted service from a grateful scholar who had made an unlucky first choice of patrons. Al-Ghawrī frequently granted amnesty to individuals he had earlier imprisoned. Admittedly, his clemency reached its peak during his eye infection. On 1 Jumādā I 919/5 July 1513, fearing blindness, al-Ghawrī granted writs of amnesty to three fiscal officials he had dismissed.[13] A former director of the mint caught counterfeiting, a previous secretary of Mamlūks who who absconded with bonus money, and a deceased dawādār's steward suspected of tampering with his master's estate were all welcomed from seclusion. Two were offered positions in the sultan's entourage while the third accepted formal retirement. Al-Ghawrī systematized a trend toward publicly condemning dīwān officials for their embezzlement, sending them to jail, and then allowing their reentry into his coterie of clients. Because they had already demonstrated their skills, individuals convicted of crimes in someone else's service were doubly valuable. Their new patron could count on their gratitude for restoration to lucrative posts along with proven talents.

Covert services can be readily discerned in chroniclers' comments on a client's conduct, often appended to an offhand statement about arrest or confiscation. A patron's unspoken expectations rarely received elaboration, however, and must be deduced from piecing together disparate bits of information about a bureaucrat's machinations. These functions can be categorized as bribery, fiscal procurement, and intelligence gathering. Since each had a long history in the Egyptian dīwāns, examples which provoked the chroniclers' rancor in the Circassian period betoken devices well-honed over time.

While publicly denouncing fiscal corruption, Qāytbāy accepted payments for offices even when the aspirant showed few qualifications for the post he sought. The sultan collected bribes from both officers and civilians wishing writs of appointment. Soon after his enthronement, as he pondered whom to assign provincial governorships, Qāytbāy granted important garrison commands in Damascus and Aleppo solely for cash.[14] Theoretically, officers competing for such assignments had demonstrated a certain level of competence to warrant their promotions. But the sultan's decisions often turned on money. Dispensing of fiscal offices closer to home raised more vexing questions of probity since abuses might incur angry protests that marred the sultan's biweekly audiences. One controversial yet illustrative case involved appointment of the amīr Yashbak al-Jamālī to the market inspectorship of Cairo in Rabīʿ II 873/ October-November 1469.[15] While Ibn Taghrī-Birdī, al-Malaṭī and Ibn Iyās concurred in their commendation of Yashbak's tenure, which lasted to 877/ 1472, al-Ṣayrafī cast a critical eye on his discharge of duties.

Claiming that Yashbak never toured markets, stalls, or workshops, al-Ṣayrafī questioned the amīr's familiarity with affairs of commerce. Rather, he allegedly relied on the advice of his assistants, "who derived from wealthy notables and holders of property." These aides focused their reports, which ostensibly listed abuses, on those "who had not given them pre-arranged bribes. Such persons were immediately apprehended, thrashed . . . and then publicly ridiculed by wearing a criminal's cap (*ṭarṭūr*). . . . Even persons weak of eyesight or suffering from influenza were exhibited in this way." How al-Ṣayrafī's denunciation stacks up against the positive, albeit briefer, entries penned by his colleagues eludes assessment. But al-Ṣayrafī did acknowledge Yashbak's piety: "He was religious, devout, observant of prayer and fasting." The historian also wryly noted that this amīr took pains to win approval of prominent figures in Cairo's judiciary. Perhaps the muḥtasib's high standing among legal authorities, stemming from his munificence to their academies, persuaded al-Ṣayrafī's fellows of his worthiness.

Yashbak's employer, Qāytbāy, certainly recognized the primacy of the amīr's hidden obligations. His office had to yield a reliable sum every month. The muḥtasib's disinterest in day-to-day assurance of standards counted for little, especially if civil notables themselves ignored Yashbak's oversights because of his generosity. Qāytbāy routinely installed persons who winked at abuses for a fee. Although plaintiffs often brandished petitions detailing corrupt practices his staff let slip, Qāytbāy gave ear only when he himself was dissatisfied with bribes his subordinates offered for their placement.[16]

Al-Ghawrī also demanded bribes when he chose a bureaucrat or promoted an amīr. Yet Ibn Iyās, upon whom we depend almost exclusively for our cognizance of al-Ghawrī's dealings, dwelled less frequently on upfront payments than al-Ṣayrafī. Nonetheless, he listed myriad instances of embezzlement. Ibn Iyās' reticence may signal al-Ghawrī's operational preferences in comparison with Qāytbāy's. His relative brevity may imply the sultan's awareness that skilled extorters should be encouraged to maximize their takes after placement. It is enlightening that one of the notorious instances of al-Ghawrī's consignment of a lucrative office for money involved a rich landlord who was plainly incompetent. In Muḥarram 918/March-April 1512, al-Ghawrī appointed one Sharaf al-Dīn ibn Rawq as supervisor of the royal storehouses (*Nāẓir al-Khazāʾin al-Sharīfa*).[17] This individual also received the privilege of inventorying the recently confiscated estate of the Jīʿān family, previously mentioned. Al-Ghawrī collected five thousand dīnārs from Ibn Rawq, fully aware of his ineptitude. Ibn Iyās stated that this man threw away vast sums for offices he could not hope to retain: "The irony of his ludicrous case was his large fortune, which he wasted on bribes that produced paltry results. He had previously attempted to buy his appointment to the Shāfiʿī qāḍīship of Egypt, but nothing came of it. Nonetheless, he had already taken to riding a horse in public and other excesses." Only two months elapsed before Ibn Rawq was stripped of the posts he had paid so dearly to obtain. Ibn Iyās attributed the short duration of his term to his unfitness: "He did not succeed, for he knew nothing about their (the storehouses') supervision, nor even how to write up receipts and disbursements. He was an addled bumbler, *always in arrears* (emphasis mine), and no one regretted his fate." Being "always in arrears," was a fault that assuredly outweighed the sums Ibn Rawq handed over initially. One may speculate on al-Ghawrī's calculated estimate of this man's short-term survival time in office, before public outcries would conveniently necessitate his removal. The sultan could predict with precision just how briefly the lout would last until events brought him down. Ibn Rawq's bribe yielded a tidy profit for an appointment that could soon be rectified with an abler replacement. Had Ibn Rawq proven himself more capable at his covert tasks and not fallen "in arrears," he might have retained his office even in the face of complaints. For procurement on the job mattered far more in al-Ghawrī's eyes than a simple bribe. The latter could be paid but once. The former was limited only by the collector's imagination.

Exploiting a dīwān office for procurement could assume several guises. Individuals might be pressured for payments in return for downscaling their tax obligations. Accounts of bureaus dispensing large budgets could be falsified to siphon off percentages from their licit purposes. Receipts from tariff or toll-collecting agencies might be reduced, leaving differences available for pocketing. Opportunities for petty embezzlement abounded if an individual were versed in collection procedures of his dīwān. But whatever the methods an official refined, his efforts were facilitated if he managed several bureaus simultaneously. The phenomenon of multiple officeholding has been scrutinized in previous studies.[18] Its proliferation during the later Mamlūk period paralleled the increased significance of covert services dīwān officials performed under conditions of fiscal crisis. An individual often controlled both the revenue-receiving and -dispensing functions of a bureau and thereby juggled accounts with impunity. Clandestine procurement on the part of dīwānī personnel predated the final decades of Mamlūk rule. Yet its augmented frequency in the narrative sources during al-Ghawrī's tenure implied the substance of its contribution to revenues he received.

That Qāytbāy relied on procurement to the same degree is more problematic. While several chroniclers reported on his reign, they castigated fewer individuals for embezzlement. Since Qāytbāy showed no more scruples than his successor over confiscating fortunes of dīwān officials who had prospered in his service, one must regard the lower incidence of denunciations with skepticism. Yet Qāytbāy did make more gestures toward fiscal propriety by apprehending bureaucrats than al-Ghawrī. These convictions may reflect his stance as a defender of Sharīʿa. Soon after his enthronement, Qāytbāy arrested Khushqadam's wazīr, Qāsim Shughayta.[19] This master of financial manipulation had risen from modest origins precisely because of his skills. He had learned the intricate byways of bribes and kickbacks during his stint as muḥtasib during Īnāl's and Khushqadam's reigns. Whether Qāytbāy seized him primarily as a show of justice or for the wazīr's enormous estate is probably moot. When Ibn Iyās wrote Qāsim's obituary twenty-eight years after his first dismissal, the historian noted that he was reinstated in 889/1484 and reconfirmed in 891/1486.[20] Qāsim may have fallen from grace temporarily following Qāytbāy's accession, but not so low that he could not recoup his losses and penetrate the upper echelons of the dīwān network once again. Ibn Iyās pointedly described Qāsim Shughayta as an adept clerk "with a capacity for performing any task. His acumen was unmatched." Even though he suffered disgrace, his expertise warranted his reappointment.

If celebrated cases of procurement were rare under Qāytbāy, they were ubiquitous under al-Ghawrī. Most incidents came to light in the context of arrests, and this circumstance sheds light on al-Ghawrī's relationship with his dependents. While we cannot discern the majority of conditions al-Ghawrī set for placement of an individual in a particular office, seizure for violating them occurred often enough to hint at their characteristics. They vividly illustrate the fine line between survival and disaster. In Dhū'l-Ḥijja 907/June-July 1502, the supervisor of the Privy Fund, Nāṣir al-Dīn ibn al-Ṣafadī, committed suicide by swallowing a compound of diamond powder rather than submit to al-Ghawrī's interrogation over "sums of money he owed but could not collect."[21] Those who curried their patron's favor supplied their quotas without fail. No one was released unscathed from an inquisition if he had not "settled his account with the sultan."[22] Everyone who supervised a lucrative department tallied up a special account known only to him and his sovereign. Al-Ghawrī allowed his wiliest financiers to occupy several offices at once for reasons cited above. One individual held the Special Bureau (*Dīwān al-Mufrad*), along with the major-domoship (*ustādārīya*), normally reserved for a senior officer, a second the army paymastership (*istifāʾ al-jaysh*) with the chancellorship (*kitābat al-sirr*), still another the guard captaincy (*ri'āsat al-nawba*) with the Special Bureau.[23] When describing the third pairing, Ibn Iyās observed that this joint appointment enabled its incumbent "to extract money in disguise."

Most of the men who attained notoriety in the dīwāns under al-Ghawrī earned such epithets as "corrupt" or "greedy." Yet neither they nor chroniclers who dwelled on their iniquities attributed their downfall to their crimes. Assiduous settling of accounts alone reassured the sultan of his officials' loyalty. Ibn Iyās used the phrase "the sultan's wrath fell on. . ." when he signaled an official's failed attempt at duping his employer. Milking the ra'īya unfairly elicited the monarch's harsh response only when their complaints discomfitted him. Cheating on the patron who installed his client in a lucrative sinecure could never be forgiven, however, and al-Ghawrī ruthlessly prosecuted officials he suspected of pocketing what they owed.[24] For those who never violated his trust, al-Ghawrī showed himself magnanimous, lavishing honors and gifts. And when circumstances compelled al-Ghawrī to dismiss an adept official whose embezzlement sparked a storm of protest, he soon resurfaced to resume his previous activities after a cooling-off period when popular memories of his misdeeds had dimmed.

Intertwined with procurement was spying, the gathering of intelligence on individuals who either posed a potential threat to the sultan or handled revenues copious enough to tempt theft. Clients whose abilities as undercover agents caught a ruler's notice had risen high in courts throughout the Muslim world long before our period. Most Mamlūk sultans relied on their aides's secret briefing to ferret out cells of intrigue. But consonant with his own penchant for conspiracy, al-Ghawrī sought out persons who showed unusual promise as denouncers. The need for spying must be weighed against its effects on the morale of courtiers. In a highly personalized bureaucracy where formal duties counted for less than clandestine service, tension between loyalty and self-aggrandizement pervaded every level of the royal establishment. Similar to the tenuousness of collegiality among amīrs, trust remained ambivalent among clerks who competed for their patrons' favor while amassing personal fortunes they hid whenever possible. The inherent nature of covert service promoted treachery and thus placed a high premium on spying. But no one was more aware of divided loyalties than the monarch who imposed them. A shrewd autocrat like al-Ghawrī might scorn fidelity and yet hold it up as the vital quality demanded of those he used to betray their fellows.

In Rabī' I 916/June-July 1510, al-Ghawrī turned on his confidant, Muḥammad ibn Su'ayda, "who had reported on the people's intrigues and gossip." "This Ibn Su'ayda had become so thick with the sultan that he sat beside him, diverting him in games of chess. He had become dreaded and hated among the populace as an accuser."[25] Al-Ghawrī heeded no complaints against this spy until a judge, Muḥyī al-Dīn ibn al-Naqīb, insinuated his insults against the throne. Ibn Suʿayda had assisted Ibn al-Naqīb in his bid for reinstatement as Shāfiʿī qāḍī, but had subsequently affronted the jurist on the matter of compensation and his litigation of suits brought by Ibn Suʿayda's cronies. Ibn al-Naqīb warned the sultan to beware the deviousness of an informer whose knowledge was dangerous. Even his patron could be embarrassed by stories such a miscreant might spread. Ibn Suʿayda had boasted of his grip over the sultan, whom "he had duped because of his own comeliness." Once alerted to Ibn Suʿayda's slander, al-Ghawrī reacted without remorse. Ibn Suʿayda was summoned to the Duhaysha, flogged, and banished to a desert oasis where he could spin his yarns before local villagers.

Perhaps the most memorable case of a denouncer whose career ended in disgrace was Shams al-Dīn ibn ʿAwaḍ, whom al-Ghawrī first incarcerated in Jumādā I 917/August 1512, but executed three years later.[26] This Ibn ʿAwaḍ's deportment typified a person who, born to poverty, became obsessed with the acquisition of power and wealth. Ibn ʿAwaḍ had been a peasant in the Delta village of Minyat Masīr when he caught the attention of district inspectors who respected his quickness of mind. He administered estates of several amīrs, including the dawādār Azdamur who presented him at the court in Cairo. Al-Ghawrī discerned unusual abilities in this rustic, despite his rude speech. He placed Ibn ʿAwaḍ in charge of the royal household and then assigned him custodianship over the Reserve Fund (*Dhakhīra*). The sultan heaped other fiscal sinecures on Ibn ʿAwaḍ's two sons.

While Ibn ʿAwaḍ's machinations yielded substantial sums he duly shared with his master, his intimidation of colleagues won him al-Ghawrī's abiding admiration. Ibn ʿAwaḍ's web of fear ensnared even muqaddamīn who dreaded his inventory of seditious rumors, all backed with evidence meticulously compiled. Ibn ʿAwaḍ outmaneuvered other courtiers who scheduled access to royal audiences and ultimately held a monopoly over petitioners the monarch heard. "Heaven and Earth thus clamored for his attention!" "He stood so close to the sultan the latter relied on him as his eyes and ears." Ibn ʿAwaḍ's ego was his undoing, however. Powerful rivals who harbored their own ambitions held him in such loathing that they set aside their differences to destroy him. A grand amīr, Khayrbak, prefect of Gharbīya Province, earned Ibn ʿAwaḍ's special animus by exercising his supervisory rights over properties there controlled by a local shaykh allied with the denouncer. When Ibn ʿAwaḍ contested Khayrbak's claims, the prefect informed al-Ghawrī that his intimate was withholding one hundred and fifty thousand dīnārs in revenue from this district alone. Incensed by the disclosure, al-Ghawrī seized Ibn ʿAwaḍ and turned him over to Zaynī Barakāt, who had connived with Khayrbak to foil a mutual enemy. Zaynī Barakāt eagerly assumed responsibility for uncovering the whereabouts of other troves the denouncer had salted away.

Although subjected to tortures, Ibn ʿAwaḍ displayed the stoic fortitude so typical of his peasant upbringing. No torment, including compression of his

skull or wedges under his fingernails, could loosen his tongue. He expired
without revealing the location of riches rumored to exceed the sultan's. Ibn
Iyās mused over this stubborn man's demise. No one attended his funeral and
his wealth remained a secret none could discover. Whether people stayed away
because they feared guilt by association the historian did not say, but he did
find the forlorn prayer reading bereft of mourners "a lesson for those who are
perceptive." Ibn ʿAwaḍ tasted the bitter fate of an agent provocateur who mis-
calculated the limits of his influence. When he angered competitors whose
rank exceeded his own, he was brought down.

The Dynamics of Clientship: Personal Expectations

In light of stress emerging from a client's hidden obligations, what ties joined
him to his patron? How were such bonds initiated and what circumstances
promoted the firming of some into indissoluble symbioses while others failed
with negative consequences for the dependent? Conditions under which ambitious civilians entered into client relations with Mamlūk officers differed
widely. But all turned ultimately on a sense of mutual advantage each would
gain. Despite proliferation of bureaucratic offices during the Circassian period,
the behavior of patron and client invariably implied their mutual awareness of
this advantage.[27] We have noted how sons frequently succeeded to a father's
post. Such positions devolved on offspring because of their presumed tutelage
at their father's side. Few sultans cared about the intrinsic advantage a civilian
family gained from inheritance of office. But they may have recognized how a
client's appreciation for a transition of this kind strengthened the personal
bonding his patron did value. The succession of a "beardless youth" such as
ʿAlāʾ al-Dīn ʿAbd al-Karīm ibn Julūd to his father's post as secretary of
Mamlūks (*kātib al-Mamālīk*) can only be explained by Qāytbāy's presumption
of his gratitude.[28] Although al-Ṣayrafī deemed the younger Julūd as "knowl-
edgeable and intelligent," he obviously brought no expertise to the job. Yet he
observed at close range his father's courting of the sultan's favor, and took
pains to mimic him. Qāytbāy often promoted sons to posts their parent had
administered "well and ably," that is with an eye for their employer's special
wishes. When Qāytbāy mused over candidates who might take on the lucrative
Army Bureau intendency (*mutawallī Dīwān al-Jaysh*) in Rabīʿ II 882/
July-August 1477, he advanced the incumbent's son Yaḥyā ibn Shākir ibn al-
Jīʿān because of the former's "good service" and the family's proven record.[29]
The junior Jīʿān had as yet no opportunity to demonstrate his own qualifications for an office so rife with embezzlement. His house's reputation as devoted
members of the sultan's faction justified his investiture. An untested youth
from a reliable family posed fewer risks than an experienced accountant whose
affiliations remained indeterminate.

Qāytbāy showered benefices on his devoted clients in ceremonials proclaiming his esteem. When the sultan's business agent, the Sharīf ʿAlāʾ al-Dīn al-Kurdī, returned from a sojourn in Damascus and Aleppo overseeing his patron's affairs there, Qāytbāy confirmed him as Syndic of the Prophet's Descendants (*Naqīb al-Ashrāf*), a sinecure yielding a comfortable income from properties endowed for support of the Prophet's lineage.[30] The sultan also granted him the townhouse formerly owned by none other than the deceased historian Ibn Taghrī-Birdī. While the residence originally belonged to Ibn Taghrī-Birdī's father, a prominent amīr, his family presumably lost their claim in favor of the sultan's close associate (*ṣāḥib*). There were few precedents for a civilian, even a sharīf, assuming title to property held by the military caste, but no one protested Qāytbāy's show of gratitude.

The importance of personal ties for securing a post extended beyond the sultan's circle. Officers whose support the sultan coveted often promoted their own candidates. Despite Qāytbāy's advocacy of litigation free from nepotism, he was susceptible to pressures his adjutants might exert. In Rabīʿ II 885/ June-July 1480, Qāytbāy dismissed the Shāfiʿī and Ḥanbalī qāḍīs, Walī al-Dīn al-Asyūṭī and Badr al-Dīn al-Saʿdī, on grounds of their corruption in inheritance rulings.[31] But since both enjoyed the atābak Azbak's favor, the marshal persuaded his sovereign to recall them. Neither had disproved charges of misconduct. Yet since one of Qāytbāy's closest colleagues willed their reinstatement, both received their offices back.

Personal connections between clients and patrons extended throughout the palace, reaching even into the harem. When Qāytbāy's intendent of aids in the vizierate (*muqaddam al-dawla*), Sharaf al-Dīn ibn Gharīb, fired his deputy, one Ibn Najā, for excessive cognizance of "secret fiscal dealings," the latter enrolled his wife in his appeals.[32] Recognizing that any open challenge against Ibn Gharīb was futile, Ibn Najā's spouse immediately sought out Qāytbāy's wife and concubines since she belonged "to their faction" (*jihatihinna*). After these ladies whispered Ibn Najā's grievances in their lord's ear, he ordered his wazīr to summon Ibn Najā for a formal hearing. When Ibn Gharīb was shown to have fired his deputy in favor of another accountant from his circle he found less threatening, Qāytbāy dropped all charges against the dismissee and restored his assets but let Ibn Gharīb's replacement stand. Two conflicting ties, one to household, the other to a superior client, were contending for the sultan's decision in this instance. He astutely resolved them without disrupting Ibn Gharīb's profitable web of associates.

A client's success in the sultan's entourage required an intuitive grasp of his implicit obligations. When an official accepted his diploma of investiture, he understood exactly what his employer expected of him. Those who advanced through this hazard-ridden hierarchy realized which acts warranted reward or punishment. If they covered their tracks, they cast no disparagement on their master. If they clumsily disclosed their machinations or ran roughshod over fellow manipulators, they discredited the entire system—and suffered a blunderer's fate. Chroniclers voiced less criticism of these tendencies during Qāytbāy's reign, and yet the phenomenon is discernible under his rule.

A controversial judicial transfer at the end of 885/February 1481 reveals how a conferee might confound his advocates once he had shown his true colors. A Damascene, one Ibn ʿAbd al-Zayn, assumed the Ḥanafī qāḍīship of Cairo following the demise of Shams al-Dīn Muḥammad al-Amshāṭī.[33] Pertinent to his formal duties, al-Amshāṭī had previously supervised charitable trusts endowed for support of instruction in Ḥanafī fiqh. When Ibn ʿAbd al-Zayn succeeded al-Amshāṭī, he displaced his son who fully expected to administer these waqfs "to mutual advantage of recipients and notables" (that is, Mamlūk patrons who doled out the funds in return for a cut). Devastated over loss of so lucrative a post, the son appealed to his sponsor, Qānṣūh, second dawādār, but initially to no avail since Qāytbāy had received positive reports about Ibn ʿAbd al-Zayn during his Syrian tour of 882. Yet once Ibn ʿAbd al-Zayn began asserting his own authority, he dismayed all his associates by stopping their special allowances and directing all waqf proceeds solely to their prescribed charities. "Every impoverished Ḥanafī . . . now received three dīnārs a *day* more or less and what was one to think of that?" Ibn ʿAbd al-Zayn fired all his predecessor's nuwwāb because he caught them accepting bribes for their legal duties. Al-Ṣayrafī, though sorely in need of employment, disqualified himself from a post subordinate to this magistrate who prevented his assistants from making a proper living. Ultimately, complaints against the "vainly self-righteous" judge, whose misguided propriety caused consternation among both colleagues and sponsors, became so strident that Qāytbāy dismissed him. Originally impressed with Ibn ʿAbd al-Zayn's devotion to the needy in Damascus, the sultan found him naively inappropriate for the realities of judicial dealings in Cairo.

One individual on al-Ghawrī's staff accomplished his master's designs so consummately that he exemplified a subordinate's understanding of his true calling. This was none other than Zayn al-Dīn Barakāt ibn Mūṣā. His first post as bailiff, having evolved from a curtain drawer who heralded the monarch's arrival at audiences, embraced functions of enforcer and ombudsman during the Circassian period. While Ibn Iyās reported no details on Zaynī Barakāt's discharge of official responsibilities, the historian dwelt on those abilities that facilitated his advancement. In 910, Zaynī Barakāt obtained his pivotal office: the market inspectorship of Cairo.[34] The muḥtasib's overt charges mattered far less than his function as a broker mediating between regime demands and producers' evasions. Zaynī Barakāt administered the Ḥisba masterfully over the next eleven years. His acceptance of gratuities from artisans and merchants who appreciated his alleviation of the government's perennial expropriations bespeaks his diplomatic skills. Zaynī Barakāt protected the interests of asset holders without skimping on his patron's take.

The popularity Zaynī Barakāt enjoyed among the masses was almost unique among civil servants of this era. Ibn Iyās often remarked about Zaynī Barakāt's stature before the commons, but provided no commentary about it. We may surmise that this man exhibited a cardinal virtue from the very beginning of his career: a keen recollection of his origins. Zaynī Barakāt never assumed airs of an aristocrat. He nurtured lines of communication with every urban quarter of Cairo and each sector of its populace no matter how meek. A man intimately familiar with Cairo's pithy street dialects, Zaynī Barakāt grasped what was transpiring in the capital's teeming warrens better than anyone else in al-Ghawrī's service. Both the commons and the sultan recognized this unique canniness and for more than a decade Zaynī Barakāt exploited his acumen with coarseness in ways no rival could equal. Barakāt cherished his reputation as an extorter whose cruelty was legendary. Yet he subjected only those his master suspected of skullduggery to his excruciating torments. To the average artisan, shopkeeper, dragoman, or customs official who accepted the efficacy of "good graft" and paid his dues, Zaynī Barakāt acted as a trusted spokesman who lightened their burdens of confiscation. A defender of stable market policies and steady rates of currency, Zaynī Barakāt posed as a champion of consumers' rights. Over the years, the masses held him in such high regard that when al-Ghawrī toyed with his expendability, they vehemently decried his expulsion.

Zaynī Barakāt's popularity may indeed have disquieted his patron. If the commons saw the sultan's aide as their defender, might his stature not become excessive, his esteem compromising his value as a coercible agent? In Ramaḍān 914/January 1509, the sultan stripped Barakāt of both the bailiffship and the ḥisba.[35] Ibn Iyās mentioned only al-Ghawrī's displeasure with Barakāt, but implied his excessive influence. Soon thereafter, the sultan dismissed his client from the rectorship he had held in the affluent khānqāh at Siryāqūs and supervision of tariffs yielded in Burullus Province.[36] All told, Barakāt found himself bereft of sixteen posts or sinecures he had accumulated. But reactions soon compelled al-Ghawrī's change of heart. Cairo's wheat supply ran short and "bread disappeared from the markets." Vendors rejected Zaynī Barakāt's replacement, who feared for his life when he ventured into the sūqs. The sultan had no choice but to reinstate his client whose connections rendered him untouchable. "Once Zaynī Barakāt was restored, the populace rejoiced and unrest ceased."

This episode allows a fascinating glimpse of a client's ingenious methods of entrenchment. Barakāt almost certainly instigated a strike among grain dealers and bread bakers in Cairo. So dependent had they become on this individual's manipulation of the ḥisba they would accept no other. Awed by Barakāt's capacity to shut down the city's staple food supply without any show of defiance, al-Ghawrī restored his offices. Henceforth, their relationship would be strained by mutual suspicion of influence mongoring and latent dis-

missal. Four years after this abortive removal, al-Ghawrī exploited smouldering jealousy on the part of rival clients to compel Barakāt's disclosure of all his
accounts.[37] Al-Ghawrī seized on the occasion of a quarrel between the
muḥtasib and the wazīr, Jamāl al-Dīn Yūsuf al-Badrī, one of Barakāt's bit-
terest enemies. Barakāt lost his composure during this episode, one of the rare
instances when he forgot his place, and reviled al-Badrī with street epithets
that appalled assembled courtiers. Al-Ghawrī turned Barakāt over to two officers for interrogation. He was held eight days while the amīrs examined his
transactions for the preceding four years. During this harrowing episode, not
one of Barakāt's erstwhile allies among the officers dared intercede. Only after
the muḥtasib agreed upon restitution of between thirty and forty thousand
dīnārs did al-Ghawrī release him. The sultan showed Barakāt no personal rancor after reminding him of his station, but draped him with a robe of honor
and left him with his offices. The mob had threatened a riot when they learned
of their esteemed inspector's reversal.

Zaynī Barakāt's career continued in like vein to his patron's dramatic end
and beyond. No one else could approach his knowledge of practical affairs nor
duplicate his talents as an extorter. Because of his myriad links with bureaucrats and marketeers, Barakāt essentially controlled the capital's vital functions. However much al-Ghawrī might resent his client's connections, he
could not run the risk of expelling him. As events abroad and the incessant
clamoring of his soldiers distracted him in these final years, the sultan could
not do without such an agent—no matter how devious. And for all his contacts, Barakāt remained outwardly the consummate client, ever mindful of
his place. Beset by no delusions over trappings of grandeur, Barakāt never
crossed his sovereign in public. After his one lapse of decorum, he revealed
no further chinks in his armor. The sultan might well have suspected his
underling's nefarious dealings, over which he himself exercised progressively
less control. In a pragmatic sense, Zaynī Barakāt may have become the most
influential man in Cairo by 1516. But he never brandished his clout in an
open insult to his master and thus gave al-Ghawrī no cause for terminating him.

So astute was this former falconer's page that, following al-Ghawrī's departure for Syria, his regent Ṭūmānbāy reconfirmed Barakāt in all his offices.
Given the realm's emergency, "no one was to oppose his authority."[38] An appropriate reward for the client who now "took charge of state affairs with none
untouched by his hand." Nor did he vanish with the demise of the Mamlūk
sultanate. Barakāt successfully adjusted to conditions of service under the new
regime. He appears on the last page of Ibn Iyās' chronicle (*Badāʾiʿ* 5, 494).
Muṣṭafā Bāshā, the Ottoman governor, reappointed Barakāt as supervisor of
tax receipts (*al-taḥadduth ʿalā al-jihāt*) from Sharqīya Province in the Delta (on
Tuesday, 29 Dhūʾl-Ḥijja 928/19 November 1522). The next day, the governor
restored Barakāt to the market inspectorship (*ḥisba*) of Cairo, an ironic yet fit-

ting conclusion for this massive work in which Barakāt occupied so prominent a place as master manipulator of the capital's commerce.

The other civilian who approached Zaynī Barakāt's influence in al-Ghawrī's circle proffered services of a markedly different kind. Sarī al-Dīn ibn al-Shiḥna's eminence during al-Ghawrī's reign denoted a jurist whose ambitions outweighed his scruples. From Ibn al-Shiḥna's first appointment as supervisor over his maternal grandfather's waqfs in 874/1469, this individual refined his talents as a litigator of charitable trusts whose judgments favored testators with expansive visions for their estates.[39] An incident in Shaʿbān 875/ February 1471 heralded Ibn al-Shiḥna's future twisting of legal principle that would attract al-Ghawrī's notice more than thirty years later. Learning that the scholar Badr al-Dīn al-Ardabīlī, who occupied several academic chairs, lay near death, Ibn al-Shiḥna set out with his father, Muḥibb al-Dīn, to pay a call of condolence.[40] Since al-Ardabīlī could claim only his son-in-law (ṣihr) as close male kin, the two Shiḥnas concocted a scheme for enlarging their own fortune while playing the role of solicitous colleagues concerned over their associate's plight.

Sitting at al-Ardabīlī's bedside, Sarī al-Dīn offered him a settlement of one hundred dīnārs and written assurance of the monthly salaries from each of his professorships so long as he lived. In return, al-Ardabīlī would consign him their titles. Since al-Ardabīlī expired three days after this encounter, his faculties may have been waning. Surely a jurist so steeped in trust procedures should have recognized the improbity of Sarī al-Dīn's act. Only waqf donors themselves, their descendants, their chosen agents or a tribunal of judges in concert could reallocate an endowed chair upon its incumbent's decease. A professorship, after all, was not its occupant's property. Sarī al-Dīn most likely thought up this ploy since his father joined him with great reluctance, allowing adulation for his son to impede his better judgment. Sarī al-Dīn enlisted al-Ardabīlī's son-in-law and four nuwwāb in his own pay as signatories of the document he drew up formalizing the transfer.

Word of so egregious a violation of principle spread rapidly, and when Qāytbāy was informed of it, he angrily summoned the deputies to explain their behavior. After the deputies and son-in-law swore to the propriety of their action, the sultan flatly rejected their protestation of honesty, claiming they had hoodwinked a dying man whose signature had been affixed after he was incompetent (*ghayr ʿaqlihi*). Some rumors alleged a forged testament, drawn up after al-Ardabīlī's death. Qāytbāy found the son-in-law's conduct more heinous than his sponsor Sarī al-Dīn's, since he was a marital relative. Holding connivance dearer than family was sinful and Qāytbāy threatened him with a public flogging. He then ordered a trial of the defendants to determine their fitness for continued duty as witnesses (*shuhūd*). Seeking incontestable evidence of coercion, Qāytbāy called in al-Ardabīlī's widow and daughter for personal testimony. The sultan wanted their version of circumstances surrounding the transfer. When asked whether al-Ardabīlī remained conscious when presented with the writ, both hedged by claiming that "he was weak" (*ḍaʿīf*). Outraged by obfuscation from everyone implicated in the affair, Qāytbāy ordered the deputies' interrogation at the hands of his officers in the barracks. Even the chancellor Ibn Muzhir could not dissuade him. Only after Sarī al-Dīn reconsidered the folly of his scheme and relinquished all claims to al-Ardabīlī's chairs in writing did Qāytbāy release their nuwwāb, who so far had borne the brunt of his investigation. The sultan seriously weighed dismissal of the senior Shiḥna from the Ḥanafī qāḍīship and asked for resumés of possible replacements. Ultimately, Muḥibb al-Dīn kept his judgeship but found his reputation stained by the son's deed. Al-Ṣayrafī summed up this sordid affair as follows: "Indeed, if magistrates of the law glorify God and his ordinances, He magnifies them. But if they care more for their own positions, they demean only themselves."

Two months after the transfer scandal, Sarī al-Dīn departed for Aleppo with his father's blessing.[41] His absence of seven months was prudent in light of his sudden notoriety. The senior Shiḥna may have decided his son's future was enhanced by an extended sojourn away, allowing sour memories to fade. But Sarī al-Dīn returned unchastened. His subsequent arrogance at the Ṣalāḥīya Madrasa where he received his first qāḍīship confirmed Qāytbāy's suspicions, who conferred no further benefices in Cairo on him.[42] Sarī al-Dīn would regain prominence only after al-Ghawrī's enthronement.

Sarī al-Dīn resurfaced in 906/1501 after a tour of judicial duty in Syria, when al-Ghawrī appointed him Ḥanafī qāḍī.[43] Despite his anomalous stature as an unknown to many of his colleagues, Sarī al-Dīn lost no time distinguishing himself as a man on the rise. His extended absence abroad having deflated none of his hauteur, Ibn al-Shiḥna soon acquired the reputation of a snob who flaunted his position in the sultan's retinue. Sarī al-Dīn's acrimonious encounters with the satirist Jamāl al-Dīn al-Salmūnī and the incarcerated treasurer Ibn Rawq indicate the diversity of his detractors. Their mutual antipathy under contrasting circumstances underscores his widespread disfavor. When Sarī al-Dīn demanded al-Salmūnī's lashing in the Ṣalāḥīya courtyard for slander, a mob gathered and threatened the qāḍī with stoning. Finding no one who intervened on his behalf, not even his patron's amīrs, Ibn al-Shiḥna swallowed his ego and rescinded the sentence.[44] Ibn Iyās acknowledged the repellence of al-Salmūnī's satire; indeed, tongue-in-cheek, he begged his reader's pardon for reproducing it. Yet the commons evidently found the satirist's depiction of Sarī al-Dīn quite timely.

Six years later, at Ibn Rawq's trial, the plaintiff accused his judicial colleagues of masking their own chicanery behind their self-righteous condemnations of him. "I do not recognize one qāḍī here fit to lead prayer!"[45] He singled out Sarī al-Dīn for particular insolence but as he was prepared for the lashing, a mob once again assembled with stones clenched in their fists. If the sentence were imposed, they would attack Ibn al-Shiḥna. The council then adjourned without a verdict. The behavior of ruffians who rudely jostled their way into Cairo's highest civil court with impunity to prevent punishment of persons they supported reveals the masses' latent power in lieu of any formal enfranchisement. But how had Ibn al-Shiḥna earned their animosity? While we cannot know for sure, his overbearing attitude and reputation for tampering with charitable trusts may have sullied his standing. Zaynī Barakāt never soiled his hands by diverting funds set aside for the believers' welfare. He confined his dealings to individuals who had themselves broken the rules of tolerable graft. Ibn al-Shiḥna, by contrast, aided his patron in embezzling assets that were inviolate.

Sarī al-Dīn's career progressed without incident for the next thirteen years. Al-Ghawrī insured his comfort with several academic sinecures.[46] When Ibn Iyās pondered Ibn al-Shiḥna's fate in his obituary, he noted his personal rapport with his sponsor, spending three nights a week in close consultation over "state affairs." But then "the sultan's wrath fell on him" in a remarkable episode that led to his ingnominous fall from grace. The event, a lurid adultery scandal, merits recounting since it highlights the fragility of a client's relationship with his master. No retainer, regardless of value, could heap ridicule on his patron.

On Saturday, 12 Shawwāl 919/11 December 1513, the wife of a Hanafī deputy judge, Ghars al-Dīn Khalīl, and her paramour joined in an illicit encounter that precipitated an unprecedented clash of wills between the sultan and his judiciary. This woman, cherished for her beauty, invited her lover, the Shāfiʿī nāʾib Nūr al-Dīn ʿAlī al-Mashālī, to her bed after Khalīl departed for a nocturnal prayer vigil at the shrine of Imām al-Layth.[47] This woman's charms were appreciated throughout the quarter apparently, since she had rebuffed advances by a second philanderer. This individual nursed his wounded pride with dire plans of revenge, and when he observed al-Mashālī slipping through the wife's front door he informed her husband. Khalīl rushed home, forced open his barred gate, and found his spouse writhing in al-Mashālī's embrace. Spurning the adulterous pair's entreaties for mercy, the cuckolded husband thrashed them both before consigning them to the grand chamberlain for punishment. Once the two confessed their guilt, the Hājib informed al-Ghawrī who found their case a convenient means of polishing his image as a guardian of public morality. But al-Ghawrī's plans ran afoul of legal authorities who jealously reserved litigation on morals cases as their prerogative.

A second Shāfiʿī deputy named Shams al-Dīn al-Zankalūnī wrote up a fatwā challenging the sultan's decision to execute the couple by stoning without due process.[48] He listed several Hadīths urging clemency that Imām al-Shāfiʿī had incorporated within his *Risāla*. According to these traditions, adulterers who freely repented their offense could be spared. Upon heated debate the chief qāḍīs, including Sarī al-Dīn, rescinded their earlier endorsement of al-Ghawrī's death sentence. When the sultan was so informed, he lost his temper. Keenly aware of invidious comparisons between Qāytbāy's illustrious reputation as a legal arbiter and his own indifference over court proceedings, al-Ghawrī had planned on exploiting the episode.

The affair's disastrous consequences for Sarī al-Dīn disclose his fatal error of judgment and the tightrope a client in his position had to walk every day. When al-Ghawrī had first convened the qāḍīs and accepted their unanimous acquiescence to his penalty, he had stunned Ibn al-Shiḥna by upbraiding him for winking at corruption among his own assistants. Whether Ibn al-Shiḥna should have sensed in this admonition a warning of al-Ghawrī's displeasure over his covert services we cannot know. But when the qāḍīs disqualified their previous verdict, the sultan singled Sarī al-Dīn out for particular vituperation. Having privately assured his master of the validity of the sentence by stoning, Ibn al-Shiḥna now sided with his peers. The man on whom al-Ghawrī had relied for more than a decade to legitimate his waqf expropriations now embarrassed him over a petty morals charge. Sarī al-Dīn must have underestimated the sultan's interest in this case, for why else would he have thrown in his lot with his judicial peers? Countless times before Ibn al-Shiḥna had countermanded their rulings when these inconvenienced his patron. He had skillfully pointed out flaws in their reasoning and shown al-Ghawrī legal justifications for his actions. Perhaps he regarded an adultery charge involving no assets as a signal opportunity for mending his fences with them. How serious his miscalculation was Sarī al-Dīn soon realized. Terrified over his sudden isolation, he begged other members of al-Ghawrī's entourage to speak for him.[49] But none dared cross the sultan when his temper was up lest they suffer the same fate. Sarī al-Dīn joined his colleagues in dismissal. Despite his efforts at ingratiation, his pleading of past service, Ibn al-Shiḥna would never again look al-Ghawrī in the face. He died two years later in seclusion, lucky to have avoided the corporeal abuse al-Ghawrī inflicted on the jurisconsult who drew up the odious fatwā.

Sarī al-Dīn's fall was a stark example of the primacy personal ties assumed in patron-client relations. Although every individual who curried favor did so by performing clandestine tasks, none survived if his loyalty wavered. In a bureaucracy that no longer operated along formal channels, covert aid and personal fealty intersected as components of a shadow system profitable to all. But every player paid a price for his cooption in this game. The sultan, as master schemer, tolerated no hint of deviance. Few of his retainers, no matter how adept, took his support for granted. Their creativity was thus confined to efforts at currying their patron's favor while maximizing immediate gain from a post in any way possible short of crossing him. Status and wealth had to be squeezed from a sinecure quickly no matter who below was trampled in the process. For if the sultan's eventual ire loomed ominously as one of the few certainties a client could expect, what realistic alternatives did he have? It is in light of these conditions of bureaucratic mobility that we assess the regime's tactics for self-preservation, which limited its capacity for change.

The Context of Royal Justice: A Contrast in Motives

As supreme arbiter of his realm, the sultan heard cases referred from lower courts at biweekly audiences. This duty, having evolved from centuries-old traditions, varied in its practice according to inclinations of individual rulers. For some, litigation was a tedious burden discharged with minimal effort for its symbolic value. Sultans who slighted their magisterial function shunted most decisions upon judicial aides: the four chief qāḍīs, senior jursiconsults (*muftīs*) and their staffs. But others laid personal stock in their vocation and participated vigorously in even the most intricate of cases, despite shortcomings in their training. Qāytbāy assumed an assertive posture in appeals sessions from the start of his reign. While his interaction with judicial subordinates caused them discomfiture on more than one occasion, none could deny the sultan's reinvigoration of royal hearings. Although al-Ghawrī found audiences with plaintiffs less appealing, he manipulated them for his ulterior purposes.

During his consolidation, Qāytbāy worked closely with judges and their adjutants. By the end of this period (ca. 877), jurists who owed him their appointments dominated the Sharīʿa courts of Cairo and its provincial capitals. Qāytbāy's motives for installing these men cannot be dismissed as simple nepotism. Even judges who showered their benefactor with praise clashed with him on any number of cases. A palpable tension over autonomy exuded from litigation when the sultan intervened. Qāytbāy himself rarely sought obsequious approbation. He did remind his subordinates time and again, however, that he wielded final say in any appellate case. While acknowledging the expertise of scholars raised to the bench, Qāytbāy often rankled over their quibbling at fine points of interpretation, which, in his eyes, disguised stalling. Considered apart from this dynamic, marked by the autocrat's interruption and his magistrates' studied delays, Qāytbāy's explosive reactions read like temper tantrums. But in the context of dominance and resistance, they imply a subtler meaning. Qāytbāy posed as a champion of Sharīʿa, an incorruptible guardian of his subjects' rights before the law. His judicial adjutants regarded his assertion of primacy with ambivalence since it challenged their own status as the collective embodiment of Sharʿī authority. Qāytbāy may well have envisioned the elevation of his reputation by assuming such an aggressive role in appellate litigation. Although the sultan treated his learned subordinates with respect, he often overrode their judgments.

Qāytbāy seized upon hearings to proclaim his own sense of legal propriety. Many cases involved supervision of charitable trusts that supported venerable institutions. In Rabīʿ I 874/September-October 1469, the sultan transferred waqfs maintaining the mosque of Ibn Ṭūlūn from the Shāfiʿī qāḍī's jurisdiction to that of a Mamlūk amīr.[50] Under the former, staff salaries had suffered inexcusable delays, as the trust's proceeds "had been devoured by his accountants." Whether an officer would dispense these revenues more effectively depended on his sovereign's intimidation. But Qāytbāy signaled his readiness to supplant even trustees designated by a waqf writ if they compromised their duties.

In these early years Qāytbāy frequently convened his justices to resolve questions over controversial theological issues, public debts left outstanding by deceased magistrates and other trust disputes.[51] A particularly acrimonious debate erupted in Jumādā II 876/October-November 1471 when descendants of Ibn Īnāl, a retainer of Sultan Jaqmaq, petitioned their right to dispense waqf yields for their grandfather's mosque, as stipulated in the original deed.[52] When the plaintiffs presented their fatwās accusing the Shāfiʿī qāḍī of usurping their authority to hire and fire madrasa personnel, an argument erupted between the judges over provisos in the document and the qāḍī's prerogatives as its nāẓir. After reaching a deadlock, the judges were compelled to yield Qāytbāy the decision. Acknowledging the grandson's claims, the sultan deferred their dispensing of revenues or replacement of staff until all back wages had been paid. His deft resolution of a knotty problem embarrassed the judges, who had haggled for hours over their respective madhhabs' perspectives on accountability. Qāytbāy, who had watched their antics with bemused cynicism, scored a telling point. An unschooled autocrat who applied simple logic to the Sharīʿa might settle a dispute far more expeditiously than savants who quarreled to demonstrate their erudition. In this and numerous other debates, Qāytbāy proved that the appellate system could not operate properly without the autocrat's abiding presence.[53]

Qāytbāy projected an aura of no nonsense control over his squabbling adjutants for broader purposes than judicial decorum. Throughout his reign Qāytbāy exploited his role as final arbiter to inculcate a sense of identity with his mission among the masses. Cases abound of the sultan chastizing bureaucrats for corruption after hearing pleas against them, or his reversing the qāḍīs' initial rulings over charitable trusts, inheritance disputes, and marriage contracts that trampled on claims a plaintiff could substantiate. We must rely largely on the opinion of al-Ṣayrafī, who attended biweekly audiences. But the consistency of praise he reported from the commons for the sultan's defense of their interests conveys a measure of success for Qāytbāy's tactic. The cases Qāytbāy chose for his intervention usually involved an official guilty of a gross, and thus noteworthy, violation or a spectacular example of tampering with funds dedicated to public welfare. In Rabīʿ II 874/October-November 1469, Qāytbāy assembled the four qāḍīs to review charges brought against the Syndic of the Prophet's Descendants.[54] Accused of withholding stipends and stymying investments through mismanagement, the syndic and his brother were ordered before the sultan who reviled them for sullying their sacred trust. When the two engaged in mutual recrimination, Qāytbāy placed them in custody and installed a respected magistrate as their successor. Al-Ṣayrafī recounted the plaintiffs' grateful accolade: "May God favor our lord the sultan, for he is paramount in justice!"

Qāytbāy took charge of cases when he calculated that his judgment on behalf of a civil supplicant augmented his stature among the commons while disclosing negligence or interest pandering among the magistrates. He had a special interest in suits brought by women whose husbands had violated their inheritance rights. On 17 Jumādā I 874/22 November 1469, the sultan sustained the claim of a wife whose husband, an ironsmith, had retained her dower after a divorce settlement and enlisted an amīr's backing. Not only did Qāytbāy uphold the divorcée's appeal but he found the Ḥanafī deputy judge who first heard the case guilty of bias.[55] Once Qāytbāy made up his mind in this affair he would not be gainsaid, despite irritation his ruling aroused among other nuwwāb who sought their own patrons' endorsement for a protest against his interference. Al-Ṣayrafī wryly observed that the deputies mended their ways "but briefly and soon took up their former behavior." But the masses appreciated Qāytbāy's gesture, since jurists in the lower courts customarily sided with partisans connected to persons influential in the royal hierarchy.

When petitioners complained of Mamlūks who committed assaults on drunken binges, Qāytbāy ordered the offenders' execution—so long as they belonged to a rival faction.[56] Bureaucrats who imposed excessive tariffs on merchants were publicly reprimanded.[57] Such displays were largely for show since the sultan himself gained handsomely from revenues his officials extracted in like fashion. Few actually lost their posts, but merely restored the loot they collected in a case that had been appealed. Yet if a bureaucrat flagrantly brandished extractions he should have concealed, Qāytbāy brusquely sanctioned his removal. Confiscation required finesse rarely served by arrogance. The expert embezzler maximized his take without compromising his patron's luster before the masses—a delicate task assuredly but requisite for survival in royal service.

Having allotted a substantial part of his estate to charitable trusts, Qāytbāy advocated assiduous distribution of waqf proceeds. Any infringement on a writ's provisos kindled the royal wrath. One of the most vivid examples occurred on 10 Rajab 876/23 December 1471, when the shaykh of the Ṣayfīya Madrasa disputed appropriation of a hall (*īwān*) within the college by its Mamlūk nāẓir for his dwelling and stable.[58] After hearing the qāḍīs haggle over the nāẓir's custodial rights versus the donor's stipulations, Qāytbāy lost his patience, summoned his mount and rode over to the college to inspect the alterations. The qāḍīs were hard pressed to follow him and made an amusing spectacle as they galloped through Cairo's streets in hot pursuit on their mules. Qāytbāy conducted an impromptu inspection of the premises, voicing his opposition to any change prejudicial to the hall's use for worship. But he took no action against the supervisor and left the case unresolved pending further investigation. This behavior typified Qāytbāy's actions in such incidents. Studied outbursts of indignation and spontaneous on-site inquiries into alleged abuses outnumbered actual convictions of accused parties, especially if they ranked high in the sultan's network. Yet these displays made for symbolic pretenses in which bureaucrats and jurists often suffered humiliation before the commons. The masses may have sensed the sham implicit in these shows but enjoyed the degradation of magistrates who hedged their principles nonetheless. And the sultan did frequently uphold the rights of legitimate petitioners. His reputation as a defender of orphans, widows, and the helpless was not without merit. Yet adjudicating their grievances usually involved petty sums, restoration of which cost him little. Public acclamation for protection of the lowly's claims was cheaply bought.

Paralleling his defense of Sharīᶜa was Qāytbāy's piety in matters of orthodoxy. Few would contend the sultan's depth of conviction, but he was alert to the positive impression his judgments made on savants and commoners. When chance created the possibility of ill-omened calendrical concurrences, such as two khuṭbas on the same Friday, Qāytbāy arbitrarily delayed the lunar month's start by a day in Cairo thereby allaying superstition.[59] When controversy simmered among jurists and theologians over the "deviant poet" Ibn al-Fāriḍ's verse, Qāytbāy backed judges who found the lyricist's opinions sound. He shrewdly noted the masses' fervid allegiance.[60] Victims of the sultan's punishments who subsequently retreated in remorse to a holy shrine often received a stipend from their persecutor who was moved by their behavior and by accolades his mercy drew.[61] Quick to shroud women walking in the streets with their shoulders bare, Qāytbāy moved more cautiously when smouldering confessional rivalries erupted into open riot. In Shawwāl 876/April 1472, a gang of Copts mutilated a mendicant North African shaykh they suspected of converting their children.[62] Fearing a counter-*pogrom* by Muslim mobs, Qāytbāy had his prefect of police proclaim a stern edict forbidding anyone to disturb "the tranquility of God's commonwealth" by taking the law into his own hands. Prosecution of the Coptic ruffians should be left to proper authorities. In Rabīᶜ I 877/August-September 1472, a deranged preacher stood in the Rumayla Square below the Citadel and announced he had received the sultan's personal assurance that the prefect would release all prisoners, regardless of offense.[63] Upon apprisal of the lunatic's raving, Qāytbāy ordered his immediate confinement to an asylum. But despite the preacher's incendiary statements, his life would be spared since God had touched his soul. Upon receiving petitions advocating demolition of a synagogue in Jerusalem, Qāytbāy convened the qāḍīs to weigh their legality.[64] He supported jurists who upheld the synagogue's continued existence since worship there had never been formally terminated. The majority of Cairo's ʿulamāʾ, while hardly advocating enhancement of Judaic observances in the empire, paused at razing an established center of Dhimmī prayer.

The consistency of Qāytbāy's adherence to orthodoxy earned him the clerics' effusive praise. Al-Ṣayrafī extolled him as "beloved of God's servants among the pious, learned, law-worthy and mystical. . . . May his munificence be glorified. His virtue, generosity, humility, submission, asceticism, spirituality, clemency, rectitude and decency; his forbearance with those apt to opposition; his benevolence, hospitality and lack of parsimony for all God's followers converge in his dazzling nobility."[65] Since no sinecure on Qāytbāy's staff sweetened al-Ṣayrafī's flattery, we may discern genuine esteem behind the florid rhetoric. In contrast with many of his Mamlūk contemporaries, Qāytbāy imbued his subjects with the conviction that their ruler personified propriety as defined in Sunna. However we may ponder the veracity of this image, the sultan astutely broadened his base of popular support by disseminating such an impression. Qāytbāy escaped much of the vituperation heaped on his successor, al-Ghawrī, by juxtaposing his fiscal profligacy against his record as an upholder of social propriety.

Few found in Qānṣūh al-Ghawrī an inclination to uphold propriety. Yet for all his disinterest in appeals sessions, al-Ghawrī grasped the importance of his role as arbiter over the courts for symbolic legitimation of his reign. The sultan made sporadic gestures to portray himself as "Guardian of Sunna." Al-Ghawrī never duplicated his predecessor's reputation in his subjects' eyes or his chroniclers' opinions. What measures he did take smacked of an ulterior motive, usually financial or vainglorious. And when a jurist set unexpected obstacles in his path, the sultan reacted with petulant tyranny Qāytbāy scorned. Al-Ghawrī indulged his penchant for self-aggrandizement even when restoring tribunal facilities that had fallen into disrepair. In Dhū'l-Qaʿda 916/ January-February 1511, the sultan razed the old justice pavilion (*dakka*) in the Citadel courtyard when its confines cramped the swarms of supplicants jostling with their petitions.[66] Although the populace admitted the existing structure's inadequacy, they held it in nostalgic awe since so many august monarchs had dispensed rulings there. Al-Ghawrī sought to assuage their unease by erecting a more splendid edifice, faced with marble and porphyry and embossed with gold. Ibn Iyās conceded the beauty of the new estrade but also noted how prominently its builder inscribed his own name on the dais. Al-Ghawrī made sure all supplicants realized who had improved their audience facility. Yet his association with the pavilion smacked of extravagance rather than engagement with plaintiffs' needs.

Al-Ghawrī's infrequent shows of amnesty or support of orthodoxy disclosed either a fiscal incentive or worry over security. When a beggar was apprehended concealing one hundred seventy gold dīnārs, a sum such a person could acquire only by theft, al-Ghawrī summoned him for interrogation.[67]

The beggar insisted the money was his by inheritance from his esteemed mother, but al-Ghawrī ignored his protestations. The sultan confiscated the gold as a trove "stolen from the Muslims" and now retrieved. While he promised the hapless beggar a modest clothing and food allowance, the latter denounced al-Ghawrī's seizure with his own cupidity: "Give me back my gold and keep your clothing!" Al-Ghawrī apparently dismissed the beggar with amused contempt since he let his affront pass with no further indictment.

Two years later, upon hearing that Christians were celebrating the start of Easter (first day of Khamsīn) by purchasing Muslim slave girls, al-Ghawrī angrily decried the acquisition of believers by Dhimmīs.[68] Yet his fine of twenty thousand dīnārs struck even Muslim purists as excessive, and certainly spoiled the Copts' holy season that year. The size of al-Ghawrī's extraction implied the sultan's exploitation of a Coptic practice offensive to Muslims solely for his own gain. This year also witnessed al-Ghawrī's harrowing eye infection. The sultan reversed many oppressive edicts he had earlier imposed on his subjects in hope of divine mercy. His release of prisoners, including convicted felons, from his dungeons suggested magnaminity inspired by terror rather than humility, an unseemly trait.[69] Avarice or duress seemed to motivate the sultan's tokens of justice.

Al-Ghawrī's inclinations toward appeasing his colleagues to bolster his position were apparent in his dealings with their clients' crimes. In Shawwāl 915/January-February 1510, two servants in Tūmānbāy's train committed homicide in fits of passion. Ignoring incontestable evidence, the Mālikī qāḍī who weighed their case refused to prosecute them once he learned their patron's identity. When the second defendant was brought before al-Ghawrī, "no one came forth to testify" and the sultan dropped all charges. "He had done murder in broad daylight after noon in the caravansaray (*wakāla*) of Barsbāy. . . . Thus did the victim's relatives and children receive no satisfaction. Final judgment rests with God."[70] To be sure, but in this life the sultan bore responsibility for dispensing justice. Al-Ghawrī made clear his priorities. Those who served his pivotal associates could break the law and go free.

But after a jurist like Sarī al-Dīn crossed his patron in a case the latter fixed on as a show of morality, his career plummeted. Why did the sex scandal of Shawwāl 919 so provoke al-Ghawrī's ire? What subliminal code had Ibn al-Shiḥna and the other qāḍīs violated to unleash such fury? Their provocation must be sought in tensions over final authority to control litigation. When the Shāfiʿī deputy, al-Zankalūmī, circulated his fatwā challenging the qāḍī's earlier acquiescence in al-Ghawrī's sentence, his act betokened more than a point of interpretation on the fate of confessed adulterers. He disparaged the sultan's image as first guardian of probity. Ibn Iyās commented that al-Ghawrī "wished to show himself severely just in this matter. He wanted it recorded in his time that he had stoned fornicators during his reign, as the Prophet had done. . . ."[71] Al-Ghawrī smarted over invidious comparisons so many savants drew between his abuse of court proceedings and Qāytbāy's renown for upholding them. Now, when a signal opportunity for rectification presented itself, his subordinates foiled his design—in the face of absolute proof. Upon learning of al-Zankalūnī's fatwā, al-Ghawrī summoned the four qāḍīs and hurled the offense in their faces: "O ye Muslims, a man enters another's house, couples with his wife, is caught with her under the sheets, confirms his guilt, signs it with his own hand, and then you change your judgment?"

The qāḍīs had reversed their earlier concurrence only after reflection on the threat to their professional autonomy the sultan's unilateral decision posed. If they submitted after one of their own junior magistrates produced an alternative ruling from the *Risāla,* they meekly demeaned a pillar of Sharīʿa before a temporal authority. The sovereign was himself sworn to uphold the revealed law as embodied by the four canonical schools. Al-Shāfiʿī presided over Egypt as her orthodox patron saint. How could the four chief justices, living symbols of consensus from his day to their own, overlook an injunction for clemency drawn from the source of their magistracy? A knotty dilemma, and one with devastating consequences. When al-Ghawrī perceived their resolve, including that of Ibn al-Shiḥna, his summary dismissal was unprecedented in the sultanate's history.[72] The sultan called forth al-Zankalūnī and accosted him with the following words: "Your ruling is ephemeral while mine is enforced!" He then had him flogged a thousand strokes, a reprisal rarely inflicted upon a member of the judiciary. Al-Zankalūnī expired after his fearful penalty, his death a reminder of where real power lay in this regime. Although the qāḍīs were spared corporeal punishment, their removal was irrevocable. None were allowed any chance for reinstatement and thus were effectively cast out of the civil elite. For their part, the two offenders were hanged outside the gate of another shaykh who had upheld al-Zankalūnī's fatwā.[71] They were suspended from a single rope with two nooses so tied that the sinners faced each other as the trap door fell open beneath them. Thus did their executions reenact their transgression. Al-Ghawrī held their lives forfeit to their crime, but backed away from lapidation.

This affair epitomized the sultan's attitude toward his role as legal arbiter. Initially seeking improvement of his image, he expected the jurists, all of whom owed him their offices, to fall in line. What did the lives of two fornicators matter in the broader scheme of covert stratagems so profitable to all concerned? When the four judges opposed him in a show of professional solidarity, they had broken the quid pro quo underlying their appointments. By proclaiming loyalty to Sharīʿa over sponsor, they shook the system of obligations and rewards on which al-Ghawrī's security was vested. No matter how respected, they too were dispensable. An affront from such notable players in the sultan's devices could not be condoned. For this ruler, justice enjoyed no more sanctity than any other largesse he dispensed. Its bestowal remained his exclusive prerogative, granted or withheld at will.

The Context of Beneficence: Piety versus Pomp

Straitened finances dissuaded neither Qāytbāy nor al-Ghawrī from heaping vast sums on religious foundations, poor relief, public ceremonials, defense installations, and pleasure pavilions. These expenditures qualify the image of bankruptcy harped upon by historians of their generations. But the parallel stops with a mutual propensity for extravagance. Contrasts between the two sultans' donations bespeak differing motives behind beneficence and dissimilar personal inclinations. Both individuals were aware of how their grants would be received, expending their largesse with well-defined constituencies in mind. The generosity of each thus falls within the redistribution of assets back into the society from which they were extracted. In this light, largesse may be interpreted as a vital leaven of predation so central to the Mamlūk economy. Yet given this shared function, Qāytbāy and al-Ghawrī were moved by antithetical impulses. For one, piety influenced his actions while for the other, display compensated for his oppression.

Chroniclers who wrote after Qāytbāy's death wistfully recalled the scope of his good works.[74] Qāytbāy never deviated from the traditional benevolence they revered. When Ibn Iyās listed the sultan's innovations, they involved temporary cancellations of an existing procedure or protocol.[75] The historian noted only one actual change in Qāytbāy's practice of expenditure: his doling out of military stipends personally to each recruit, no matter his rank. This single divergence from previous custom underscored Qāytbāy's equation of duty with remuneration. The sultan also impressed upon every soldier in his army a keen awareness of his commander's concern for his welfare and his performance. The revocations, on the other hand, signal Qāytbāy's lack of interest in costly tableaux which served no purpose but ostentation.

Qāytbāy figured prominently in processions to and from the Citadel. These progressions rendered the monarch visible before his subjects and proclaimed the grandeur of his station. When Qāytbāy returned to Cairo from a Delta tour in 873/1469, he wore ceremonial finery and passed through the Bāb al-Naṣr on a tapestry of yellow silk.[76] Al-Ṣayrafī disputed Ibn Taghrī-Birdī's cynical assessment of the procession. The latter saw the commons' accolades as a facade obscuring their misery. Any joy they manifested represented scant diversion from daily suffering. Al-Ṣayrafī, however, saw in the masses' reception genuine appreciation for the sultan's generous mien. Whether Qāytbāy remained aloof from vanity during his progressions we cannot know. But chroniclers always associated them with acts of magnaminity or celebration of thanksgiving for God's clemency. One of Qāytbāy's grander parades commemorated his recovery from his first leg fracture in 876/1471.[77] The sultan's capacity to ride a horse after such an injury at his age symbolized his restored competence as war leader. The cavalcade terminated at the Citadel mosque where he presided over Friday prayer, a ritual he missed only when abroad.

Earlier the same year, Qāytbāy disclosed the depths of his piety in an impromptu act during an outing. On 14 Rabīʿ II/30 September, the sultan encountered the funeral train of a low-class woman proceeding toward the oratory just north of the Bāb al-Naṣr.[78] Upon hearing the mourners' keening, Qāytbāy dismounted, ordered his retinue to follow suit, and led prayers over the deceased's casket. Both al-Ṣayrafī and Ibn Iyās (who wrote his version decades later, on hearsay) found the episode exceptional, since Mamlūk autocrats rarely demeaned themselves by participating in obsequies of their poorest subjects. Each marveled at Qāytbāy's concern. A fellow Muslim's decease merited the obsequies even the sultan's lordly peers received in a state funeral. No equivalent act of humility was ever attributed to al-Ghawrī.

Sultans customarily bestowed largesse in dress reviews, festivals of the Muslim calendar, and on an ad hoc basis to the indigent. Hearkening back to the Classical Age, their generosity was posited on the blessedness of alms giving, an obligation for all believers but particularly those God had allotted great wealth. Qāytbāy restored practices of robe distribution and money bonuses to judges, scholastics, and divines twice a year: during the Prophet's birthday in Rabīʿ I and the holy month of Ramaḍān.[79] The court traditionally observed the latter period of fasting with a festive reading of the complete corpus of Prophetic Traditions of al-Bukhārī. Qāytbāy elevated this custom to an imposing (and fatiguing) ceremonial in the Citadel. In 888/1483, he commissioned the embroidery of a vast tent to enclose reciters and listeners.[80] The sultan spent in excess of thirty thousand dīnārs on this marquee, which had no equal in any Muslim court. Most of Qāytbāy's lavish expenditures promoted rituals or structures devoted to religious service, whereas we shall note al-Ghawrī's preference for festivals or edifices that advertised the regime's beneficence in more secular ways.

When Qāytbāy was informed of catastrophes inflicted on his subjects, he provided them assistance. In 876/1472, a baladīya woman gave birth to quadruplets, all of whom survived. Although a miraculous event, their arrival left her family destitute. The father carried all four infants to the Citadel and showed them to Qāytbāy during audience. So moved was the sultan, whom fate denied a large family, that he gave the man ten dīnārs (a windfall for an individual who rarely saw a gold coin in a year) and five irdabbs of wheat.[81] Qāytbāy made such gestures spontaneously, except when the Ottoman expeditions pressed him during the nineties. His good will was seen as heartfelt by the masses, enhancing his image as a paragon of generosity in an abstemious age. Al-Ghawrī made similar bestowals, but less frequently. And when he did, he had calculated their impact, scheduling them when he sensed seditious currents.

Qāytbāy's architectural patronage assumed legendary proportions even in his own lifetime. No monarch since al-Nāṣir Muḥammad invested equivalent sums in such an array of monuments and restorations extending from Cairo to Aleppo and the Ḥijāz. The former sultan presided over a healthier financial system yielding larger revenues more dependably. The typology of Qāytbāy's monuments merits scrutiny since it denotes his motives for endowment. Qāytbāy began construction of new edifices and repair of extant ones from his enthronement year. While the pace of his projects varied over following decades, the sultan persisted with his patronage until his death. The list of structures (see chapter 7, note 28) reveals an almost exclusive focus on religious, welfare, commercial, and defense foundations in descending order of frequency. Although Qāytbāy embellished Citadel halls and set up modest belvederes in Cairo's environs or at his hunting stations in the Fayyūm, few palaces were ordered. The only complex raised to commemorate his own name was his imposing madrasa-mausoleum, which he dedicated in Rajab 879/November-December 1474.[82] All the others he built for God's service and prosperity of His commonwealth.

The sultan, of course, announced his patronage with inscriptions inscribed prominently over entryways and around rotundas of īwān domes. Qāytbāy sought to renew at least the facade of grandeur his regime had once evoked. If this could not be duplicated in the later fifteenth century, he could hearken back to earlier glory days when the empire's monuments were synonymous with its temporal power.[83] Qāytbāy's abiding interest in the edifices of Islam's three holiest shrines: Mecca (the *Kaʿba*), Medina (the Prophet's Mosque and Tomb), and Jerusalem (Dome of the Rock), all of which lay within his domain, exemplified his custodianship of orthodoxy. Qāytbāy regarded himself as a mujaddid, a renewer whom God had granted power and wealth. His concept of revival meant exactly that: restoration of past glories in a tradition of spiritual unity looking back to the early caliphs and the unified Islamic Empire. Qāytbāy's identity with these shrines, to which all his competitors came as contrite pilgrims, cannot be doubted. When the sultan received an exhausted messenger who had ridden to Cairo in forced stages on a racing dromedary with a report that the Prophet's Mosque in Medina had suffered fire damage ignited by lightning, he wept profusely and ordered repairs with his own money.[84] No thought of requisition entered his mind; the responsibility was his.

This personal sense of duty was so consistent that the man's obsession with his mission cannot be doubted. But Qāytbāy's intensity of belief did not belie practical objectives. Beyond bolstering the regime's image before rival monarchs, the sultan shrewdly calculated that his soldiers could not accuse their master of selfishness when they plotted rebellion for no higher purpose than greed. Property holders could not label their ruler a spendthrift who bled them for nothing more than self-aggrandizement. Savants could not condemn his expropriations as violations of Islamic law if their proceeds contributed toward enhancement of institutions nurturing their own class. This practical side of Qāytbāy's endowment program should be kept in mind when his stance as a pious conservator is weighed. Since it contrasts with al-Ghawrī's objectives, the latter's unsavory reputation among the ʿulamāʾ was predictable. But al-Ghawrī's projects, vain as they were, embodied goals no less rational and certainly more intriguing.

Al-Ghawrī had little taste for traditional rituals of piety. The Ramaḍān readings of Bukhārī's corpus that so captivated his predecessor now lapsed to their former modest venue. Al-Ghawrī curtailed the bestowal of ceremonial robes Qāytbāy had lavished on devout attendents.[85] While the nāẓir al-khāṣṣ was publicly condemned for their tawdry quality, everyone knew from whom he took his marching orders. Al-Ghawrī's charitable offerings to the indigent were consonant with his pragmatic attitudes toward largesse overall. The sultan confined most of his alms to ceremonies celebrating his mausoleum-hospice complex just west of the Azhar Square. Only when he offered thanks for his recovery from an infection of his eyelids did he distribute equivalent sums with no thought of his monument.[86]

Rituals allowing copious display resonated with al-Ghawrī's inclination toward the masquerade of majesty. Wearisome intonations of Ḥadīth weighed heavily on all but the most stalwart. But processions associated with Ḥajj observances stimulated al-Ghawrī's imaginative faculties. Only a minute segment of the population could attend devotional functions at the Citadel, whereas musterings of pilgrims ready to depart for the holy cities or paradings of the Kaʿba Mantle thrilled throngs of local residents and awed foreign visitors joining the Cairo caravan. Qāytbāy had deliberately downplayed Ḥajj displays, inviting Ibn Iyās' lament over the people's sense of loss when deprived of this ceremony symbolizing Egypt's centrality in the annual rite of unity to which all Muslims gathered. Al-Ghawrī, on the other hand, perceived the effect of such spectacles and exploited the mantle cavalcade as a token of his regime's munificence. Once he felt confident of his own security by 912/1507, he elaborated the Maḥmal procession into a multistaged affair with prescheduled stops through the capital for the tapestry to be shown.[87] His revived lancers' corps, drilled to precision, delighted spectators, native and foreign, with their cadences. Al-Ghawrī took a proprietory interest in embellishing tombs of all the prophets within his realm. In 919 and 921/1513 and 1515 he commissioned seven silk tapestries for their sanctuaries and ordered a celebration honoring the most esteemed after Muḥammad himself, Ibrāhīm al-Khalīl ("the Friend").[88] The chief steward (*khādim*) of his mausoleum at Hebron led the processions heralded by timbalists and trumpeters. A company of der-

vishes whirled in ecstasy before the tapestry howdahs borne on dromedaries—
truly scenes to enthrall the masses. Yet they paled before the pilgrimage
departure of 920/1514, in which the sultan's wife and son participated.

On 17 Shawwāl/5 December, Ibn Iyās vented his sarcasm as he described
the sultan's ostentation for this occasion.[89] Four batallions set out from the
Rumayla Square for the Pilgrim's Lake: those of Jānibak Qarā, caravan commander (*bāsh*), a scion of a previous monarch, the sultan's son and wife, and
the head of the Maḥmal cavalcade. While all four dazzled spectators, the third
was truly remarkable. Ibn Iyās stated that al-Ghawrī assigned it the royal standards while the other three could display only subordinate blazons. The prince
and khawand hardly traveled as humble penitents. More than twenty camels
bore their personal effects, which included porcelain table service, vases of la-
pis lazuli, crystal goblets and gold cutlery. Even a copper bathtub embossed
with silver spigots was loaded onto a dromedary.

Al-Ghawrī's choice of the caravan to mark his offspring's debut as an adolescent was understandable and the robes embroidered with gold thread the
prince received came from his father's wardrobe. Yet no favored officials lacked
for splendid mantles either, in contrast with the cheap drapes handed out during Ḥadīth recitals. The procession's unabashed luxury struck Ibn Iyās as callous in times of hardship for ordinary pilgrims. And the sight provided by the
royal bathing vessel swaying precariously on a disgruntled camel's back he
found ridiculous. The khawand herself did not even participate in the parade,
but departed the Citadel via a postern gate early the next morning and secretly
joined the company at the Pilgrim's Lake. Her palanquin, crafted specially for
the event at a cost of twenty thousand dīnārs, had made its way empty through
the streets. Once the caravan reached the holy cities, the behavior of al-Ghawrī's
spouse and son made a mockery of pious gratuity. Showered with costly gifts
by the amīr of Mecca, neither reciprocated in kind. The royal entourage wal-
lowed in ease during the prescribed rites as other participants paid exorbitant
prices for accommodations and food. Neither the prince nor khawand made
any charitable donations on their journey or sojourn. "No one spoke well of
them, since the princess failed even to offer water at rest stations, as the khawand al-Khaṣṣbakīya, Qāytbāy's spouse, had done when she made the Ḥajj.
Al-Ghawrī's wife granted fellow pilgrims no morsel of sugar nor bit of pastry
to stave off thirst. All those in her train complained of her penury. Still, blame
lay not with her but the sultan, her husband, who was among the stingiest of
God's creatures. . . . His son was too young to grant anything on his own
volition." *Badāʾiʿ* 4, p. 441, l. 10. Yet withal, Ibn Iyās judged the Cairo departure a propagandistic triumph since it suitably impressed local inhabitants
who were temporarily diverted from threats abroad, and ambassadors who allegedly marveled at this monarch's pomp.

Sensitive as he was to the impact of his pilgrimage galas, al-Ghawrī
showed little interest in constructing houses of public worship. The roster of

his contributions to pious foundations, noticeably shorter than Qāytbāy's, focuses on his own tomb, located at the site of the former Hatmaker's Market (*Sūq al-Sharābishiyīn*). (See chapter 7, note 41.) Aside form this edifice, controversial as it was, the sultan made only three donations elsewhere: a minaret at the Azhar, a hospice-madrasa in Mecca and a small mosque in the Hippodrome precinct he renovated.[90] His namesake, called al-Ghūrīya to this day, impressed observers for its innovative features (a minaret with four separate turrets at its summit and a vast circular chamber in its Ṣūfī hospice) but also invited their criticism for its benefactor's untoward methods. A man who craved instant glory, al-Ghawrī stripped other structures of costly decorative stone and wood for his monument's adornment.[91]

Expropriating the site itself from a former eunuch guardian of apprentice Mamlūks, one Mukhtaṣṣ, the sultan denied him any space for burial in its courtyard. He then ordered the adjustment of a waqf governing an adjacent property that supported another madrasa to facilitate his demolition of neighboring buildings. Brushing aside protests over his tampering with an immutable trust, al-Ghawrī sought divine emanation on the spot by transferring relics of the Prophet from their Nile shrine.[92] He pressured the ʿulamāʾ into issuing a fatwā legalizing this change of repository, despite its violation of the founder's endowment deed. The sultan also sent down the ʿUthmānī Koran, to which he attached particular veneration. Several other revered copies found a new home in the shrine. This man's obsession with accumulating physical objects idolized for their baraka or commissioning tableaux in his mausoleum struck contemporaries as ironic. Ibn Iyās noted how assiduously al-Ghawrī planned details of the relics' placement near his future tomb, and pondered details of khuṭba preachings while ignoring the illicit implications of his trust expropriations. Persistent structural defects, including a tilt in the huge minaret necessitating its demolition and reconstruction, signaled the All-High's displeasure with this edifice some had dubbed the *"Masjid al-Ḥarām"* (Sinful Mosque), a pointed word play on the revered shrine in Mecca.[93]

Al-Ghawrī himself had directed work on his mosque in absentia, so haunted was he over danger outside the Citadel and possibly his bad name. He delayed paying a visit to the complex for nine years before he inspected it and presided over Friday service.[94] The sultan often ignored hallowed traditions when his interests required, but he remained peculiarly sensitive about public reprobation. Al-Ghawrī put off his first visit almost a decade in part from worry over epithets the mob might hurl at him as he rode by. But sour memories died hard, and rancor over the vast complex plagued him to the end of his life. Nonetheless, criticism never impelled a change in his attitude toward expropriation. The implicit contradiction between worry over popular condemnation and perseverance with policies incurring it emerges as one of the persistent enigmas surrounding al-Ghawrī's behavior.

Such contradictions figured less vividly in the sultan's secular projects. From 909/1503, when his mausoleum neared completion, al-Ghawrī initiated works of renovation or new construction that over the following decade beautified Cairo in ways few former rulers had envisioned. Al-Ghawrī built palaces and kiosks from Rawḍā Island to al-Maṭarīya and Būlāq along the Nile shore. His venture in the Khān al-Khalīlī market enhanced mercantile activity there. But while the palaces, as private dwellings, benefitted the sultan's retainers and the wakālas turned him personal profits, he implemented several designs that served a broader spectrum of society. Two inspired special praise: the Hippodrome Gardens below the Citadel and the Nilometer complex at the southern tip of Rawḍā.

Al-Ghawrī began altering the Hippodrome (*Maydān*) in Ṣafar 909/July-August 1503.[95] Over the next four years, he extended the precinct with a new casement wall further out in the Rumayla Square, imported several varieties of aromatic shrubs and trees from Syria, and installed an aqueduct to irrigate the orchards and fill the reflecting pool before his pavilion. Ibn Iyās pointedly reminded his readers of al-Ghawrī's extravagance, which allegedly ran to eighty thousand dīnārs. But he also extolled the gardens' consummate effect when completed. As the seedlings matured and blossomed, they transformed a sunbaked polo field into a recreational wonder. The kiosks and belvederes surrounding the pool offered guests a vista hitherto unknown in the heart of a large city. Qāytbāy, for all his patronage of religious architecture, provided his capital with nothing remotely comparable. The verses that circulated in the Ṣafavid realm deriding the gardens indicate how far its fame had spread.[96] Shah Ismāʿīl's pundits might ridicule its instigator but his refined taste could not be denied. The Hippodrome Orchards were beautiful. If, in the eyes of his rivals, an autocrat deviated from military tradition by sponsoring such effeteness, so be it. But a competitor's scorn smacked of secret envy over a marvel that brought the sultan renown elsewhere.

Al-Ghawrī's restoration of the Nilometer hall and its adjacent mosque, construction of a palace, and additions of riverside pavilions surrounding them also won him acclaim.[97] Al-Ghawrī laid great stock in his function as God's first supplicant in Egypt who prayed for the annual flood. He therefore exhibited more personal solicitude for the Nilometer than for any religious foundation in Cairo, transforming ancient rituals and prayer vigils into spectacles the masses could join. For the Nilometer was indeed a popular forum where subjects from all classes congregated. Al-Ghawrī staged many of his fireworks pageants at the site. His penchant for throwing a party on a scale massive enough to enchant the entire city clearly betokened personal inclinations his predecessor eschewed.[98] Al-Ghawrī also revealed himself a master of distraction who preoccupied his subjects with displays lest they dwell unduly on his fiscal abuses. No one downplayed the sultan's arbitrary rule. But most appreciated his fabulous shows and Bacchanalian receptions because they enlivened their humdrum existence. Long after al-Ghawrī's shortcomings as a monarch or failure as a guardian of his realm had faded, memories of his soirées persisted as a felicitous moment in an otherwise troubled era. Did Ibn Iyās' censure of al-Ghawrī as "the stingiest of God's creatures" address all dimensions of his behavior? His common subjects probably thought otherwise.

Al-Ghawrī combined a huckster's instincts with a connoisseur's tastes. A ruler who drew artists and poets into his circle, the sultan genuinely enjoyed their company and talents. He clearly found them more congenial than the savants who so titillated Qāytbāy with their legal minutiae and scholastic trivia.[99] Al-Ghawrī was capable of gestures that disclosed a keen aesthetic sensitivity. On New Year's Day of 916 (I Muḥarram/10 April 1510), he welcomed all the muqaddamūn to the Hippodrome pavilion where he presented each one with a rose from an embroidered napkin (*fūṭa*).[100] The sultan sniffed the petals before offering them to the amīrs individually. Ibn Iyās searched the annals of his precursors but could find no comparable ceremony. A man who made oppression a high art and dealt with his peers as enemies could also show exquisite glimmerings of hospitality.

Such gestures did not compensate for the sultan's overriding greed, and Ibn Iyās never rescinded his harsh judgment of al-Ghawrī's reign. Many of his renovations, attractive as they were, remained edifices to his personal gratification. Yet even these offered artists and literateurs a venue to perform and recite. Al-Ghawrī presided over many evenings graced by music and verse in his belvederes, and those soirées he restricted to powerful guests bespoke the sultan's skilled use of flattery and nuance. Al-Ghawrī could not equal Qāytbāy's moral authority or commander's status. But he understood the foibles of human vanity, exploiting them with a master's touch. As an autocrat fated to dole out a shrinking payroll among soldiers whose avarice had run amok, al-Ghawrī could not resolve his financial dilemma. He could stave off its more drastic consequences, however, by ingratiating potential rivals. For all their ostentation, ceremonials cost much less than military bonuses. Despite allegations of frivolity, al-Ghawrī's shows must be seen in the context of his innovative attempts at coping with irremedial problems.

The military review stood out as the most memorable ceremonial of Qāytbāy's tenure. For al-Ghawrī such consistories almost uniformly projected his humiliation before unruly praetorians who obdurately defied reform. Al-Ghawrī's receptions, on the other hand, proclaimed his generosity in a setting more consonant with his delight in luxury and splendor. If these ceremonies deemphasized the importance of troop musters and reduced his competitors' influence, so much the better. Since survival remained al-Ghawrī's ultimate goal, his rivals' diminished stature counted for more than their effectiveness in battle. Despite the risks such a perspective entailed, al-Ghawrī was fully prepared to gamble his fate. Until Selim's aggression loomed on the horizon, the sultan had more to fear at home from his own soldiers than abroad. Moreover, his public festivals could ameliorate his greedy image. They certainly impressed on the masses an awareness of his rule, a sense of what it offered them tangibly. At a time of cynicism over fiscal oppression, which affected the rich far more than the poor, al-Ghawrī's fetes played on his subjects' need for diversion. Since the regime could not abandon its extractions, the commons could expect no relief. But they might find solace in their sovereign's galas, to which he welcomed them all, high or low.

The Context of Confiscation: Routinizing the Ad Hoc

Such galas were hosted in the midst of less genial events. Both Qāytbāy and al-Ghawrī extracted revenues from their officials and subjects when pressed by their troops. These measures had evolved from temporary expedients into fixed procedures yielding reliable sums. Precise analysis of this transformation is complicated by its clandestine nature. No bureaucrat ostensibly received his commission for embezzlement. No quota of graft was appended to his brevet of appointment. And while chroniclers grimly tallied monies squeezed from officials, one cannot presume their listing of every dīwānī whose accounts the regime scrutinized. Moreover, the figures we do have of funds extracted from bureaucrats or the masses during crisis levies cannot be compared against replete tax figures, since the latter have not endured. Contemporary observers dwelled at greater length on funds pulled from recalcitrant officials than on any formal sources of revenue.

It is their pointed emphasis on confiscation as a process that so strongly implies its centrality in the budget during the late Circassian period. When Ibn Taghrī-Birdī and Ibn Iyās, writing decades apart, summarized Qāytbāy's flaws, they uniformly dwelled on his arbitrary seizures. Ibn Iyās found Qāytbāy's emergency "futures tariffs" ill-disguised expropriation of profits not yet realized.[101] Ibn Taghrī-Birdī, a firsthand witness of what he criticized, condemned Qāytbāy's attitude when he contemplated financing his first expedition against Sūwār in Dhū'l-Qaʿda of 872[102]:

> The Sultan lamented the paucity of money in the treasury, the short supplies
> in the magazines. He realized it was incumbent upon him to expend bonus
> money on the officers and troops mustering for battle. . . . He therefore or-
> dered the qāḍīs, caliph, and ʿulamāʾ to convene before him the next day to
> consult on how the funds were to be collected from merchants, waqf super-
> visors and iqṭāʿ holders. The sultan had resolved upon extractions from the
> populace which were unprecedented. The latter spent the night in terror over
> future calamities. Everyone harbored troubling thoughts over the monarch's
> avarice, his minimal regard for notables of his realm. This ruler exhibited a
> choleric temper marked by violent tantrums, inconstant whim and lack of

solicitude for those mediating on his behalf or who ventured a contesting opinion. For the sultan never gave credit to anyone else for advice. Rather, from his youth his character tended toward unilateral actions according to what he perceived as valid. He never accepted someone else's view, or judgments from council. . . . When he ordered the magistrates to advise him on fundraising, everyone knew he would seize the money one way or the other with no one swaying his resolve. There is no protection, save from God the All-High.

Yet if Qāytbāy's subjects sensed where the ultimate power of coercion lay, why did that source bother with rites of consultation over its legitimacy? Qāytbāy always deliberated with the highest legal agents of his realm. The apparent paradox acquires a rationale if the process of confiscation is weighed in its attendant guise of punishment for equivocation or corruption. Extraordinary taxes and mass levies were invariably justified on grounds of state security and dubious loyalty of sullen commons who bore their alien rulers little affection. The officials whom the monarch installed were routinely accused, mulcted, exiled, and then reinstated. The rhythm of appointment, dismissal, and restoration was so consistent that we may assume a deliberate, if covert, system of reciprocal duties and profits—hidden behind a facade of retribution. Both patron and client stood to gain from this arrangement provided each played by its intuitive rules.

But did all players abide by these conditions? Were the sultan's minions immune from the avarice their patron and his fellows embodied? And had artisans, merchants, or cultivators perfected techniques of obfuscation so well by the later fifteenth century that even this means of extortion no longer generated revenues sufficient to satisfy their appetites? These are queries that must inform our discussion.

For Qāytbāy, confiscation never disengaged itself from exigency. Whatever the validity of Ibn Taghrī-Birdī's castigation, the sultan regarded extortion as an expedient. His vitriolic outbursts bespeak an abiding conviction in a process that could be sustained if its constituents did their part. That Qāytbāy regarded his extractive prerogative as incontestable cannot be doubted. Soon after his enthronement, Qāytbāy seized property in Anbāba across from Būlāq held by the caliph, titular head of state, as an iqtāʿ and conferred it upon his colleague, Jānibak Ḥabīb, recently recalled from exile in Anatolia and in need of an income.[103] Although this champion of Sharīʿa had usurped property rights of his spiritual superior, Qāytbāy exhibited no concern over muttered censure. Installation of comrades mattered far more than transgressions against a powerless figurehead who still retained enough rental income to support his stature at court. This kind of appropriation, which actually reclaimed caliphal allotments made by previous rulers from the royal fisc, had occurred since the early Islamic era and represented no innovation. Nor did sporadic sale of offices or acceptance of bribes from ambitious officials seeking greater prestige deviate from time-honored practices.[104] It was troopers' demands that triggered Qāytbāy's augmentation of his procurers' networks. Seizure of caliphal estates or sale of posts could not generate the sums they devoured.

Qāytbāy convened his advisors before the Sūwār expeditions of the seventies and Ottoman campaigns of the mid-nineties. Chroniclers, two of whom attended these stormy sessions, dwelled on tensions erupting during their proceedings. Qāytbāy initiated the Sūwār councils by requesting a detailed summary of the realm's shortfall from his chancellor, Ibn Muzhir.[105] The kātib al-sirr dutifully outlined the monarch's military needs and the empty treasury his precursors had left him. He then announced the sultan's intent to tap all surplus profits, rents, and waqf yields, allowing artisans, merchants, and charitable trusts no gain for the year. Whether the sultan expected meek acquiescence from council members accepting a fait accomplit the historians do not specify, although most of the assembled legists murmured their assent at the outset. But when the Ḥanafī shaykh Amīn al-Dīn Yaḥyā al-Aqsarāʾī stood up to denounce the sultan's plan, other dissenting voices were raised. Let the monarch collect funds from his fellow militarists' coffers first before bleeding charitable hospices. Even Ibn Muzhir then hedged against the advocacy he had been obliged to preach. Qāytbāy was forced to adjourn the session with no endorsement for his scheme.

But, of course, the expropriation went ahead and the money was raised. Levies charged against pious foundations in particular redistributed assets accumulating for the ʿulamāʾs benefit over decades and did not spell foreclosure for any specific institution. Al-Aqsarāʾī, after all, was rector of the affluent Ashrafīya Barsbāy Madrasa and thus hardly offered a disinterested opinion. The councils were more noteworthy for the light they shed on Qāytbāy's obsession with legal formalities and manifestation of scholastic self-interest clothed in terms emphasizing rights of Muslims trampled upon by fellow believers. Ibn Taghrī-Birdī honed in on individuals most deeply implicated in the affair—bureaucrats whom Qāytbāy charged with implementing his plan. They would bear the brunt of his wrath if they failed in their tasks or concealed their gains:

> Those who feared confiscation the most were (propertied) notables, generators of assets, and officeholders fearing the fate of al-Ṣābūnī (a senior official subjected to interrogation). He had been allowed to descend from confinement to raise part of what the sultan expected from him. Nothing remained for him thereafter, while those classes who possessed few resources to be tapped had nothing to lose and went on unaffected. Most belonged to the commons.[106]

Of the myriad clerks who tallied figures in the dīwāns, several acquired notoriety because of their sovereign's favor or ire. Their career profiles illustrate the vulnerability involved with lucrative positions their patron alternately bestowed or withdrew. When Qāytbāy assumed the sultanate, he garnered his first bonus trove from two persons prominent in Khushqadam's administration: the latter's dawādār, Khayrbak, and his officer of council, Shihāb al-Dīn Aḥmad ibn al-ʿAynī. Khayrbak's mulcting and exile followed predictable demotions inflicted upon a former monarch's intimates. But al-ʿAynī's fate revealed tensions inherent in the symbiosis between military patrons and civilian clients. Al-ʿAynī was a grandson of the eminent historian Badr al-Dīn Maḥmūd and therefore reaped his family's longstanding ties with the Mamlūk elite.[107] Enjoying Khushqadam's esteem as "one of his own sons," al-ʿAynī became a "true master of the realm." But his immense fortune, accumulated in less than five years, provoked Qāytbāy's special umbrage. Al-ʿAynī had become too rich too fast and had curried support from Khushqadam's Mamlūks with lavish benefices. The new sultan thus oversaw his degradation with the same relish as he laid bare his estate.[108] Qāytbāy personally lashed al-ʿAynī when the latter protested destitution after his initial losses. The sultan's agents had ascertained his covert wealth at two hundred thousand dīnārs artfully concealed in trusts or properties held in numerous associates' names. Khushqadam's arch-procurer also kept a lengthy list of bribers who protected their own hoards by paying him handsomely. Qāytbāy coveted this list and would not rest until al-ʿAynī divulged it. Over the next several months, the two waged a war of intimidation and endurance remarkable for the one's brutality and the other's obduracy. But Qāytbāy persevered until he wrung almost four hundred thousand dīnārs from his predecessor's aide, and tracked down most of his partners' graft. Al-ʿAynī's fate typified the prospects of officials who rose high in a former ruler's coterie and thereby became marked men in his successor's eyes. From Qāytbāy's viewpoint, al-ʿAynī had secreted the realm's assets, which must be once again placed at its disposal.

Following Qāytbāy's consolidation, four individuals masterminded much of the regime's extortion. One presided over the vizierate repeatedly in his patron Yashbak's shadow. The others took turns with him in the vizierate or the controllership of the Privy Fund (*al-Khāṣṣ*), a department enlarged during the Circassian period as the sultan's private fisc. These individuals were: Qāsim Shughayta, discussed earlier, Shams al-Dīn Muḥammad al-Ahnāsī, Zayn al-Dīn ʿAbd al-Raḥmān ibn al-Kuwayz, and Tāj al-Dīn ʿAbd-Allāh ibn al-Maqsī. For some twenty-five years these men concocted extractive schemes, designed "futures" taxes, implicated owners of hidden estates and jockeyed with one another for the same posts. Each served time in jail, endured public humiliation as spoilsmen, braved threats of torture, but survived to resume office.[109] Collectively, they represented the sharpest fiscal minds Qāytbāy could exploit, and while he demeaned them he could never do without them. Chroniclers derided them as shameless opportunists. Yet despite their unsavory records, all received grudging accolades as adept financiers who garnered funds when the state till was empty. They served their master in two capacities: procurement and scapegoatism. All four disclosed troves cleverly disguised. They deflected the public's censureship from Qāytbāy himself, who could sustain his image as a guardian of Sharīʿa by prosecuting his own minions' skulduggery. A mutually convenient relationship since all four surmounted their ordeals intact. Qāytbāy's successor saw more lucrative possibilities in such arrangements.

When Selim Yavuz's accountants entered Aleppo Citadel after the Marj Dābiq victory, they were astounded at the treasure al-Ghawrī hauled with him from Cairo.[110] Whatever that enigmatic man's motives, the extent of his hoarded wealth contrasted with the insolvency he had pleaded before his restive troops sixteen years before. Then, al-Ghawrī could rely on no convenient troves stashed away by a predecessor's adjutants.[111] Qāytbāy had already exhausted most reserves he might have tapped. Qāytbāy's ephemeral successors had no opportunity for replenishing the fisc. Al-Ghawrī therefore enjoyed no grace period before his day of reckoning with soldiers who would decide his fate. He resorted immediately to extortion because no other option presented itself. Yet the proverbial riches Selim chanced upon represented royal hoarding of centuries and long predated al-Ghawrī's reign. When he succumbed to the Ottoman in 922, al-Ghawrī had not bought off his troops' sedition by whittling away at this hidden reserve. For sixteen years he staved off fiscal disasters far worse than Qāytbāy had faced in 872 while preserving, and even augmenting, the royal hoard. How did he manage this achievement?

Aside from his blood relative and alter ego, Ṭūmānbāy, few officers developed a rapport with al-Ghawrī. But several hit upon innovative schemes to extort larger sums from broader segments of society than had Qāytbāy's clients. The distinction between collegial tie and collusion in graft contrasts sharply with the genuine camaraderie at the apex of Qāytbāy's entourage. No one personified tensions between the sultan and his adjutants more than Qāyt al-Rajabī, his first marshal. We have already considered this officer's role in al-Ghawrī's enthronement. But the atābak's indispensable contribution derived from his oversight of confiscations in Cairo that kept al-Ghawrī's regime afloat.[112] Al-Ghawrī exiled Qāyt in 910, three years after the marshal rescued him from bankruptcy. Once the sultan had noted his atābak's overtures to the viceroy of Damascus, he was removed—no matter how valued his previous service. Al-Ghawrī and Qāyt al-Rajabī were bound solely by convenience. When the latter saw his own advancement tied with the former's ensconcement, he employed his formidable skills in his liege-lord's cause. When their interdependence became less binding, mutual antipathy prevailed and their relationship soured. Expedience mattered, rapport did not. Al-Ghawrī's dealings with most other high-ranking officers paralleled his demotion of Qāyt.[113] Since his subordinates perceived their expendable status, they responded in kind. But the system Qāyt helped implement continued unabated until al-Ghawrī's defeat. Its effects would be discernible centuries later.

This system, stripped of chroniclers' heated rhetoric, involved heightened monitoring of rich families who had refined concealment, mulcting members of Mamlūk houses previously spared as inviolate, and broadening the reach of confiscation to embrace the commons whose penury had heretofore spared them the regime's notice. The first two aspects of this program represented straightforward intensification of extant ploys. Civilians who profited from their clientship and yet retained an aura of respectability had always been ripe for extortion in emergencies. Al-Ghawrī, however, placed several eminent families under indefinite surveillance, siphoning off their gains with unremitting fervor until he was satisfied they had been decimated. A prime example were members of the Jī'ān clan, previously discussed. Beginning in Rabī' I 908/September-October 1502, al-Ghawrī placed the family's patriarch, Ṣalāḥ al-Dīn Yaḥyā, under arrest until he yielded a sum the sultan's spies found commensurate with his suspected hoard. Over the next decade, the sultan extracted more than half a million dīnārs from prominent Jī'ānīs without once substantiating a corruption charge against them.[114] One of his extorters, 'Abd al-'Aẓīm, the moneychanger, might accuse Ṣalāḥ of embezzling the state treasury, but his libel was never sustained in court. In fact, al-Ghawrī, rarely bothering with trumped-up legal formalities, relentlessly kept up his intimidation until the family divulged its wealth in return for peace. The tactic succeeded, for the Jī'ānīs had indeed secreted a vast fortune which they divulged only when cowed by unrelieved harassment. Impoverishment might rank above misery on a scale of absolute degradation, yet its stifling effect on the propertied classes lasted long beyond al-Ghawrī's oppression.

Qāytbāy had not totally ignored estates guarded by individuals traditionally spared vicissitudes of intra-Mamlūk rivalries. He exhibited little remorse when he hounded the Lady Sāda for an "obligatory gift" in 874/1470.[115] But Qāytbāy respected patrimonies entrusted to female relatives of deceased competitors who had deliberately specified their wives or daughters as custodians. Qāytbāy relied on his own spouse's skills as manager of their vast properties—held jointed by testament of surviving trust deeds.[116] Since Islamic inheritance laws governed only a Mamlūk's personal effects, male members of the caste colluded with their female counterparts to preserve estates for their descendants. But al-Ghawrī began undermining this tacit arrangement. He took his first tentative steps at compromising the immunity of Mamlūk women from confiscation when he arrested Qāytbāy's concubine, mother of his son and heir, in 907.[117] From then on, his boldness paralleled his growing need, and he extended his mulctings beyond real estate. The sultan pilfered bridal trousseaus for jewelry, fined eminent women singers whose fame hinted at substantial assets and impounded charitable donations set aside for orphans or widows. Al-Ghawrī disdained the reprobation his measures predictably invoked, but his policy must be judged for its efficacy rather than its improbity. Did such extractions, petty at face value, yield sums worth the efforts they incurred? While the chroniclers provide few precise amounts, their frequency implies al-Ghawrī's conviction of their utility.

Al-Ghawrī and his aides showed their real flair for ingenuity as they broadened the scope of mass confiscations, concocted new imposts, tightened their grip over subordinates, and closed off loopholes through which both producers and collectors had slipped in the past. The new administration inaugurated its creative voracity with the New Year's confiscation of 907/1502.[118] Following his strident morning council with the qāḍīs, and his subsequent closeting with Ibn al-Shiḥna, al-Ghawrī convened Qāyt al-Rajabī and several other officers to divide up their extortive duties. The marshal assumed responsibility for summoning waqf supervisors and iqtāʿ holders. Pensioners, including widows or orphaned daughters, reported to the exchequer (*wakīl Bayt al-Māl*). Owners of houses, tenements, and shops let to rent proceeded to the dawādār Miṣirbāy. Any individual who avoided his subpoena was brought to trial. Eight other officers took charge of interrogating wealthy families, including the Jīʿānīs, and canvassed Cairo's districts. Detailed files of payees had been compiled in advance by the sultan's procurers who estimated the covert riches of each, as well as his probable tactics of deception. All victims were to be questioned twice: first, at a time formally scheduled, and, second, unexpectedly when they believed themselves off the hook, rejoicing in the assets they had saved. Elders of the Christian and Jewish communities were included in their sweep and disclosed projected incomes of their flocks. Ibn Iyās remarked on the remorselessness of this levy. Under the menace of impending troop revolt, Qāyt al-Rajabī's soldiers forced their way into homes without warrants, subjected women to strip searches on the suspicion of jewelry hidden in body orifices, closed down mosques until they signed over their waqf proceeds, and even threatened patients in the Manṣūrī Hospital. The searches degenerated into a general riot of looting by slaves and street hooligans following on the extorters' heels. But they generated a substantial amount of money. Al-Ghawrī received five hundred thousand dīnārs from ten-months' waqf yields and pension payments alone. His take amply covered the troops' bonuses, and once their demands were met he could rest easy. Public disturbances might depress the economy and traumatize the masses but the sultan's survival rested on his soldiers' sufferance. Mass confiscations remained a viable option for him and a palpable threat to his subjects until he departed Cairo for Syria. Despite his desperate situation, al-Ghawrī had not touched a fils (copper coin) of the royal hoard he inherited. The levy fulfilled his needs with plenty to spare. His private trove he would protect for the Ottomans to plunder.

Like Qāytbāy, al-Ghawrī gathered his coterie of extorters whose position depended entirely on the revenues they uncovered. Their names have already figured prominently in this study: ʿAlī ibn Abī'l-Jūd, Zaynī Barakāt ibn Mūsā, Shams al-Dīn ibn ʿAwaḍ, and Sarī al-Dīn ibn al-Shiḥna. While their profiles of chicanery broadly paralleled those of Qāytbāy's aides, they were distinguished by more audacity and less certainty. Qāytbāy and Yashbak assuredly browbeat their officials. Yet the humiliation these men experienced was more symbolic than real—meted out for public mollification. Al-Ghawrī, by contrast, worked with no partner in arms like Yashbak, at least until his nephew came of age, and regarded all his clients with the same ambivalence. Al-Ghawrī's agents, excepting Zaynī Barakāt, came to violent ends at his hands. When their usefulness no longer matched the antipathy they provoked from his soldiers, al-Ghawrī turned on them and they suffered a scapegoat's fate. For Qāytbāy, scapegoatism was part of the implicit contract both sides recognized. Few lost their lives or forfeited their fortunes because of it. Al-Ghawrī's retainers, on the other hand, usually faced a catastrophe when they fell from favor. Few of the notorious regained their posts no matter what their previous contributions had been.

Al-Ghawrī may well deserve the castigation Ibn Iyās and others heaped on him. And yet, weighed objectively, his behavior merits respect for its effectiveness. Al-Ghawrī did not lack for capable persons who eagerly sought to enter his service, whatever the risks they ran. His reprisals never checked the ambitions of fresh candidates. His supply of clients clawing their way up through the ranks to penetrate his inner circle remained steady. By eliminating those who succeeded too well, Al-Ghawrī could cool the heated tempers of his soldiery, upon whom he inflicted much the same abuse. So hated did his agents become, again with Zaynī Barakāt's exclusion, that mock arrests and exiles no longer requited the troopers' lust for revenge. Moreover, al-Ghawrī would not tolerate competition in hoarding. All of his prominent extorters persisted in attempts at feathering their own nests, at their patron's expense.[119] Since al-Ghawrī staved off bankruptcy with confiscated funds, he was proclaiming via his elimination of aides that extortion had now become a royal monopoly. Al-Ghawrī's fiscal experiments were not limited to confiscation. But since his other ploys remained rudimentary, he could not dispense with seizure as his reliable source of revenue. Accordingly, no subordinate could vie with him for retention of mulcted assets.

The Context of Cruelty: Duplicity's Price

Of the images from the Mamlūk era haunting the consciousness of modern Egyptians, few evoke more turbulent emotions than the abuse these praetorians heaped upon their ancestors. The Mamlūk elite amply merited the respect they won on the battlefield, often against formidable odds. Their generosity on behalf of religion, scholarship, and welfare was proverbial by any preindustrial standard. And yet the Mamlūks are remembered as masters of cruelty. Anyone familiar with narratives of the later Mamlūk period cannot ignore their incessant harping on brutal treatment, which, at first glance, seems to have been applied randomly. But so ubiquitous is the phenomenon of elite abuse in history that no one group can claim a monopoly over it. Simplistic condemnation of perpetrators reveals little about motives behind systematic cruelty, individuals who suffered the brunt of it, or its long-term legacy. That Qāytbāy, al-Ghawrī, and their colleagues dealt harshly with subordinates emerges from almost every leaf of contemporary histories. Despite profound spiritual convictions, their unruffled demeanor implies their conception of cruelty as an expedient, a lever justified by circumstance.

For the Mamlūks, whose barracks socialization steeped them in the politics of violence, cruelty figured large in their hierarchy of values. Mercy in the face of competition counted as a sign of weakness, an invitation for one's rivals to seize the initiative and dash not only individual ambitions but those of comrades as well. Spectacular acts of barbarity betokened something of the theatrical, a propensity for exhibiting extremes of behavior that might cow even the most formidable of enemies.[120] Yet atrocities among peers represented the savagery of equals who could give as nastily as they received. Cruelty inflicted upon clients was patently one-sided, a power of coercion or prohibition one party monopolized as a gain over the other. Omnipresent as it might seem, abuse of subordinates occurred as an aspect of rivalry only by association. Patrons meted it out most often in reprisal for suspected treachery. They defined treachery as a violation of implicit expectations for covert service a subordinate accepted when he entered into a client relationship. As the later Mamlūk state struggled to ward off insolvency, sultans and adjutants became obsessed with the prospect of minions hoodwinking them at their own game. Assets squeezed from the masses that both patron and client exploited were being concealed by methods employed ostensibly for the former's exclusive benefit. Moreover, behind this immediate, and seemingly irremedial, dilemma lurked an even more disquieting possibility. Clandestine schemes of parasitic extraction that had mutually profited bureaucrats and militarists since the time of Ṣalāḥ al-Dīn were now proving inadequate for the needs, or greed, of either.

The depths of suspicion pervading the outlook of all participants in this process were vividly apparent in preemptive arrests at a new reign's outset. When Qāytbāy began dismantling his predecessor's apparatus, he seized fortunes of all those tainted by clientage. As Qāytbāy interrogated Khushqadam's aides, he wasted no time investigating their culpability.[121] Success on behalf of their former master sufficed to confirm their treason. Loyalty to a peer rival automatically disqualified either for a place in the new autocrat's team. But before they were eliminated, the assets they garnered for that rival's enterprise must be recovered. Qāytbāy's personal abuse of al-ʿAynī or Yashbak's oppression of Ibn ʿAbd al-Razzāq whom he replaced as major-domo, symbolized their hostility toward clients who were their peer-rival's appendages. The peer had died but so long as his followers closeted his assets, they might rally his soldiers against the new order. Presumably, only a forthright disclosure of those assets would have saved al-ʿAynī or Ibn ʿAbd al-Razzāq from the travails they experienced by pleading destitution. Qāytbāy and Yashbak knew the system too well to believe protestations, and they persevered until everything was disclosed. Thus, while Ibn Taghrī-Birdī or Ibn Iyās might blanch over al-ʿAynī's fate, neither found it untoward. Al-ʿAynī acquired riches reserved as the military caste's preserve. He enjoyed them only so long as his patron reigned because, in fact, they remained his master's by right. Al-ʿAynī could manipulate them solely as his master's instrument. Any attempt at concealment was equated with treason.

But Qāytbāy did not limit cruelty to those in his predecessor's service. Throughout his reign, he repeatedly harassed his closest civilian aides for money. These individuals had cast their lot with him. All had succeeded admirably at the covert tasks their sovereign demanded. Yet when the sultan suspected them of withholding a portion of their embezzlements, he treated them as backstabbers who ungratefully transgressed the rules of their relationship. This conviction of deceit on the patron's part is essential to our comprehension of cruelty. When Qāytbāy exploded in rage at his wazīr, al-Ahnāsī, he railed at the latter's lachrymose guise of penury.[122] Qāytbāy and Yashbak were well apprised of what this office typically yielded over a given period. Al-Ahnāsī's pleas reeked of obfuscation. He was stubbornly resigned to his racking, which produced only two thousand dīnārs before his release. Ibn Taghrī-Birdī noted that al-Ahnāsī "returned home outwardly chastened but privately intent upon regaining the vizierate." For torture rarely inhibited an ambitious bureaucrat from seeking reinstatement and dabbling in murky waters time and again. Qāsim Shughayta was flogged on numerous occasions when Qāytbāy suspected him of keeping his own proper share. But he invariably reemerged when the regime had need of his skills. Abuse suffered by Qāytbāy's reliable procurers whose talents were indispensable must be distinguished from more severe reprisals imposed on those the regime marked for execution. These were more likely to have engaged in espionage for a foreign enemy or sullied their ruler's honor.[123] While torments borne by the sultan's fiscal agents were onerous, they threatened limb more than life. Clients who staked their fortunes in the sultan's cause accepted harrowing episodes in his inquisitors' chambers as an inevitable consequence of their own chicanery. The threat of torture prohibited few from seeking reentry. Their persistence in the face of adversity underscores differences between modern sensibilities and perspectives of those living in other times. What may strike the contemporary mind as intolerable may well have been endured as a normative price for success.

When we contemplate cruelty under al-Ghawrī, similarities in affliction are qualified by contrasts in motives. Revenue and security underlay all
of al-Ghawrī's devices. If anything, he approached torture with more vehemence but less passion than Qāytbāy. Al-Ghawrī systematized the harassment
of his fiscal agents so effectively that one suspects a direct correlation between
intensity inflicted and money hoarded. Discovery of a few thousand dīnārs
laundered within a waqf supervisor's account logs merited a lashing.[124]
Further up the scale, when a currency manipulator offered only half of what
al-Ghawrī's counterspies knew he had collected, the level of torture rose to a
body racking of skull compression in a vice.[125] In both instances, the offender
could not sustain excessive injury since he must survive for payment of his
debt. But when al-Ghawrī sought a massive sum, representing an agent's
lifetime accumulation, he gave his inquisitors free rein. Shamuwāl, a Jewish
moneylender, and his wife, the prime suspect in his duplicity, suffered so
terribly that they expired—but not before they had divulged the whereabouts
of half a million dīnārs they had stashed away.[126] The sultan had determined
that the size of Shamuwāl's trove outweighed any future service he might
provide. Nonetheless, before the moneychanger died, al-Ghawrī dragged out
valuable details about holdings of Cairo's Jewish community.[127] The grisly
outline of al-Ghawrī's tactics bespeak not only regularized torture but its refined application at an expert's hands. The master touch of Zaynī Barakāt
guaranteed divulgence of assets before death and consequent loss of lucrative
information.

Yet al-Ghawrī and his arch-inquisitor perfected their unique brand of fear
less for the exquisite torments they devised than for the precariousness of their
subordinates. Unlike Qāytbāy, al-Ghawrī turned against several of his most
productive agents purely for tactical reasons. Extorters who initially intrigued
the sultan with their schemes found themselves abandoned if officers too powerful to annoy detected them sniffing uncomfortably close to their own
hoards.[128] Whatever their duplicity, these individuals fulfilled the clandestine
requirements of their offices. Al-Ghawrī eliminated them when they amassed
fortunes approaching his own (and thereby challenged his capacity to purchase
loyalty), or compromised the interests of pivotal colleagues. Al-Ghawrī's
behavior thus raises the question of whether he played by the rules they accepted by compulsion. Neither Qāytbāy nor al-Ghawrī invented confiscation or torture as policies. But al-Ghawrī's actions suggest his growing dis-
enchantment with the system he inherited by default. This process by itself
could no longer meet his fiscal needs. Its inadequacy compelled a radical intensification of both cruelty and betrayal. Al-Ghawrī's experiments with alternative procedures should be interpreted in light of his callous attitude
toward aides who had striven within the existing system. Since this man no
longer found them so essential, he dispensed with even the most able when
circumstances warranted.

Notes

1. As per *Badāʾiʿ* 5, p. 72, l. 18.

2. William Popper, *Egypt and Syria under the Circassian Sultans,* University of California Publications in Semitic Philology, vol. 15 (Berkeley, 1955), 96–98 for decline of the vizierate (*wizāra*); modification of controllership of Privy Funds (*niẓārat al-Khāṣṣ*); enhancement of the Special Bureau (*niẓara Dīwān al-Mufrad*); rise of controllership of Financial Bureaus (*Dīwān al-Dawla*) as co-signatory of fiscal edicts with *wazīr;* decline of Exchequer (*wakīl Bayt al-Māl*) as major-domo's (*ustādār*) powers are enlarged.

3. On the nature of client or "dyadic" relationships, see Carl H. Landé, "The Dyadic Basis of Clientism," in S. W. Schmidt, ed. *Friends, Followers and Factions: A Reader in Political Clientism* (Berkeley, 1977), xix, on the function of clientism in noncorporate groups, the lack of boundaries between such groups, and xx, for problems of reliability; E. Gellner, "Patrons and Clients," in *Patrons and Clients in Mediterranean Societies* (London, 1977), who notes (3) that a patronage system always belongs to some "pays réel" ambivalently conscious of not being the "pays légal." Gellner regards patronage as likely in a partially centralized state or defective bureaucracy. John Waterbury, "An Attempt to Put Patrons and Clients in their Place," (in *Patrons and Clients in Mediterranean Societies*), 322, interprets patron-client networks as strategies for maintenance or aggrandizement on a patron's part, coping or survival on a client's part.

4. *Inbāʾ*, p. 151, l. 12.

5. Ibid., p. 207, l. 8.

6. Ibid., p. 218, l. 15.

7. Ibid., pp. 392, l. 18; 398, l. 5; *Badāʾiʿ* 3, p. 68, l. 3.

8. *Inbāʾ*, p. 489, l. 1.

9. See Bernadette Martel-Thoumian, *Les civils et l'administration dans l'état militaire mamlūk (ixᵉ/xvᵉsiècle)* (Damascus: IFD, 1991), 295–319, for the activities of this prominent family.

10. *Badāʾiʿ* 3, p. 209, l. 10.

11. *Badāʾiʿ* 4, p. 72, l. 6.

12. Ibid., p. 82, l. 14.

13. Ibid., p. 319, l. 20.

14. *Rawḍ,* f. 178, l. 2. In Shaʿbān 872/February–March 1468, the commandantship of the Damascus Citadel went to one Yashbak al-Sayfī ʿAlī Bāy

for a fee of five thousand dīnārs, while the same post in Aleppo was allotted to Timurbāy, brother of Almās, in return for six thousand dīnārs. Many regional posts were parceled out in this way. In Ṣafar 874/August–September 1469, the chamberlain of Ṭarābulus paid ten thousand dīnārs for his appointment. See *Inbā'*, p. 130, l. 3; *Rawḍ*, f. 247-b, l. 4.

15. *Ḥawādith* 4, p. 694, l. 16; *Inbā'*, *p. 41, l. 15; Rawḍ*, f. 211-b, l. 15; *Badā'i'* 3, p. 25, l. 2.

16. When Qāytbāy granted the lucrative syndicate of the Prophet's Descendants (*niqābat al-Ashrāf*) in Damascus to a prominent merchant of the town, he withheld the customary robe confirming the appointment "because the aspirant did not pay up what had been customarily charged for the office." (*Inbā'*, p. 497, l. 16; Dhū'l-Ḥijja 885/February–March 1481). This office assigned its incumbent authority over all endowments and properties donated toward support of the Prophet's Descendants. Mamlūk sultans routinely expected a handsome payment when they bestowed the sinecure. Ultimately, this individual was dismissed and exiled, ostensibly for his hostility toward one of Qāytbāy's judicial protégés in Damascus.

17. *Badā'i'* 4, p. 257, l. 18; 264, l. 1.

18. On multiple officeholding, see Martel-Thoumian, *Civils et l'administration*, 92–97 (who does not deal with covert fiscal matters); Petry, *Civilian Elite*, 201–04.

19. *Ḥawādith* 4, p. 626, l. 13; *Rawḍ*, f. 179, l. 30; *Badā'i'* 3, p. 10, l. 6.

20. *Badā'i'* 3, p. 307, l. 7.

21. *Badā'i'* 4, p. 29, l. 15.

22. Ibid., p. 40, l. 17 (Rabī' I 908/September–October 1502: the case of Ṣalāḥ al-Dīn ibn al-Jī'ān who escaped torture only because he met the sum demanded of him); 42, l. 19 (Rabī' II 908/October–November: a supervisor of charitable trusts who owed "debts" unaccounted for); 144, l. 1 (Ramaḍān 914/December 1508–January 1509: Jewish director of mint accused of hoarding sixty thousand dīnārs embezzled from his patron).

23. *Badā'i'* 4, pp. 82, l. 19; 181, l. 7; 217, l. 21.

24. For example, in Dhū'l-Qa'da 918/January–February 1513, al-Ghawrī fined his agent of the army (*naqīb al-jaysh*) ten thousand dīnārs because he allowed a subordinate, the inspector of Manfalūṭ, to disappear with his district's extractions. The sultan accused the naqīb of collusion with the kāshif and demanded that he make good the sum, along with a fine for his breach of loyalty. "This naqīb al-jaysh intrigued against those who sought audiences

with the sultan and prejudiced their hearings. He was well versed in all sorts of evil practices. Thus does the recompense equal the perfidious deed." Perhaps, but al-Ghawrī turned against this man only because he connived with an underling, an unforgivable act. See *Badāʾiʿ* 4, p. 289, 1. 14. Earlier that year, al-Ghawrī seized the property of his intendent of the larder (*sharabdār*) for allegedly stealing from his master's own provisions. The sultan pursued his interrogation without mercy because "his trusted staff had betrayed his confidence." See *Badāʾiʿ* 4, p. 263, 1. 7.

25. *Badāʾiʿ* 4, p. 185, 1. 16.

26. Ibid., pp. 235, 1. 6; 250, 1. 12; 376, 1. 20; 382, 1. 10; 387, 1. 8.

27. On comparable dynamics of patron-client relations in medieval Iran, see Roy P. Mottahedeh, *Loyalty and Leadership in an Early Islamic Society* (Princeton, 1980).

28. *Ḥawādith* 4, p. 672, 1. 16; *Inbāʾ*, p. 8, 1. 10; *Badāʾiʿ* 3, p. 18, 1. 15 (3 Muḥarram 873/24 July 1468).

29. *Badāʾiʿ* 3, p. 133, 1. 19.

30. *Inbāʾ*, p. 239, 1. 5 (29 Jumādā II 875/23 December 1470).

31. *Badāʾiʿ* 3, p. 168, 1. 6.

32. *Inbāʾ*, p. 286, 1. 9.

33. Ibid., p. 491, 1. 16.

34. *Badāʾiʿ* 4, p. 75, 1. 2.

35. Ibid., p. 144, 1. 9; 146, 1. 10.

36. See Petry, *Civilian Elite*, 341.

37. *Badāʾiʿ* 4, p. 274, 1. 10 (Jumādā II 918/August–September 1512).

38. *Badāʾiʿ* 5, p. 79, 1. 19 (Shaʿbān 922/August–September 1516).

39. *Inbāʾ*, p. 134, 1. 12.

40. Ibid., p. 248, 1. 10.

41. Ibid., p. 279, 1. 2.

42. Ibid., pp. 359, 1. 11; 360, 1. 9; 361, 1. 4; 370, 1. 7.

43. *Badāʾiʿ* 4, p. 7, 1. 3; 85, 1. 11.

44. Ibid., p. 112, 1. 7 (Ramaḍān 913/January–February 1503).

45. Ibid., p. 299, 1. 22.

46. *Badā'iʿ* 4, pp. 135, l. 7 (Jumādā I 914/August–September 1508: rectorship over the Ṣarghitmishīya Madrasa); 183, l. 2 (Ṣafar 916/May–June 1510: son's appointment as nāẓir of the Manṣūrī Hospital, supported by one of the largest waqfs in Cairo).

47. *Badā'iʿ* 4, p. 340, l. 20.

48. Ibid., p. 343, l. 23.

49. Ibid., p. 345, l. 22.

50. *Inbā'*, p. 141, l. 4.

51. Ibid., pp. 186, l. 4 (Muḥarram 875/June–July 1470: the perennial question of the poet, Ibn al-Fāriḍ, whose verses challenged established canons of orthodoxy); 223, l. 12 (Rabīʿ II 875/September–October: council over debts left by deceased Mālikī qāḍī).

52. Ibid., p. 352, l. 16. Al-Ṣayrafī personally observed this acrimonious debate and copied down its participants' arguments. The proceedings were infused with barely concealed hostility between the three judges. The sultan seized upon their disagreements to assert his own prerogative.

53. Other salient examples of Qāytbāy manipulating his fractious judicial network: *Badāiʿ* 3, p. 62, l. 12 (Muḥarram 876/June–July 1471: Sultan dispossesses progeny of Shaykh of Mu'ayyadī Mosque, although they are entitled to the office by waqf writ; defies his cabinet of judges); *Inbā'*, p. 333, l. 15; *Badā'iʿ* 3, p. 63, l. 13 (Rabīʿ I 876/August–September: Sultan reforms procedure for appeals, which are to be heard first by deputy judges before referral to the royal tribunal; Nuwwāb castigated for shirking responsibilities); *Inbā'*, pp. 371, l. 22 (Rajab 876/December 1471–January 1472: Sultan interrogates the four chief justices and their deputies over allegations of corrupt trial proceedings; numerous dismissals); 391, l. 16; *Badā'iʿ* 3, p. 66, l. 20 (same month: During biweekly audience, sultan flogs his nāẓir al-khāṣṣ for cheating three plaintiffs; attendant qāḍīs rebuked for dragging their heels in reporting his abuses); *Inbā'*, p. 436, l. 2 (Dhū'l-Ḥijja 876/May–June 1472: During monthly greeting audience, sultan denies Ḥanafī qāḍī a look through a European magnifying glass; assertion of royal primacy; qāḍī insulted); *Badā'iʿ* 3, pp. 79, l. 16 (Rabīʿ II 877/September–October 1472: Sultan accuses Muḥibb al-Dīn Ibn al-Shiḥna of embezzling waqf funds from the estate of Sultan Barqūq); 168, l. 6 (Rabīʿ II 885/June–July 1480: Sultan dismisses his Shāfiʿī and Ḥanbalī qāḍīs when they delay settlement without justification); 183, l. 13 (Rajab 886/August–September 1481: Sultan dismisses Mālikī and Shāfiʿī qāḍīs along with kātib al-sirr Ibn Muzhir over drawn-out harangue in audience; Mālikī judge and chancellor restored); 228, l. 18 (Rabīʿ II 891/April–May 1486; Sultan curbs fees charged by audience bailiffs for entry); 259, l. 1

(Muḥarram 891/January–February 1486: Sultan limits independent authority of deputies to the Shāfiʿī and Ḥanafī judges, especially with regard to prison sentencing).

54. *Inbāʾ*, pp. 141, l. 11; 142, l. 15. Al-Ṣayrafī observed that, in fact, Qāytbāy soon restored the syndic to his post, once he had squared his accounts. Apparently, after a show of justice, a mutually acceptable arrangement was reached. If the syndic were an astute manipulator of assets, his skills were too valuable to waste by dismissal.

55. Ibid., p. 153, l. 16.

56. Ibid., p. 193, l. 1 (Muḥarram 875/June–July 1470; Mamlūk bisected for shooting arrows while drunk).

57. Ibid., pp. 261, l. 12 (Ramaḍān 875/February–March 1471: Sultan compels wazīr to return money collected from tariff he imposed on shoemakers); 362, l. 19 (Jumādā II 876/November–December 1471: slipper merchants protest wazīr's extractions); 367, l. 18 (same month: Sultan hears petitions from water carriers whose salaries are in arrears); 377, l. 16 (Rajab 876/December 1471–January 1472: Sultan demands accounting from muḥtasib of Alexandria and his wife who have mulcted merchants); 387, l. 19 (same month: Sultan rebukes muḥtasib of Cairo for his corruption); 397, l. 9 (Shaʿbān 876/January–February 1472: merchant accusees qāḍī of claiming his inheritance unjustly); 400, l. 21 (same month: plaintiff accuses guard captain of brutality and extortion); 476, l. 1 (Rabīʿ I 877/August–September 1472: Sultan hears complaints from merchants who accuse muḥtasib of undercutting their sales by setting prices below market value to favor his own partisans); *Badāʾiʿ* 3, pp. 105, l. 22 (Dhūʾl-Ḥijja 879/April–May 1475: Sultan executes inspector of Buḥayra Province and his secretary for embezzlement); 165, l. 13 (Rabīʿ I 885/May–June 1481: Sultan fires muḥtasib after hearing charges of latter's negligence).

58. *Inbāʾ*, pp. 379, l. 10; 383, l. 14. The shaykh, ʿUthmān al-Khaṭṭāb, came under scrutiny himself when the sultan determined he had also altered the īwān without regard for the waqf provisos governing its use. But the fact of Qāytbāy's final ruling against the shaykh's constructions rather than the nāẓir's confirmed the sultan's shrewd assessment of political realities involved if he disgraced a powerful amīr. The shaykh's piety had been conveniently exposed as disguised self-interest.

59. *Ḥawādith* 4, p. 643, l. 1 (Dhūʾl-Ḥijja 872/June–July 1468).

60. *Inbāʾ*, p. 190, l. 5 (Muḥarram 875/June–July 1470: Sultan's relative claims to have beheld Ibn al-Fāriḍ in vision); *Badāʾiʿ* 3, p. 47, l. 9 (same month: Sultan sides with qāḍīs who accept Ibn al-Fāriḍ as sound).

61. *Inbā*, p. 190, l. 14 (Muḥarram 875/July 1470: Sultan cuts off petitioner who then takes up residence in the Azhar Hospice; sultan grants him pension).

62. *Badā'iᶜ* 3, p. 67, l. 11 (Rajab 876/December 1471–June 1472: on strict rules governing public attire for women); *Inbā*, p. 424, l. 5 (Shawwāl 876/March–April: furor over alleged attempts at converting Coptic children).

63. *Inbā*, p. 481, l. 18.

64. *Badā'iᶜ* 3, p. 102, l. 20 (Ramaḍān 879/January–February 1475).

65. *Inbā*, p. 339, l. 19 (Rabīᶜ II 876/September–October 1471).

66. *Badā'iᶜ* 4, p. 203, l. 8.

67. Ibid., p. 250, l. 21 (Dhū'l-Qaᶜda 917/January–February 1512).

68. Ibid., p. 297, l. 6 (20 Muḥarram 919/March–April 1513).

69. Ibid., pp. 303, l. 12 (Ṣafar 919/April–May 1513: eminent female prisoners released); 316, l. 12 (29 Rabīᶜ II 919/4 July 1513: eighty prisoners liberated in one day; unprecedented. Some inmates reveal their degradation: One individual refused any barbering or grooming and his hair resembled a harpy's. Even the sultan's stubborn procurer Ibn Rawq sees the light of day because of al-Ghawrī's alarm).

70. Ibid., p. 168, l. 9.

71. Ibid., p. 343, l. 10 (16 Shawwāl 919/15 December 1513).

72. Ibid., pp. 346, l. 14 (29 Shawwāl 919/28 December 1513: al-Zankalūnī flogged); 347, l. 3 (same day: Sultan departs for Qalyūb to snub the four qāḍīs; civil litigation ceases); 348, l. 1 (1 Dhū'l-Qaᶜda 919/29 December: Sultan refuses to relent over dismissal); 348, l. 11 (2 Dhū'l-Qaᶜda/30 December: Sultan initiates replacement proceedings; interviews candidates).

73. Ibid., p. 349, l. 9 (7 Dhū'l-Qaᶜda/4 January 1514).

74. *Rawḍ*, f. 171-b, l. 26 (Qāytbāy's biography, summary of his military stipends, charitable donations, and building projects covers more than thirty lines of script); al-Sakhāwī, *Dhayl*, f. 283; l. 4 (Dhū'l-Qaᶜda 901/July–August 1496: author extols Qāytbāy's exceptional legacy of respect and admiration); *Jawāhir al-Sulūk*, f. 402-b, l. 4 (same month: Anonymous author links sultan's generosity to his troops with his capacity to unite them).

75. Ibn Iyās, *ᶜUqūd*, f. 242-b, l. 14.

76. *Inbā*, p. 75, l. 19.

77. *Badā᾽iᶜ* 3, p. 62, l. 24.

78. *Inbā᾽*, p. 338, l. 16; *Badā᾽iᶜ* 3, p. 63, l. 20.

79. On robe conferrals: *Rawḍ*, f. 250-b, l. 30 (Shawwāl 874/April–May 1470: Sultan orders his nāẓir al-khāṣṣ to restore robes to all meritorious officials); *Inbā᾽*, p. 213, l. 3; *Badā᾽iᶜ* 3, p. 53, l. 11 (Rabīᶜ I 875/August–September 1470: robe bestowals during Mawlid al-Nabawī); *Inbā᾽*, pp. 259, l. 16 (Ramaḍān 875/February–March 1471: civil notables receive robes); 407, l. 1; *Badā᾽iᶜ* 3, pp. 68, l. 23 (Ramaḍān 876/February–March 1472: Sultan distributes more than one thousand dīnārs to ᶜulamā᾽); 83, l. 10; 93, l. 7; 122, l. 5; 137, l. 10; 170, l. 5; 196, l. 19; 206, l. 22; 220, l. 8; 243, l. 13 (references to subsequent Bukhārī readings).

80. *Badā᾽iᶜ* 3, p. 200, l. 19.

81. Ibid., p. 72, l. 6.

82. Ibid., p. 100, l. 8.

83. For the context of Qāytbāy's architectural patronage, see Amy Whittier Newhall, "The Patronage of the Mamluk Sultan Qa᾽it Bay, 872–901/1468–1496," (Ph.D. diss., Fine Arts, Harvard University, 1987), chap. 3, 61–84.

84. *Badā᾽iᶜ* 3, p. 187, l. 18 (Ramaḍān 886/October–November 1481).

85. *Badā᾽iᶜ* 4, pp. 88, l. 14 (Ramaḍān 911/January–February 1506: Sultan cancels Bukhārī reading in Qāytbāy's great tent; affair becomes "insignificant"); 104, l. 10 (Shawwāl 912/February–March: cheap festival robes); 247, l. 11 (Ramaḍān 917/November–December 1511: festival robes of poor quality); 286, l. 15 (Ramaḍān 918/November–December 1512: shoddy festival robes; reduced in quantity by 50 percent); 340, l. 4 (Ramaḍān 919/October–November 1513: poor quality of festival robes: ghāyat al-waḥāsha); 478, l. 9 (Ramaḍān 921/October–November 1515: festival robes of disgraceful appearance; nāẓir al-khāṣṣ held responsible); *vol. 5*, p. 24, l. 19 (Rabīᶜ I 922/April–May 1516: gala Mawlid al-Nabawī celebrated due to sultan's alarm over Ottoman menace).

86. *Badā᾽iᶜ* 4, pp. 126, l. 21 (Ramaḍān 913/January–February 1508: Sultan inspects new aqueduct, visits shrines, distributes alms); 141, l. 18 (8 Shaᶜbān 914/2 December 1508: Sultan grants money to vagabonds who have been harassing visitors to his Hippodrome Gardens); 170, l. 20 (Dhū᾽l-Ḥijja 915/March–April 1510: Sultan grants poor money during festival in Maṭarīya); 244, l. 1 (24 Shaᶜbān 917/16 November 1511: Sultan bestows alms at his madrasa); 285, l. 21 (19 Ramaḍān 918/18 November 1513: Sultan grants orphans special clothing at his madrasa); 331, l. 22 (4 Shaᶜbān 919/5

October 1513: Sultan wears formal headdress to celebrate recovery; votive offering); 399, l. 12 (Ramaḍān 920/October–November 1514: Sultan orders new outfits for orphans housed at his madrasa only, no others).

87. On al-Ghawrī's Maḥmal cavalcades: *Badāʾiʿ* 4, pp. 127, l. 10 (8 Shawwāl 913/10 February 1508: the new Kaʿba Mantle and awning for Abraham's Tomb in Hebron displayed); 288, l. 1 (18 Shawwāl 918/27 December 1512: Ḥajj caravan departs amidst festivities); 343, l. 17 (17 Shawwāl 919/16 December 1513: departure of Maḥmal caravan in pomp, observed by princes from Takrūr).

88. *Badāʾiʿ* 4, pp. 337, l. 9; 480, l. 21.

89. For Ibn Iyās' detailed description of the 920 Ḥajj caravan, see *Badāʾiʿ* 4, pp. 409, l. 11–411, l. 20; 432, l. 22–433, l. 14; 439, l. 11–440, l. 19.

90. *Badāʾiʿ* 4, pp. 160, l. 2; l. 13; *vol. 5*, p. 93, l. 23. The sultan also dredged out wells and repaired rest houses on the Pilgrim's Road from ʿAqaba to Mecca in the Ḥijāz.

91. *Badāʾiʿ* 4, pp. 52, l. 19 (Dhū'l-Ḥijja 908/May–June 1503: completion of structure); 58, l. 10 (1 Rabīʿ II 909/23 September 1503: dedication).

92. Ibid., p. 68, l. 15 (Jumādā I 910/October–November 1504).

93. Ibid., pp. 84, l. 4 (Jumādā I 911/September–October 1505: minaret tilt); 249, l. 12; 299, l. 10; 307, l. 2 (Shawwāl 917/December 1511–January 1512, Ṣafar 919/April–May 1513: Rabīʿ I 919/May–June: Crack appears in mausoleum dome; demolition required).

94. Ibid., p. 236, l. 10 (3 Jumādā II 917/7 September 1510).

95. Ibid., pp. 56, l. 3; 60, l. 10 (redesign of playing field, enlargement of casement wall); 102, l. 8 (Shaʿbān 912/December 1506–January 1507: aromatic shrubs and trees planted); 110, l. 5 (Dhū'l-Ḥijja 912/April–May 1507: construction of aqueduct for irrigation and pool supply).

96. Ibid., p. 222, l. 1 (Rabīʿ I 917/May–June 1511).

97. *Badāʾiʿ* 5, p. 94, l. 16; Popper, *Cairo Nilometer,* 27–28.

98. On al-Ghawrī's receptions and spectacles at Nilometer, see *Badāʾiʿ* 4, pp. 250, l. 14 (14 Dhū'l-Qaʿda 917/2 February 1512: Sultan hosts amīrs to reception; each in private tent); 254, l. 21 (Muḥarram 918/March–April 1512: Sultan offers banquet attended by singers, jugglers and buffoons); 275, l. 23 (13 Jumādā II 918/26 August 1512: Sultan commissions fireworks display; barge carrying several thousand candles, rockets and sparklers anchored offshore; cost: twenty thousand dīnārs; property holders along shore provide torches to illuminate homes; effect "unprecedented during any former reign").

99. When Ibn Iyās entered the decease of eminent artists in his chronicle, he noted their status at court. See *Badā'i'* 4, pp. 8, 1. 11 (Shawwāl 906/April–May 1501: obituary of female vocalist, "respected by notables and dignitaries"); 130, 1. 4 (Dhū'l-Qa'da 913/March–April 1508: Innovative musician recasts musical poems in short verses, "revolutionizes musical style"); 258, 1. 11 (9 Ṣafar 918/26 April 1512: obituaries of two female vocalists esteemed at court); 401, 1. 11 (18 Ramaḍān 920/6 November 1514: death of sultan's intimate, skilled musician); *vol. 5*, p. 66, 1. 21 (5 Sha'bān 922/3 September 1516: obituary of eminent book dealer, associate of sultan). 'Abd al-Bāsiṭ al-Malaṭī extolled his sovereign's appreciation for "melodies which delighted the heart and inspired the soul." (*Majmū' al-Bustān*, f. 8, 1. 12).

100. *Badā'i'* 4, p. 176, 1. 16.

101. *Badā'i'* 3, p. 331, 1. 1 (Dhū'l-Qa'da 901/July–August 1496: Qāytbāy's obituary).

102. *Ḥawādith* 4, p. 635, 1. 15.

103. *Ḥawādith* 4, p. 633, 1. 3 (Dhū'l-Qa'da 872/May–June 1468); *Rawḍ*, r. 181-6, 1. 30; *Badā'i'* 3, p. 13, 1. 7.

104. *Badā'i'* 3, p. 40, 1. 13 (Rabī' II 874/October–November 1469: obituary of Mālikī qāḍī who purchased office); *Inbā'*, pp. 152, 1. 12 (Jumādā II 874/December 1469–January 1470: appointment of paymaster's son, a Muslim Copt, as replacement for bribe of one thousand dīnārs); 383, 1. 9 (Rajab 876/December 1471–January 1472: Sultan grants fiscal offices in Jidda for bribes; some as high as thirty thousand dīnārs); 406, 1. 16; 423, 1. 11 (1 Ramaḍān 876/11 February 1472: Sultan appoints Shāfi'ī qāḍī of Damascus for payment of thirty thousand dīnārs); *Badā'i'* 3, p. 120, 1. 1 (Rabī' I 881/June–July 1476: obituary of chief Shāfi'ī Qāḍī al-Makīnī who purchased his office); Ibn al-Ḥimṣī, *Ḥawādith*, f. 70-b, 1. 3 (Muḥarram 883/April–May 1478: Sultan appoints Ḥanafī qāḍī of Damascus for bribe of eight thousand dīnārs); *Inbā'*, p. 504, 1. 4 (23 Dhū'l-Ḥijja 885/23 February 1481: Syndic of Prophet's Descendants in Damascus accused of buying office); *Badā'i'* 3, pp. 243, 1. 9 (Ramaḍān 892/August–September 1487: Sultan installs the Shāfi'ī qāḍī al-Makīnī in shaykhship of Khashshābīya College for bribe); 257, 1. 18 (Dhū'l-Qa'da 893/October–November 1488: Muslim Copt appointed army controller of Damascus for bribe).

105. *Ḥawādith* 4, pp. 636, 1. 8; 641, 1. 21 (Dhū'l-Qa'da 872/May–June 1468); *Rawḍ*, f. 183, 1. 2; *Badā'i'* 3, p. 13, 1. 21.

106. *Ḥawādith* 4, p. 683, 1. 19 (16 Rabī' I 873/4 October 1468). On 'Alā' al-Dīn ibn al-Ṣābūnī's fate, see *Inbā'*, pp. 149, 1. 12; 150, 1. 14.

107. *Badā'i'* 4, p. 57, 1. 9.

108. On al-ʿAynī's mulcting, see *Ḥawādith* 4, p. 618, l. 24; *Rawḍ*, f. 174-b, l. 17; *Badāʾiʿ* 3, p. 6, l. 12 (Rajab 872/January–February 1468: al-ʿAynī's initial summons); *Ḥawādith* 4, pp. 621, l. 9 (Jumādā II 872/ December 1471-January 1472: Sultan demands two hundred thousand dīnārs from al-ʿAynī); 623, l. 10; *Rawḍ*, f. 178, l. 17; *Badāʾiʿ* 3, p. 9, l. 5 (3 Shaʿbān 872/27 February 1468: Sultan flogs al-ʿAynī to compel revelation of stashed assets).

109. On vicissitudes of their careers: *Ḥawādith* 4, p. 626, l. 13; *Rawḍ*, f. 179, l. 30; *Badāʾiʿ* 3, p. 10, l. 6 (Shaʿbān 872/February–March 1468: Qāsim Shughayta, advanced by Yashbak, now dismissed from vizierate); *Ḥawādith* 4, p. 627; *Rawḍ*, f. 180, l. 22; *Badāʾiʿ* 3, p. 11, l. 4 (same month: al-Ahnāsī replaces him); *Ḥawādith* 4, p. 651, l. 5; *Rawḍ*, f. 187, l. 6 *Badāʾiʿ* 3, p. 17, l. 14 (Dhū'l-Ḥijja 872/June–July: al-Ahnāsī arrested, fined and mulcted); *Ḥawādith* 4, p. 651, l. 12; *Rawḍ*, f. 187, l. 21 (same month: Qāsim Shughayta resurfaces); *Badāʾiʿ* 3, p. 19, l. 9 (Muḥarram 873/July–August 1468: Ibn al-Kuwayz recalled from exile in Anatolia, whence Khushqadam had sent him); *Ḥawādith* 4, p. 681, l. 3; *Inbāʾ*, p. 20, l. 11; *Rawḍ*, f. 205, l. 2; *Badāʾiʿ* 3, p. 21, l. 21 (Rabīʿ I 873/September–October: al-Ahnāsī dismissed from vizierate again; replaced by Qāsim); *Ḥawādith* 4, p. 682, l. 17 (same month: Yashbak assumes formal vizierate but imposes extortive policies on Qāsim's advice; cuts meat rations; manipulates wheat prices); *Inbāʾ*, p. 24, l. 5 (same month: Qāsim reduces stipends to awlād al-nās and ʿulamāʾ); *Inbāʾ*, p. 163, l. 6; *Rawḍ*, f. 250-b, l. 12; *Badāʾiʿ* 3, p. 44, l. 6 (18 Ramaḍān 874/ 21 March 1470: Al-Zaynī ibn al-Kuwayz replaces Tāj al-Dīn ibn al-Maqṣī as nāẓir al-khāṣṣ; latter in hiding to avoid mulcting); *Inbāʾ*, p. 164, l. 11; *Rawḍ*, f. 250-b, l. 32; *Badāʾiʿ* 3, p. 44, l. 19 (17 Shawwāl 874/19 April: Ibn al-Kuwayz' brother, al-Badrī, appointed contractor for royal projects [muʿallim al-ṣināʿ]; *Inbāʾ*, p. 208, l. 15; *Badāʾiʿ* 3, p. 52, l. 22 (27 Ṣafar 875/25 August 1471: Ibn al-Maqṣī replaces Ibn al-Kuwayz as nāẓir al-khāṣṣ; latter accused of administering according to diviners' whims); *Inbāʾ*, pp. 214, l. 5 (Rabīʿ I 875/ August–September 1470: Yashbak flogs Qāsim for secretly profiting from illegal grain sales and not sharing); 217, l. 14; 226, l. 1 (Rabīʿ II 875/ September–October: Yashbak forces Qāsim to pay fine of five thousand dīnārs; one month later, Qāytbāy restores him); 270, l. 16; 279, l. 13 (Shawwāl 875/ March–April 1471: Ibn al-Kuwayz released from jail after paying "debts"); 281, l. 5 (same month: Qāsim takes refuge in house of Ibn Muzhir; seeks Qāytbāy's pardon in guise of Ṣūfī penitent); 318, l. 16 (7 Muḥarram 876/26 June 1471: Ibn al-Maqṣī reinstated as nāẓir); *Badāʾiʿ* 3, pp. 108, l. 4 (Rabīʿ I 880/July–August 1475: Ibn al-Maqṣī appointed major-domo and reconfirmed as nāẓir al-khāṣṣ); 168, l. 17 (Jumādā I 885/July–August 1480: Ibn al-Maqṣī disgraced, pardoned, then executed for malfeasance; widely mourned); 197, l. 1 (Shawwāl 887/December 1482: Qāsim resurfaces after

"long seclusion;" invested with niẓārat al-dawla); 207, l. 4; 208, l. 5 (Rabīʿ II 889/April–May 1484: Qāsim appointed wazīr); 234, l. 7 (Dhū'l-Qaʿda 891/October–November 1486: Qāsim dismissed from vizierate and al-dawla; accounts sequestered); 249, l. 20 (Rabīʿ II 893/March–April 1488: Qāsim restored to al-dawla); 292, l. 19 (Shawwāl 897/July–August 1492: Qāsim dismissed from al-dawla); al-Sakhāwī, *Dahyl*, f. 221-b, l. 25 (Dhū'l-Qaʿda 897/August–September: Qāsim mulcted of five thousand dīnārs); *Badāʾiʿ* 3, p. 307, l. 7 (Jumādā II 900/February–March 1495: Qāsim's obituary; Ibn Iyās notes origin as baker [*khabbāz*], skillful initiatives as wazīr).

110. *Badāʾiʿ* 5, pp. 42, l. 2; 75, l. 6 (Rabīʿ II 922/May 1516; Shaʿbān 922/August–September 922).

111. *Badāʾiʿ* 4, p. 13, l. 22 (Dhū'l-Ḥijja 906/June–July 1501).

112. Ibid., p. 73, l. 1 (16 Rajab 910/23 December 1504: Qāyt al-Rajabī's arrest for treason; summary of his innovative extortion); *vol. 5*, p. 18, l. 17 (Ṣafar 922/March-April 1516: twelve years after Qāyt's arrest, the taxes he implemented are cancelled to inspire loyalty in sultan's absence).

113. For examples of other senior officers who fell afoul of their sovereign: *Badāʾiʿ* 4, pp. 119, l. 19 (20 Jumādā II 913/27 October 1507: obituary of Azdamur al-Dawādār, highly respected but al-Ghawrī arrests staff and inventories estate); 208, l. 11 (6 Muḥarram 917/5 April 1511: obituary of Ṭarābāy al-Sharīfī, guard captain, hated as confiscator of waqfs); 358, l. 23 (5 Muḥarram 920/2 March 1514: sultan arrests his major-domo, Jānībak, accused of stealing revenues, and fines him thirty-five thousand dīnārs); 380, l. 2 (6 Jumādā I 920/29 June: Sultan fires Jānībak on corruption charges); 428, l. 24 (7 Dhū'l-Ḥijja 920/23 January 1515: Jānībak tortured to compel divulgence of assets); 476, l. 1 (13 Ramaḍān 921/21 October 1515: Prefect tortures Jānībak again; Ibn Iyās considers him worthy of his fate and "vilest of God's creatures" but also an epitome of his master's regime).

114. On Jīʿānī intimidation: *Badāʾiʿ 4, pp. 40, l. 17 (Rabīʿ I 908/4* September 1502: Ṣalāḥ al-Dīn replaced after initial fine; no charge); 136, l. 21 (Jumādā II 914/September–October 1508: ʿAbd al-ʿAẓīm's charge of embezzlement against Ṣalāḥ; one hundred thousand dīnārs collected); 152, l. 17 (7 Ṣafar 915/27 May 1509: Shihāb al-Dīn Aḥmad fined without charge); 156, l. 12 (his release after payment); 179, l. 5 (15 Muḥarram 916/24 April 1510: Ṣalāḥ's obituary enumerating his distinctive services and unjustified confiscations); 235, l. 21 (Jumādā I 917/July–August 1511: Sultan releases two members of clan after payments); 309, l. 7 (Rabīʿ I 919/May–June 1513: Jīʿān home robbed by Mamlūks; prefects investigation an excuse for more appropriation).

115. *Badāʾiʿ* 3, p. 46, l. 17.

116. See chapter 7.

117. On the concubine's forced payments: *Badā'i'* 4, p. 20, l. 12. Other examples: pp. 159, l. 22 (Rabī' II 915/July–August 1509: Sultan arrests female staff of Qāytbāy's concubine; suspected of hoarding); 285, l. 11 (Ramaḍān 918/November–December 1512: Sultan fines female singer five thousand dīnārs); 301, l. 11 (Ṣafar 919/April–May 1513: Sultan impounds stipends set aside for orphans of plague victims); 442, l. 17 (13 Ṣafar 921/29 March 1515: Sultan seizes princesses' inheritances and trousseaus to raise troop stipends); *vol. 5,* p. 32, l. 8 (Rabī' II 922/May–June 1516: Sultan confiscates amīr's estate left to his daughter).

118. *Badā'i'* 4, p. 14, l. 13; *Ta'rīkh al-Jarākisa,* f. 68, l. 14.

119. In Dhū'l-Qa'da of 915/February-March 1510, al-Ghawrī accused several of his fiscal officials "of dragging their feet with regard to payments they owed him." He went over their accounts personally and demanded six hundred thousand dīnārs on the spot. "They descended beside themselves as if drunk, although none had touched any alcohol." See *Badā'i'* 4, p. 169, l. 2.

120. Robert Irwin has mused perceptively about the theatrical quality of violence within the Mamlūk elite. See *Middle East,* 86–90.

121. On al-'Aynī's fate, see note 108. For Yashbak's mulcting of Ibn 'Abd al-Razzāq, see *Inbā',* p. 143, l. 8; *Badā'i'* 3, p. 40, l. 13 (28 Rabī' I 874/1 October 1469).

122. *Ḥawādith* 4, p. 681, l. 3; *Rawḍ,* f. 205, l. 2; *Badā'i'* 3, p. 21, l. 21 (9 Rabī' I 873/27 September 1468).

123. For example, the fate of Aḥmad ibn al-Dīwan al-Ḥalabī who, in Jumādā II 894/May 1489, was convicted of selling military secrets to the Ottomans. Qāytbāy interrogated him in Cairo and ordered him flayed alive. See *Badā'i'* 3, p. 265, l. 24.

124. *Badā'i'* 4, p. 61, l. 21 (Sha'bān 909/January–February 1504: case of the qāḍī Burhān al-Maqdisī). Jurists rarely suffered brutalities heaped on bureaucrats but al-Ghawrī respected rank less than efficiency.

125. Ibid., p. 147, l. 13 (Dhū'l-Qa'da 914/February–March 1509: 'Abd al-'Aẓīm al-Ṣayrafī was so tortured, but only enough to loosen his tongue. Given the risk of death because of excess, this kind of abuse required an expert's touch).

126. Ibid., p. 235, l. 2 (Jumādā I 917/August–September 1511).

127. Ibid., p. 244, l. 12 (Ramaḍān 917/November–December 1511). Ibn Iyās mentioned the Orthodox (*Rabbān*) and Karaite (*Qarrā'*) communities

along with prominent merchants whom Shamuwāl implicated. Collectively, they yielded an additional one hundred thousand dīnārs.

128. Ibid., p. 23, l. 17 (Rajab 907/January–February 1502: case of Ṣalāḥ al-Dīn ibn al-Junayd, who devised a plan sure to yield two hundred thousand dīnārs "without inconvenience." Al-Ghawrī's amīrs threatened revolt if he were retained. Al-Ghawrī then paraded Ṣalāḥ nude on a camel and had his tongue cut out).

7

Surmounting Crisis: Covert Innovation

"For indeed, Sultan al-Ghawrī entertained many original ideas—more than his predecessors."[1] With this offhanded remark, appended to his description of al-Ghawrī's Hippodrome beautification, Ibn Iyās touched on a characteristic he would emphasize repeatedly. Despite his reputation as a conspirator, al-Ghawrī's innovative measures set him apart from other members of his caste. Rudimentary as they may have been at his death, these policies attracted the attention of observers because they were so unusual. Almost uniformly condemned by his soldiery, al-Ghawrī's tentative steps at creating an alternative military unit financed with sequestered funds represent the first experiment of its kind since Baybars al-Bunduqdārī had integrated Mongol renegades (*Wafidīya*) into his army more than two hundred years earlier.[2]

And this trial in military recruitment was only the most unsettling of al-Ghawrī's schemes. He would revive a defunct lancers' unit, commission new weaponry, whittle away at iqṭāᶜ allotments, which provided his rivals income to challenge his own status as senior landlord of the realm, and initiate the creation of a private fisc by appropriating blocks of endowed (*waqf*) properties for his personal exploitation. What success al-Ghawrī would have reaped from these experiments we cannot know since fate intervened too soon. Their attempts nonetheless recall the validity of that timeless adage: "Necessity is the mother of invention." But which necessities ranked highest in al-Ghawrī's scheme of priorities?

The Military Innovations: Supplanting the Intractable

Ever alert to opportunities for show, al-Ghawrī brooded over the image of languor his army projected in the later Circassian period. Qāytbāy had instituted reviews of the troopers' combat readiness he supervised personally. Al-Ghawrī was more concerned about appearances than substance. Ever since Khushqadam had dispensed with cavalry exercises (*al-Furūsīya*), troopers had lost the fine edge of mounted archery and lance casting that had brought them renown throughout the Musim world.[3] High velocity drills compelling a horseman's placement of an arrow or lance in a small target while at full gallop dated back to the Samarrā era in Baghdād and reinforced the Mamlūks' awareness of their venerable traditions. When such exercises were discontinued, morale waned and soldiers found time on their hands for contemplating revolt. Al-Ghawrī certainly weighed these considerations when he reinstituted the crack lancers' corps of Baybars' day by drilling them formally in the Hippodrome. Ibn Iyās remarked about his motives: "The sultan resolved upon restoring the Maḥmal procession in Rajab, accompanied by lancers parading as per ancient tradition. The custom had been abolished in 872 during al-Ẓāhir Khushqadam's reign. Consequently, lance-casting expertise waned. The sultan renewed this tradition to take credit for it so that he would be recalled among rulers as its reviver."

Al-Ghawrī, as in other circumstances, accurately gauged the impression precision drills executed by splendidly outfitted lancers would make on domestic and foreign observers. The performers, carefully screened by four senior officers, donned red uniforms designed early in the Mamlūk regime.[4] In addition to their spectacular feats of spear casting, they performed daring acrobatic stunts on their chargers. As they raced by the sultan's reviewing pavilion, they would momentarily dismount, kiss the earth before him, and reseat themselves without breaking stride. These displays thrilled spectators, not the least ambassadors of rival rulers the sultan wished to intimidate. Daunting emissaries with his cavalrymen's adroitness mattered greatly to al-Ghawrī. Once the archers and lancers corps attained a high level of competence, the sultan routinely showed them off. Whether their feats drew awed responses because of precision or new martial tactics concocted by al-Ghawrī's trainers Ibn Iyās did not specify, but he reported the amazement they provoked among foreign dignitaries.

Emissaries from the Ottoman and Ṣafavid monarchs allegedly marveled at what they saw—and rushed home with elaborate reports to discomfit their masters.[5] How profoundly moved these visitors were by a lavish show performed by warriors who had not tested their maneuvers on the battlefield one can only guess, but by all accounts the lancers' performances made dazzling theatre. Al-Ghawrī himself seems to have been content with display of this venture since Ibn Iyās makes no mention of his extending intensified training procedures down through his soldiers' ranks. The crack lancers served at Marj Dābiq but al-Ghawrī held them in reserve until the last minute, as he did with all his favored units. Veterans took the brunt of the combat and nursed their resentment at being expendable—a sentiment the traitor Khayrbak, Viceroy of Aleppo, would exploit with devastating consequences. Al-Ghawrī, true to his regime's deferral of hostilities, employed a wide variety of stalling tactics of which the cavalry drills were a prominent example. In an age when advantages of superior firepower could not yet be ascertained, the precision of highly trained archers and lancers still evoked an impression of invincibility. Even if al-Ghawrī exploited this perception as a facade masking his army's myriad defects, he could entertain realistic hopes for its effectiveness.

Despite his proclivity for ostentation, al-Ghawrī did not confine his experiments to ceremonies. He began exploring more substantive means of aggrandizing his military strength. His attempts at creating a viable artillery unit impressed contemporary observers as ludicrous, and certainly caused their instigator no end of frustration. Their repeated trials, however, bespeak al-Ghawrī's growing awareness of his vulnerability when faced with rapid changes in military technology throughout Europe and closer to home at the Ottoman court.[6] Chroniclers referred only once to an artillery experiment during Qāytbāy's reign.[7] Yashbak al-Dawādār, who supervised general armaments planning, included the test in a demonstration of naphtha explosives he put on at the Rumayla Square. From al-Ṣayrafī's description, which dwelt on the masses' derision of the spectacle, Yashbak rather than Qāytbāy, who observed his marshal's trials with bemusement, would seem to have intended the cannon as a viable weapon.

Al-Ghawrī, by contrast, stubbornly persisted with artillery testing in the face of repeated failures and his adjutants' disdain. From Rajab 913/ November-December 1507 to the final months before he set out for Aleppo in 922, al-Ghawrī cast artillery pieces at a foundry in Cairo, transported them to al-ʿĀdil Ṭūmānbāy's mausoleum at al-Raydānīya, north of town, and fired them off across the plain. Whence his engineers acquired their models Ibn Iyās did not say, but in light of incessant clashes with European mariners whose ships were outfitted with cannon, the Mamlūk regime certainly had the opportunity to capture specimens. While techniques of molding brass or iron pieces capable of sustaining explosions without shattering remained elusive, al-Ghawrī skimped neither on material or staffers. The huge size of his early units rendered them almost immobile. As they traversed the city, subsurface sewer mains collapsed causing delays and injuries.[8] Once they arrived at the test site, pieces often failed so miserably they embarrassed their sponsor. When al-Ghawrī invited his retinue to witness a firing on 13 Jumādā II 916/17 September 1510, "not a single unit held up."[9] All fifteen burst, scattering shrapnel in every direction. The sultan was so depressed he canceled the banquet he had planned and nursed his disappointment alone in the Citadel. But setbacks never dissuaded him. Experiments continued on a regular basis; by mid-917/August 1511 units were holding up and their accuracy improving.[10] Al-Ghawrī began founding large numbers and in Muḥarram 922/February-March 1516 he sent off two hundred that had withstood firing to garrison Alexandria.[11]

Yet given his success at founding cannons, al-Ghawrī vacillated over their use. Willing to deploy them in his Suez expeditions in concert with the Ottomans, he withheld them from his campaign against Selim. Since the Ottomans turned the tide of battle only after they fired their own artillery and muskets on the Mamlūk cavalry, al-Ghawrī's omission could be interpreted as a fatal strategic blunder. But so formidable was opposition to any deviation from traditional combat methods within his army that the sultan might have exacerbated mutinous sentiments already smoldering if he introduced his own artillery. The logistics of hauling such cumbersome juggernauts over so great a distance may also have given him pause. In any case, al-Ghawrī's elaborate experiment in artillery building never came to fruition on the battlefield.

Midway through 916/January 1511, Ibn Iyās began mentioning a "Fifth Corps" (*al-Ṭabaqat al-Khāmisa*) of infantrymen recruited outside normal cadres of Mamlūk trainees.[12] This new corps emerges furtively in narrative sources. Ibn Iyās brought it up primarily in the context of its stipend funding, use of firearms, venue of service, and vehemence of hostility on the part of regulars. Nowhere does he provide an extended explanation of al-Ghawrī's motives behind its formation. But he drops enough hints for plausible hypotheses. The corps' appellation itself derived from a special fifth pay session following the four days during which line troops and reservists drew their salaries. Designation of a separate time for Fifth Corpsmen underscored the brigade's status distinct from the Mamlūk elite. Members did not belong to traditional divisions of the military: the *Sulṭānī* or Royal Mamlūks (including both purchased recruits [*mushtarawāt*] and veterans [*qarāniṣa*] who had served other rulers), the *Sayfīya* or troopers in retinues of grand amīrs, and reservists (*al-Ḥalqa*).[13] Exactly who was pressed into this motley brigade escapes precise identification since chroniclers often repeated derogatory remarks about their quality on the part of regulars who loathed them.[14] Beneath the recruits' vituperation one may discern a high percentage of freeborn foreigners from Iran or Turkistan, and reservists who had flunked their fitness tests. Al-Ghawrī found their defects no obstacle, apparently, since he intended them to try out muskets (*arquebuses*) for the first time in his reign. While keen eyesight for marksmanship may have counted in their training, bow drawing and lance casting did not.[15]

None of the corpsmen, who numbered approximately three hundred in their first musters, rode a horse and consequently received any *iqṭāʿ* money. Al-Ghawrī had already been diminishing his reliance on iqṭāʿ rents to pay military stipends. As early as 912/1506, he promoted one Arikmās min Ṭarābāy, former viceroy of Damascus, to the rank of Muqaddam and soon granted him the influential amīrship of council (*Imārat al-Majlis*).[16] But Arkimās did not receive a fief commensurate to his exalted rank. Rather, al-Ghawrī conferred upon him a salary of one thousand dīnārs per month and one thousand irdabbs of wheat per annum from the Dhakhīra Reserve Bureau. It is no happenstance that this Arikmās was assigned responsibility for training the Fifth Corps in their new weaponry and maneuvers. Having been gradually weaned away from dependence on the land allotments that, even as usufruct, gave senior officers a measure of autonomy, which the sultan interpreted as rivalry, he was al-Ghawrī's natural choice to preside over a trial battalion paid with funds from outside traditional sources. Ibn Iyās noted al-Ghawrī's steady eroding of iqṭāᶜs parceled out to amīrs in standard service. By Shaᶜbān 918/October-November 1512, he was systematically reducing the grants awarded even his most senior muqaddamīn.[17] Was this money earmarked for members of the Fifth Corps? Ibn Iyās did not elucidate, but the possibility exists since he did elaborate on the recruits' outrage over Fifth Corps stipends.

In Ṣafar 920/April 1514, the julbān stationed themselves outside the courtyard where the corpsmen had lined up for their payments.[18] As the latter filed out, the recruits confronted them with drawn weapons and confiscated one Ashrafī dīnār from each. "Thus did soldiers of the Fifth Corps suffer severe humiliation that day at the recruits' hands, but the sultan could do nothing to restrain them. Some seized a corpsman's whole stipend, while others took only an Ashrafī and returned the remainder. Those who kept the entire jamakīya fled off with it." The julbān's behavior strongly implies their sense of being shortchanged for the benefit of upstarts who might undermine their privileged position if the sultan had his way unthwarted. Whatever the validity of their fears, the regulars were aware that al-Ghawrī always found funds to pay his new brigade while protesting poverty in the face of their own bonus demands. Since savings he realized from iqṭāᶜ manipulations could not meet all his fiscal needs, the sultan quite likely raised much of the Fifth Corps' stipend money from expropriated assets, which by this time had reached substantial proportions. Thus we behold a new experimental unit funded largely via unofficial revenues. These corpsmen received nothing but cash. They could rely on no propertied holdings as a means for alleviating their dependence on their sponsor. Having astutely observed that the iqṭāᶜ system invariably whetted his regulars' competitive appetites, al-Ghawrī resolved on compensating his new corps with funds he collected from his extortion network. Loyalty among professional soldiers was purchased and rarely offered out of camaraderie. But members of the Fifth Corps were given to understand that their futures were intimately linked to their benefactor's cause—and his alone. If they wavered, they would fall prey to their enemies' tender mercies.

Al-Ghawrī assigned the Fifth Corps field duties only twice during their brief existence: first as part of the force he dispatched to guard Suez from the Portuguese in mid-919/September-October 1513, and second as a contingent within the naval venture to India in Jumādā I 921/June-July 1515.[19] The locations of both tours are telling. Neither involved corpsmen in Cairo where they would presumably arouse the ire of their Mamlūk rivals and provoke a revolt. Al-Ghawrī may well have intended the Fifth Corps as an alternative prop for his own security. But if so, his deployment of them far away from those most likely to depose him defies a ready explanation. Even in these two expeditions the exact nature of the corpsmen's expected service is unclear. That they alone would employ the sultan's new muskets emerges as their only tangible duty. Since the Ottoman janissaries at Suez were outfitted with similar firearms, al-Ghawrī may have wished to show their admiral, Salmān, that his soldiers could also field these weapons. But Ibn Iyās' brevity leaves a question mark over the corpsmen's other activities.

Their conspicuous absence from al-Ghawrī's host during his march toward Marj Dābiq discloses a more perplexing enigma. Ibn Iyās dwelled at length on the several battalions departing Cairo in Rabīᶜ II 922/May 1516 for al-Raydānīya where they bivouacked before advancing on Syria.[20] Nowhere does he mention the Fifth Corps' presence. The Egyptian force consisted entirely of Sulṭānī recruits or veterans, Sayfīya troopers and reservists—all traditional figures in the Mamlūk hierarchy. Why did al-Ghawrī exclude the Fifth Corps from this showdown on which his fate rested?

David Ayalon has argued vigorously for the corps' sole intended service against Portuguese raiders in the Red Sea.[21] Their confrontations would take place aboard ship or in distant ports negating the transport of horses and fodder. Since their opponents would carry firearms, they perforce bore similar equipage. The imminent Ottoman conflict was reserved for Mamlūk regulars who disdained any use of firearms whatsoever and would tolerate the presence of no despised musketmongers. While Ayalon's case is lucid, he overlooks an alternative interpretation of his own logic. If well-trained non-Mamlūk arquebusiers ever turned their weapons on their "masters and creators," armed only with "horses, bows, swords and lances" (82), the corps' patron might well benefit from his peers' destruction in a time of crisis. Let us recall that to the end, al-Ghawrī feared deposition by his own Mamlūks more than any other threat, including Selim. Did he wish to husband the corps for his own safety at home in the advent of a defeat he might survive, or even a victory his regulars might seize upon to demand a reward he could not pay? Both this and Ayalon's scenarios are possible, and yet they leave us in the realm of conjecture. As with al-Ghawrī's other innovations, the Fifth Corps' real purpose is obscured in the sources' lacunae. Yet Ibn Iyās' cryptic remarks about them do underscore their tenuous status. Beset with overriding pressures of bankruptcy, factionalism,

and impending invasion, al-Ghawrī could not concentrate his inventive energies on transforming the Fifth Corps from a "hodge-podge of threads and tatters" into a crack arquebus regiment. To his fateful departure, he may have
remained undecided about how he might best use them, or against whom.
Indecision surrounding his novel endeavors allegedly characterized al-
Ghawrī's behavior throughout the reign. Whether irresolution marked his
most covert fiscal schemes as well raises questions of equal complexity.

Fiscal Innovations: Waqf Manipulation as Investment Strategy

Qāytbāy and al-Ghawrī invested massively in charitable trusts throughout
their reigns. Together, they authorized a third of all trust documents surviving
from the Mamlūk period.[22] Formally granted for the benefit of the Muslim
community, these documents disclose an impressive roster of activities promoting piety, scholasticism, and welfare. Yet upon scrutiny, they also reveal
strategies of investment their donors never openly acknowledged. These tactics
so closely parallel the financial dilemmas confronting both sultans that their
interrelationship cannot be dismissed as circumstantial.[23] Their implications
significantly qualify the overt purposes for which trusts were endowed and the
options for Egypt's creative use of her capital assets at the end of the Middle
Ages. While the following observations make no definitive claims, they rest
on a body of evidence unique for the window of insight it offers. In their sum,
the trusts deeds compiled by Egypt's last autocrats tell a sobering tale of short-
range ingenuity but long-term myopia.

The charitable trust evolved over centuries into a complex institution. As
the primary provider of benevolent services in sedentary Muslim societies that
administered substantial reserves of real estate and agrarian property, the waqf
endowment embraced a large share of a state's assets. Because of its dual function as a charitable foundation and a shelter of estates, the waqf was progressively refined to facilitate its donor's altruistic wishes and patrimonial
objectives. By the high Middle Ages, few endowments fit neatly into the ideal
categories of "charitable" (*khayrī*) or "familial" (*ahlī*). Most furthered both objectives according to stipulations laid down by a donor and approved as consistent with Sharʿī principles by one or more magistrates versed in waqf
litigation. Although a waqf was theoretically granted in perpetuity, a feature
enhancing its appeal as a guardian of estates, it could be modified by a variety
of transactions. A waqf could be sold (*bayʿ*), substituted for equivalent real
estate (*istibdāl*), reassigned (*intiqāl*), alienated or transferred (*tamlīk*), so long
as the value of its original principal remained equivalent and its charitable
yield undiminished.[24] Donors could, within limits fixed by inheritance codes,
set aside properties specifically for their descendants' support. More often,
they designated a family member as waqf supervisor (*nāẓir*), charged with al-

location of the endowment's proceeds and the right of choosing subsequent directors—thus presumably ensuring control over the waqf's proceeds within the lineage down through later generations. These refinements promoting a waqf's flexibility developed as a consequence of the trust's ad hoc status in Sharīʿa. While interpreted by analogy as a fundamental manifestation of the Fourth Pillar of Charity incumbent upon believers, the waqf itself is not mentioned in Koran. Examples of welfare donations first appear in Ḥadīth literature, acquiring their sanctity by Prophetic approval rather than Divine pronouncement. Since freedom of legal interpretation grows inversely to the primacy of legal source, the waqf's legitimacy as a procedure confirmed by tradition rather than revelation promoted its malleability. By the later Middle Ages in the central Islamic lands, the charitable trust had become simultaneously the bastion of public welfare and the protector of estate integrity in an environment rife with threats to each.

The very ploys for extracting revenues from unofficial sources elaborated in preceding chapters posed dire threats to the cohesion of estates. All holders of property, civilian and military, were alert to such ploys since it was they who plied them. The proliferation of investments in charitable trusts must be seen as a consequence of their anxiety. A waqf endowment represented the safest shelter allowable under Islamic law. Once granted to promote the common good, a trust transcends the will of temporal governments, which, ideally, will not obstruct its provisos as specified by its donor. In practice, Muslim regimes did confiscate waqf properties sporadically, but only under circumstances of national emergency. A ruler might tamper with waqfs under dire need, but he invited widespread criticism if he did so. Moreover, he would set an ominous precedent for his own estate he amassed for his heirs. In Mamlūk Egypt, the incidence of mass waqf alienation remained rare until the late Circassian period. To the reign of al-Ghawrī, appropriation occurred intermittently but always as an exceptional measure, a last resort. Thus, in an uncertain fiscal environment, placement of one's assets and real estate in a charitable trust with stipulation for its permanent supervision by descendants did not offer absolute protection. No strategy could preclude the regime's interference under some guise. But a waqf endowment remained the best haven available, and the most likely to assure survival of the family fortune over time.

Given the limitation of individual title over state domains (all allotted as iqtāʿs) to usufruct, the Mamlūk elite found the charitable trust an attractive means of providing a legacy for their heirs. That waqf endowments were in principle tax-free enhanced their allure. Yields could be subjected to taxation but property stipulated in a writ as the source of such proceeds was immune to assure its perpetuity.[25] Finally, a waqf generated reliable income. Only fixed property could be placed in trust, in a fashion assuring the steadiest annual return. The waqf was never designed to promote aggressive capital

growth but rather to provide inviolable support of a beneficial service. To individuals who found themselves candidates for mulcting by state authorities,
assurance of a dependable legacy for their progeny took precedence over other
options for investment that might magnify the original asset but subject it to
greater risk as well.

Extant waqf deeds granted by Qāytbāy and al-Ghawrī underscore similarities and contrasts between their respective use of the charitable trust. These
differences strongly imply al-Ghawrī's departure from traditional means of estate building pursued by his predecessors. Even though we cannot assume the
completeness of these documents, they disclose Egypt's penultimate sovereign
groping his way toward construction of a private fisc sheltered by the sanctity
of its properties and subject to his exclusive use. Al-Ghawrī's massive waqf
expropriations thus accorded with two of his overriding objectives: securing
reliable revenues and freedom to spend them as he saw fit. Comparison of the
two sultans' writs highlights their antithetical methods while also indicating
the rudimentary state of al-Ghawrī's experiment when it was abruptly terminated by Marj Dābiq.

Qāytbāy began buying property and placing it in trusts long before his
enthronement. The earliest surviving deed in his name dates from 29 Dhū'l-
Qaᶜda 855/23 December 1451, seventeen years in advance of his succession.[26]
Qāytbāy, then an amīr, was titled simply al-Sayfī ibn ᶜAbd-Allāh al-
Maḥmūdī. He purchased 26.7 percent of an agrarian tract in Nāḥiyat
Salamūn, Gharbīya Province, for eleven hundred dīnārs.[27] Since the property
does not appear in his later deeds designating its yield for support of a foundation, the purchase may have been reserved for Qāytbāy's personal estate.
From this time until the year before his death, Qāytbāy acquired a vast array
of urban real estate and rural holdings the bulk of which he assigned to his
waqf donations. These intricate deeds, several of which are inscribed on rolls
exceeding twenty meters in length, date from 24 Jumādā II 879/5 November
1474 to 15 Dhū'l-Ḥijja 895/30 October 1490. They support fourteen charitable foundations, including the sultan's mausoleum-mosque (*jāmiᶜ al-madfan*)
located in the Desert Cemetery (*Ṣaḥrā'*) east of Cairo, several public fountains,
orphanages, district mosques in the capital or Delta, and a college (*madrasa*)
in Jerusalem.[28] While these do not embrace the full roster of Qāytbāy's magnanimous offerings as mentioned in the narrative literature, their endowment
programs do depict the sultan's allocation priorities. (See appendices 5 and 6.)

Qāytbāy's primary writ, issued on 24 Jumādā II 879/5 November 1474
and amended several times subsequently, lists properties supporting his tomb
complex, three fountains in the city, two primary schools, his mosque in
Gharbīya Province and an irrigation wheel in Minūfīya district.[29] The first
institution, which received the waqf yield's largest share, should be interpreted as the employer and benevolent agency it was. The deed outlines in
detail the staff of religious functionaries, mystics, scholastics, and custodians

who sustained its daily devotional, pedagogical, and welfare operations. All of these individuals were salaried in dirhams (presumably copper *fulūs*), worth only a minute fraction of an Ashrafī.[30] But collectively, they and the supplies they purchased absorbed well over a million dirhams annually for this foundation alone.

Despite predictable favoritism for his mausoleum, Qāytbāy was obsessed with communal welfare on a much broader scale, as noted previously. The other foundations supported by his endowments received a substantial percentage of their yields and cannot be dismissed as mere shelters concealing his private holdings. Qāytbāy was especially interested in the mosque he established on Rawḍā Island, south of the central city, and his Jerusalem academy.[31] He inspected construction work on his fountains and the Rawḍā edifice personally and called his stewards or engineers to account for the expense money they received.[32] The one glaring lacuna in Qāytbāy's charitable documents involves the enormous donation he made during the Mawlid of 877/1471 to pilgrims and mendicants resident in Medina.[33] The sum al-Ṣayrafī and Ibn Iyās reported paralleled monies Qāytbāy reserved for his large foundations but cannot be confirmed from surviving archival evidence. Nonetheless, discounting this omission, comparison of amounts calculated for yields and expenses reveal interesting trends in Qāytbāy's allocation preferences.

Trust writs supporting the eight foundations described in Qāytbāy's primary donation generated an estimated annual income of 58,600 dīnārs.[34] Annual disbursements on these charities amounted to 4082 dīnārs, or 7 percent of the yield. (See appendices 5 and 6.) Even if the expense estimate undercalculates revenues provided for student stipends, staff salaries, and operational supplies by half—an unlikely error rate—the total would still amount to only 14 percent. Clearly, the great majority of generated income from the waqf writs, roughly 90 percent of the total, was not devoted to the writ's stated functions. Since the deeds simultaneously provided for the welfare of Qāytbāy's family and retainers, one might assume that they collected all the difference. But in fact, the writs often allow discretion within the lineage. Amounts reserved for specific persons vary widely from a majority of residual to mere pittances. And the sums they allot for supervisory personnel represent only minute fragments of total income.[35] Allocation of the majority share of income thus remained undesignated in the documents. What reasoning lay behind such a difference between yield and expenditures can only be surmised, but we can hardly assume that either the discrepancy or silence occurred as a consequence of oversight. The care evidenced in defining, locating, and tallying the properties, or in outlining expenditures precludes that possibility. And the elaborate witnessing of every transaction in each writ by the realm's most senior magistrates precludes any chance of misstatement. The documents specify what their donor and his aides designated—no more, no less. Qāytbāy's other deeds expended higher proportions of their yields on their foundations, but overall they generated much less income. (See appendix 6.) The vast revenues, comparable to a significant segment of the realm's total receipts, emerged from writs sustaining the first eight foundations.

What then were Qāytbāy's undeclared purposes for this income? Since presumably the revenue was no longer tallied in any government register nor subject to formal tax, one assumes that it flowed into a private reserve, the sultan's personal fisc. The Bureau of Charitable Trusts, headed by its supervisor—a royal appointee, exercised jurisdiction only over monies stipulated in an original deed for specific foundations. He possessed no legal claim over any excess beyond those amounts. Whether rectors of institutions receiving these revenues could make any demands against this surplus is indeterminate from archival or narrative evidence. Yet their tapping of a large proportion also begs credibility. Not owning the trust itself, they merely administered revenue it specified for their foundations. Circumstances therefore point toward the donor alone and his close advisers deciding the use of these majority shares.

What might such use encompass? This study has elaborated at some length on fiscal dilemmas confronting the regime, problems that superficially defied resolution. Given shortfalls caused by shrinking of formal income sources and proliferation of concealment or hoarding tactics devised by income producers, the system could not overtly meet demands made against it. But if Qāytbāy relied progressively on a private fisc generated from waqf surpluses, neither he nor anyone in concert with him explained how he did so. While the chronicles dwell on Qāytbāy's sporadic appropriation of waqf yields to meet military costs, these incidents remained ad hoc and confined to official expenditures. The sultan's disregard for protests from foundation rectors may indicate his awareness of the contrast between income and expense. By the fifteenth century, waqf-supported foundations probably embraced the largest troves of nonmilitary assets in the realm. Most could survive a mulcting or two. Still, the narrative authors make no mention of Qāytbāy defraying his own debts by drawing on a trust-based reserve. They describe only the Special Bureau (*Dīwān al-Mufrad*) or the Privy Fund (*Dīwān al-Khāṣṣ*), primarily in the context of their failure at generating funds over and beyond what traditional sources could provide. The accelerating frequency of arrests experienced by directors of these two bureaus attests to their incapacity at fulfilling their patron's needs. In light of the sources' studied vagueness during Qāytbāy's reign, and their endorsement of his professed rectitude in fiscal matters, we must turn to al-Ghawrī's policies for clearer hints about a process that remained elusive even under his initiative.

Before speculating about al-Ghawrī's experiments, the contribution of Qāytbāy's spouse Fāṭima merits attention, for she too emerges as one of the salient figures in the archival sources. Fāṭima's obituary notice lays emphasis on her immense estate (*tarika ḥāfila*).[36] Ibn Iyās states that she presided as mistress over the imperial court for thirty years and possessed her own quarters. But he also notes that, following her husband's decease, she was subjected to indignities because of her wealth. The julbān recruits dared invade her suburban dwelling by the Āq Ṣunqur Bridge to demand a bonus. They heaped insults on her and threatened assault if she did not accede. When Qāytbāy's heir, al-Nāṣir Muḥammad, learned of their brazenness, he forbade any Mamlūk to approach her residence on pain of death. The julbān believed that Fāṭima had participated in a conspiracy to murder Qānṣūh Khamsmiʾa, whom she had married following his enthronement to protect her estate. Although Fāṭima's involvement was never proved, her vulnerability remained. She therefore sought security by yet another marriage—to al-ʿĀdil Ṭūmānbāy—which lasted only two months. Fāṭima's health declined rapidly after this affair, and she died in Būlāq on 22 Dhūʾl-Ḥijja 909/6 June 1504.

Some thirty-nine deeds granted by Fāṭima alone have been preserved. As with her contemporaries, this collection of documents may only represent a remnant of Fāṭima's total endowment program. Nonetheless, the sample still extant does suggest her investment strategy. The longest writ, Fāṭima's own primary waqf,[37] drawn up well into her career, repeats many properties listed in individual bills of sale that exhibit both shares and prices. Indeed, most of the remaining documents identify Fāṭima's purchases.[38] The earliest dates from 21 Rabīʿ I 878/15 August 1473, the last from 27 Rajab 909/15 January 1504, just months before her death. She spent a total of 16,500 Ashrafī dīnārs and ten thousand silver (not copper) dirhams over this thirty-year period. According to surviving deeds, Fāṭima was most actively engaged in acquisition of real estate between 894 and 896 (1488-1491), which period also witnessed the first signs of her husband's declining vigor. Fāṭima may well have been alarmed over her security after Qāytbāy fractured his leg three years earlier and have begun to plan for future exigencies. The properties she bought divide into two-thirds commercial or rental structures in Cairo, with clusterings in the Āq Ṣunqur (where she made her private home outside the Citadel), Bāb Shaʿrīya and Būlāq districts (total purchase value 9900 dīnārs); and one-third agricultural land in Gharbīya (Delta), Ashmūnayn (Upper Egypt) and al-Maṭarīya (north of Cairo) (total purchase value 6400 dīnārs). While all of this property was clearly differentiated from that of her husband, Fāṭima bought shares in real estate partially owned by powerful amīrs, trusted colleagues of her husband's faction. Prominent among these were Qāytbāy's relative, Baybars al-Rajabī, and Muḥammad, son of the former Dawādār Bardibak.[39] She therefore seems to have hedged against the threat of confiscation were he to die suddenly. Of course, upon her own demise, al-Ghawrī assumed title to all her property. The transfer was completed in one day, under the supervision of Sarī al-Dīn ibn al-Shiḥna: 24 Ṣafar 910/6 August 1504, terminating one of the larger Mamlūk fortunes of the age.[40]

Yet Fāṭima maintained her control over this estate until her passing—no mean feat. Despite his avarice, al-Ghawrī waited until the widow's death before seizing her assets. And he could claim with justice that no legal heirs survived her. Whether Fāṭima secretly agreed to will her property to al-Ghawrī if he respected her position until her death is not clear, but stands as a reasonable hypothesis. If the sultan respected Fāṭima's rights during her lifetime, one may assume that he had been assured some profit in return. It is this tension between testator's rights and expropriator's designs that emerges from their strained relationship. The profile of Fāṭima's investments depict a skilled partner contributing to her husband's efforts at enlarging a fiscal preserve and an astute politician sheltering an estate upon his demise. Al-Ghawrī may have learned more from Fāṭima's tactics than he did from Qāytbāy's grandiose benevolence.

What was al-Ghawrī in the process of learning before fate cut short his designs? Preceding his enthronement, little concrete can be surmised. In contrast with Qāytbāy, al-Ghawrī placed nothing in trusts during his career as an officer. His earliest alleged purchases date from 907, several months after his accession. But from then on to his departure for Marj Dābiq, al-Ghawrī engaged in an unprecedented acquisition of waqf properties. The three hundred writs bearing his name constitute almost a third of archival materials left from the entire Mamlūk period. Yet despite this wealth of documentation, al-Ghawrī's charitable donations are far more restricted than Qāytbāy's. Al-Ghawrī issued only one major votive deed. Although its scope is impressive, the writ supports but four charities, concentrating its benefits overwhelmingly on the first: the sultan's own mausoleum and mystic hospice (*al-Qubba wa'l-Khānqāh al-Ghawrīya al-Sharīfa*) located in the Hatmaker's Bazaar (Sūq al-Sharābishiyīn).[41] We have already noted widespread cynicism over al-Ghawrī's parasitic means of adorning this luxurious complex, which rose rapidly under his impatient goading of construction crews and interior decorators. Nonetheless, al-Ghawrī did not skimp on largesse he reserved for this self-aggrandizing monument.

From early 907 to the first transaction of his primary waqf deed, dated 26 Muḥarram 909/21 July 1503, al-Ghawrī amassed a network of properties so large they generated an estimated annual yield approaching fifty-three thousand Ashrafī dīnārs. By the end of 914/April 1509, he had added holdings that provided thirty-one thousand more per annum. Thus, by 915, during an interval of seven years, this man gathered a trove of assets providing roughly eighty-three thousand dīnārs annually, all sheltered in a blanket trust dedicated ostensibly to his mausoleum. (See appendices 7 and 8.) Of al-Ghawrī's three other charitable bequests, only the flood gauge, mosque, and belvedere of the Nilometer on the southern tip of Rawḍā Island received any appreciable income (approximately seven hundred dīnārs annually). The other two were minimal: twelve thousand dirhams (approximately forty dīnārs) granted yearly to the senior eunuch custodian (*shaykh al-khuddām*) of the Holy Sanctuary at

Mecca and five hundred-plus dīnārs every twelve months for the sultan's corpse-washing font at the base of the Citadel. But even yearly expenditures on al-Ghawrī's mausoleum, embodiment of his ostentation, were dwarfed by the trove's unused output. In 914, apparently a watershed year for al-Ghawrī's fiscal program, his mausoleum-hospice actually received slightly less than six thousand dīnārs annually, 7 percent of the total. The parallel with the ratio between yield for and expenditures on Qāytbāy's tomb is obvious. In both cases, more than 90 percent was left as unassigned income. Similar to the lack of specific provisos governing this majority in Qāytbāy's major writ, Awqāf 882 makes no mention of how most of its surplus is to be utilized. Statements assuring the support of al-Ghawrī's wife, son and future descendants are linked to relatively minimal sums or proportions. Given the deed's precision of property and expense itemization, all witnessed by the sultan's senior legates, oversight may also be discounted. One is therefore again left with the presumption that this surplus flowed into the sultan's private fisc, no strings attached. But by al-Ghawrī's time, both narrative and archival sources provide substantive evidence that this hypothesis merits more than an impression's consideration.

We have already dwelled on Ibn Iyās' alarm over al-Ghawrī's expropriation of waqf yields to defray his troops' bonus demands. Confronted by their first rebellion in Dhū'l-Ḥijja 906/June-July 1501, the sultan consulted with both his dīwānī and jurist advisers on how he might acquire the money after Qāytbāy had left him an empty treasury.[42] Following initial opposition from the four qāḍīs, Sarī al-Dīn ibn al-Shiḥna ascended later in the day for a private audience in which a procedure for taking over yields was worked out. The sultan's marshal, Qāyt al-Rajabī, then assumed direction over the collection sweep, assigning his subordinates responsibility for districts throughout the city. Ibn Iyās, while our sole commentator on these events, remarked more pointedly about the sultan's intentions than did any of Qāytbāy's chroniclers: "The sultan sought to confiscate waqfs of mosques, colleges, and other benevolent foundations, *leaving them funds sufficient to cover daily operations only* (emphasis mine). As an incentive to the amīrs responsible for the expropriations, he planned to grant them trust properties in their own names—thereby alienating them permanently." Although Ibn Iyās depicted this confiscation as a measure unparalleled for its wickedness and called the All-High's wrath down on al-Ghawrī's head, the mulcting must be assessed in light of the yield-expense ratio above. If the enormous surpluses generated by Qāytbāy's and al-Ghawrī's trusts provide a concrete indicator of proportions, the latter's assumption of either a six- or twelve-month cumulative yield for Cairo's waqf institutions still left them with most of their assets intact—ripe for mulcting again when the need arose. The litany of apocalypse chanted so stridently by the narrative authors should therefore be tempered by the documentary evidence of a large residual surviving even the most severe extractions. But did al-Ghawrī collect enough money from these sweeps to assuage his soldiers' avarice? Did assuagement constitute the sum total of his objectives? Before speculating on this matter, the profile of al-Ghawrī's acquisitions merits scrutiny.

Since al-Ghawrī granted only one major trust instrument, amended and enlarged through several transactions down to 922 and beyond, all the others issued in his name differed in purpose and scope. These three-hundred-odd documents certify sale, substitution, transfer, and repossession procedures for discrete properties. Unlike the primary waqf writ, they spell out the properties' prices—although rarely in the certificate legalizing al-Ghawrī's acquisition. Many of these deeds list agreements tracing purchases initiated during the preceding century. But the dates associated with al-Ghawrī's assumption are much more concentrated and bespeak a highly efficient process by which whole series of accumulated writs were transferred in a single session. The documents, 262 of which supported the sultan's mausoleum or his other three foundations, embraced urban real estate almost exclusively. Few of the extensive rural holdings, located from Upper Egypt to Central Palestine and exhibited in the main writ, appeared in these deeds. Presumably alienated from iqṭāʿ allotments (all included in the cadaster summaries drawn up by Ibn al-Jīʿān or Ibn Duqmāq, summarized by Halm), these agrarian tracts were acquired via a separate procedure undocumented beyond chroniclers' allusions. The grouping of deeds according to these dates also emphasizes the fragmentary nature of this collection, illuminative as it is. One cannot assume that these dates represent al-Ghawrī's complete procedure of expropriation. Many other deeds, probably an indeterminate majority, have been lost. Those remaining do run the full gamut of income-producing real estate in the capital during the later Middle Ages.[43] More than 60 percent of them resurfaced in the several transactions of Awqāf 882, painstakingly demarcated by their "purchase" dates.

The writs' early transactions certifying an original purchase spanned more than a century. Typically, the first or even second buyers were civilians of means, but as the property changed hands it came into the proximity of al-Ghawrī's extorters. The critical transition phase involved individuals from both the bureaucratic and military elites who themselves were dabbling with trust speculation. Although three hundred deeds were ultimately procured by al-Ghawrī's agents, the list of those who submitted their assets to him directly embraced only 115 persons. Most bore titles indicating military rank or dīwān post. These individuals appeared in the penultimate transaction and here the data are both more focused and enlightening.

Of the 115, twenty-seven were discernible in the narrative sources, or 24 percent. All were mentioned, and often discussed at length, in the context of their confiscation at al-Ghawrī's hands.[44] Former executive officers, confidential secretaries, and other bureaucrats figured prominently. Most salient, and a signal exemplar of al-Ghawrī's strategy, was none other than Khayrbak al-Sharīfī, one of the sultan's former confidants and treasurers.

Depicted by Ibn Iyās as the sultan's "master of troves" (*amīr al-khazāʾin*) until his death on 9 Ramaḍān 920/28 October 1514,[45] this man was deeply involved with his sponsor in joint ventures suggesting privatization of waqf properties. Between 20 Muḥarram 910/3 July 1504 and 6 Rabīʿ I 920/1 May 1514, the khāzindār "sold" over one hundred units of property to his sovereign at front prices totalling more than thirty-two thousand dīnārs.[46] Roughly half of these were agrarian iqṭāʿ tracts the treasurer had alienated from the Army Bureau. Since under law they officially belonged to the state as its collective capital, they could not be auctioned off at any price. The cadasters listed average annual yields from them rather than market values. But since the transfer deeds dated on 27 Shawwāl 914/18 February 1509 listed the Army Bureau chief (*nāẓir al-jaysh*), Muḥyī al-Dīn al-Qaṣrawī as wakīl, we may assume that this individual, whom Khayrbak had recommended to al-Ghawrī for the office, readily submitted to his pressure and signed over the allotments.

The documents thus reveal a fascinating glimpse into one dimension of the process by which state properties passed out of its jurisdiction into the sultan's personal trust reserve. Heretofore, the chronicles have only hinted at how the alienation took place. The documents disclosed its occurrence fully sanctioned under the aegis of appropriate dīwān authorities. Outwardly, neither Khayrbak nor al-Ghawrī violated the laws of state or God as they whittled away at the realm's font of usufruct properties their competitors used for their own challenges. The "prices" Khayrbak collected should be interpreted more as his facilitation fees than as any indicator of the real value these lands might command on the open market—which certainly would have exceeded thirty-two thousand dīnārs. Indeed, all prices associated with al-Ghawrī's acquisitions must be regarded with caution. They warrant more credibility as liaison money than measures of worth.

And all of these transactions ensued in a murky environment of mutual deceit and nest feathering. Khayrbak himself concealed funds al-Ghawrī deposited with him for safekeeping, and ran his own extortion racket on the side, compromising his partner's devices. When Ibn Iyās penned Khayrbak's obituary, he described the sultan's astonishment over his treasurer's closeted estate, the contents of which he had never divulged.[47] So incensed was al-Ghawrī at his erstwhile lieutenant's treachery that he proclaimed him a miser who bled the Muslims, cancelled customary recanting of Koranic verses for salvation over his grave, and prohibited distribution of any penitential offerings in his name. Khayrbak's skulduggery may well have motivated al-Ghawrī's assumption of the khāzindār's functions himself after the treasurer's death. The sultan's decision to empty the Citadel vaults and transport their contents to Aleppo where he could guard them personally also underscores doubts over his adjutants' custodianship in his absence. If these hoards were left behind, he might return home to find the fruits of his labors alienated even if he survived his confrontation with Selim.

The plot thickens as patterns of transaction dates unfold. The transferrals of property to al-Ghawrī and their subsequent registry in his mausoleum testament took place en masse. Of the 262 deeds dedicated to his primary foundation, more than a third were appropriated in 914/1509 alone, the year al-Ghawrī completed the second phase of his main writ. Sixty-eight documents entered his mausoleum trust on a single day: 20 Ṣafar 911/23 July 1505. Fifty-two more joined them on 18 Rabīʿ II 922/1 June 1515 shortly before his departure. The overwhelming preponderance of these two dates does not imply the entirety of al-Ghawrī's expropriations, but they do reveal coincidences and procedures. That al-Ghawrī saw fit to cancel his oppressive monthly futures taxes in Ṣafar 922/March-April, Ibn Iyās dismissed as a last ditch good will gesture typical of the sultan's craven attempts at buying loyalty rather than earning it.[48] But al-Ghawrī's capacity to endure the loss of seventy-six thousand dīnārs in annual revenue puzzled him. The sultan's confidence in his solvency becomes more plausible in light of his gaining a trove of valuable real estate six weeks later. Beyond such felicitous concurrences of chronology, the deeds display the mechanisms of expropriation. And emerging as their leading expediter was none other than Sarī al-Dīn ibn al-Shiḥna.

This qāḍī, whom al-Ṣayrafī chided for raw ambition and Ibn Iyās condemned decades hence for finessing legal sanctions of waqf manipulation, acted either as presiding judge or first witness in more than a hundred of these documents. He first appeared in a deed dated 14 Ṣafar 907/29 August 1501, shortly after his appointment as Ḥanafī justice.[49] From that time to his ignominious dismissal and possibly beyond, Ibn al-Shiḥna served his sovereign more consistently than any of his colleagues on the bench. Although the language of his transactions is formulaic, Sarī al-Dīn oversaw procedures he certified as legitimate under Sharīʿa. Given the discrepancy between output and expenditure, we may assume that Ibn al-Shiḥna deftly avoided any undue disruption of benevolent services as a consequence of his machinations. But the fact that not a single price was quoted for his sovereign's "purchases" gives pause for reflection. The texts of such launderings read as follows:

> The entirety of the site described above was transferred to the possession (*milk*) of our Sovereign Sultan al-Ghawrī from the possession of _______, as a lawful (*Sharʿī*) transfer according to lawful (principles) of sale at a price mutually accepted by the aforementioned seller, a legal contract in fullness and perfection (*bi'l-tamām wa'l-kamāl*) from assets of our Sovereign Majesty, in his Royal Name, as the above dated bill of sale on Damascene paper guarantees.[50]

While this case specifies no foundation as a charitable objective, the following specimens make clear where most acquisitions were directed:

> The entirety of _______, and what it encompasses by its boundaries described (above), became a trust (*waqf*) among the aggregate trusts of our Sovereign Majesty, Sultan al-Ghawrī, may his Name be exalted, for maintenance of the Royal and Sultanic College (*Madrasa*) located in the Hatmakers' Quarter (*Sharābishiyīn*).

A more detailed designation:

> All of the _______, and what it encompasses within its boundaries described (above), was certified as a lawful waqf among the aggregate trusts of our Sovereign Majesty, Sultan al-Ghawrī, may his Name be exalted, for maintenance of the Royal and Sultanic College (*Madrasa*), its Mausoleum (*Qubba*), its Hospice (*Khānqāh*), its School (*Maktab*), and its Fountain (*Sabīl*), which our Sovereign Majesty, may his Name be exalted, founded; and for (support of) learned savants (*arbāb al-shaʿāʾir*), esteemed shaykhs (*al-sādā al-mashāʾikh*), mystics (*al-ṣūfīya*), orphans (*al-aytām*), custodial staff (*arbāb al-wazāʾif*) and (other) specified emoluments (*al-jawāmik al-murattaba*) appertaining thereto by clear and explicit provision in His (al-Ghawrī's) royal trust deed inscribed on Ḥamā paper.[51]

Nowhere do these representative waqf certificates, or the transferrals preceding them, spell out a concrete sum. Only deals "at a mutually accepted price" (*bi-thamani ḥālin maqbūḍin*) approved by "legal proxy" (*tawakkul Sharʿī*) are mentioned. Since all the persons the chronicles confirmed who relinquished property to al-Ghawrī had experienced dismissal, arrest, and confiscation, the validity of these phrases rings rather hollow. Nor do Ibn Iyās' comments about Ibn al-Shiḥna's services nurture an impression of his solicitude for payment guarantees under law. Rather, he dwelled on the qāḍī's skilled advice and the intensity of his patron's wrath when the former betrayed his loyalty.[52] Whether the victims of al-Ghawrī's compulsory sales received nothing whatever for the assets they lost is less likely than partial compensation linked to their release. This second option coincides with trends toward mutual complicity described in chapter 6. A jurist like Ibn al-Shiḥna could set his signature to certificates containing the proceding phrases without literal violation of principles he was sworn to uphold. Ibn al-Shiḥna loomed large in these transactions but he did not monopolize them. Other magistrates approved the transfers and front "sales" masking al-Ghawrī's expropriations. By no means does Ibn Al-Shiḥna bear sole responsibility. Yet his prominence in the archival documents, when coupled with his notoriety in the chronicles, warrants his assignation as a prime architect of his master's devices.

The matter of Sarī al-Dīn's dismissal, so luridly described by Ibn Iyās, may be qualified by his ongoing presence in the archival sources. Although the great majority predate his fall from grace in Shawwāl 919, several reveal him continuing either as presiding judge or prime witness until shortly before his death in Rajab 921. While Ibn al-Shiḥna certainly lost his prestigious

post as senior Ḥanafī jurist and his comfortable academic sinecures, his expertise as a waqf litigator may have persuaded al-Ghawrī to retain him in his
more covert function. Nonetheless, his abiding signature does deflate Ibn Iyās'
sweeping claim that the sultan "never beheld his face thereafter." Perhaps al-
Ghawrī so loathed Sarī al-Dīn that he never received him again. But the ex-
qāḍī's services may have carried a residual value the monarch could not easily
dismiss. If they remained concealed, he could perform them without any formal reconciliation.

What do these developments connote about al-Ghawrī's growth as an aggressive rentier, if not a covert capitalist? They surely parallel his lengthy con-
sultations with the procurers he has advanced. While precise knowledge of
their discussions is irretrievable, al-Ghawrī did not lack for astute advisers to
help craft his programs or encourage him once he had resolved on a course of
action. Ibn Iyās implicates Sarī al-Dīn so heatedly that his involvement is obvious, but we have traced the schemes of several other dīwānīs who worked
closely with their patron before he toppled them. Given their disparities, all
rose to the bureaucracy's summit because of their finesse at extortion. Their
tactics, when compared with al-Ghawrī's trust acquisitions, complement his
creation of a private fisc in the guise of a vast waqf trove over which he held
exclusive title. Since amendments to Awqāf 882 disclose hasty "pastes-on"
wherein all properties are added indiscriminately with no attempt at their in-
tegration into the expenditure section nor at concealment of their crude graft-
ing, the procedure remained rudimentary throughout. Beyond accumulation,
it does not seem to have advanced toward more sophisticated means of coor-
dinating acquisitions or maximizing their yield. But we have already seen how
lucrative their income was. Al-Ghawrī's waqf manipulations thus point to his
conception of the pious foundation as a secure depository above all else, a kind
of bank in an age ignorant of the concept. Granted by the military elite, with
the monarch as prime donor, charitable trusts of the Mamlūk era enjoyed respect primarily for the relative inviolability of their assets. From al-Ghawrī's
perspective, he never surrendered ownership over his bestowals and chose this
particular medium for its security. Siphoned in time of need, a trust repository
represented the least vulnerable haven he could devise for his trove's safekeeping. In light of the glaring discrepancy between yield and outlay, al-Ghawrī's
tactic did not egregiously infringe upon his trusts' formal purpose. He could
build up a clandestine fisc primarily from their undesignated income.

Whether al-Ghawrī actually tapped his secret reserve to stave off rebellion
cannot be ascertained with any degree of accuracy despite the correlation between need and appropriation. The narrative sources stress his reliance primarily on seemingly ad hoc confiscations of annual or semi-annual staff monies
to meet bonus demands or expedition costs. Ibn Iyās' single reference to al-
Ghawrī selling any portion of his waqf property is significant for its unique-
ness and the sultan's vexation[53]:

On Sunday the fifth (of Rajab 917/2 September 1511), the sultan convened only the julbān recruits in the courtyard. He rebuked them, saying: "I shall abdicate the sultanate and you may acclaim whom you will." The stand-off continued into the afternoon until the sultan finally agreed to a bonus for his purchased Mamlūks, but only in the amount of forty dīnārs each. Several officers remonstrated with the sultan, urging him to avoid worse trouble by raising the bonus to fifty. But the sultan responded that he could not now afford that level. The debate continued until the monarch finally granted fifty dīnārs per soldier. He was compelled to sell properties and lands he had placed in waqf to support his madrasa. The sultan had no other choice at this time since the treasuries were void of funds and he could temporarily find no other means of procuring the money to alleviate the crisis.

Since personal survival outranked all other priorities, al-Ghawrī reluctantly took this expedient. Yet he did so but once, and only when he saw no other option for escaping deposition. The anxiety this experience caused al-Ghawrī may have heightened his resolve to harbor his trove for more compliant subordinates.

Only a year earlier Ibn Iyās first mentioned the experimental Fifth Corps—in the context of its stipend funding. The historian dwelt on sources known to him: monies formerly designated exclusively for Sulṭānī Mamlūks that the monarch was steadily, if furtively, eroding. Also at this time, al-Ghawrī stepped up his reduction of iqṭāᶜs. The intersection of these developments with al-Ghawrī's waqf appropriations, and his ire over giving a portion of his new reserve up in the face of revolt, mutually betoken his intended use of its proceeds outside the formal military establishment. The latter al-Ghawrī now regarded primarily as a bastion of self-interest and sedition, ambivalent over service in the field and disinclined to obey commands.

Do all these disparate phenomena, once pieced together, reveal a budding master plan by which the iqṭāᶜ system would be scrapped outright once the sultan garnered the means to replace it? Did al-Ghawrī contemplate phasing out the most intractable elements of the Mamlūk corps once he had trained a viable alternative? Did he envision his financial liberation from the incessant crises that had plagued his entire executive career in the creation of a fiscal preserve he alone controlled? We cannot resolve these queries for certain. David Ayalon would have us believe that such thoughts never crossed the mind of anyone embedded in the military elite, so enslaved by the mentality of caste supremacy. Yet admitting the speculative nature of these hypotheses, which can never be proved conclusively barring new sources, they present an alternative explanation for al-Ghawrī's behavior that rationalizes decisions his contemporaries saw only as menacing and more recent analysts dismissed solely as erratic. Both the ᶜulamāʾ and Mamlūk hierarchies had every reason to detest al-Ghawrī's stratagems. In hindsight, and the luxury of immunity from their consequences, we may interpret them as signs of genuine innovation, however tentative. They certainly add a new dimension to our understanding of al-Ghawrī's deviation from time-honored traditions that had pampered entrenched elites so handsomely for so long.

It is this confluence of events, heretofore noted only in isolation, that explains at least in part al-Ghawrī's unenviable stature as a defiler of Islam. No such experiments are discernible in Qāytbāy's policies, and he received his contemporaries' acclaim as Islam's conservator. We cannot assume that al-Ghawrī's efforts promised viable prospects for long-term success. Still, groping as they were, they disquieted all those committed to upholding the past. Even al-Ghawrī's nephew, Ṭūmānbāy, hearkened back to Qāytbāy's stance when he took power. His codicil concluding his uncle's waqf, transaction seven,[54] deviates sharply from the deed's earlier allotments to endow several traditional charities conspicuously absent from al-Ghawrī's donations. Their provisos, tacked onto the main writ, may bespeak Ṭūmānbāy's shame over his uncle's neglect of institutions revered in the minds of pious believers. But shame, however warranted, does not discount the ingenuity implicit in al-Ghawrī's allocations. If they hint at clandestine investment strategies, their instigator fully merits his reputation as an innovator singular in his time. What long-term impact they might have historians can debate. That Qānṣūh al-Ghawrī defied rigid custom by initiating them earns him more than castigation as an arch-villain among Egypt's autocrats.

Notes

1. *Badā'i'* 4, p. 103, l.1.

2. D. Ayalon, "The Wafidīya in the Mamlūk Kingdom," *Islamic Culture* 25 (1951): 89–104.

3. *Badā'i'* 4, p. 59, l. 21 (Jumādā I 909/October-November 1503); D. Ayalon, "Notes on the Furūsīya Exercises and Games of the Mamlūk Sultanate," *Studies in Islamic History and Civilization*, Scripta Hierosolymitana 9 (1960): 47–53.

4. On the red uniforms: *Badā'i'* 4, pp. 72, l. 10 (9 Rajab 910/16 December 1504); 201, l. 16 (11 Dhū'l-Qaʿda 916/9 February 1511); the acrobatic Furūsīya stunts: 151, l. 17 (Muḥarram 915/April-May 1509).

5. On ambassadors' observations of drill ceremonials: *Badā'i'* 4, pp. 124, l. 10 (27 Shaʿbān 913/1 January 1508: Ṣafavid emissary hosted at lancers' drill returns "posthaste" to his patron in Iran); 145, l. 12 (4 Shawwāl 914/26 January 1509: ambassador from Baghdād awed by drill exercises); 163, l. 23;

164, l. 20 (Rajab-Sha'bān 915/October-December 1509: Ottoman Prince Qurqud beholds lancers); 201, l. 16 (11 Dhū'l-Qa'da 916/9 February 916: Viceroy of Aleppo [future traitor] watches lancers' feats); 230, l. 3 (19 Rabī' I 917/6 June 1511: Ṣafavid ambassador "marvels" at lancers' drills); 391, l. 6 (6 Rajab 920/27 August 1514: Ottoman emissary hosted at lancers' drill).

6. D. Ayalon, *Gunpowder and Firearms in the Mamluk Kingdom* (London, 1956), 48–52. Ayalon notes the focus of artillery on defense of coastal ports, particularly Alexandria.

7. *Inbā'*, p. 271, l. 1 (9 Shawwāl 875/31 March 1471).

8. *Badā'i'* 4, pp. 191, l. 17 (6 Jumādā II 916/10 September 1510: enormous size and weight); 260, l. 21 (8 Rabī' I 918/24 May 1512: artillery piece causes street collapse).

9. Ibid., p. 192, l. 10.

10. Ibid., p. 238, l. 1.

11. *Badā'i'* 5, p. 14, l. 1.

12. *Badā'i'* 4, p. 200, l. 15; Ayalon, *Gunpowder,* 71–83.

13. D. Ayalon, "Studies on the Structure of the Mamlūk Army—I," *BSOAS* 15 (1953): 204–05.

14. On 20 Ṣafar 920/16 April 1514, Al-Ghawrī's elite guard, the khāṣṣakīs, threatened revolt, accusing their patron of reneging on their stipends to pay his Fifth Corpsmen, whom they dismissed as "a hodge-podge of threads and tatters" (*mulaffaqīn shay' khiyāṭ wa-shay' bakhāniqī*) See *Badā'i'* 4, pp. 369, l. 3; 206, l. 3 (Dhū'l-Qa'da 916/January-February 1511: Ibn Iyās describes their membership more soberly as Turkmān, Persians, reservists, and others of low stature).

15. Ibn Iyās, while discussing al-Ghawrī's muster of the Fifth Corps for his Suez expedition against the Portuguese in Rabī' I 919/May-June 1513, described their outfits as follows: "They wore coats of mail, helmets and swords in their belts. Among them were musketeers (*arquebusiers*). Their numbers amounted to three hundred men." (The parallels with equipage of contemporary European troops is clear.) See *Badā'i'* 4, p. 308, l. 3.

16. *Badā'i'* 4, 100, l. 18; for appointment of Arikmās as unit commander, p. 308, l. 3.

17. Ibid., p. 283, l. 2.

18. Ibid., p. 370, l. 9.

19. For the Suez expedition, *Badā'i'* 4, p. 331, l. 7; 335, l. 7; 337, l. 6; on the India maritime expedition, pp. 458, l. 1–466, l. 15.

20. *Badā'i'* 5, pp. 38, l. 10–44, l. 17.

21. Ayalon, *Gunpowder*, 80–82.

22. Muḥammad Amīn lists thirty-seven documents for Qāytbāy, but after duplicates are accounted for twenty-two supported his fourteen foundations. Thirty-nine appear under his spouse Fāṭima's name; three hundred three under al-Ghawrī's, only one of which is a major waqf writ. (See note 41.) These represent roughly a third of the thousand documents surviving from the Ayyūbid and Mamlūk periods.

23. Muḥammad Amīn has produced the most comprehensive study of the Waqf institution in medieval Egypt to date: *Al-Awqāf wa'l-Ḥayāt al-Ijtimā'īya fī Miṣr* (The Waqfs and Social Life in Egypt) (Cairo, 1980). His observations, particularly on pp. 320–72, are of critical importance but based primarily on impressionistic judgments of individual cases. L. Fernandes has commented on propagandistic motives behind royal support of large mystic hospices. See her "Some Aspects of the Zāwīya in Egypt at the Eve of the Ottoman Conquest," *AI* 19 (1983): 9–17; *The Evolution of a Sufi Institution in Mamluk Egypt: the Khanqah*, Islamkundliche Untersuchungen series, 134 (Berlin, 1988).

24. On benevolent services supported by waqf, see G. Makdisi, *The Rise of Colleges: Institutions of Higher Learning in Islam and the West* (Edinburgh, 1981), 35–74; on regulation of waqf transfer: H. Cattan, "The Law of Waqf," in M. J. Khadduri and H. J. Liebesny, eds. *Law in the Middle East*, 1: *Origins and Development of Islamic Law* (Washington, 1955), chap. 8; W. Heffening, "Wakf," *EI¹* 4: 1096–1103.

25. Taxation of waqf yields was an issue that provoked controversy among legal authorities. See Amīn, *Awqāf*, 69–130.

26. Amīn # 116: DW, Maḥfaẓa 18, ḥujja 111 (Halm, *Ägypten* 2, 568).

27. Trust donors usually purchased shares of a property. This tendency was pronounced with regard to agrarian land, which had been surveyed in cadasters from ancient times. The most recent of these, and the register in force for *iqṭā'* allocations during the Circassian period, was the cadaster (*rawq*) commissioned by Sultan al-Nāṣir Muḥammad (1309–1340), summarized by Ibn Duqmāq: *Kitāb al-Intiṣār li-Wāsiṭat 'Iqd al-Amṣār* in 809/1406 and Sharaf al-Dīn Yaḥyā ibn al-Jī'ān (of the wealthy family which suffered at al-Ghawrī's hands): *Al-Tuḥfat al-Sanīya bi-Asmā' al-Bilād al-Miṣrīya*, ca. 885/1480. Each village or agrarian district placed in *iqṭā'*, from the Mediterranean to Aswān, was divided as a unit into twenty-four portions according to annual yield computed as "army" (*jayshī*) dīnārs, a currency of account designating rents col-

lected for the Army Bureau and paid out to the amīr assigned the allotment. A jayshī dīnār was worth approximately four-fifths (80 percent) of an Ashrafī gold dīnār, the highest value coin of the Circassian period. As these allotments were progressively alienated, the original division of twenty-four was subparcelled into smaller sections with each transaction. Percentages in this analysis were computed from resultant fractions. See Halm, *Ägypten* 1, A: Introduction.

28. Qāytbāy's foundations (compare with Newhall, *Patronage,* 264–65):

1. Mausoleum-mosque (*jāmiᶜ al-madfan*) located in the Desert Cemetery (*Ṣaḥrāʾ*) east of Cairo, quarter of Sīdī ᶜAbd-Allāh al-Minūfī.
2. Cistern (*ṣahrīj*), fountain (*sabīl*) outside Fāṭimid district, quarter of al-Rabᶜ al-Ẓāhirī.
3. Primary school (*kuttāb*) associated with # 2.
4. Fountain (*sabīl*) in the quarter of the Ibn Ṭūlūn Mosque.
5. Mosque (*jāmiᶜ*) located in Nāḥiyat Salamūn, Gharbīya Province, but no proven association with deed in note 26 (Halm, *Ägypten* 2, 568).
6. Irrigation wheel (*sāqiya*) located in Nāḥiyat Manawahla, Minūfīya Province (Halm, *Ägypten* 2, 369).
7. Marbled fountain (*sabīl murakhkham*) located in the Azhar quarter, Street of the Turks (*Darb al-Atrāk*).
8. Primary school (*kuttāb*) associated with # 7.
9. Mosque (*jāmiᶜ*) located in Damietta (*Thaghr Dumyāṭ*).
10. Hospice (*zāwiya*) located near the Ṣūfī Khānqāh at Siryāqūs, Qalyūbīya Province.
11. Mosque (*jāmiᶜ*) located in Nāḥiyat Disūq, Gharbīya Province (Halm, *Ägypten* 2, 497–98).
12. College (*madrasa*) located near the Chain Gate (Bāb al-Silsila), Jerusalem.
13. Mosque (*jāmiᶜ*) located in the south side (*jihat al-Qiblīya*) of Ghazza, quarter of al-Tuqjī's Bath.
14. Mosque (*jāmiᶜ*) located on Rawḍa Island, Old Cairo (*Miṣr*) District.

29. Amīn # 475: AW 886 qadīm; partially published by L. A. Mayer, *The Buildings of Qāytbāy as Described in His Endowment Deed,* fascicule 1, text and index (London, 1938).

30. Due to incessant debasement policies legislated by Circassian sultans, copper dirhams fluctuated widely in weight and value. But their rough equivalency to an Ashrafī dīnār was three hundred to one after 1462. See E. Ashtor, *Histoire des prix et des salaires dans l'orient médiévale* (Paris: S.E.V.P.E.N., 1969), 278.

31. Supported by Amīn # 222: DW 33/210, dated 15 Dhū'l-Ḥijja 895/ 27 October 1490, and Amīn # 467: AW 887 qadīm, transactions 1 (4 Rabīᶜ II 877/8 September 1472) and 2 (25 Shawwāl 883/19 January 1479).

32. For the fountain: *Rawḍ*, f. 249-b, l. 22; *Badāʾiʿ* 3, p. 43, l. 2
(1 Shaʿbān 874/3 February 1470); *Inbāʾ*, p. 387, l. 10 (17 Rajab 876/30
December 1471). For the Rawḍā Mosque: *Badāʾiʿ* 3, p. 182, l. 9 (Rabīʿ II
886/May–June 1481); the Jerusalem College: *Badāʾiʿ* 3, p. 218, l. 8 (Jumādā II 890/June-July 1485: appointment of rector shaykh and dedication
entourage).

33. Described by al-Ṣayrafī during the Prophet's Birthday celebration, 11
Rabīʿ II/15 September: *Inbāʾ*, p. 478, l. 18. Ibn Iyās discusses an identical
donation, but dates it eight years later: *Badāʾiʿ* 3, p. 164, l. 1. Al-Ṣayrafī,
who personally observed the ceremony, is more reliable.

34. Deeds Amīn # 475: AW 886 qadīm, transactions 1–3; 550: AW
890 qadīm, transaction 3 (12 Rabīʿ II 880/15 August 1475), 198; DW 28/
187, transaction 1 (27 Ramaḍān 884/12 December 1479); 551: AW 611
jadīd, transaction 1 (28 Ṣafar 890/16 March 1485); 237: DW 36/225, transaction 5 (8 Shawwāl 918/17 December 1512). In lieu of prices for urban real
estate, which waqf writs do not include, value was estimated at one thousand
dīnārs per unit (averaging three properties each), calculated from prices provided for comparable properties in sale deeds. Annual disbursements were
computed at 10 percent of estimated value. Agrarian tracts were located in
Halm, *Ägypten*, 1 and 2; annual yields calculated according to shares reported
in deeds from totals provided by Ibn Duqmāq and Ibn al-Jīʿān.

35. See Jonathan Berkey, *The Transmission of Knowledge in Medieval Cairo*
(Princeton, 1992), 136–37, for stipends of nuẓẓār.

36. *Badāʾiʿ* 4, p. 64, l. 6.

37. Amīn # 506: AW 775 jadīd.

38. See C. F. Petry, "Class Solidarity vs. Gender Gain: Women as Custodians of Property in Later Medieval Egypt" in *Women in Middle Eastern History: Shifting Boundaries in Sex and Gender*, ed. N. Keddie and B. Baron (New
Haven, 1991), 141–42, n. 45.

39. Amīn # 510: AW 77-A jadīd, *Badāʾiʿ* 3, p. 189, l. 22; Amīn #
438, 439: AW 209, 490 jadīd, *Rawḍ*, f. 175, l. 23.

40. The assumptions are designated as transfers (*intiqāl*) or gifts (*hiba*).
They name al-Ghawrī as executor of Fāṭima's estate and place all properties
within the sultan's waqf supporting his mausoleum-hospice known as the
Ghūrīya.

41. Amīn # 652: AW 882 qadīm:

transaction 1, p. 9: trust (*waqf*) for foundations 1 (*qubba/khānqāh:* Cairo) and 2
(*jāmakīya khādim al-ṭawashīya:* Madīna) (26 Muḥarram 909/21 July 1503)

transaction 2, p. 275: addition (*ziyāda*) to foundation 1 (27 Shawwāl 914/18 February 1509)

transaction 3, p. 429: transfer (*intiqāl*) to foundation 1 (25 Dhū'l-Qaʿda 916/23 February 1511)

transaction 4, p. 459: trust (*waqf*) for foundation 3 (*sabīl al-muʾminīn*) (26 Muḥarram 909)

transaction 5, p. 479: addition (*ziyāda*) to foundation 3 (17 Rabīʿ II 922/20 May 1516)

transaction 6, p. 485: trust (*waqf*) for foundation 4 (*miqyās*) (18 Rabīʿ II 922/21 May)

transaction 7, pp. 522–71: trust (*waqf*) granted by Ṭūmānbāy, executor of al-Ghawrī's will, in support of foundations 5–11 (*al-Ḥaram al-Sharīf:* Mecca; *al-Qubba al-Nabawīya, al-Rawḍā al-Sharīfa, al-Ḥaram al-Sharīf:* Madīna; *Simāṭ Ibrāhīm:* al-Khalīl [Hebron]; *Jāmiʿ ʿAmr ibn al-ʿ Āṣ:* Miṣr; *jāmiʿ al-Azhar:* Cairo)

42. *Badāʾiʿ* 4, pp. 13, l. 22; 14, l. 13; *Taʾrīkh al-Jarākisa,* f. 68, l. 14.

43. Property items placed in trust yielded rents on a monthly or annual basis. Most common were stalls (*ḥawānīt*) hired by individual shopkeepers. Al-Ghawrī let out more than one thousand by the end of 914. Other types appearing frequently: markets (*aswāq*), manufacture halls (*qāʿāt*), caravansarays (*wakālāt*), warehouses (*ḥawāṣil*), dwellings (*ṭibāq*), inns (*khānāt*), magazines (*makhāzin*), merchant emporia (*fanādiq*), sugar kitchens (*maṭābikh*); stables (*iṣṭablāt*), bakeries (*afrān*), baths (*ḥammāmāt*), gardens (*junaynāt*), oil or cane presses (*maʾāṣir*), granaries (*shūnāt*).

44. In addition to Khayrbak al-Sharīfī:

Shihāb Aḥmad ibn al-Jīʿān, former kātib al-sirr: Amīn # 475: AW 886 qadīm, transaction 11; *Badāʾiʿ* 4, pp. 144, l. 15; 152, l. 17; 156, l. 12; 181, l. 7; 183, l. 16.

Shihāb Aḥmad al-Qarāfī, nāẓir al-jaysh: Amīn # 634, 638, 642: AW 197, 457, 182 jadīd; *Badāʾiʿ* 4, p. 43, l. 16.

Shams Muḥammad ibn Muzāḥim, nāẓir al-iṣṭabl: Amīn # 647, 656: AW 551, 202 jadīd; *Badāʾiʿ* 4, pp. 35, l. 3; 97, l. 20.

Shams Muḥammad ibn Taghrī-Birmish, son of wazīr: Amīn # 784, AW 392, jadīd; *Badāʾiʿ* 4, pp. 47, l. 18; 105. l. 4; 299, l. 17.

Shams Muḥammad al-Ḥulaybī al-Faraskūrī al-Khawājā: Amīn # 626, 689, 705, 704, 706, 730, 772, 776, 780: AW 183, 451, 113, 75, 388, 164, 174, 330, 374 jadīd; *Badāʾiʿ* 4, pp. 282, l. 16; 373, l. 4.

Shams Muḥammad al-Tājir: Amīn 779, 660: AW 372, 688 jadīd; *Badāʾiʿ* 4, p. 373, l. 4.

Sharaf Yaḥyā ibn ʿAwaḍ, son of Shams al-Dīn: Amīn # 475: AW 886 qadīm, transaction 12; *Badāʾiʿ* 4, p. 376, l. 20; 382, l. 10; 387, l. 8.

Sharaf Yaḥyā ibn ʿAbd al-Laṭif, son of eminent merchant: Amīn # 475: AW 886 qadīm, transaction 9; *Badāʾiʿ* 4, p. 100, l. 12.

ʿĀʾishā bint Khāṣṣbak, wife of Aqbirdī, sister of Khawand Fāṭima and al-Nāṣir Muḥammad: Amīn # 599, 615: AW 404, 134 jadīd; *Badāʾiʿ* 4, pp. 39, l. 2; 43, l. 20; 242, l. 15.

ʿAbd al-Laṭīf ibn ʿAbd-Allah, al-Amīr al-Zimām: Amīn # 399, AW 534 jadīd; *Badāʾiʿ* 4, p. 19, l. 15.

ʿAlam Yaḥyā ibn al-Jīʿān: Amīn # 633, AW 423 jadīd; *Badāʾiʿ* 4, pp. 40, l. 17; 136, l. 21.

ʿAlī al-Bakrī al-Ṣughayr: Amīn # 585, AW 618 jadīd; *Badāʾiʿ* 4, pp. 170, l. 11; 234, l. 17.

Abū Bakr ibn ʿAbd al-Qādir, son of nāẓir al-dawla: Amīn # 403, AW 186 jadīd; Ḥawādith 4, p. 626, l. 13.

Abūʾl-Faḍl ibn Kātib Gharīb: Amīn # 328, AW 524 jadīd; *Inbāʾ*, p. 4, l. 11; *Badāʾiʿ* 4, p. 373, l. 9.

Jamāl ʿAbd-Allāh, bawwāb al-Duhaysha: Amīn # 350, 831, 832, AW 140, 159, 514 jadīd; *Badāʾiʿ* 5, p. 78, l. 21.

Jamāl Yūsuf al-Alwāḥī, bawwāb al-Duhaysha: Amīn # 593, AW 111 jadīd; *Badāʾiʿ* 5, p. 81, l. 3.

Muḥammad ibn al-Sayfī Taghrī-Birmish: Amīn # 680, 681, AW 101, 432 jadīd; see entry for Shams Muḥammad ibn Taghrī-Birmish.

Muḥyī ʿAbd al-Qādir al-Qaṣrawī, nāẓir al-jaysh: Amīn # 839, AW 105 jadīd: *Badāʾiʿ* 4, pp. 79, l. 1; 112, l. 1; 376, l. 4; 434, l. 21; 5, p. 5, l. 5.

Mukhayr Muḥammad al-Khaydarī al-Jawharī, son of Damascene qāḍī: Amīn # 360, 370, 667, 749, 752, AW 188, 553, 370, 356, 375 jadīd; *Inbāʾ*, p. 423, l. 11.

Nāṣir Muḥammad ibn Taghrī-Birmish: Amīn # 274, 731, 458, 717, 754, 756, 759, 769, 749, 741, 742, 743, 753, 314, 620, 811, 814, 366, DW 41/361, AW 148, 363, 119, 338, 129, 362, 132, 356, 331, 314, 208, 328, 532, 500, 528, 201, 103 jadīd; see entry for Shams Muḥammad ibn Taghrī-Birmish.

Nāṣir Muḥammad ibn Khāṣṣbak, brother of donor Khawand Fāṭima: Amīn # 469, AW 707 jadīd; see entry for ʿĀʾishā bint Khāṣṣbak.

Ramaḍān ibn Sulaymān, mukhtār to Sultan Qāytbāy: Amīn # 676, AW 381 jadīd; *Badāʾiʿ* 3, p. 280, l. 1; 4, p. 342, l. 18.

Sayfī Anaṣbāy, ḥājib al-ḥujjāb: Amīn # 435, AW 428 jadīd; *Badāʾiʿ* 4, p. 98, l. 11.

Sayfī Dawlatbāy al-Muqaddam: Amīn # 719, AW 36 jadīd; *Badāʾiʿ* 4, p. 261, l. 9.

Sayfī Jānībak al-Kamālī al-Ustādār: Amīn # 685, AW 442 jadīd; *Badāʾiʿ* 4, pp. 217, l. 21; 358, l. 23; 392, l. 22; 428, l. 24; 431, l. 17; 476, l. 1.

Sayfī Tānībak al-Jamālī al-Khāzindār: Amīn # 610, 699, 624, 625, 628, AW 60, 403, 425, 721, 142 jadīd; *Badāʾiʿ* 4, p. 6, l. 10.

Sayfī Timurbāy: Amīn # 677, AW 769 jadīd; *Badāʾiʿ* 4, pp. 12, l. 6; 80, l. 13.

45. *Badāʾiʿ* 4, p. 398, l. 16.

46. Deeds Khayrbak turned over to al-Ghawrī (most entries were shares of a unit): Amīn # 658, AW 117 jadīd (20 Muḥarram 910/3 July 1504): agrarian tract (*arḍ*), 100%.

659, AW 176j (same date): 24 agrarian tracts, shares vary from 3 to 33%.

657, AW 452j (5 Dhū'l-Ḥijja 910/9 May 1505): 5 magazines (*makhāzin*), 100%.

#690, AW 444j (same date): 1 structure (*bināʾ*), 100%, 1 agrarian tract, 100%.

#693, AW 108j (20 Ṣafar 911/23 July 1505): 1 agrarian tract, 100%.

#661, AW 521j (1 Rabīʿ I 911/2 August 1505): 1 agrarian tract, 50%.

#662, AW 157j (same date): 1 agrarian tract, 50%.

#735, AW 382j (1 Rabīʿ I 914/30 June 1508): 1 agrarian tract, 100%.

#384, AW 537j (27 Shawwāl 914/18 February 1509): 1 hall (*qāʿa*), 75 %, 4.2%.

#385, AW 549j (same date): 1 hall, 75%.

#564, AW 327j (same date): 1 site (*makān*), 9.7%.

#598, AW 219j (same date): 1 dwelling (*sakan*), 100%.

#603, AW 320j (same date): 1 dwelling, 100%.

#606, AW 550j (same date): 1 dwelling, 100%.

#630, AW 333j (same date): 3 rooms (*maqʿad*), 33.3%.

#698, AW 350j (same date): 1 agrarian tract, 50%.

#700, AW 128j (same date): 1 site, 100%.

#712, AW 97j (same date): 1 dwelling, 25%.

#713, AW 220j (same date): 1 townhouse (*qaṣr*), 75%.

#720, AW 163j (same date): 1 caravansaray (*wakāla*), 50%.

#721, AW 402j (same date): 1 dwelling, 100%.

#729, AW 342j (same date): 3 rooms, 33.3%.

#732, AW 317j (same date): 6 upper-story rooms (*ṭabaqa*), 1 hall, 5 sites, 1 bakery (*furn*), 58.3%.

#736, AW 343j (same date): 6 sites, 41.7–80%.

#766, AW 358j (same date): 1 dwelling, 100%.

#774, AW 321j (same date): 1 dwelling, 100%.

#775, AW 329j (same date): 1 agrarian tract: island (*jazīra*), 8.8%.

#781, AW 380j (same date): 1 dwelling, 100%.

#782, AW 389j (same date): 4 sites, 100%.

#785, AW 389j (same date): 5 sites, 80–100%; 1 bakery, 5 upper story rooms, 100%.

#786, AW 529j (same date): 1 dwelling (*dār*), 100%.

#788, AW 552j (same date): 1 agrarian tract, 100%.

#663, AW 594j (2 Rabīʿ I 915/20 June 1509): 1 agrarian tract, 8.3%

#798, AW 150j (3 Rabīʿ I 915/21 June 1509): 1 hall, 100%.

#530, AW 385j (20 Rabīʿ I 916/27 June 1510), 1 dwelling, 100%.

#800, AW 629j (1 Ṣafar 919/8 April 1513): 1 dwelling, 1 apartment (*rabʿ*), 100%.

#805, AW 390j (1 Rabīʿ II 919/6 June 1513): 3 agrarian tracts, 5.6–12.5%.

#629, AW 216j (22 Rabīʿ II 919/27 June 1513): 2 agrarian tracts, 75%.

#579, AW 322j (1 Jumādā I 919/5 July 1513): 2 agrarian tracts, 5.6–8.3%.

#829, AW 511j (6 Rabīʿ I 920/1 May 1514): 2 agrarian tracts, 0.9–33.3%.

47. *Badāʾiʿ* 4, p. 405, l. 2. The sultan's nephew, Ṭūmānbāy, and muḥtasib, Zaynī Barakāt, conducted the assessment. Even by standards of hoarding routine in this age of concealment, the extent of Khayrbak's holdings stunned the court. More than eighty thousand gold (not debased *jayshī*) dīnārs appeared in his coffers. Al-Ghawrī had deposited half a million dīnārs from his own purse with Khayrbak for safekeeping when his eye infection seemed impervious to treatment. Following his recovery, al-Ghawrī had received none of this money back. Khayrbak apparently died without heirs since he drew up no will. But neither had he made provision for payment of funds due persons who presented vouchers from the state treasury. As the inventory progressed, caches of weapons embossed in gold or silver, precious stones, pearls, and luxury apparel came to light. Collectively, their value was estimated at one hundred thousand dīnārs. More than one thousand robes (*thawb*) of Baʿlabakkī cloth, fine woolens, ermine, squirrel and sable pelts, silk draperies, and velvet tunics were discovered, evaluated at fifty thousand dīnārs. These collections, all hidden in the khāzindār's palace, had once belonged to the trousseaus of sixteen deceased princesses that Khayrbak had sequestered during al-Ghawrī's reign. But not a bolt of cloth had he shared with his patron. "The treasurer had amassed herds of horses and draft animals beyond counting. He had taken over rental rights to inns, apartment complexes, commercial structures and shops throughout Cairo and had extracted revenues from them exceeding ten thousand dīnārs per annum—*with no provision for claims of heirs* (emphasis mine)." When the dawādār and muḥtasib finally completed their inventory, Khayrbak's closeted holdings were estimated at four hundred thousand dīnārs, excluding the half million al-Ghawrī had deposited. "Yet despite his enormous fortune, God never inspired Khayrbak, even on the verge of death, to bequeath some small token to his former master's (*ustādh*) son, the impoverished scion of Khushqadam, as alleviation for his penury. Nor had he, preserver of

the fisc, discharged his personal debts. Such behavior verified his stinginess and no one mourned his passing. He may have departed this world but could not be assured of salvation in the next. Only God grants that dispensation."

48. *Badāʾiʿ* 5, pp. 17, l. 20; 18. l. 17.

49. Amīn # 613, AW 486 jadīd.

50. Amīn, # 668, AW 406 jadīd, dated 20 Ṣafar 911/23 July 1505.

51. Amīn #673, 674, AW 437, 165, jadīd (duplicate copies, the second with more replete certificate), both dated as in n. 50.

52. *Badāʾiʿ* 4, pp. 345, l. 12; 470, l. 1.

53. Ibid. p. 241, l. 18.

54. See n. 41. Foundations 5–11 were endowed solely by Tūmānbāy.

8

CONCLUSIONS

If al-Ghawrī rates a place in history as something more than an ogre of rapacity, what judgment do he and those around him who quickened his creative instincts warrant? The preceding chapters have identified clandestine stratagems these individuals concocted for tapping funds from a society adept at their concealment. Whatever their ulterior motives, they were eminently rational. The devices al-Ghawrī and his associates applied to stave off insolvency evolved from exigencies of circumstance, not from proclivity of ethnicity. Every participant in this precarious drama was driven by perceived necessity. The system that engulfed them offered few alternative options. Those who managed to surmount the adversities they encountered did so by outscheming their rivals, not by confronting root causes.

Yet the chroniclers who alluded to their stratagems indulged in no frivolous banter. Their denunciations disclosed abiding defects in the regime that dominated their society. These authors wrote in somber tones, their remarks reiterating myriad variants on a pervasively dismal theme. The tactics their overlords masterminded brought on a decline palpable and immediate, not ephemeral or remote. Our authors leveled criticisms at tangible flaws; they rarely engaged in "poetic lament." What kinds of evidence did these chroniclers offer to substantiate their castigations? Which actors in this drama did they allow us to observe? Superficially appraised, most enjoyed elite status at or near the apex of Egypt's ruling hierarchy. The foregoing analysis has revealed bureaucrats, jurists, officers and scholastics—but few artisans, dragomen, farmers or merchants. Those who actually crafted wares, harvested crops, or marketed commodities figured modestly in chronicles of the Mamlūk age. We are thus minimally informed about their mundane activities, which collectively sustained the domestic economy.

Still, many of the memorable characters in this study made their way to notoriety from exceedingly humble backgrounds. Even the monarchs who sanctioned their wiles started out as slaves. Those who eagerly served them as clients usually caught their glance while chafing at humdrum callings. And with due acknowledgment of the regime's propensity to install sons in a father's sinecure for continuity of a parent's expertise, the chroniclers depicted no entrenched aristocracy in either the civilian or military hierarchies. Autocrats who survived to consolidate their grip on authority rose within the ranks, having amply proved their martial ability and personal force. Their civil officials attracted their notice because of adroitness not pedigree. The chroniclers therefore presented an array of characters who derived from a broad spectrum of Egyptian society. While their paths to influence varied, they depicted a system wide open to the clever and ambitious. However their antics are judged, they indicated widespread mobility. The later Mamlūk sultans presided over no closed bureaucracy.

If the chroniclers allow few glimpses of producers at work, they fulsomely enlighten us as to how those covetous of their assets went about tapping them. The hints historians give suggest in sum the tactics revenue procurers refined to garner monies their sponsors demanded. No one contemplating both the diversity of these ploys and their frequency can ignore the preponderant place such stratagems occupy in the narrative sources. One concludes that these devices loomed large in the chroniclers' consciousness and, from their scale of priorities, merited the space they assigned them.

These asides and veiled references depicted a process to which the historians attributed erosion of the public's confidence in their future prospects, the absence of growth-oriented ventures and the general malaise of their times. While data for day-to-day workings of the economy were scanty, the chroniclers gave ample evidence for harassment of revenue generators. Fiscal procurement as an obligation imposed by a patron in return for appointment emerged so vividly that it must be assessed as a primary goal rather than an ad hoc expedient.

The measures described by our historians consistently point to a bureaucratic mindset in which creativity and ingenuity focused on means of ferreting out hoarded assets. By stark contrast, the chroniclers rarely discussed innovative techniques of production. Experimentation is noteworthy for its scarcity, mentioned almost exclusively in terms of its attendant risks, the vulnerability it assured anyone who lost sight of his overriding goal: secreting what he had stashed away. The process depicted in this study bears responsibility for the outlook of both producers and extractors in later Mamlūk society. Neither innovation nor parasitism are "natural" to a culture. One or the other assumes preeminence in the context of a system that evolved because of historic circumstances.

In Mamlūk Egypt, the chroniclers' anecdotes disclose ubiquitous hoarding that, at the least, isolated a certain proportion of capital assets and blocked them from more active deployment. Such behavior rarely connotes aggressive investment in ventures conducive to economic growth or technical change. Rather, it implies the equation of prosperity with vulnerability. If these devices of obfuscation are weighed in the broader setting of predation and stasis encouraged by the ruling caste, the paradox of decline in the midst of potential prosperity is in part resolved. A regime dedicated to upholding the status quo rarely encourages entrepreneurship.

The system described in preceding chapters was self-generated, conceived and implemented internally with little influence from outside. Those who routinely attribute Egypt's persistent contemporary dilemmas exclusively to foreign intervention have yet to confront the abundant evidence for stasis Egypt's own historians of the later Middle Ages laid before them. Yet their criticisms neither implicate the Islamic religion per se nor detract from the agility of militarists or bureaucrats. Nowhere did Islam, either in theory or in practice, figure actively in regime parasitism or producer deflection. While many predators and victims were profoundly devout, fervor of faith bolstered their zeal or obduracy but inspired few of their ploys. Qāytbāy's avowed piety surely justified in his own mind the oppressive means he exploited to rescue his regime from the abyss. But he found no instruction in Islamic precedents for his tactics. As for al-Ghawrī, his dearth of interest in pious display was pointedly associated with his propensity for innovation.

And adroitness merits admiration, however it reflected on the values these individuals cherished. Their behavior may have contributed to a mentality that inhibited growth or innovation as such concepts are understood in the modern West. But these actors certainly exhibited an élan as they coped with or, on occasion, surmounted the odds against them. How, in the final analysis, do we judge a shrewd mulcter like Qāsim Shughayta, a master inquisitor like Zaynī Barakāt, or a learned manipulator like Ibn al-Shiḥna? What verdict do we pronounce on Qāytbāy as conservator of institutions past their prime or al-Ghawrī as an innovator whose experiments were more impelled by survival than vision? Their stratagems may have promoted Egypt's waning as a world power, but they do not depict a society bereft of its vitality or will to persevere. Those acquainted with social realities of the contemporary Egyptian state will discern in their wiles many behavioral traits alive and well today. These engage as much as they bemuse.

The system postulated in this study may have emerged as the only practical means by which members of the Mamlūk regime elite ensured their preferred status or their profligate lifestyles. If we have castigated the ruling elite

and its cadres for a dubious legacy, we must also inquire about the feasibility
of an opportunistic risk-oriented approach. Jean-Claude Garcin, in a thought-
ful essay on the "blockage" of medieval Muslim society from capitalistic development, ponders the limited options open to Islamic governments in the
Eastern Mediterranean or Southwest Asia at the end of the Middle Ages.[1] He
muses over the advantages in resources enjoyed by Western European states on
the threshhold of the commercial revolution:

> Beside the refinement, and even the slightly foolish ostentation, of the East-
> ern weapons of war, the European suits of armour at the end of the Middle
> Ages, with their jointed plates, their rivets and screws, already testified to a
> technical mastery in tools for working metal, which it was soon going to be
> possible to apply to more productive instruments. With what sort of iron
> would the Muslim artisans have been able to perfect their techniques? In
> what naval shipyards could they have been trained in discovering better de-
> signs for ships, when wood had to be imported very expensively as needed,
> and when it was a strategic material? What new kind of plough should have
> been invented, when modern instruments later occasionally proved to be too
> rough, and for what sort of agricultural surface? Egypt, the centre of the
> Moslem Empire, had at the time a utilizable land surface no larger than that
> of Holland. In such conditions, was a "Near East Miracle" conceivable? The
> end of medieval times highlights the worn-out state of this old world that
> was the inheritor of the ancient world, the scene in its day of so much
> progress, but not grown poor and bereft of the great resources upon which
> was built the power of Europe. Should we really be astonished if the next
> stage in human development came about in countries that were still new and
> vast, with abundant natural wealth that was almost untouched? Such an eco-
> nomic development in the Near East of that time would have truly deserved
> the term "miracle" if it had occurred.

Garcin's comments certainly give one pause before holding up the Egyptian
Mamlūk regime to invidious comparisons with its European contemporaries.

And yet Garcin's perspective does not dispel nagging questions. Is poverty of resources sufficient to explain rampant parasitism described in the preceding pages? Was the Nile Valley any more "worn-out" in the fifteenth
century than in the ninth, the first, or the halcyon episodes of the Pharaonic
era? A utilizable surface no larger than Holland perhaps, but one still replen-
ished by the richest flood alluvium of any riverine system on earth. Few chroniclers lamented Egypt's loss of agrarian fecundity, but they all vehemently
decried its mismanagement and exploitation. It is almost a truism to identify
a society's human capital as its greatest resource. This study has provided ample evidence of human ingenuity at all levels of the productive process. Yet
such ingenuity addressed the squeezing of profits from an economy both producers and exploiters accepted as fixed with few prospects for growth. Regardless of current rationales for Egypt's alleged decline at the dawn of the modern

age, a static concept of potential still emerges from the judgments of indigenous observers as the pervasive worldview in the Mamlūk State on the eve of its conquest.

These assessments were applied differentially to the two monarchs whose personalities so dominated events of this period. Their policies embodied opposing concepts of royal authority and executive style, which contemporary observers praised or decried as such. Al-Ashraf Qāytbāy saw his mission fully within parameters of behavior set by his predecessors long before. Even alleged innovations he adopted under pressure of need never exceeded conceptual limits fixed earlier in the regime's evolution. Qāytbāy was indeed revered by both Mamlūk colleagues and civilian clients because they found in his actions the reassurance of proven precedent. In the final analysis, reassurance outweighed the piety Qāytbāy so genuinely espoused. Qāytbāy reinvigorated an inertia-bound system of military power and bureaucratic procedure. His horizons did not extend beyond principles he inherited from bygone days.

Individuals who wield power according to customary norms of authority invariably invoke acclaim from those whose interests are enhanced by prolongation of the status quo. All the chroniclers who assessed their rulers' performance belonged to social groups that profited from continuing the old order in Cairo. Their incessant criticisms of the Mamlūk regime railed against surface ills but rarely condemned underlying causes. And when the latter were confronted, the historians offered no alternatives to remedy them. The chroniclers' admiration for Qāytbāy was thus predictable. His stoic resolve in the face of calamity resonated with their appreciation of a protector's defiance before enemies but humility before God. Qāytbāy radiated the assurance of one whose role demanded custodianship of a system that had worked reasonably well for many decades, and guardianship of a realm that had long stood as a bastion of safety in a turbulent world. Even Ibn Taghrī-Birdī's castigations were provoked by the vagaries of succession at the outset of his reign. That Qāytbāy contemplated not a single new idea about the governance of his regime not one of his biographers found blameworthy.

Qānṣūh al-Ghawrī, whom most of his contemporaries found wanting by comparison, exhibited more than deficiencies of an uncharismatic personality. Juxtaposed against the myriad cases his critics listed of abuse, corruption, and extraction are an equal number of ideas impressive for their ingenuity. Upon reflection over the stridency of condemnation in Ibn Iyās' remarks, one is struck by the sultan's shrewd assessment of where individuals adroit in hoarding of assets stashed—and consequently idled—their resources. Although Ibn Iyās lamented at length the decline of Egypt's agrarian, artisanal, and commercial productivity, he never acknowledged the connection between hoarded assets and inactive wealth. While al-Ghawrī warrants no recognition as even a protocapitalist aware of this linkage, he was impelled by dilemmas he perceived as both inimical and irremedial to ponder an assault against customary patterns of military hierarchy and property control. The alarm such an attempt, however tentative, aroused among al-Ghawrī's peers is palpable on every page or manuscript leaf of period descriptions. Acceptance of their depictions verbatim has led later historians to echo their tirades as ample proof that a tyrannical regime was haplessly mired in ills of its own making.

My own reading of this dismal record has led me to its qualified revision. At the very least, Qāytbāy's august stature merits rethinking in light of his contemporaries' relief over his preservation of their world, while al-Ghawrī's image as a tyrant of avarice calls for reassessment in light of their worries about the implications of his innovations. When al-Ghawrī experimented with artillery, recruited new military units from outside the Mamlūk caste, or manipulated waqfs to pay them, he was denounced for either wasting his time or sullying the rights of those whom God had ordained to govern society. That these measures, inchoate as they were, might suggest al-Ghawrī's toying with their replacement is never openly admitted by any of his commentators. Yet one wonders whether the intensity of their protests was motivated by subliminal fears of sweeping change, a prospect appealing to no one content with the way things were.

Rare were al-Ghawrī's actions depicting a monarch impelled by noblesse oblige. Nor does our evidence imply a grand design on his part for building a "new Egypt." Yet our sources, narrative and archival, do provide poignant examples of al-Ghawrī's frustration over his incapacity to function as the kind of commander in chief Qāytbāy had been. There are hints embedded in these vivid episodes and fiscal ploys that al-Ghawrī resented the bankruptcy his predecessor bequeathed him as much as he did Qāytbāy's pious deportment. The latter was odious because of personal aversion or simple jealousy while the former was dangerous for the strictures it imposed. Ire is as profound an incentive for change as admiration, perhaps more profound since it encourages departure from past precedent. Worship of a precursor promotes replication of his policies, while aversion induces departure from them.

Thus, even in the quagmire of stasis there appeared tokens of propensity for change at the final hour. The devices of al-Ghawrī, enigmatic architect of innovation, tempt speculation over what might have been. Had fate and harem intrigue placed a less pugnacious individual on the throne of ʿUthmān, might al-Ghawrī have survived to refine his hesitant first steps? Had Selim chosen coexistence with his southern rival, how would al-Ghawrī's groping experiments have fared? Would they have matured into substantive reform? We cannot know. The conservatism of al-Ghawrī's heir apparent, Ṭūmānbāy, suggests a preference for restoration of the past's trusted inertia with a vengeance, an abiding hope that the world order remain obligingly fixed.

It did not so remain, and the Ottomans played out their hegemonic designs with devastating success. But their victory terminated neither Egypt's domestic economy nor her military hierarchy, at least at its medial levels.

Egypt, Syria, and the Ḥijāz continued to play an integral role in commerce of the Eastern Mediterranean, Southwest Asia and Northeast Africa. The Mamlūk system was stripped of its autocrat but not its cadres of officers who adapted quite adroitly to their new masters. In coming centuries, the boldest among them would reassert their autonomous rule over Egypt within the fragmenting Ottoman imperium.

Nonetheless, our sources do not impart a reawakening of the aggressive competition that had inspired carftsmen, marketeers, and property holders during Egypt's earlier centuries of commercial ascendancy. Similar impulses motivated their counterparts in Western Europe, poised as they were on the brink of a technical revolution unprecedented in world history. When, in closing, one ponders Egypt's peculiar evolution at the end of its traditional era, one is tempted to ask "why not?" This study has presented hypotheses in response to that query. To what extent their implications reflect on Egypt's modern potential for self-transformation in the face of persistent inertia exceeds the historian's competence. But as noted above, any observer alert to social conditions in Egypt today will detect many parallels with actions of the individuals brought to life in these chapters. Neither their stamp on the past nor their influence on the future should be overlooked, for to do so would belittle the intriguing heritage of a complex and vital society.

Note

1. J.-C. Garcin, "The Mamlūk Military System and the Blocking of Medieval Moslem Society," in Jean Baechler *et al*, ed., *Europe and the Rise of Capitalism* (Oxford, 1988), 128.

APPENDICES

Key

Sources:

B: *Badāʾiʿ*
Dh: *Dhayl* (al-Sakhāwī)
H: *Ḥawādith*
I: *Inbāʾ*
JS: *Jawāhir al-Sulūk*
R: *Rawḍ*
TJ: *Taʾrīkh al-Jarākisa*

Measures:

dhr: dhirāʿ = cubit, .58 meter in Egypt
dn: dīnār (Ashrafī)
dr: dirham (copper), 300 = 1 dn
fd: faddān = 4200.83 m^2
ir: irdabb = 198 liters in Egypt
is: iṣbaʿ = finger, 3.125 cm in Egypt
nf: niṣf fiḍḍa = 1/2 silver dr = 18 cu dr
qn: qinṭār = 100 rt
qr: qīrāṭ = dry measure, .064 liter in Egypt
rt: raṭl = 449.28 grams in Egypt

————: no amount reported
CM: Coptic month
sd: same date
tr: transaction

Appendix 1: Nile Flood Levels during Qāytbāy's Reign

Date	Level
1. 29 DQ 872/ 20 Jun 1468 CM: 26 Būna H 641, l. 18; R f. 185, l. 7	Low level: 6 dhr, 14 is
28 DH 872/ 29 Jul 1468 H 651, l. 7; R f. 187, l. 7; B3 17, l. 5	Rise delayed three days; alarm
DH 872/ Jul 1468 H 656, l. 4	Crest: 18 dhr, 6 is
2. 16 Mh 873 6 Aug 1468 CM: 12 Misurī H 674, l. 13; I 11, l. 2; R f. 202, l. 1; B3 19, l. 3	Flood surge: 16 dhr, 2 is
4 Sf 873/ 24 Aug 1468 R f. 202, l. 16	Rise delay; alarm and crop price rise
10 Sf 873/ 30 Aug 1468 R f. 203, l. 32	Crest (low): 18 dhr, 12 is
20 Sf 873/ 9 Sep 1468 H 677, l. 1	Crest mispredicted; 20 dhr expected
sd, CM: 18 Tūt I 15, l. 1	Premature drop responsible for low crest
DH 873/ Jun-Jul 1469 H 716, l. 7; I 79, l. 17	Low level: 5 dhr, 22 is High level: 19 dhr, 8 is
3. 4 Sf 874/	Flood surge: 16 dhr, 4 is

| | 13 Aug 1469
CM: 20 Misurī | |
| I 127, l. 8; R f. 247, l. 16 | | |

| | 8 Sf 874/
17 Aug 1469
CM: 24 Misurī | Delay; Nilometer annointed with perfume |
| B3 38, l. 6 | | |

| | 20 R1 874/
27 Sep 1469
CM: 1 Bāba | Crest: 19 dhr, 6 is |
| R f. 247-b, l. 21 | | |

| | 17 J1 874/
22 Nov 1469 | Violent rain; canals overflow; markets inundated |
| I 152, l. 16 | | |

| | 20 DH 874/
20 Jun 1470
CM: 26 Būna | Rise of 5 is, from level of 6 dhr, 20 is |
| R f. 251-b, l. 5 | | |

| 4. | 16 Sf 875/
14 Aug 1470
CM: 21 Misurī | Flood surge: 16 dhr, 18 is erratic; alarm |
| I 203, l. 9 | | |

| | 19 Sf 875/
17 Aug 1470 | Rise: 16 dhr, 2 is dyke opening; relief and celebration |
| I 205, l. 4 & 20; B3 52, l. 15 | | |

| | 7 R1 875/
3 Sep 1470
CM: 7 Tūt | Rise ceases |
| I 211, l. 15 | | |

| | 25 R1 875/
21 Sep 1470 | High level: 16 dhr, 20 is |
| I 215, l. 16 | | |

| 5. | 1 Mh 876/
20 Jun 1471
CM: 26 Būna | Low level: 6 dhr, 8 is |
| I 316, l. 14; B3 61, l. 8 | | |

| | 21 Sf 876/
9 Aug 1471
CM: 26 Misurī | Crest: no figures; arrested |
| I 329, l. 14; B3 63, l. 7 | | |

17 R1 876/   Crest: 19 dhr, less 1 is
3 Sep 1471
CM: 5 Tūt
I 334, l. 8

1 R2 876/   High level: 18 dhr, 20 is
17 Sep 1471
I 337, l. 10

28 DH 876/   Alluvium (*ṭīn*) measured: 3 qr, 1 per dhr
6 Jun 1472
CM: St. Michael's Feast
I 446, l. 3

6.   7 R1 877/   Crest: no figures
11 Aug 1472
CM: 21 Misurī
B3 76, l. 3

27 R1 877/   Alluvium measured: 19 qr, slight diminution
1 Sep 1472
CM: 12 Būna
I 484, l. 9

7.   5 R1 878/   Crest: 16 dhr, 12 is
31 Jul 1473
CM: 5 Misurī
11 R1 878/   High level: 19 dhr, 12 is rapid rise
6 Aug 1473
B3 90, l. 17

8.   R1 879/   Violent storm
Jul-Aug 1474
CM: St. Michael's Eve
B3 97, l. 4

sd   Crest: no figures but late; alarm
CM: 20 Misurī
B3 97, l. 14

9.   R2 880/   Crest: no figures
Aug 1475
CM: 12 Misurī
B3 108, l. 19

10.   R2 881/   Crest: no figures
Aug 1476
CM: 3 Misurī
B3 120, l. 15

11. R2 882/ Crest: no figures but early
     Aug 1477
     CM: 1 Misurī
B3 133, l. 4

     J1 882/ High level: 20 dhr, 21 is; extremely high
     Aug-Sep 1477
     CM: Bāba (end)
B3 134, l. 11

12. R2 883/ Crest: no figures
     Jul-Aug 1478
     CM: 4 Misurī
B3 146, l. 16

     sd High level: 17 dhr, 0 is; delayed rise
B3 146, l. 17

13. 3 J1 884/ Off-date surge
     23 Jul 1479
     CM: 29 Abīb
     5 J1 884/ Crest: 17 dhr, 6 is
     25 Jul 1479
B3 155, l. 4

     J2 884/ High level: 19 dhr, 20 is
     Aug 1479
B3 157, l. 17

14. J2 885/ Crest: no figures
     Aug-Sep 1480
B3 169, l. 7

15. J2 886/ Crest: no figures
     Jul-Aug 1481
     CM: 15 Misurī
B3 183, l. 10

     Rm 886/ Rainstorm; off-season
     Oct-Nov 1481
     CM: late Bāba
B3, p. 187, l. 13

16. J1 887/ Crest: no figures
     Jun-Jul 1482
B3 195, l. 19

17. R2 888/ Low level: 6 dhr, 4 is
     Jun 1483

B3 201, I. 20

       Rj 888/   Crest: no figures
       Aug 1483
       CM: 18 Misurī
B3 203, l. 16

18.   Rj 889/   Crest: no figures
       Jul-Aug 1484
       CM: 22 Misurī
B3 209, l. 5

       J2 889/   Rapid rise; then normal
       Jul 1484
B3 208, l. 4

       $b 889/

                        High level: 17 dhr, 22 is very low; much land
       Aug-Sep 1484   dry
B3 209, l. 20

       Rm 889/   Off-season rise; after low flood
       Sep-Oct 1484
B3 211, l. 3

19.   J1 890/   Low level: 8 dhr, 20 is; unusually high
       May-Jun 1485
B3 217, l. 22

       $b 890/   Crest: no figures
       Aug-Sep 1485
       CM: 20 Misurī
B3 219, l. 5

       DQ 890/   Off-season rise: 1 dhr
       Nov-Dec 1485
       CM: 13 Hātūr
B3 211, l. 11

20. $b 891/
       Aug 1486   Crest: 16 dhr, 20 is; subsequent rise over 3
       CM: 18 Misurī   days: to 49 is, very high
B3 230, l. 22

21.   Rj 892/   Rise ceases; alarm
       Jul 1487
       CM: 9 Abīb
B3 241, l. 20

       $b 892/   Crest: no figures

Jul-Aug 1487
CM: 12 Misurī
B3 242, l. 23

22. $b 893/   Crest: no figures
       Jul-Aug 1488
       CM: 11 Misurī
B3 254, l. 19

23.   30 $b 894/   Crest: no figures
       28 July 1489
B3 267, l. 4

       1 Rm 894/   Dyke opening; early fast break due to heat
       29 Jul 1489
B3 267, l. 6

24.   Sf 895/   Freezing temperatures
       Dec 1489-
       Jan 1490
B3 268, l. 16

       $b 895/   Low level: 7 dhr, 8 is
       Jun-Jul 1490
B3 273, l. 15

       10 Rm 895/   Crest: no figures but one-day surge of 33 is
       28 Jul 1490
       CM: 4 Misurī
B3 274, l. 5

       Rm 895/   Crest: 16 dhr, 8 is
       Aug 1490
       CM: 4 Misurī
Dh f. 202-b, l. 1

25.   1 $w 896/
       8 Jul 1491   Crest: no figures but dyke opened on 2 $w
       CM: 14 Misurī   because of ʿĪd al-Fiṭr
B3 284, l. 9

26.   DQ 897/   Crest: no figures
       Aug-Sep 1492
B3 293, l. 1

27.   Mh 898/   Hailstorm; crop damage
       Oct-Nov 1492
B3 294, l. 5

       $w 898/   Crest: no figures

          Jul-Aug 1493
B3 296, l. 13

28.   R2 899/   Snow in Alexandria
          Jan-Feb 1494
B3 299, l. 10

          17 Rm 899/   Crest: no figures; early
          21 Jun 1494
Dh f. 250-b, l. 5

          DQ 899/   Rise ceases; alarm; wheat price rise
          Aug 1494
B3 304, l. 7

29.   DQ 900/   Crest: no figures; Azbak's last dyke ceremony
          Jul-Aug 1495
B3 310, l. 6

30.   DQ 901/   Crest: no figures
          Jul-Aug 1596
B3 323, l. 9

Appendix 2: Staple Crop/Food Prices during Qāytbāy's Reign

	Date	Staple	Price
1.	$w 872/	Grain price increase	
	Apr-May 1468	wheat	600 dr/ir
		fūl beans	200 dr/ir
		barley	240 dr/ir
		bread	1 1/2 dr/raghīf loaf
		rice	1500 dr/ir
		samn oil	24 dr/rt
		sesame oil	24 dr/rt

H 628, 1. 6; R f. 180-b, 1. 3; B3 11, 1. 20

	Date	Staple	Price
2.	1 DQ 872/	Crop blight in Delta;	
	23 May 1468	price increase	
	CM:1 Bashans		

H 630, 1. 3

	Date	Staple	Price
3.	DH 872/	Grain price increase;	
	Jun-Jul 1468	sultan opens granaries	
		wheat	700 dr/ir
		fūl beans	200 dr/ir
		barley	300 dr/ir

H 643, 1. 6; B3 16, 1.24

	Date	Staple	Price
4.	10 Sf 873/	Delayed flood; grain	
		price increase; controls	
	30 Aug 1468	imposed to no effect	
		wheat, officially	400 dr/ir
		wheat, actually	750 dr/ir
		barley	300 dr/ir
		fūl beans	200 dr/ir

H 676, 1. 3; I 13, 1. 10; R f. 202-b, 1. 33; B3 19, 1. 19

	Date	Staple	Price
5.	1 R2 873/	Grain price increase;	
	19 Sep 1468	small crop due to rapid	
	CM:22 Tūt	flood drop	
		wheat	900 dr/ir
		barley	660 dr/ir

| | | |
| | | fūl beans | 400 dr/ir |

H 678, l. 16; I 17, l. 1 & 5; R f. 104, l. 1; B3 21, l. 9

6.   20 R1 873/   Grain prices set down;
      8 Oct 1468   price gouging
                      wheat   400 dr/ir

I 28, l. 13

7.   R2 873/   Grain price increase;
      Oct-Nov 1468   famine threat
                      wheat   900 dr/ir
                      barley   450 dr/ir
                      fūl beans   450 dr/ir
                      bread   500 dr/rt

H 687, l. 18; I 32, l. 1

8.   1 J2 873/   Grain price increase;
      17 Dec 1468   erratic shifts
      CM:22 Kayhak   wheat   900 dr/ir; up 100 dr from
                                               J1

H 696, l. 12; I 46, l. 6; R f. 212-b, l. 2; B3 25, l. 24

9.   1 Rj 873/   Grain prices stable in
      15 Jan 1469   Egypt; rising in Syria
                      wheat   20 dn/gharāra sack
                      barley   10 dn/sack

H 699, l. 1, 700, l. 21; I 53, l. 16

10.   1 Rm 873/   Grain prices exorbitant in
      15 Mar 1469   Syria; lower in Egypt
                      wheat (H 59, l. 11)   33 dn/sack in Syria
                      wheat (B3 30, l. 11)   40 dn/sack in Syria
                      wheat   600 dr/ir
                      barley   300 dr/ir
                      fūl beans   300 dr/ir

H 706, l. 1; I 61, l. 5; R f. 219, l. 19

11.   J1 874/   Grain price increase but
      Nov-Dec 1469   no shortage; Yashbak's
                      expedition to Upper Egypt
                      drives up prices due to
                      requisition demand
                      wheat   1200 dr/ir
                      barley   700 dr/ir
                      fūl beans   700 dr/ir
                      hay   300 dr/load
                      bread   7 dr/rt

I 152, l. 7; R f. 248-b, l. 16; B3 41, l. 16

12.	J2 874/ Jan 1470 Dec 1469	Grain price increase; shortage	
	R f. 248-b, l. 31		
13.	Rj 874/ Jan-Feb 1470	Grain prices high due to Yashbak's hoarding in Up- per Egypt wheat barley fūl beans	1200 dr/ir 1200 dr/ir 1200 dr/ir
	I 159, l.1; B3 42, l. 10		
14.	1 Rm 874/ 4 Mar 1470	Sultan opens granaries to reduce prices wheat, officially wheat, actually barley, officially barley, actually bread, officially bread, actually	1000 dr/ir 1300 dr/ir 600 dr/ir 900 dr/ir 6 dr/rt 9 dr/rt
	I 162, l. 1; R f. 250, 14; B3 43, l. 13		
15.	Mh 875/ Jun-Jul 1470	Grain price increase Fine (*ṭayyib*) wheat Coarse wheat Flour barley fūl beans	900 dr/ir 800 dr/ir 220 dr/ir 380 dr/ir 350 dr/ir
	I 187, l. 4; B3 47, l. 4		
16.	Rj 875/ Dec 1470-Jan 1471	Grain prices low bread	 1 dr/rt
	B3 55, l. 22		
17.	DQ 876/ Apr-May 1472	Grain price increase due to Mamlūk muḥtasibs Flour barley	 100 dr/measure of 50 rt (up from 70) 70 dr/measure
	I 431, l. 1		
18.	4 R1 877/ 9 Aug 1472	Sultan sets food prices to quiet populace angry at muḥtasib	
	I 477, l. 9		

19.   Mh 878/   Food prices low; prosperity
         May-Jun 1473   meat   8 dr/rt
                            flour   4 nf/measure

B3 89, l. 9

20.   J2 879/   Grain shortage; bread
         Oct-Nov 1474   scarce

B3 100, l. 5

21.   Mh 888/   Grain shortage;
         Feb-Mar 1483*   price increase

B3 199, l. 14

22.   J1 889/   Food prices low
         May-Jun 1484   wheat   1/2 dn/ir
                            flour   4 nf/measure of 50 rt

B3 207, l. 21

23.   DQ 889/   Cotton scarce; expensive
         Nov-Dec 1484   cotton   2400 dr/qn

B3 213, l. 3

24.   DH 889/   Birsīm (clover) price
         Dec 1484-   increase
         Jan 1485   birsīm   10 dn/fd

B3 213, l. 7

25.   Mh 891/   Grain, fodder, water prices
         Jan-Feb 1486   high due to low Nile
                            birsīm   12 dn/fd
                            fodder   400 dr/100 bushel

B3 224, l. 14

26.   DQ 891/   Rice price increase
         Oct-Nov 1486   rice, previously   6 dn/ir
                            rice, presently   12 dn/ir

B3 234, l. 16

27.   Mh 892/   Food prices rise steeply;
         Dec 1486-   famine
         Jan 1487   wheat   6 dn/ir
                            flour   450 dr/measure of 50 rt
                            Sultan opens granaries;
                            sells wheat at   5 dn/ir
                            Wheat price drop due to
                            import
                            wheat   4 dn/ir

B3 237, l. 20, 238, l. 16

28.	R1 892/ Feb-Mar 1487 B3 239, l. 17	Salt price increase due to hoarding	
29.	Rm 896/ Jul-Aug 1491 B3 284, l. 7	Food stocks abundant wheat	1 dn/3 ir
30.	$w 897/ Jul-Aug 1492	Food prices low wheat fūl beans wheat barley fūl beans rice sugar wheat, previously fūl beans, previously	10 nf/ir 10 nf/ir 120 dr/ir 118 dr/ir 84 dr/ir 500 dr/ir 8 dn/qn 180 dr/ir 150 dr/ir
	Dh f. 221-b, l. 1		
31.	Rj 899/ Apr-May 1494 Dh f. 241-b, l. 30	Late Nile rise; prices sta- ble due to controls	
32.	Rm 899/ Jun-Jul 1494 B3 302, l. 12	Melon prices drop melon	2 nf/camel load
33.	Rj 900/ Mar-Apr 1495 B3 308, l. 5	Grain prices low; abundance wheat	3 dn/ir
34.	DQ 900/ Jul-Aug 1495 B3 310, l. 8	Bread prices low bread	3 dr/8 loaves
35.	R2 901/ Dec 1495- Jan 1496 B3 318, l. 15	Grain prices very low wheat flour	1 dn/5 ir 3 nf/measure of 50 rt

---

*Note nine-year gap.

Appendix 3: *Nile Flood Levels during al-Ghawrī's Reign*

Date	Level
1. 18 Mh 907/ 3 Aug 1501 CM:9 Misurī B4 18, 1. 18	Crest: no figures
2. 27 Mh 908/ 2 Aug 1502 CM:8 Misurī	Crest: 71 is
1 R2 908/ 4 Oct 1502 B4 36, 1. 7, 42, 1. 3	High level: 20 dhr, 5 is
3. 8 Sf 909/ 2 Aug 1503 CM:9 Misurī B4 55, 1. 22	Crest: no figures
R2 909/ Sep-Oct 1503 CM:Tūt B4 59, 1. 6	High level: 19 dhr, 11 is low; dry land
Rj 909/ Dec 1503- Jan 1504 B4 60, 1. 18	Delta storm; crop damage
4. Sf 910/ Jul-Aug 1504 B4 66, 1. 2	Rise ceases six days; alarm and hoarding
7 R1 910/ 18 Aug 1504 CM:25 Misurī B4 66, 1. 9	Crest: 17 dhr, 5 is
5. 2 R1 911/	Crest: high but no figures; even surge

3 Aug 1505
CM:9 Misurī

B4 81, l. 9

J1 911/   High level: 20 dhr, 11 is
Oct 1505

B4 83, l. 1

6.   28 Mh 912/   Low level: 7 dhr, 10 is (10 is higher
        20 Jun 1506   than 911 low)

B4 94, l. 21

        20 R1 912/   Crest: no figures
        10 Aug 1506
        CM:20 Misurī

B4 96, l. 22

        J1 912/   High level: 19 dhr, 2 is
        Sep-Oct 1506

B4 99, l. 22

7.   R1 913/   Crest: 70 is surge in three days
        Jul-Aug 1507
        CM:10 Misurī

B4 117, l. 15

        J1 913/   High level: 18 dhr, 1 is
        Sep-Oct 1507

B4 120, l. 7

8.   Sf 914/   Low level: 6 dhr, 10 is
        Jun 1508

B4 132, l. 5

        R2 914/   Rapid surge: 50 is; 90 is rise over three
        Jul-Aug 1508   days
        CM:11 Misurī
        CM:14 Misurī   Crest: no figures

B4 133, l. 17

        J2 914/   High level: 19 dhr; holds to 20 Bāba
        Sep-Oct 1508

B4 137, l. 6

        DH 914/   Poultry epidemic
        Mar-Apr 1509

B4 149, l. 4

9.   R1 915/   Low level: 6 dhr, 18 is; higher than 914
        Jun-Jul 1509   lower by 8 is

B4 156, l. 15

        R2 915/   Crest: no figures but very high
        Jul-Aug 1509
        CM:14 Misurī
B4 159, l. 20

        DH 915/   Prayers to lower crest
        Mar-Apr 1510
B4 172, l. 2

10.   13 R1 916/   Low level: 7 dhr, 10 is; higher than 915
        20 Jun 1510   lower by 10 is
B4 184, l. 12

        7 J1 916/   Crest: no figures but late and slow
        12 Aug 1510
        CM:20 Misurī
B4 188, l. 8

        J 2 916/   High level: 17 dhr, 21 is
        Sep-Oct 1510   low, land dry; heavy alluvium
B4 193, l. 19

        Rm 916/   Intense cold; hailstorms damage crops
        Dec 1510
B4 198, l. 22

        DQ 916/   Crop blight
        Jan-Feb 1511
B4 202, l. 16

11.   24 R1 917/   Low level: 6 dhr
        21 Jun 1511
B4 220, l. 5

        11 J1 917/   Rise ceases before crest; sultan alarmed
        6 Aug 1511
B4 230, l. 22

        12 J1 917/   Crest: no figures; praise for sultan's
        7 Aug 1511   prayers at Nilometer
B4 231, l. 14

        24 J1 917/   Postcrest rise to: 18 dhr, 8 is
        19 Aug 1511
B4 234, l. 14

        3 Rj 917/   High level: 19 dhr, 9 is
        26 Sep 1511
        CM:27 Tūt

B4 241, l. 11

| 12. | 6 R2 918/
21 Jun 1512 | Low level: 6 dhr |

B4 265, l. 5

12 J1 918/
21 Jul 1512
CM:1 Misurī

Crest: 16 dhr, 10 is; record, same as 883
Postcrest rise next day: 17 dhr, 4 is

B4 273, l. 4

18 Rj 918/
29 Sep 1512
CM:1 Bāba

High level: 20 dhr, 8 is

B4 281, l. 4

13.   5 J2 919/
8 Aug 1513
CM:14 Misurī

Crest: 16 dhr, 5 is

B4 325, l. 9

14.   26 R2 920/
20 Jun 1514

Low level: 6 dhr, 12; lower than in 919

B4 379, l. 1

23 J2 920/
14 Jul 1514

Crest: 16 dhr, 2 is

B4 389, l. 9

24 J2 920/
15 Jul 1514
CM:23 Misurī

Postcrest rise: 17 dhr, 16 is

B4 389, l. 13

10 $b 920/
30 Sep 1514

High level: 19 dhr, 15 is

B4 396, l. 10

15 $b 920/
5 Oct 1514

Claim that peak higher by 11 is than in 919

B4 396, l. 21

15.   7 J1 921/
19 Jun 1515

Low level: 7 dhr, 4 is

B4 457, l. 3

18 J2 921/
30 Jun 1515

Crest: no figures but strong

B4 462, l. 5

21 Rm 921/

Flood lasts too long; crop damage

        29 Oct 1515
        CM:1 Hātūr
B4 477, l. 23

16.   23 Sf 922/   Off-season rise; flash floods in Upper
        28 Mar 1516   Egypt
B5 21, l. 14

        19 J1 922/   Flood slow and low; alarm
        20 Jun 1516
B5 52, l. 3

        21 J2 922/   Crest: no figures but early
        22 Jul 1516
        CM:27 Abīb
B5 56, l. 5

        2 Rm 922/   High level: 20 dhr
        29 Sep 1516   Flood too long
        CM:1 Bābā
B5 84, l. 3

Appendix 4: Staple Crop/Food Prices during al-Ghawrī's Reign

	Date	Staple	Price
1.	R2 912/ Aug-Sep 1506 B4 99, l. 4	Grain/food price increase	——
2.	Rj 914/ Oct-Nov 1508 B4 139, l. 7	Grain/food shortage wheat hay	 500 dr/ir 1 dn/camel load
3.	DH 914/ Mar-Apr 1509 B4 150, l. 2	Crop shortage due to year- length cold wheat	 2 dn/ir
4.	R1 916/ Jun/Jul 1510 B4 184, l. 14	Onion price increase onions	 22 nf/qn
5.	Sf 917/ May 1511 B4 217, l. 15	Grain price increase; scarcity due to low Nile and rat infestation wheat	 1 dn/ir
6.	Rj 917/ Sep-Oct 1511 B4 241, l. 11	Grain/fodder prices high despite strong flood birsīm	 5 dn/ir
7.	Rm 917/ Nov-Dec 1511 B4 246, l. 19	Sugar shortage; price rise of confections	
8.	DH 917/ Feb-Mar 1512	Prosperous year despite severe cold that drives prices up wheat	 2 dn/ir

B4 253, l. 4

9.   J1 918/   Abundant harvest due to
          Jul-Aug 1512   record flood, yet grains
                           costly; author cannot ex-
                           plain

B4 274, l. 1

10.   Rm 918/   Fuel wood/charcoal scarce
          Nov-Dec 1512
B4 284, l. 5

Appendix 5: Estimated Annual Receipts (EAR) from Trusts Granted by Qāytbāy

	Date	Deed	EAR
F* 1–8	24 J2 879/ 5 Nov 1474	AW 886q, tr 1	24,083 dn
	27 J2 879/ 8 Nov 1474	AW 886q, tr 2	3700 dn
	sd	DW 20/125	100 dn
	12 R2 880/ 15 Aug 1475	AW 890q	100 dn
	27 Rm 884/ 12 Dec 1479	AW 886q, tr 3	300 dn
	sd	DW 28/187	3000 dn
	28 Sf 892/ 23 Feb 1487	AW 611j, tr 1	400 dn, 26,820 dn
	8 \$w 918/ 17 Dec 1512	DW 42/270	100 dn
F 1–8	Total EAR:		58,600 dn
F 9	22 DH 881/ 10 Apr 1477	AW 889q, tr 1	2000 dn
F 10	25 \$w 874/ 27 Apr 1470	AW 912q, tr 1	1246 dn
F 11	13 Rm 886/ 5 Nov 1481	AW 810q, tr 1	112 dn
F 12	5 R2 877/ 9 Sep 1472	AW 887q, tr 1	2000 dn
F 13	25 \$w 883/ 19 Jan 1479	AW 887q, tr 2	600 dn

| F 14 | 15 DH 895/ | DW 33/210 | 1100 dn |
| | 27 Oct 1490 | | |

*See chapter 7, note 28 for foundation (F) details.

Appendix 6: Estimated Annual Disbursements (EAD) from Trusts Granted by Qāytbāy

	Deed	EAD
F 1–8	AW 886q, tr 1	3690 dn
	AW 886q, tr 2	42 dn
	AW 611j, tr 1	350 dn
F 1–8 total EAD:		4082 dn
F 9	AW 889q,	407 dn
F 10	AW 912q, tr 1	12 dn
F 11	AW 810q, tr 1	276 dn
F 12	AW 887q, tr 1	138 dn
	AW 887q, tr 3	675 dn
F 12 total EAD:		813 dn
F 13	AW 887q, tr 2	148 dn
F 14	DW 33/210	430 dn

Appendix 7: Estimated Annual Receipts (EAR) from Trusts Granted by al-Ghawrī

	Date	Deed	EAR
F* 1–2	26 Mh 909/ 21 Jul 1508	AW 882q, tr 1	52,787 dn
	27 $w 914/ 18 Feb 1509–18 R2 922/ 21 May 1516	AW 882q, tr 2–6 & addi- tions	31,093 dn
F 1–2 Total EAR:			82,880 dn
F 3	26 Mh 909/ 21 Jul 1508	AW 882q, tr 4	180 dn
F 4	18 R2 922 21 May 1516	AW 882q, tr 6	400dn
	22 $w 910/ 28 Mar 1505	AW 344j, tr 2	75 dn
	10 J2 918/ 23 Aug 1512	AW 36j, tr 1	70 dn
	10 $b 921/ 19 Sep 1515	AW 341j, tr 2	20 dn
F4 Total EAR:			560 dn

F 5–11 supported by Ṭūmānbāy, AW 882q, tr 7

*See chapter 7, note 41 for foundation (F) details.

Appendix 8: Estimated Annual Disbursements (EAD) from Trusts Granted by al-Ghawrī

	Deed	*EAD*
F 1–2	AW 882q, tr 1	5977 dn
F 3	AW 882q, tr 4	336 dn
	AW 882q, tr 5	180 dn
F 3 Total EAD:		516 dn
F 4	AW 882q, tr 6	696 dn
F 5–11	AW 882q, tr 7	284 dn

WORKS CITED

I. Narrative Sources

Ibn Ḥajar al-ʿAsqalānī. *Inbāʾ al-Ghumr bi-Anbāʾ al-ʿUmr.* Edited by Ḥasan Ḥabashī. 3 vols. Cairo, 1969–1972 (GAL 2 83).

al-ʿAynī *ʿIqd al-Jumān fī Taʾrīkh Ahl al-Zamān.* In process of publication. Edited by Maḥammad Amīn. Cairo, 1987- (Gal 2 65; Suppl. 2 51).

al-Baʾūnī. *al-Lamḥa al-Ashrafīya waʾl-Bahja al-Sanīya.* Ms. Paris: Bibliothèque nationale, fonds arabe, 1615 (GAL 2 54; Suppl. 2 67).

Ibn Duqmāq. *al-Jawhar al-Thamīn fī Siyar al-Khulafāʾ waʾl-Salāṭīn.* Ms. Cairo: Dār al-Kutub, 1522 Taʾrīkh.

————. *Nuzhat al-Anām fī Taʾrīkh al-Islām.* Ms. Cairo: Dār al-Kutub, 1740 Taʾrīkh (GAL 2 50; Suppl. 2 49–50).

al-Ghazzī. *al-Kawākib al-Sāʾira bi-Manāqib ʿUlamāʾ al-Miʾa al-ʿĀshira.* 3 vols Beirut, 1979 (GAL 2 291).

Al-Ḥalabī. *Durr al-Ḥabab fī Taʾrīkh Aʿyān Ḥalab.* Ms. Vienna: Codex Vinobonensis Palatinus, Mxt. 667 [Flügel 1184] (GAL 2 368).

Ibn al-Ḥimṣī. *Ḥawādith al-Zamān wa-Wafayāt al-Shuyūkh waʾl-Aqrān.* Ms. Istanbul: Feizullah, 1438 (GAL Suppl. 2 41).

Kitāb Ithbāt Dalālāt Muḥammad ibn al-Marḥūm al-Malik al-Ashraf Qāytbāy. Ms. Istanbul: Topkapi Saray, 2960.

Ibn Iyās. *Badāʾiʿ al-Zuhūr fī Waqāʾiʿ al-Duhūr.* Edited by M. Mustafa, H. Roemer, H. Ritter. vols. 3–5. Cairo and Wiesbaden, 1960–1963; abridged version: *ʿUqūd al-Jumān fī Waqāʾiʿ al-Azmān.* Ms. Istanbul: Aya Sofya, 3311.

————. *Nuzhat al-Umam fīʾl-ʿAjāʾib waʾl-Ḥikam.* Ms. Istanbul: Aya Sofya, 3500 (GAL 2 295; Suppl. 2 405).

Jawāhir al-Sulūk fīʾl-Khulafāʾ waʾl-Mulūk. Ms. London: British Museum, 6854 (GAL 2 42; Suppl. 2 53).

Ibn al-Jīʿān. *Al-Qawl al-Mustaẓraf fī Safar Mawlānā al-Malik al-Ashraf.* French translation by H. Devonshire. IFAO Bulletin 20 (1922): 2–40 (GAL 2 38; Suppl. 26).

Ibn Khaldūn. *al-Muqaddima.* English translation by F. Rosenthal. 3 vols. New York, 1958.

ʿAbd al-Bāsiṭ al-Malaṭī. *Majmūʿ al-Bustān al-Nūrī li-Ḥaḍrat Mawlānā Sulṭān al-Ghurī.* Ms. Istanbul: Aya Sofya, 4793.

————. *al-Rawḍ al-Bāsim fī Ḥawādith al-ʿUmr waʾl-Tarājim.* Ms. Vatican arabo, 729.

————. *al-Risāla al-Laṭīfa tashtamilu ʿalā Dhikri man Waliya Miṣr min al-Salāṭīn.* Ms. Istanbul: Laleli, 2044 (GAL 2 54; Suppl 2 52).

al-Maqrīzī. *Ighāthat al-Umma bi-Kashf al-Ghumma.* Cairo, 1940.

————. *al-Mawāʿiẓ waʾl-Iʿtibār bi-Dhikr al-Khiṭaṭ waʾl-Āthār.* 2 vols. Cairo, 1853–1854 (GAL 2 48; Suppl. 2 36–37).

al-Sakhāwī. *al-Ḍawʾ al-Lāmiʿ fī Aʿyān al-Qarn al-Tāsiʿ.* Edited by Ḥusām al-Qudsī. 12 vols. Cairo, 1934.

————. *al-Dhayl al-Tāmm ʿalā Duwal al-Islām.* Ms. Tūnis: Dār al-Kutub al-Waẓīfa, 6856 (GAL 2 43; Suppl. 2 31–32).

al-Jawharī al-Ṣayrafī. *Inbāʾ al-Haṣr fī Abnāʾ al-ʿAṣr.* Edited by Ḥasan Ḥabashī. Cairo, 1970.

————. *Nuzhat al-Nufūs waʾl-Abdān fī Tawārīkh al-Zamān.* Edited by Ḥasan Ḥabashī. 3 vols. Cairo, 1971–1973 (GAL Suppl. 2 41).

Ibn Taghrī-Birdī. *Ḥawādith al-Duhūr fī Madā al-Ayyām waʾl-Shuhūr.* Edited by William Popper. Vol. 7, nos. 1–4 of University of California Publications in Semitic Philology. Berkeley, 1930–1931.

————. *al-Manhal al-Ṣāfī waʾl-Mustawfī baʿd al-Wāfī.* In process of publication. Edited by Muḥammad Amīm, Cairo, 1984–.

————. *al-Nujūm al-Zāhira fī Mulūk Miṣr waʾl-Qāhira.* Edited by William Popper. Vols. 5–7, 12, 14, 17–19, 22 of University of California Publications in Semitic Philology. Berkeley, 1915–1960 (GAL 2 51–52).

Taʾrīkh al-Malik al-Ashraf Qāytbāy. Ms. Paris: Bibliothèque nationale, fonds arabs 5916 (GAL 2 38; Suppl. 2 26).

Ibn Ṭūlūn. *Iʿlām al-Warā bi-man Wulliya Nāʾiban min al-Atrāk bi-Dimashq.* Edited by ʿAbd al-ʿAẓīm Khaṭṭāb. Cairo, 1973.

————. *Mufākahat al-Khillān fī Ḥawādith al-Zamān.* Edited by Muḥammad Muṣṭafā. 2 vols. Cairo, 1962–1964.

II. Archival Sources

M. Amīn, *Catalogue des documents d'archives du Caire de 239/853 à 922/ 1516* Cairo 1981 (Amīn).

Dār al-Wathāʾiq al-Qawmīya, Cairo (DW).

Wizārat al-Awqāf, Cairo (AW); *jadīd* (j); qadim (q).

Amīn 116: DW 18/111	Amīn 134: DW 20/125
198: DW 28/187	222: DW 33/210
225: DW 42/270	237: DW 36/225
274: DW 41/261	314: AW 532j
328: AW 524j	344: AW 517j
350: AW 140j	360: AW 188j
366: AW 103j	370: AW 553j
384: AW 537j	385: AW 549j
398: AW 405j	399: AW 534j
403: AW 186j	435: AW 428j
438: AW 209j	439: AW 490j
452: AW 912j	457: AW 519j
458: AW 363j	467: AW 887q
469: AW 707j	475: AW 886q (main writ of Qāytbāy)
476: AW 888q	486: AW 889q
506: AW 775j	507: AW 810q
510: AW 77-a j	530: AW 385j
550: AW 890q	551: AW 611j
564: AW 327j	579: AW 322j
585: AW 618j	593: AW 111j
598: AW 219j	599: AW 404j
603: AW 320j	606: AW 550j
610: AW 60j	613: AW 486j
615: AW 134j	620: AW 500j
624: AW 425j	625: AW 721j
626: AW 183j	628: AW 142j
629: AW 216j	630: AW 333j
633: AW 423j	634: AW 197j
638: AW 457j	642: AW 182j
647: AW 551j	652: AW 882q (main writ of al-Ghawrī)

656: AW 202j
657: AW 452j
658: AW 117j
659: AW 176j
660: AW 688j
661: AW 521j
662: AW 157j
663: AW 594j
667: AW 370j
668: AW 406j
673: AW 437j
674: (duplicate of #673)
676: AW 381j
677: AW 769j
680: AW 101j
681: AW 432j
685: AW 442j
689: AW 451j
690: AW 444j
691: AW 344j
693: AW 108j
698: AW 350j
699: AW 403j
700: AW 128j
704: AW 75j
705: AW 113j
706: AW 388j
712: AW 97j
713: AW 220j
717: AW 119j
719: AW 36j
720: AW 163j
721: AW 402j
729: AW 342j
730: AW 164j
731: AW 148j
732: AW 317j
735: AW 382j
736: AW 343j
741: AW 331j
742: AW 314j
743: AW 208j
749: AW 356j
752: AW 375j
753: AW 328j
754: AW 338j
756: AW 129j
759: AW 362j
766: AW 358j
769: AW 132j
772: AW 174j
774: AW 321j
775: AW 329j
776: AW 330j
779: AW 372j
780: AW 374j
781: AW 380j
782: AW 389j
784: AW 392j
785: AW 398j
786: AW 529j
788: AW 552j
798: AW 150j
800: AW 629j
804: AW 341j
805: AW 390j
811: AW 528j
814: AW 201j
822: AW 511j
829: AW 340j
831: AW 159j
832: AW 514j
839: AW 105j.

III. Secondary Studies

Abu-Lughod, Janet L. *Before European Hegemony; The World System A.D. 1250–1350.* Oxford, 1989.

Allouche, Adel. *The Origins and Development of the Ottoman-Ṣafavid Conflict.* Berlin, 1983.

Amīn, Muḥammad M. *Al-Awqāf wa'l-Ḥayāt al-Ijtimāʿīya fī Miṣr.* Cairo, 1980.

—————. *Catalogue des documents d'archives du Caire de 239/853 à 922/1516.* Cairo, 1981.

Ashtor, Eliyahu. *Histoire des prix et des salaires dans l'orient mediévale.* Paris, 1969.

—————. "Ḳāʾit Bāy," *Encyclopaedia of Islam.* Vol. 4. 2d. ed.

—————. *Levant Trade in the Later Middle Ages.* Princeton, 1983.

—————. *A Social and Economic History of the Near East in the Middle Ages.* Berkeley. 1976.

Ayalon, David. "Aspects of the Mamlūk Phenomenon: A. The Importance of the Mamlūk Institution; B. Ayyūbids, Kurds and Turks." *Der Islam* 53 (1976): 196–225; 55 (1977): 1–32.

—————. "The Circassians in the Mamlūk Kingdom." *Journal of the American Oriental Society* 69 (1939): 135–47.

—————. "Egypt as a Dominant Factor in Syria and Palestine during the Islamic Period." In *Egypt and Palestine: A Millennium of Association,* edited by Amnon Cohen and Gabriel Baer, 31–37. New York, 1984.

—————. "L'esclavage du Mamlouk." *Oriental Notes and Studies 1.* Jerusalem. 1951.

—————. *Gunpowder and Firearms in the Mamluk Kingdom.* London, 1956.

—————. "Names, Titles, and 'Nisbas' of the Mamluks," *Israel Oriental Studies* 5 (1975): 189–232.

—————. "Notes on the Furūsīya Exercises and Games of the Mamlūk Sultanate." *Studies in Islamic History and Civilization,* Scripta Hierosolymitana 9 (1960): 31–62.

—————. "Le régiment bahriya dans l'armée mamelouk." *Revue des Études Islamiques* (1951): 133–41.

—————. "Studies on the Structure of the Mamlūk Army—I." *Bulletin of the School of Oriental and African Studies* 15 (1953): 203–28.

————. "The Wafidīya in the Mamlūk Kingdom." *Islamic Culture* 25 (1951): 89–109.

Bacharach, Jere L. "Palestine in the Policies of Tulunid and Ikhshidid Governors of Egypt." In *Egypt and Syria; A Millennium of Association*, edited by Amnon Cohen and Gabriel Baer, 51–65. New York, 1984.

Berkey, Jonathan. *The Transmission of Knowledge in Medieval Cairo*. Princeton, 1992.

Cahen, Claude. *Makhzūmīyāt, études sur l'histoire économique et financière de l'Égypte médiévale*. Leiden, 1977.

Canard, Marius. "Le traité de 1281 entre Michel Paleologue et le Sultan Qalāʾūn." *Byzantion* 10 (1935): 669–80.

————. "Un traité entre Byzance et l'Égypte au xiiie siècle et les relations diplomatiques de Michel viii Paleologue avec les sultans mamlouks Baibars et Qalāʾūn." In *Mélanges Gaudefroy-Demombynes*, 197–224. 1934–1945.

Cattan, Henry. "The Law of *Waqf*. "Chap. 8 in *Law in the Middle East*. Vol. 1, *Origins and Development of Islamic Law*, edited by M. J. Khadduri and H. J. Liebesny. Washington, 1955.

Darrag, Ahmad. *L'Égypte sous le règne de Barsbay*. Damascus, 1961.

Dölger, Franz. "Der Vertrag des Sultans Qalāʾūn von Ägypten mit dem Kaiser Michael Palaiologos," In *Serta Monacensia*. Leiden, 1952.

Ehrenkreutz, Andrew S. "The Fatimids in Palestine, Unwitting Promoters of the Crusades." In *Egypt and Palestine; A Millennium of Association*, edited by Amnon Cohen and Gabriel Baer, 66–72. New York, 1984.

————. *Saladin*. Albany, 1972.

Escovitz, Joseph H. *The Office of Qāḍī al-Quḍāt in Cairo under the Baḥrī Mamlūks*. Berlin, 1984.

Fernandes, Leonor. *The Evolution of a Sufi Institution in Mamluk Egypt: the Khanqah*. Berlin, 1988.

————. "Some Aspects of the Zāwiya in Egypt on the Eve of the Ottoman Conquest." *Annales Islamologiques* 19 (1983): 9–17.

Garcin, Jean-Claude. "The Mamluk Military System and the Blocking of Medieval Muslim Society." In *Europe and the Rise of Capitalism*, edited by J. Baechler et al, 119–23. Oxford, 1988.

Gellner, Ernest. "Patrons and Clients." In *Patrons and Clients in Mediterranean Societies*, edited by Ernest Gellner and John Waterbury, 1–6. London, 1977.

al-Ghaytānī, Jamīl. *Al-Zaynī Barakāt.* Cairo, 1985. English translation by Farouk Mustafa. New York, 1989.

Goitein, Solomon D. *A Mediterranean Society: The Jewish Communities of the Arab World as Portrayed in the Cairo Geniza.* Vol. 1, Economic Foundations. Vol. 4, Daily Life. Berkeley, 1967, 1983.

Haarmann, Ulrich. "Miṣr: 5. The Mamlūk Period." *Encyclopaedia of Islam.* Vol. 8. 2d. ed.

————. "The Sons of Mamluks as Fief-holders in Late Medieval Egypt." In *Land Tenure and Social Transformation in the Middle East,* edited by Tarif Khalidi, 141–68. Beirut, 1984.

Hanna, Nelly. *An Urban History of Bulāq in the Mamlūk and Ottoman Periods.* Cairo, 1983.

Halm, Heinz. Ägypten nach den Mamlukischen Lehenregistern. Vol. 1, *Oberägypten und das Fayyūm.* Vol. 2, *Das Delta.* Wiesbaden, 1979, 1982.

Heffening, W. *"Wakf." Encyclopaedia of Islam.* Vol. 4. 2d. ed.

Heyd, Wilhelm. *Histoire de commerce du Levant au moyen âge.* Translated by F. Reynaud. Leipzig, 1885–86.

Hitti, Philip. *The History of the Arabs.* 8th ed. London, 1963.

Hodgson, Marshall. *The Venture of Islam.* Vol. 2. Chicago, 1979.

Holt, P. M. *The Age of the Crusades: The Near East from the Eleventh Century to 1517.* London, 1986.

————. "Ḳānṣawh al-Ghawrī," *Encyclopaedia of Islam.* Vol. 4. 2d. ed.

————. "Qalawun's Treaty with Genoa in 1290." *Der Islam* 57 (1980): 101–08.

————. "Some Observations on the Abbasid *Caliphate* of Cairo." *Bulletin of the School of Oriental and African Studies* 47 (1984): 501–07.

————. "The Treaties of the Early Mamluk Sultans with the Frankish States." *Bulletin of the School of Oriental and African Studies* 43 (1980): 67–76.

Humphreys, R. Stephen. "The Emergence of the Mamlūk Army." *Studia Islamica* 45 (1977): 67–100; 46 (1977): 147–82.

————. "Mamluk Dynasty." In *Dictionary of the Middle Ages,* edited by Joseph R. Strayer, vol. 8, 73–74. New York, 1987.

Inalcik, Halil. *The Ottoman Empire: The Classical Age, 1300–1600.* New York, 1973.

Irwin, Robert, *The Middle East in the Middle Ages: The Early Mamluk Sultanate, 1250–1382*. London, 1986.

Kammerer, A. *La mer rouge, l'Abyssinie et l'Arabie depuis l'antiquité*. Cairo 1935.

Labib, Subhi Y. "Ein Brief des Mamluken Sultans Qaitbay an dem Dogen von Venedig aus dem Jahre 1473." *Der Islam* 32 (1980): 324–29.

———. *Handelsgeschichte Ägyptens im Spätmittelalter (1171–1517)*. Wiesbaden, 1965.

Landé, Carl H. "The Dyadic Basis of Clientism." In *Friends, Followers and Factions; A Reader in Political Clientism*, edited by Steffen W. Schmidt, xiii–xxxvii. Berkeley, 1977.

Lapidus, Ira M. "Ayyubid Religious Policy and the Development of Schools of Law in Cairo." In *Colloque international sur l'histoire due Caire*, 279–86. Cairo, 1969.

———. *Muslim Cities in the Later Middle Ages*. Cambridge, 1967.

Little, Donald P. "Relations between Jerusalem and Egypt during the Mamluk Period according to Literary and Documentary Sources." In *Egypt and Palestine; A Millennium of Association*, edited by Amnon Cohen and Gabriel Baer, 73–93. New York, 1984.

Lyons, M. C., and D. E. P. Jackson. *Saladin; The Politics of the Holy War*. New York, 1982.

Makdisi, George. *The Rise of Colleges: Institutions of Higher Learning in Islam and the West*. Edinburgh, 1981.

Mandaville, Jon. "The Muslim Judiciary of Damascus in the Late Mamluk Period." Ph.D. diss. Near Eastern Studies, Princeton University, 1969.

Martel-Thoumian, Bernadette. *Les civils et l'administration dans l'état militaire mamlūk (ixe/xve siècle)*. Damascus, 1991.

Mayer, L. A. *The Buildings of Qāytbāy as Described in His Endowment Deed*. Fascicule I: Text and Index. London, 1938.

Meyerson, Mark D. *The Muslims of Valencia in the Age of Fernando and Isabel: Between Coexistence and Crusade*. Berkeley, 1991.

Minorksy, Vladimir. "The Aq-quyunlu and Land Reforms." *Bulletin of the School of Oriental and African Studies* 17 (1955): 449–62.

Mordtmann, J., and L. Menage. "Dhū'l-Ḳadr." *Encyclopaedia of Islam*. Vol. 2. 2d. ed.

Mottahedeh, Roy P. *Loyalty and Leadership in an Early Islamic Society.* Princeton, 1980.

Newhall, Amy Whittier. "The Patronage of the Mamluk Sultan Qaʾit Bay, 872–901/1468–1496." Ph.D. diss. Fine Arts, Harvard University, 1987.

Petry, Carl F. *The Civilian Elite of Cairo in the Later Middle Ages.* Princeton, 1981.

————. "Class Solidarity vs. Gender Gain: Women as Custodians of Property in Later Medieval Egypt." In *Women in Middle Eastern History; Shifting Boundaries in Sex and Gender,* edited by Nikki Keddie and Beth Baron, 122–42. New Haven, 1991.

————, and Stanley Mendenhall. "Geographic Origins of the Civil Judiciary of Cairo in the Fifteenth Century." *Journal of the Social and Economic History of the Orient* 21 (1978): 52–74.

————. "A Paradox of Patronage during the Later Mamluk Period." *The Muslim World* 53 (1983): 182–207.

Popper, William. *Egypt and Syria under the Circassian Sultans.* University of California Publications in Semitic Philology 15. Berkeley, 1955.

————. *The Cairo Nilometer: Studies in Ibn Taghrī-Birdī's Chronicles of Egypt.* University of California Publications in Semitic Philology 12. Berkeley, 1951.

Rabie, Hassanein. *The Financial System of Egypt. A. H. 564–741/A. D. 1169–1341.* Oxford, 1972.

————. "Political Relations between the Safavids of Persia and the Mamluks of Egypt and Syria in the Early Sixteenth Century." *Journal of the American Research Center in Egypt* 15 (1978): 75–81.

————. "Some Technical Aspects of Agriculture in Medieval Egypt." *The Middle East, 700–1900: Studies in Economic and Social History,* edited by A. L. Udovitch. Princeton, 1981.

Raymond, André. *Artisans et commerçants du Caire au XVIIIᵉ siècle.* Damascus, 1973.

Roemer, H. R. "The Safavid Period." In *The Cambridge History of Iran,* edited by P. Jackson, vol. 6, 189–232. New York, 1986.

Salibi, K. S. "The Banu Jamāʿa: A Dynasty of Shāfiʿite Jurists in the Mamluk Period." *Studia Islamica* 9 (1958): 97–109.

————. "Listes chronologiques des grands cadis de l'Égypte sous les mamlouks." *Revue des Études Islamiques* 25 (1957): 81–125.

Sauvaget, J. "Noms et surnoms de Mamelouks." *Journal Asiatique*. 238 (1950): 31–58.

Scanlon, George. "Fusṭāṭ Expedition Preliminary Report." *Journal of the American Research Center in Egypt*. 1968, 1: 11 (1974), 81–92; 2: 12 (1975), 69–90; 1971, 1: 13 (1975); 2: 17 (1980), 77–96; 1972, 1: 18 (1981), 57–84; 2: 19 (1982), 119–30; 1978: 21 (1984), 1–38.

Serjeant, R. B. *The Portuguese off the South Arabian Coast*. London, 1963.

Schimmel, Annemarie. "Kalif und Kadi im Spätmittelalterlichen Ägypten." *Die Welt des Islams* 24 (1942): 1–128.

Shoshan, Boaz. "On the Relations between Egypt and Palestine, 1382–1517 A.D." In *Egypt and Palestine; A Millennium of Association*, edited by Amnon Cohen and Gabriel Baer, 94–101. New York, 1984.

Sobernheim, M. "Ḳāʾitbey." *Encyclopaedia of Islam*. Vol. 2

———. "Ḳānṣūh." *Encyclopaedia of Islam*. Vol. 2.

Thorau, Peter. *Sultan Baibars I. von Ägypten*. Wiesbaden, 1987.

Wallerstein, Immanuel. *The Modern World System; Capitalist Agriculture and the Origins of the European World-Economy in the Sixteenth Century*. New York, 1976.

Wansbrough, John. "A Mamluk Commercial Treaty concluded with the Republic of Florence." In *Documents from Islamic Chanceries*, edited by Samuel Stern, 39–49. Oxford, 1965.

———. "The Safe-Conduct in Muslim Chancery Practice." *Bulletin of the School of Oriental and African Studies* 34 (1971): 20–35.

———. "Venice and Florence in the Mamluk Commercial Privileges." *Bulletin of the School of Oriental and African Studies* 28 (1965): 483–523.

Waterbury, John. "An Attempt to Put Patrons and Clients in their Place." In *Patrons and Clients in Mediterranean Societies*, edited by Ernest Gellner and John Waterbury, 329–42. London, 1977.

Wiet, Gaston. *L'Égypte arabe*. Vol. 4 in *L'Histoire de la nation égyptienne*, edited by Gabriel Hanotaux. Paris, 1937.

Winter, Michael. *Society and Religion in Early Ottoman Egypt; Studies in the Writings of ʿAbd al-Wahhāb al-Shaʿrānī*. New Brunswick, 1982.

Wittek, Paul. *The Rise of the Ottoman Empire*. London, 1938.

Woods, John. *The Aqqoyunlu: Clan, Confederation, Empire*. Chicago, 1976.

Yelsin, Mehmet, "Dīvān-i Qanṣawh al-Ghawrī: A Critical Edition of an Anthology of Turkish Poetry Commissioned by Sultan Qanṣawh al-Ghawrī (1501–1516)." Ph.D. diss. Inner Asian and Altaic Studies, Harvard University, 1993.

Islam: and economy, 222; al-Ghawrī defiles, 210

Islamic law: no corporate ties, 132; violations, 161; and waqfs, 197

Ismāʿīl al-Anbābī, Sīdī, mawlid, 118

Ismāʿīl Ṣafawī: agents, 25; ambition, 24; and al-Ghawrī, 53–54; on Hippodrome, 164; imperialism, 31; as Ṣūfī, 50

Istanbul: and Cairo, 34, 60; and imperialism, 52; messenger from, 46; sultan of, 48; and Sūwār, 43. *See also* Constantinople

Italy: and Black Sea trade, 46; mercantilism, 31; seafaring from, 56

Jabal Nāblus, taxes from, 107

Jahān Shāh, and Uzun Ḥasan, 45

Jānibak al-Ustādār, arrest, 80

Jānibak Ḥabīb, iqtāʿ of, 167

Jānibak Qarā, caravan commander, 162

Jānibak Qulaqsīz: capture, 15, 43; removes observers, 75

Jānibakīya College, al-Abshīhī in, 134

Janissaries, at Suez, 195

Jaqmaq, al-Ẓāhir: Mamlūks of, 88; promotes Qāytbāy, 14; retainer, 152; and Shāh Rukh, 47; and troop salaries, 84

al-Jāzānī, rebels, 40–41

Jazīra, as buffer, 30

Jazīra Island, trade fair in, 118

Jerusalem: edifices, 160; protection, 30; Qāytbāy's college in, 198–99; Resurrection Church in, 55; synagogue in, 154; under Damascus, 35

Jews: in Alexandria, 120; confiscation, 172, 176

Jīʿān Family: confiscation, 171–72; estate, 138. *See also* Ibn al-Jīʿān

Jidda: garrisons, 40; Portuguese at, 59

Jihād, declaration, 33

Jīza canal, bridges, 115

Jīza Province: Hazanbul tribe in, 108; Yasār tribe in, 111

Jizya. *See* capitation tax

Jordan River, under Damascus, 35

Judaic observance, and ʿulamā, 155

judges, and Qāytbāy, 151

judiciary, in Syria, 36

julbān: bonus, 209; and Fifth Corps, 194; and Ibn Kātib Gharīb, 91; pay demands, 91; raid Fāṭima's house, 201; riots, 75, 91. *See also* recruits

jurists, and al-Ghawrī, 157

jurist-scholars, in Syria, 36

justice, under Qāytbāy, 17

justice pavilion, and al-Ghawrī, 155

Kaʿba: al-Jāzānī in, 41; mantle, 47, 161; and Qāytbāy, 160; and savants, 40; and Uzun Ḥasan, 47

Kamarān Islands, and Portuguese, 60

Kanbāya, ruler of, 59

al-Karak: and Banū Lām, 39; under Damascus, 35

al-Karakī, Burhān al-Dīn, quarrel, 134

Kārimī merchants, as free agents, 117–18

Kashshāf. *See* inspectors

Kātib al-Sirr: and Qāytbāy, 91; at Sūwār councils, 168; Ibn Muzhir as, 134. *See also* chancellorship

Khalīl, Ghars al-Dīn, wife of, 149

Khalīl, son of Uzun Ḥasan, 49

Khamsīn, as Easter, 156

Khān al-Khalīlī, and al-Ghawrī, 164

Khaṣṣakīs: and al-Ghawrī, 92; as governors, 35; Qāytbāy as, 14

Khawjas, fortunes, 118

Khawand, wife of al-Ghawrī, 162

Khayrbak al-Dawādār, confiscation, 169

Khayrbak al-Miʿmar, and Banū Ibrāhīm, 41

Khayrbak, prefect, and Ibn ʿAwaḍ, 141

Khayrbak, al-Sharīfī, and waqfs, 205

Khayrbak, viceroy, betrays al-Ghawrī, 25, 192

khuddām, in Ḥijāz, 40

khushdāsh: Azbak as, 19; Timurbughā as, 14, 16

Khushqadam, al-Ẓāhir: aides, 174; and cavalry, 191; and Khayrbak al-Dawādār, 169; Mamlūks, 169; promotes Qāytbāy, 14; and Qāsim Shughayta, 139; and troop salaries, 84

khuṭbas: at al-Ghawrī's tomb; on same Friday, 154

Kizilbāsh, as raiders, 50

Koran, and waqfs, 197